Symmetry in Process Optimization

Symmetry in Process Optimization

Guest Editors

Aleksandar Djordjevic
Miladin Stefanović

MDPI

Basel • Beijing • Wuhan • Barcelona • Belgrade • Novi Sad • Cluj • Manchester

Guest Editors
Aleksandar Djordjevic
Faculty of Engineering
University of Kragujevac
Kragujevac
Serbia

Miladin Stefanović
Faculty of Engineering
University of Kragujevac
Kragujevac
Serbia

Editorial Office
MDPI AG
Grosspeteranlage 5
4052 Basel, Switzerland

This is a reprint of the Special Issue, published open access by the journal *Symmetry* (ISSN 2073-8994), freely accessible at: https://www.mdpi.com/journal/symmetry/special_issues/GV8S9L38DJ.

For citation purposes, cite each article independently as indicated on the article page online and as indicated below:

Lastname, A.A.; Lastname, B.B. Article Title. *Journal Name* **Year**, *Volume Number*, Page Range.

ISBN 978-3-7258-7278-7 (Hbk)
ISBN 978-3-7258-7279-4 (PDF)
https://doi.org/10.3390/books978-3-7258-7279-4

Contents

symmetry

MDPI

Editorial

Symmetry in Process Optimization

Aleksandar Djordjevic * and Miladin Stefanovic

Faculty of Engineering, University of Kragujevac, Sestre Janjic 6, 34000 Kragujevac, Serbia; miladin@kg.ac.rs
* Correspondence: adjordjevic@kg.ac.rs

Editorial

This Special Issue, 'Symmetry in Process Optimization', brings together recent theoretical and applied studies demonstrating how the principles of symmetry can be systematically exploited to enhance optimization methods, improve computational efficiency, and increase robustness across diverse scientific and engineering domains. In complex optimization problems—characterized by combinatorial explosion, structural constraints, and heterogeneous data—symmetry-aware modeling provides a principled mechanism for reducing redundancy and improving tractability [1–13].

The relevance of symmetry in scheduling and production systems is particularly evident. The contributions included in this Special Issue address constrained parallel machine scheduling [1], while related research in the broader literature demonstrates how metaheuristic frameworks—such as modified Harris Hawks optimization [11] and artificial bee colony algorithms [12]—can effectively exploit structural symmetries in machine scheduling. Arc-flow formulations further show how symmetry can be embedded in exact optimization models for uniform parallel machine problems [13]. Collectively, these works reinforce the importance of symmetry in both heuristic and exact scheduling methodologies.

In manufacturing and additive production systems, symmetry plays a critical role in design, process planning, and surface optimization. The studies included in this Special Issue investigate machining symmetry [5] and topology optimization combined with part orientation strategies in additive manufacturing [6]. These approaches align with broader investigations into symmetry applications in metal additive manufacturing processes [14] and medical modeling via additive manufacturing [15], where geometric symmetry directly influences mechanical performance and functional accuracy.

Machine learning and computer vision represent another prominent axis of symmetry-aware optimization. Within this Special Issue, symmetry-enhanced few-shot segmentation [2] and hardware-optimized real-time image dehazing systems [9] demonstrate how symmetry can improve model consistency and efficiency. Complementary studies in the literature further highlight the importance of symmetric feature representations in semantic segmentation [16], infrastructure defect detection [17], generative adversarial dehazing networks [18], and asymmetry-guided object detection frameworks [19]. These works collectively illustrate how embedding symmetry into deep architectures improves generalization and robustness.

Control systems and dynamical modeling also benefit from the principles of symmetry. Fractional-order control strategies [7] and symmetry-optimized dynamical beam analysis [8] demonstrate how symmetric system modeling enhances stability and analytical tractability. Related research in permanent magnet synchronous motor control shows how symmetry-aware sliding mode control [20] and uncertainty/disturbance estimation strategies [21] improve precision and robustness in servo systems.

Finally, symmetry in decision-making and reconstruction frameworks can be addressed using fuzzy matrix optimization models [10] and symmetry-based 3D reconstruction using genetic algorithms [3], further emphasizing the versatility of the principles of symmetry in computational intelligence and engineering design.

Together, the contributions included in this Special Issue and the related works cited above demonstrate that symmetry is not merely a mathematical abstraction, but a unifying structural principle that enhances optimization across scheduling, manufacturing, machine learning, control, and decision-making systems. By bridging theoretical foundations with real-world applications, this Special Issue highlights the transformative potential of symmetry-aware optimization in addressing contemporary scientific and industrial challenges.

We anticipate that this Special Issue will serve as a valuable reference for researchers and practitioners and will stimulate continued interdisciplinary research at the intersection of symmetry theory and process optimization.

Conflicts of Interest: The authors declare no conflicts of interest.

References

1. Ben Abdellafou, K.; Zidi, K.; Ghaban, W. Scheduling Intrees with Unavailability Constraints on Two Parallel Machines. *Symmetry* **2026**, *18*, 103. [CrossRef]
2. Guo, L.; Li, X.; Wang, J.; Tong, Y.; Xiao, J.; Zhou, R.; Li, L.-H.; Zhou, Q.; Li, K.-C. Symmetry-Aware Superpixel-Enhanced Few-Shot Semantic Segmentation. *Symmetry* **2025**, *17*, 1726. [CrossRef]
3. Mitić, P.; Kočović, V.; Mišić, M.; Stefanović, M.; Đorđević, A.; Pantić, M.; Projović, D. A Novel Approach in 3D Model Reconstruction from Engineering Drawings Based on Symmetric Adjacency Matrices Using DXF Files and Genetic Algorithm. *Symmetry* **2025**, *17*, 771. [CrossRef]
4. Kučera, O.; Píštěk, V.; Fomin, O.; Kučera, P.; Sagin, S. Measuring Device for More Precise Mistuning Identification of Integrated Bladed Discs. *Symmetry* **2025**, *17*, 717. [CrossRef]
5. Straka, Ľ. Optimization of Qualitative Indicators of the Machined Surface in Symmetrical Machining of TS by WEDM Technology. *Symmetry* **2025**, *17*, 229. [CrossRef]
6. Malbašić, S.; Đorđević, A.; Živković, S.; Džunić, D.; Sokolović, V. Topology Optimization, Part Orientation, and Symmetry Operations as Elements of a Framework for Design and Production Planning Process in Additive Manufacturing L-PBF Technology. *Symmetry* **2024**, *16*, 1616. [CrossRef]
7. Bistak, P.; Bélai, I.; Bélai, I., Jr.; Vrancic, D.; Huba, M. Application of a Fractional Order PI Controller for a Speed Servo Drive Control. *Symmetry* **2024**, *16*, 1543. [CrossRef]
8. Umer, M.; Olejnik, P. Symmetry-Optimized Dynamical Analysis of Optical Soliton Patterns in the Flexibly Supported Euler–Bernoulli Beam Equation: A Semi-Analytical Solution Approach. *Symmetry* **2024**, *16*, 849. [CrossRef]
9. Ngo, D.; Kang, B. A Symmetric Multiprocessor System-on-a-Chip-Based Solution for Real-Time Image Dehazing. *Symmetry* **2024**, *16*, 653. [CrossRef]
10. Bekesiene, S.; Mashchenko, S. On Maximum Guaranteed Payoff in a Fuzzy Matrix Decision-Making Problem with a Fuzzy Set of States. *Symmetry* **2024**, *16*, 510. [CrossRef]
11. Ewees, A.A.; Al-qaness, M.A.A.; Abd Elaziz, M. Enhanced Salp Swarm Algorithm Based on Firefly Algorithm for Unrelated Parallel Machine Scheduling with Setup Times. *Appl. Math. Model.* **2021**, *94*, 285–305. [CrossRef]
12. Lei, D.; He, S. An Adaptive Artificial Bee Colony for Unrelated Parallel Machine Scheduling with Additional Resource and Maintenance. *Expert Syst. Appl.* **2022**, *205*, 117577. [CrossRef]
13. Kramer, A.; Iori, M.; Lacomme, P. Mathematical Formulations for Scheduling Jobs on Identical Parallel Machines with Family Setup Times and Total Weighted Completion Time Minimization. *Eur. J. Oper. Res.* **2021**, *289*, 825–840. [CrossRef]
14. Uralde, V.; Veiga, F.; Aldalur, E.; Suarez, A.; Ballesteros, T. Symmetry and Its Application in Metal Additive Manufacturing (MAM). *Symmetry* **2022**, *14*, 1810. [CrossRef]
15. Bader, C.; Oxman, N. Recursive Symmetries for Geometrically Complex and Materially Heterogeneous Additive Manufacturing. *Comput.-Aided Des.* **2016**, *81*, 39–47. [CrossRef]
16. Dzhezyan, G.; Cecotti, H. Symmetrical Filters in Convolutional Neural Networks. *Int. J. Mach. Learn. Cybern.* **2021**, *12*, 2027–2039. [CrossRef]

https://doi.org/10.3390/sym18030510

17. Zhu, Y. Edge Defect Detection of Network Image by the Application of Modal Symmetry. *Wirel. Pers. Commun.* **2022**, *127*, 561–576. [CrossRef]
18. Zhao, W.; Zhao, Y.; Feng, L.; Tang, J. Attention Optimized Deep Generative Adversarial Network for Removing Uneven Dense Haze. *Symmetry* **2022**, *14*, 1. [CrossRef]
19. Wang, S.; Zhang, L.; Ma, H.; Zhao, J. YOLOv8n-ASA: An Asymmetry-Guided Framework for Helmet-Wearing Detection in Complex Scenarios. *Symmetry* **2025**, *17*, 2124. [CrossRef]
20. Che, Z.; Yu, H.; Mobayen, S.; Ali, M.; Bartoszewicz, A.; Bouteraa, Y. A Singular Perturbation Approach-Based Non-Cascade Sliding Mode Control for Surface-Mounted PMSMs. *Appl. Sci.* **2022**, *12*, 10500. [CrossRef]
21. Nguyen, T.T.; Nguyen, T.H.; Jeon, J.W. Explicit Model Predictive Speed Control for Permanent Magnet Synchronous Motor with Torque Ripple Minimization. *IEEE Access* **2023**, *11*, 134199–134210. [CrossRef]

https://doi.org/10.3390/sym18030510

symmetry

MDPI

Article

Scheduling Intrees with Unavailability Constraints on Two Parallel Machines

Khaoula Ben Abdellafou [1,2,*], Kamel Zidi [3] and Wad Ghaban [3]

1 Higher Institute of Applied Mathematics and Computer Science, University of Kairouan, Kairouan 3100, Tunisia
2 Research Lab LR17ES05, Modeling of Automated Reasoning Systems (MARS), Higher Institute of Computer Sciences and Communication Technologies (ISITCom), University of Sousse, Sousse 4011, Tunisia
3 Applied College, University of Tabuk, Tabuk 71491, Saudi Arabia; k_zidi@ut.edu.sa (K.Z.); wghaban@ut.edu.sa (W.G.)
* Correspondence: khaoula.abdellafou@ismaik.rnu.tn

Abstract

This paper considers the two parallel-machine scheduling problem with intree-precedence constraints where machines are subject to non-availability constraints. In the literature, this problem is considered to be an open problem of unknown complexity. The proposed solution proves that the problem under consideration has polynomial complexity. Periods of machine unavailability are predetermined, and both task execution and inter-task communication are modeled as requiring one unit of time. The optimization criterion central to this study is the minimization of the makespan. Such a scheduling challenge is directly applicable to manufacturing environments, where production equipment can be intermittently offline for reasons such as unscheduled repairs or planned preventative maintenance. Adopting a unit-time task model offers a valuable framework for subsequently scheduling larger, preemptable jobs.This work presents a new method, called Scheduling Intrees with Unavailability Constraints (SIwUC), which operates by aggregating tasks into distinct groups. The analysis establishes that the SIwUC algorithm produces optimal schedules and reveals how the underlying problem architecture and its solutions demonstrate a symmetrical property in the distribution of tasks across the two parallel machines. This paper demonstrates that the proposed SIwUC algorithm builds optimal schedules and highlight how the problem structure and its solutions exhibit a form of symmetry in balancing task allocation between the two parallel machines.

Keywords: scheduling; parallel computing; unavailability; processors; SIwUC algorithm

1. Introduction

In classical scheduling , it is commonly assumed that a fixed set of machines or processors remains continuously available throughout the entire planning horizon [1,2]. However, this assumption is often unrealistic in practical environments, where machine availability may be affected by maintenance operations [3], unexpected breakdowns [4], or other operational constraints [5,6]. As a result, scheduling problems with machine non-availability have attracted considerable attention in the literature where different problems were treated such as scheduling where only a limited number of identical processors are available [7], scheduling on uniform parallel machines with periodic unavailability constraints [8,9], scheduling on distributed systems [10,11], and scheduling with communication costs [12,13].

In parallel, the scheduling of unit execution time (UET) tasks [14] has been extensively investigated due to its relevance for modeling preemptable and fine-grained tasks [15,16]. Moreover, precedence constraints and, in particular, intree structures naturally arise in many applications such as parallel computing and workflow scheduling, where communication delays between tasks cannot be neglected such as in the problem of scheduling precedence-constrained tasks [17] and the problem of scheduling-related jobs [18].

Despite these advances, the combined consideration of unitary tasks with intree-precedence constraints, communication costs, and machine non-availability remains largely unexplored.

Motivated by this gap, this paper addresses the problem of scheduling N unit execution time tasks related by intree-precedence constraints with unit communication costs on two identical parallel machines, where one machine is subject to non-availability periods. Using the three-field notation introduced by Graham et al. [19], the problem is denoted as $P2|intree, pi = 1, c = 1, nr - a|Cmax$. This problem has not been previously investigated, and neither its computational complexity nor an optimal solution method has been reported in the literature.

The contributions in this paper are as follows:

- Prove that the complexity of the treated problem is polynomial and does not have an open complexity.
- Propose an optimal algorithm with polynomial complexity.
- Prove the optimality of the proposed algorithm by a set of theorems and lemmas.

The paper is structured as follows: A review of related work is detailed in Section 2, while Section 3 provides a formal description of the problem under study.The proposed SIwUC solution is introduced and explained in Section 4, followed by its evaluation on two illustrative examples in Section 5. Section 6 provides the optimality proof for the algorithm. The paper concludes in Section 7 with a summary and suggestions for future research directions.

2. Related Works

This research examines a dual-constrained scheduling problem that combines communication delays with precedence and non-availability period constraints. Although these constraints have been studied separately in the past, there is not a perfect way to combine them. The new heuristic, Adapted CBoS (ACBoS), is introduced in this section after each constraint has been reviewed separately. For studying the behavior of this heuristic, a new lower bound is proposed to carry out a comparison between ACBoS and the lower bound.

2.1. Scheduling with Unavailabilities

The study of scheduling with non-availability constraints was first conducted by Lee et al. [20,21]. They proved that it is an NP-Hard problem to schedule independent tasks with non-unitary execution times on identical machines while taking unavailability periods into account [22–24].

The study also proved that there is not a single, universal approximation algorithm for this issue. This is due to the fact that certain situations can be created in which only an optimal schedule produces a makespan that is acceptable; in these cases, any algorithm that is not optimal would perform arbitrarily poorly. Lee therefore made the simplifying assumption that a machine is always available. Lee showed that the classical Longest Processing Time (LPT) algorithm achieves a worst-case bound of $(m+1)/2$ under this assumption and when machine j has a single unavailability period $[sj, tj]$ (where $0 \leq sj \leq tj$) within the scheduling horizon.

https://doi.org/10.3390/sym18010103

In [25], the authors study a scheduling scenario that does not allow more than half of the machines to be down at any given time. Given this setting, the authors prove that the LPT heuristic has a performance ratio of at most 2. In [26], the same results are extended to a situation where up to λ machines can be down at once, that is, $1 \leq \lambda \leq m - 1$.

In this generalized setting, the authors show the performance ratio of LPT is guaranteed to be upper-bounded by the study of scheduling with non-availability constraints was first conducted by Lee et al. [20,21]. They proved that it is an NP-Hard problem to schedule independent tasks with non-unitary execution times on identical machines while taking unavailability periods into account [22].

In [8], the authors address the scheduling problem involving two processors, each of which experiences a single interval of unavailability. They proposed exponential time algorithms that gives optimal solutions and showed, through experiments, that their algorithms generate good results especially in practical cases.

2.2. Scheduling Task Problems with Precedence Constraints and Communications

The CBoS algorithm [27] (Cluster-Based Scheduling) is a polynomial-time optimal algorithm for scheduling intree-structured tasks on two identical processors under UECT constraints.

Characteristics:

- Assign the root always to processor P1.
- Identify clusters (subtrees) that can be entirely assigned to P2.
- Balance load between P1 and P2 while minimizing communication delays (by keeping predecessor–successor pairs together when beneficial).

Advantages:

- Polynomial time for two processors.
- Minimizes communication by clustering-related tasks.
- Load balancing through R parameter.
- Optimal for many intree structures under UECT constraints
- Simple to implement.

Limits:

- Only for two processors.
- Assumes unit execution and communication times.
- May not be optimal for all intree structures.
- Does not extend easily to m > 2 processors.

Algorithm steps:

- R computing, which is the number of tasks that will be assigned to the processor P2.
- Cluster selection for P2.
- Processor P1 scheduling.
- Processor P2 scheduling.

CBoS algorithm can be summarized as in Algorithm 1:

https://doi.org/10.3390/sym18010103

Algorithm 1 Clusters determination algorithm

Input: Intree T-tree, Integer N
Output: Tasks allocated to P_2

Begin
    Integer $R \leftarrow \lfloor (n-2)/2 \rfloor$
    Integer $currentLevel \leftarrow 2$
    while $R > 0$ **do**
        $L \leftarrow \{T \mid T$ not marked and $T \in currentLevel\}$
        Sorted in decreasing order by weight
        if $|L| > 1$ **then**
            Let T_i be the first task in L such that $w(T_i) \le R$
            if such a T_i exists **then**
                cluster(T_i) is allocated to P_2
                cluster(T_i) is marked
                $R \leftarrow R - w(T_i)$
                T_i is removed from L
            else
                $currentLevel \leftarrow currentLevel + 1$
            end if
        else
            Let T_i be the only task of L
            $R \leftarrow \min(R, \lfloor (w(T_{alone} - 1)/2 \rfloor)$
            $currentLevel \leftarrow currentLevel + 1$
        end if
    end while
End

In the following Figure 1, an example of scheduling an intree by the CBoS algorithm is presented:

$$Number\ of\ tasks = 18 \text{ and } [18-2]/2 = 8.$$

R is initialized to 8. In this example, the CBoS algorithm assigns 3 subtrees to the processor $P2$. The sum of tasks of the three subtrees is 8 and the rest is allocated to the processor $P1$.

The computed schedule is described by Figure 2.

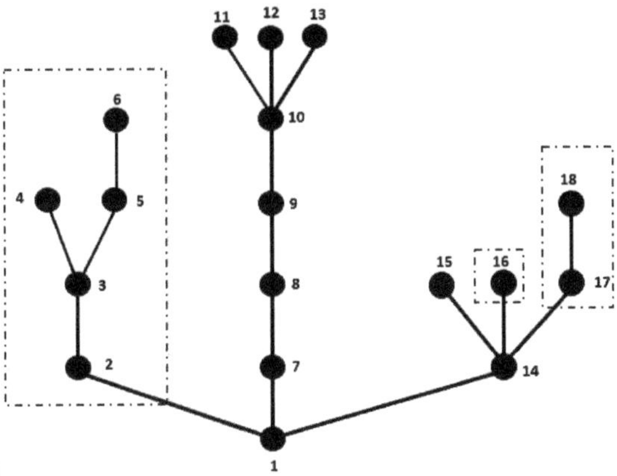

Figure 1. Task graph of the instance.

https://doi.org/10.3390/sym18010103

P1	11	12	13	10	9	8	15	7	14	1
P2	16	18	17	6	5	4	3	2		

Figure 2. Optimal schedule.

2.3. Problem of Scheduling Tasks with Unavailabilities and Precedence Constraints

In the current literature, there is no best algorithm for scheduling precedence-constrained jobs on processors that are unavailable for certain time periods. In [5], the authors proposed a method to address this problem, specifically considering scheduling UECT intrees on two identical processors, called P1 and P2, both of which may experience unavailability periods multiple times.

The new algorithm named Adapted CBoS (ACBoS) is based on the original CBoS algorithm. The most important difference between the two algorithms is how ACBoS cal-culates the parameter R, which is the upper bound on the number of jobs that can be assigned to processor P2 in any optimal schedule. The algorithm computes the value for R as follows:

a. Initialization
Let N denote the total number of tasks in the intree.
Set $R = 0$ as the task count allocated to $P2$.
Set $t = 0$ as the discrete time slot index.
b. Processor availability scanning:
At each time slot t, the availability states of P1 and P2 are evaluated.
c. Task assignment when P1 is available:
If P1(t) is available, decrement N by 1, corresponding to the assignment of one task to P1.
d. Task assignment when P2 is available:
If P2(t) is available, decrement N by 1 and increment R by 1, representing the assignment of one task to P2.
e. Time progression
After processing the availability at time t, increment t by 1. If both processors are unavailable at t, increment t until at least one becomes available.
f. Iteration condition
Repeat steps be until $N \leq 3$.
g. Boundary case N = 3
   - If both P1(t) and P2(t) are available, we simulate assigning two tasks (one to each processor): set N = N − 2 and R = R + 1.
   - If only P1(t) is available, we simulate assigning one task to P1: set N = N − 1 (no change to R).
   - If only P2(t) is available, we simulate assigning one task to P2: set N = N − 1 and R = R + 1. In each case, t is incremented after the simulated assignment to reflect time progression.

h. Final case N = 2
Increment R by 1 if P1 is unavailable at both t and t + 1, indicating that a task must be assigned to P2 due to consecutive unavailability of P1.

The algorithm terminates by returning R, which serves as an adaptive upper bound for task allocation to P2 under intermittent processor unavailability.

The two processors continue to be simulated until N = 0. At this point, the ACBoS algorithm continues in the same manner as the original CBoS algorithm.

https://doi.org/10.3390/sym18010103

Steps of R computing (for the considered ACBoS algorithm) are illustrated by Algorithm 2:

Algorithm 2 R computing algorithm

```
Input: v : root of the intree
Output: R
N ← number of tasks in the intree
t ← 0, R ← 0
while N > 3 do
    if P_1(t) then
        N ← N − 1
    end if
    if P_2(t) then
        N ← N − 1
        R ← R + 1
    end if
    t ← t + 1
end while
while P_1(t) and P_2(t) do
    t ← t + 1
end while
if N = 3 then
    if P_1(t) then
        if P_2(t) then
            R ← R + 1
            N ← 1
        else
            N ← 2
            t ← t + 1
        end if
    else
        N ← 2
        R ← R + 1
        t ← t + 1
    end if
end if
if N = 2 then
    while P_1(t) and P_2(t) do
        t ← t + 1
    end while
    if P_1(t) and P_1(t + 1) then
        R ← R + 1
    end if
end if
return R
```

In order to study the behavior of this algorithm, a lower bound is proposed and a comparison between ACBoS and the lower bound is carried out. The proposed lower bound can be summarized as in Algorithm 3.

https://doi.org/10.3390/sym18010103

Algorithm 3 Bound computation algorithm

$N \leftarrow$ number of tasks in the intree
bound $\leftarrow 0$ ▷ current time slot
while $N > 0$ **do**
  if $P_1(t)$ **then**
    $N \leftarrow N - 1$
  end if
  if $P_2(t)$ **then**
    $N \leftarrow N - 1$
  end if
  bound $\leftarrow$ *bound* $+ 1$
end while
return *bound*

The simulation of the heuristic [28] shows that it gives good results for instances of large trees (Figure 3) but mediocre results for chain instances (Figure 4).

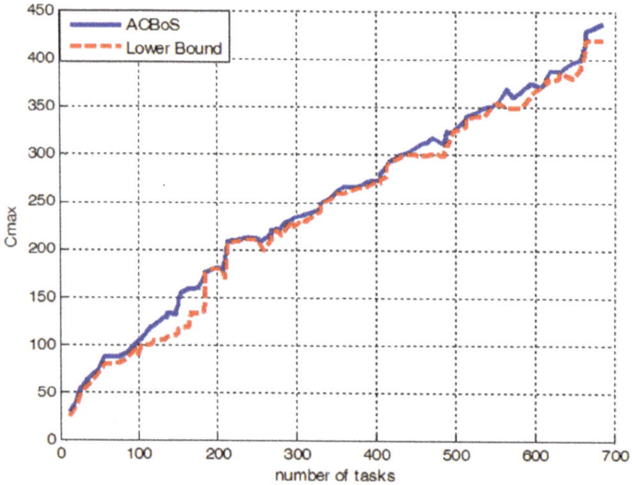

Figure 3. Simulation of ACBoS heuristic.

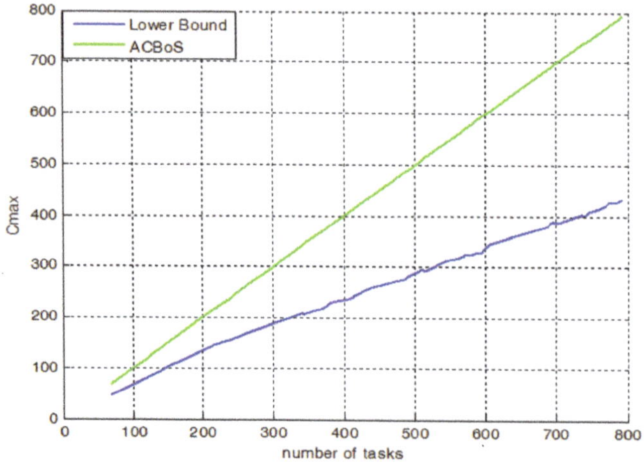

Figure 4. Simulation of ACBoS heuristic.

https://doi.org/10.3390/sym18010103

Figure 4 illustrates that the disparity in makespan between the lower bound and the ACBoS algorithm widens as the number of tasks increases. Additionally, the computational complexity of this problem specifically for schedules involving multiple unavailability periods on both machines remains an open research question.

3. Problem Formulation

We are given the following:

- Tasks: N tasks, numbered 1, 2, . . . , N.
- Precedence relation: These tasks form an intree (also called intree or converging tree).

An intree:

- Each task has at most one immediate successor (children point to a parent in terms of precedence, but precedence arrows go from predecessor to successor in scheduling terms).
- In precedence terms: each task can have multiple predecessors but only one successor (except the root task, which has no successor). So, the successor is the task that must wait until all its predecessors finish. leaf tasks are the ones with no predecessors (incoming arcs), and they all point toward one root. So, in scheduling, a predecessor must finish before a successor starts.

Execution time:

- Every task takes unit time to execute (UET = Unit Execution Time).

Communication cost:

- If a task Ti and its immediate successor Tj are scheduled on different processors, then after finishing Ti, we must wait one unit of communication delay before Tj can start.
- If they are on the same processor, no communication delay occurs. Otherwise, communication time is Unit (UCT = Unit Communication Time).
- Communication is only between predecessor–successor pairs.

Processors:

- Two identical processors are available to schedule tasks. The first processor denoted P1, which is always available, and the second processor P2, subjected to unavailability periods.

Objective:

- Minimize total schedule length (makespan) subject to precedence, communication, and resource constraints.

Notation:

- Using the three-field notation introduced by Graham et al. [19], the problem is denoted as $P2|intree, pi = 1, c = 1, nr - a|Cmax$.

An example of scheduling under UECT assumption and UET assumption is provided to explain the difference between these (Figure 5).

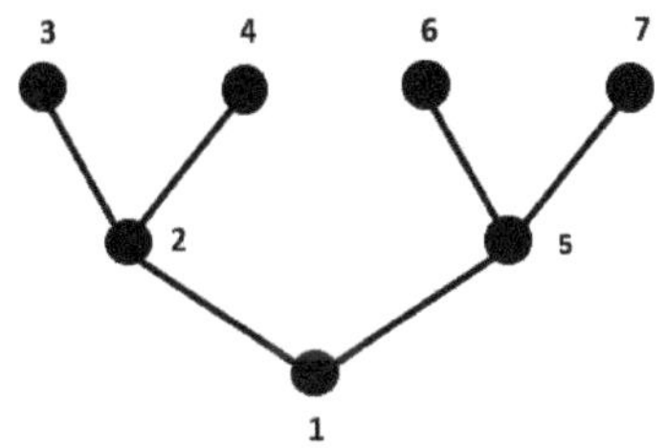

Figure 5. Task graph.

https://doi.org/10.3390/sym18010103

Figure 5 represents the N tasks related by intree-precedence constraints. All execution time of tasks is considered to be unitary.

Figure 6 represents a scheduling under UET assumption and Figure 7 represents a scheduling under UECT assumption.

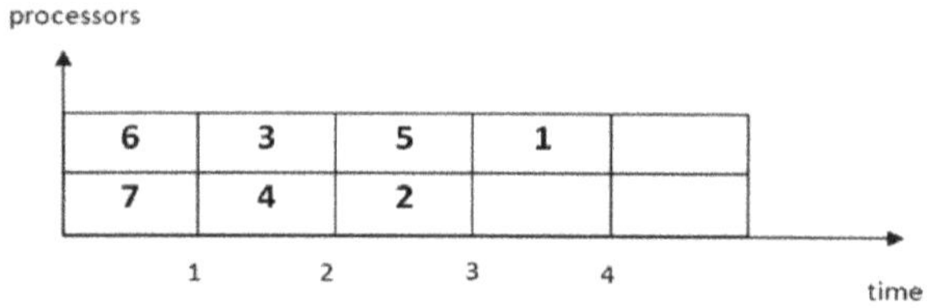

Figure 6. Sheduling under UET assumption.

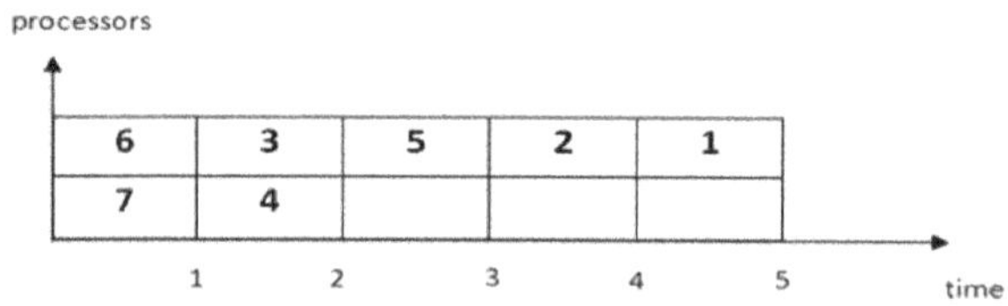

Figure 7. Scheduling under UECT assumption.

The first schedule assumes negligible communication overhead between tasks, regardless of processor assignment, thus focusing solely on precedence constraints. In contrast, the second schedule imposes a unit communication cost for dependent tasks executed on different processors. This restriction prevents task 2 from starting at the second time unit because its predecessor, task 3, runs on P1 while it is assigned to P2.

The objective of this work is to schedule N intree-structured tasks across two identical machines, respecting precedence relations to minimize the makespan. The schedule must also account for unavailability periods on one machine, with the constraint that each machine processes only one task at a time.

4. The Proposed Scheduling Algorithm: Scheduling Intrees with Unavailability Constraints (SIwUC)

In this section, we introduce a polynomial algorithm for minimizing the makespan of UECT intrees on two identical processors (P1 and P2), where one of them is subject to non-availability constraints. Without loss of generality, the processor subject to unavailabilities is denoted P2.

4.1. Principle of the Algorithm

The core strategy of the algorithm is to maximize the workload assigned to processor P2, subject to its scheduled downtime. Once P2 has been loaded to capacity, the remaining tasks are distributed to P1 or partitioned between both processors, based on the structural characteristics of the given task set.

Before presenting the complete algorithmic procedure, we introduce a set of dominance rules that govern task assignment and ordering.

Theorem 1. *A schedule that eliminates idle time on processor P1 is considered dominant. This means that any optimal schedule exhibiting idle periods on P1 can be reconfigured without increasing the makespan into an equally optimal schedule where P1 operates continuously with no idle intervals.*

https://doi.org/10.3390/sym18010103

Proof of Theorem 1. Consider an optimal schedule with idleness on $P1$ (Figure 8). □

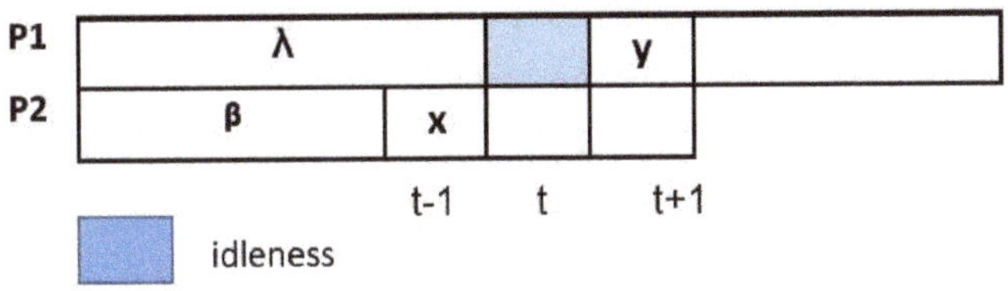

Figure 8. Optimal schedule.

The idle time on $P1$ in this case originated from a communication delay introduced between task X and its single successor, task Y.

Specifically, X was processed on $P2$ at time $t-1$, while Y was scheduled on $P1$ at time t. Although X may have had multiple predecessors, the last of these completed by time $t-3$, leaving sufficient room to reassign X from $P2$ at $t-1$ to $P1$ at t without violating any communication constraints or increasing the makespan.

This transformation illustrates a general principle: schedules that eliminate idle time on $P1$ dominate those that do not, since any schedule with idle periods can be reconverted without worsening the makespan into one where $P1$ operates continuously.

Theorem 2. *Consider an optimal schedule represented by Figure 9 in which processor P2 exhibits idle time.*

This situation arises because task Y, a predecessor of task X, was only executed on P1 starting at time $t-1$. Due to the inherent properties of the intree structure, Y can have at most one successor, which is task X. As a result, Y can be relocated from P1 at time $t-1$ to P2 at time t without violating any constraints, as all predecessors of Y are completed by time $t-2$. Consequently, reassigning Y to P2 at time t eliminates the initial idle interval on P2. While this shift may introduce new idle time on P1, Theorem 1 guarantees that idle periods on P1 can be removed without increasing the overall makespan. Moreover, this removal does not reintroduce the original idle interval on P1. Therefore, by combining the reassignment of Y to P2 with the elimination of P1's idle time, we obtain a revised schedule in which both processors operate without any idle intervals, preserving optimality.

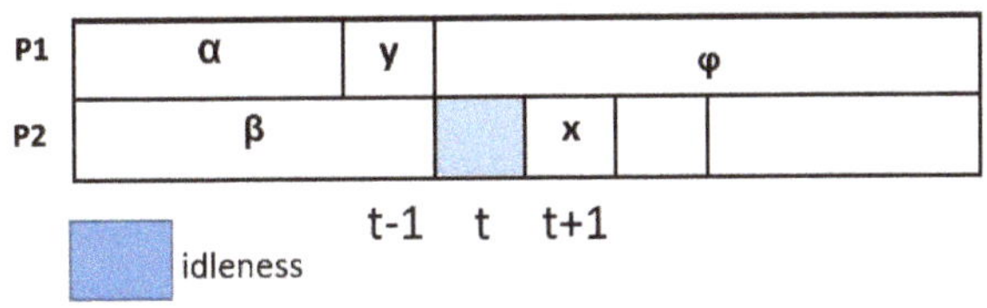

Figure 9. Optimal schedule.

4.2. Description of the Proposed Method

4.2.1. First Step: R Computing

The parameter R is designed to act as a tight upper bound for the number of tasks that can be assigned to processor P2 within the SIwUC (Scheduling with Unavailability Constraints) algorithm. The earlier bound of $\left[\frac{n-2}{2}\right]$ established in the CBoS algorithm no longer applies, since processors may now be subject to intermittent unavailability periods. To address this, we introduce a new iterative procedure to compute R.

https://doi.org/10.3390/sym18010103

We initialize $R = 0$ and then incrementally increase R by verifying whether any task in the intree can be feasibly assigned to P2 without inducing idle time on P1. This feasibility check is repeated iteratively; each time a valid task is found, R is increased by one. The procedure terminates when no additional task can be assigned to P2 without violating the idle-free condition on P1. The value of R at termination is adopted as the final bound. Before elaborating on the algorithm, we introduce two conditions that must be satisfied for any task to be eligible for assignment to P2.

First necessary condition: C1 In a scheduling without idleness, if a task T can be executed on the processor P2 at time t, then

P2(t) is true.
Level (T) $\leq$ N − NB(t)

Proof of C1. Consider a task T scheduled on P2 at time t.

In the intree, there are N − level(T) tasks that are not successors of T. For the schedule to be feasible, this number must be sufficient to occupy all time slots that require filling. Specifically, these slots include the following:

- NB(t) − 1 slots on P2 before time t (excluding the slot occupied by T itself);
- The slot on P1 at time t.

Because all successors of T incur a communication delay at time t, the slot on P1 at t must be taken by a task that is not a successor of T. Therefore, we obtain the following necessary condition

$$N - level(T) \geq NB(t) - 1 + 1.$$

□

Second necessary condition: C2

In any given schedule, if a task T can be executed on the processor P2 at the slot t, then

P2(t) is true
and
$weight(T) \leq NB(t) - 2ift > 1$
$weight(T) = 1ift = 1$

Proof of C2. The algorithmic step establishes the upper bound R, representing the maximum number of tasks that can be allocated to processor P2 without introducing idle time on processor P1. This bound is determined via an iterative analysis of the intree structure. A candidate task T is considered eligible for assignment to P2 only if it satisfies two key conditions C1 and C2. Each time a task meets both criteria, R is incremented. The logical foundation for these assignment conditions rests on the observation that a task T placed on P2 faces two obstructions that limit the execution of its entire subtree at specific times:

1. The execution of task T cannot be performed because there is a blocking condition of task T with regards to time; the insertion of its successor(s) can only occur after it has completed execution.
2. The execution of task T cannot be performed at $t - 1$ with regard to the communication cost between processors; when a successor(s) of task T is scheduled to execute on P1, there is a one-unit delay for message transmission once task T is complete on P2.

https://doi.org/10.3390/sym18010103

Here, we have calculated the maximum possible value for R. At the next scheduling stage, the algorithm will try to form a schedule for P2 containing R tasks and a schedule for P1 containing N-R tasks; if this does not succeed in creating a feasible schedule, the algorithm falls back to allocating all remaining tasks to P1. □

R computing algorithm can be summarized as in Algorithm 4.

Algorithm 4 *R* Computation

```
Input: Intree Tree, Integer N
Output: Integer R
B ← true                                              ▷ 1 operation
t ← 1                                                 ▷ 1 operation
R ← 0                                                 ▷ 1 operation
p ← 0                                                 ▷ 1 operation
while B = true do                                     ▷ N − 5 comparisons
    if P_2(t) then                                    ▷ N − 5 evaluations
        if t = 1 then                                 ▷ N − 5 comparisons
            p ← 1                                     ▷ N − 5 assignments
        else
            p ← R + (t − 1)                           ▷ N − 5 assignments
        end if
        if in Tree exists an unmarked task T_i such that
    w(T_i) ≤ p and level(T_i) ≤ N − (t + R + 1) then  ▷ 7N(N − 5) operations
            if level(T_i) = N − (t + R + 1) then      ▷ 5(N − 5) comparisons
                mark all tasks in the tree except the successors of T_i   ▷ 2(N − 1)(N − 5) operations
            end if
            R ← R + 1                                 ▷ 2(N − 5) operations
            mark T_i                                  ▷ 2(N − 5) operations
        else
            B ← False                                 ▷ N − 5 assignments
        end if
    end if
    if t + R > N − 5 then                             ▷ 3(N − 5) comparisons
        B ← False
    end if
    t ← t + 1                                         ▷ 2(N − 5) operations
end while
remove task markings for all tasks in the intree      ▷ N operations
return R
```

4.2.2. Second Step: Schedule Construction

The Figure 10 introduces the core task assignment algorithm which represented by. The fundamental principle guiding this algorithm is to distribute tasks between processors P1 and P2 so as to minimize the overall makespan.

To achieve this, we employ a multi-case heuristic tailored to reduce communication delays and, most critically, to evenly balance the computational workload across both processors. Maintaining a balanced load prevents either processor from becoming a bottleneck, which is essential for minimizing the total schedule length.

https://doi.org/10.3390/sym18010103

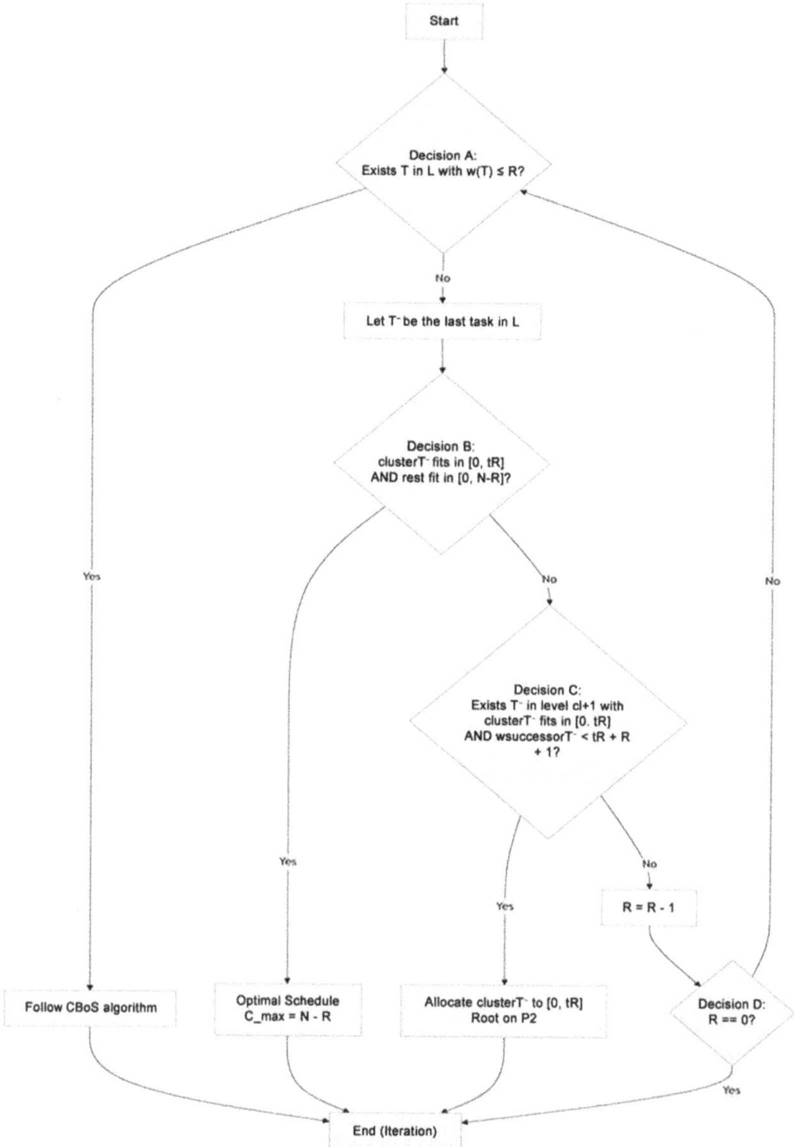

Figure 10. Flowchart of the proposed algorithm. L: The list of candidate tasks. R: The current upper bound for the number of tasks on P2. w(T): The weight or processing time of task T. cluster(T): The set of tasks in the subtree rooted at T. t(R): A function that maps the value R to a specific time point on P2. N: The total number of tasks. C_{max}: The makespan (total schedule length). level cl + 1: A specific level in the intree graph. The complexity of SIwUC algorithm is O (N2).

5. Complete Examples

In this section, two complete examples are described. In the first one, we consider an instance of intree and scheduling environment such that the optimal schedule assigns the root to the processor P1. Then, in the second example, we present another instance of intree such that the optimal schedule allocates the root to the processor P2.

https://doi.org/10.3390/sym18010103

5.1. Example 1

In this example, we consider an instance with 16 tasks as illustrated by Figure 11 and a scheduling environment as described by Figure 12.

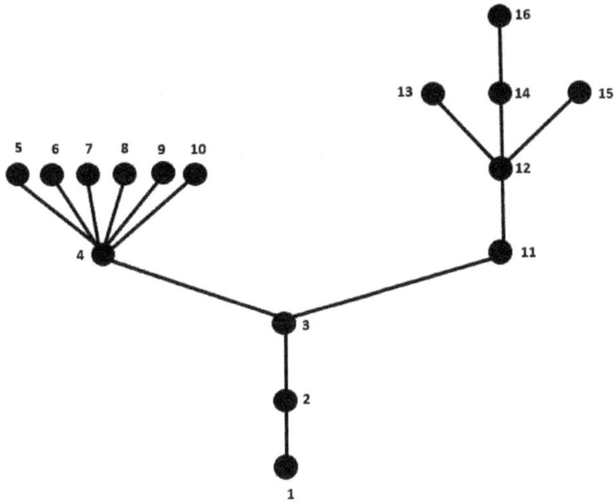

Figure 11. Instance of the intree.

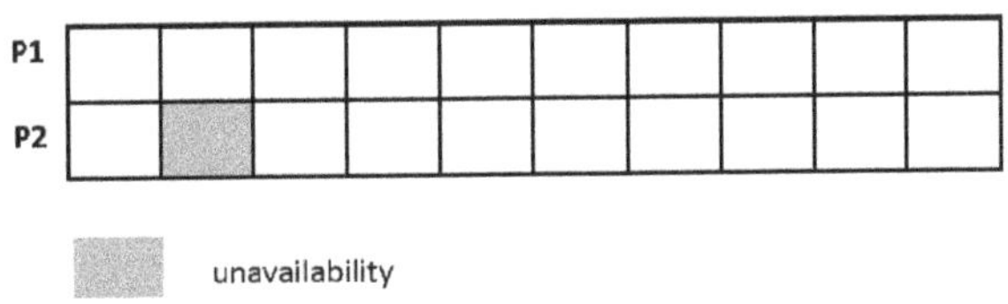

Figure 12. Machine profile.

- R computing steps

Table 1 presents the calculation details of R, which represents the maximum number of tasks that can be assigned to the P2 processor.

Table 1. Iteration values of the algorithm parameters.

Iteration (t)	$P_2(t)$	p Value	R Value
1	true	1	1
2	false	1	1
3	true	3	2
4	true	5	3
5	true	7	4
6	true	9	5

- Schedule Computing steps

Table 2 presents the details in the scheduling calculation, step by step.

https://doi.org/10.3390/sym18010103

Table 2. Execution steps of the algorithm.

Level	List L	Satisfied Condition	Chosen Task	R	Marked Tasks
2	$\{2\}$	1. All tasks in L have weights higher than R. 2. $NB(t(R)) < N - cl$. 3. $cl := cl + 1$.		5	
3	$\{3\}$	1. All tasks in L have weights higher than R. 2. $NB(t(R)) < N - cl$. 3. $cl := cl + 1$.		5	
4	$\{4, 11\}$	1. All tasks in L have weights higher than R. 2. $NB(t(R)) < N - cl$. 3. $cl := cl + 1$.		5	
5	$\{5, 6, 7, 8, 9, 10, 12\}$	1. In L exists a task T_i such that $w(T_i) \leq R$.	12	0	$\{12, 13, 14, 15, 16\}$

- Computed schedule

The Figure 13 presents the optimal schedule where 5 tasks are assigned to the processor P2 and 11 tasks are assigned to P1.

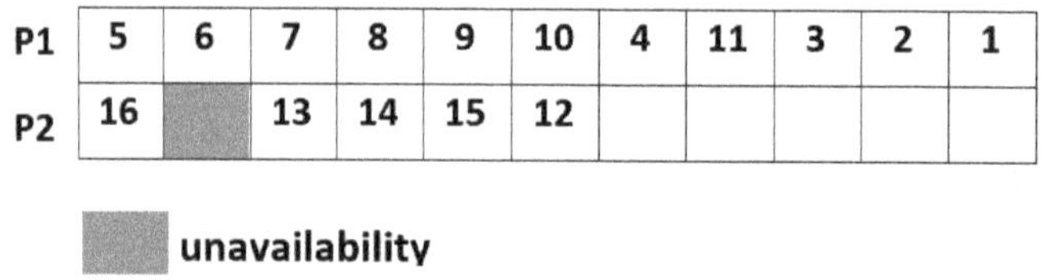

Figure 13. Optimal schedule.

5.2. Example 2

In this example, we consider an instance with 7 tasks as illustrated by Figure 14 and a scheduling environment as described by Figure 15.

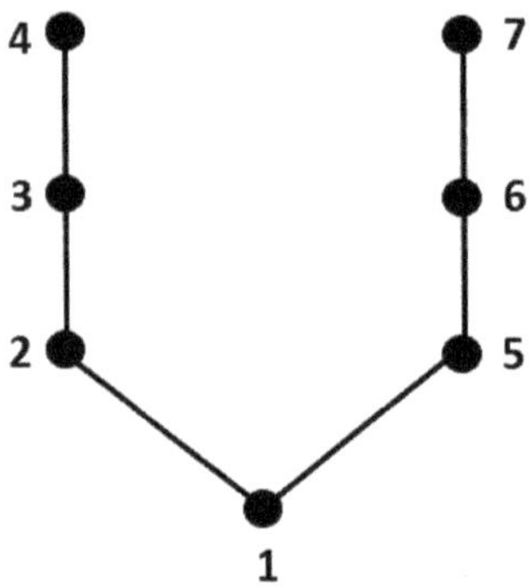

Figure 14. Instance of the intree.

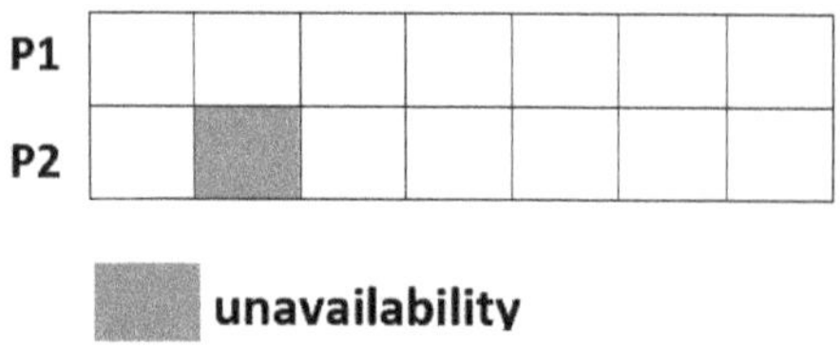

Figure 15. Machine profile.

https://doi.org/10.3390/sym18010103

Step 1: **Initialization**: The algorithm initializes $R := 2$, as determined by Algorithm 4. This parameter R quantifies the remaining communication capacity or available time slack for task scheduling.

Step 2: **Level Selection**: The current processing level is set to $c_l := 2$, establishing the baseline for subsequent scheduling decisions.

Step 3: **Task List Identification**: The scheduler identifies the task set $L = \{5, 2\}$ for processing. Notably, all tasks in L have weights exceeding the current resource constraint R.

Step 4: **Resource Verification**: Based on the condition $NB(t(R)) = N - c_l$, the scheduler examines the next processing level to locate a task T whose corresponding cluster, cluster(T), can be feasibly scheduled within the time interval $[0, 3]$.

Step 5: **Cluster Assignment**: Cluster 3 is determined to be schedulable within $[0, 3]$. This assignment satisfies the feasibility conditions since $w(2) < 6$ and processor P_2 maintains availability (experiencing no unavailability periods) during the subsequent interval $[3, 5]$.

Step 6: **Resource Update**: Following the successful allocation of cluster 3, the remaining resource R is decremented to zero, reflecting the complete utilization of available resources.

Step 7: **Chain Scheduling**: The residual task set $\{7, 6, 5, 2, 1\}$ undergoes sequential chain scheduling: tasks are assigned to processor P_1 during $[0, 3]$, then to processor P_2 during $[3, 5]$, ensuring efficient processor utilization and meeting timing constraints.

The optimal computed schedule is described by Figure 16:

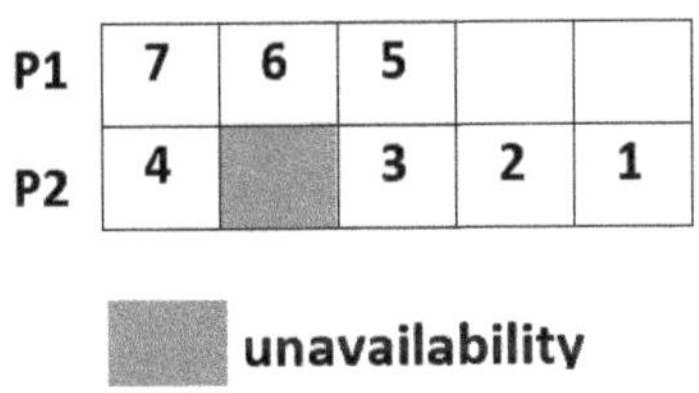

Figure 16. Optimal schedule.

5.3. Example 3

In this example, we consider an instance with 22 tasks as illustrated by Figure 17 and a scheduling environment as described by Figure 18.

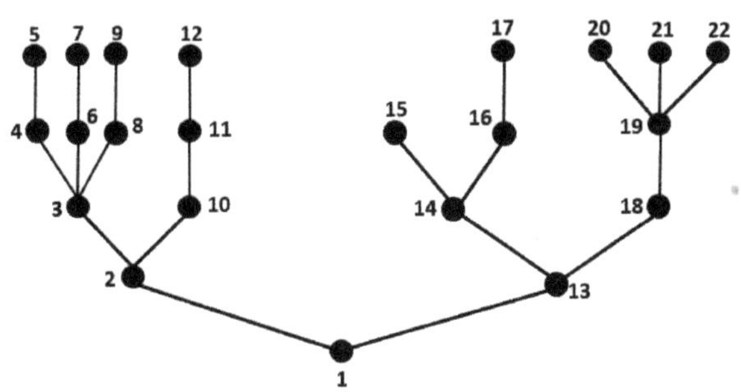

Figure 17. Instance of the intree.

https://doi.org/10.3390/sym18010103

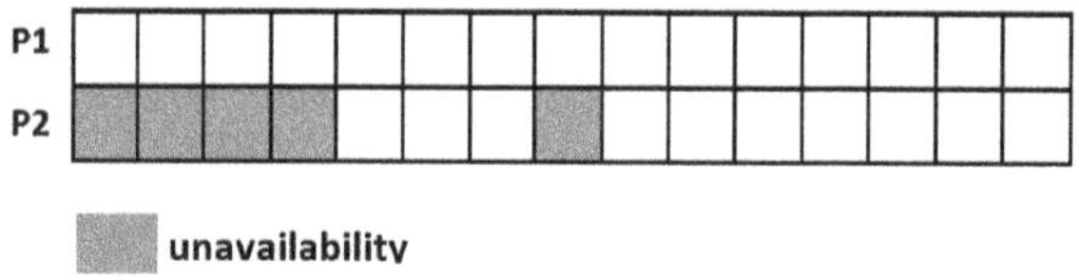

Figure 18. Machine profile.

For a number of tasks equal to 22, the value of R calculated by Algorithm 3 is equal to 7, and the optimal schedule calculated by Algorithm 4 is represented by Figure 19. Indeed, the subtree rooted by task T3 is allocated to P2, and the remaining tasks are assigned to P1.

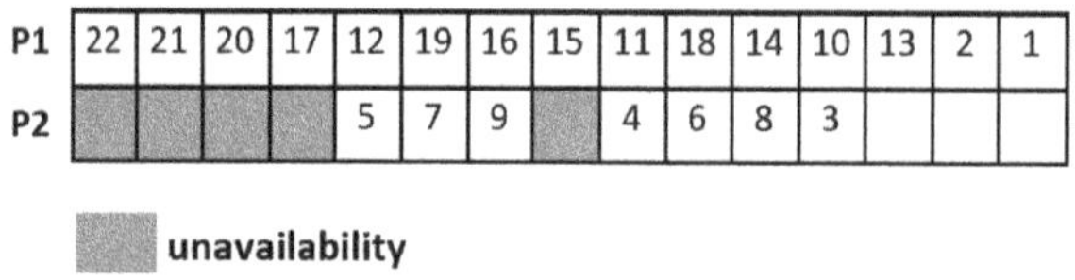

Figure 19. Optimal schedule.

6. Optimality Proof

Lemma 1. *An optimal schedule cannot initially assign more than R tasks to the processor P_2.*

Proof. The parameter R, derived from the initial algorithm, represents the upper bound on tasks assignable to P_2 while maintaining a schedule with no idle time on P_1. Under the assumption that the root task of the intree is allocated to P_1, the makespan achieved by such a schedule is $N - R$, where N denotes the total number of tasks. This section aims to demonstrate that this makespan is optimal.

For contradiction, suppose a schedule exists that assigns $R + 1$ tasks to P_2. By the definition of R, at least one of these $R + 1$ tasks violates one or both conditions (C1 or C2) required for a non-idle schedule on P_1. Consequently, P_1 must experience idle time due to that task. Given the intree structure and the communication delays between tasks, this idle time will not be isolated; rather, it will propagate, leading to at least two distinct idle periods on P_1. As a result, the makespan would increase to at least $(N - R) + 1$. This contradicts the optimal makespan of $N - R$, thereby confirming that the maximum feasible R yields $C_{max} = N - R$, which is indeed optimal. □

Lemma 2. *The schedule computed by SIwUC algorithm is without idleness on the processor P_1.*

Proof. Constraints C1 and C2 form the foundational criteria for assigning tasks to processor P_2. By adhering to these constraints during task allocation, it is guaranteed that processor P_1 will not encounter any idle periods resulting from the distribution of work to P_2. Consequently, any schedule constructed in compliance with C1 and C2 will maintain continuous execution on P_1 without interruptions.

Moreover, Theorem 1 addresses schedules that deviate from C1 and C2 by providing a corrective mechanism: any idle interval on P_1 can be resolved by transferring an appropriate task currently scheduled on P_2 to P_1. The steps explained by the flowchart in Figure 10 incorporates this principle by enforcing conditions C1 and C2 during initial task assignment, and when idle time arises on P_1, by applying the transformation prescribed in Theorem 1 to reassign work from P_2 to P_1, thereby restoring an idle-free schedule. □

Lemma 3. *The schedule computed by SIwUC algorithm is without idleness on the processor P_2.*

Proof. It is impossible that that a time slot t would be able to violate either of the necessary conditions (C1 or C2) at the same time that its following time slot, $t+1$, meets both conditions. In particular, if a necessary condition is not met at time t, it cannot be met at any subsequent time slot $t+k$, where $k \geq 1$.

First case: At time t, the first necessary condition (C1) is not satisfied: there exists no task T in the tree such that $\text{level}(T) \leq N - NB(t)$. C1 remains not satisfied for all future times $t+k$ ($k \geq 0$) because $NB(t+k) > NB(t)$.

Second case: At time t, the second necessary condition (C2) is not satisfied: there exists no task T in the intree such that $\text{weight}(T) \leq NB(t) - 2$ and $\text{level}(T) \leq N - NB(t)$. Observe that for $k > 0$, both $NB(t+k)$ and $\text{weight}(T)$ increase by at least 2 between t and $t+k$. Therefore, at time t, C2 does not hold.

The completion of task T that occurs at some future moment (C2) and satisfies both conditions is completed at time $(t+k)$. Task T meets the level requirement at time $(t+k)$ ($\text{level}(T) \leq N - NB(t+k)$). Therefore, it has also met the relaxed level requirement at a previous point in time, time t ($\text{level}(T) \leq N - NB(t)$). In order to have violated C2 at time t, task T must have violated the weight requirement for that task ($\text{weight}(T) > NB(t) - 2$). To satisfy C2 at time $(t+k)$, we must have a weight requirement that satisfies C2 ($\text{weight}(T) \leq NB(t+k) - 2$) in order to satisfy $NB(t+k) > NB(t)$. Additionally, any newly available task that becomes available at $(t+k)$, which causes an increase in $NB(t)$, will automatically violate the level requirement ($\text{level}(T)$). Thus, C2 is not able to satisfy the task due to contradictions. □

Lemma 4. *If it is not possible to assign a hole cluster to P_2 (i.e., tasks of the cluster will be allocated to P_1 and P_2) or the root cannot be assigned to P_1 and the rest of tasks can be allocated without idleness, then the makespan of the schedule is optimal.*

Proof. Once all tasks are assigned to their respective processors, the resulting schedule achieves an optimal makespan of $N - R$. □

Lemma 5. *If it is not possible to obtain a schedule without idleness when the root is allocated to the processor P_1 and the root cannot be assigned to P_2, then a decrease of R is the only solution.*

Proof. Reducing R is necessary when processor P_1 has idle time and assigning the root task to P_2 would increase the makespan.

For this reason, in the definition of R, we speak about the maximum number of tasks that can be allocated to P_2 and not the exact number of tasks that can be allocated to P_2. □

7. Conclusions and Future Works

The problem of scheduling intrees with unit execution time on two processors where one of these is subjected to unavailability periods is studied in this paper. In this paper, a new optimal algorithm is proposed for this problem.

The proposed algorithm is entitled SIwUC.

An optimal proof of the proposed SIwUC algorithm is presented. Depending on the instance of the graph and the scheduling environment, the optimal schedule assigns the root to the processor P1 or the processor P2.

The two cases are treated in this paper. The obtained results emphasize how the scheduling solutions exhibit a form of symmetry in balancing tasks between the two processors despite unavailability constraints.

As future work, this problem can be extended to the case of unavailability on both processors or a number of machines greater than two.

https://doi.org/10.3390/sym18010103

Author Contributions: Conceptualization, K.B.A.; formal analysis, K.B.A. and K.Z.; methodology, K.B.A. and W.G.; software, K.B.A.; validation, K.B.A. and K.Z.; writing—original draft preparation, K.B.A.; writing—review and editing, K.B.A., K.Z., and W.G.; visualization, K.B.A. and W.G.; supervision, K.Z. and W.G.; project administration, K.Z. All authors have read and agreed to the published version of the manuscript.

Funding: This research received no external funding.

Data Availability Statement: Data is contained within the article.

Conflicts of Interest: The authors declare no conflicts of interest.

References

1. Abdellafou , K.B.; Sanlaville, E.; Mahjoub, A.; Korbaa, O. Scheduling UECT trees with communication delays on two processors with unavailabilities. *IFAC-PapersOnLine* **2015**, *48*, 1790–1795. [CrossRef]
2. Bal, P.K.; Mohapatra, S.K.; Das, T.K.; Srinivasan, K.; Hu, Y.-C. A joint resource allocation, security with efficient task scheduling in cloud computing using hybrid machine learning techniques. *Sensors* **2022**, *22*, 1242. [CrossRef] [PubMed]
3. Garg, H.; Rani, M.; Sharma, S.P. Preventive maintenance scheduling of the pulping unit in a paper plant. *Jpn. J. Ind. Appl. Math.* **2013**, *30*, 397–414. [CrossRef]
4. Liao, C.-J.; Chen, W.-J. Scheduling under machine breakdown in a continuous process industry. *Comput. Oper. Res.* **2004**, *31*, 415–428. [CrossRef]
5. Sanlaville, E.; Mahjoub, A.; Guinand, F. Scheduling problems on parallel machines with communicating tasks and unavailability. In Proceedings of the 15th Congress of the French Society of Operations Research and Decision Support (ROADEF), Marseille, France, 26–28 February 2014.
6. Bamatraf, K.; Gharbi, A. Variable Neighborhood Search for Minimizing the Makespan in a Uniform Parallel Machine Scheduling. *Systems* **2024**, *12*, 221. [CrossRef]
7. Munier Kordon, A.; Kacem, F.; de Dinechin, B.D.; Finta, L. Scheduling an interval ordered precedence graph with communication delays and a limited number of processors. *RAIRO-Oper. Res.* **2013**, *47*, 73–87. [CrossRef]
8. Kaabi, J.; Harrath, Y. Scheduling on uniform parallel machines with periodic unavailability constraints. *Int. J. Prod. Res.* **2019**, *57*, 216–227. [CrossRef]
9. He, S.; Wu, J.; Wei, B.; Wu, J. Algorithms for tree-shaped task partition and allocation on heterogeneous multiprocessors. *J. Supercomput.* **2023**, *79*, 13210–13240. [CrossRef]
10. Shukur, H.; Zeebaree, S.R.M.; Ahmed, A.J.; Zebari, R.R.; Ahmed, O.; Tahir, B.S.A.; Sadeeq, M.A.M. A state of art: Survey for concurrent computation and clustering of parallel computing for distributed systems. *J. Appl. Sci. Technol. Trends* **2020**, *1*, 148–154. [CrossRef]
11. Ben Abdellafou, K.; Hadda, H.; Korbaa, O. An improved tabu search meta-heuristic approach for solving scheduling problem with non-availability constraints. *Arab. J. Sci. Eng.* **2019**, *44*, 3369–3379. [CrossRef]
12. Fuentes, Y.O.; Kim, S. Parallel computational microhydrodynamics: Communication scheduling strategies. *AIChE J.* **1992**, *38*, 1059–1078. [CrossRef]
13. Amoura, A.K.; Bampis, E.; Konig, J.-C. Scheduling algorithms for parallel Gaussian elimination with communication costs. *IEEE Trans. Parallel Distrib. Syst.* **1998**, *9*, 679–686. [CrossRef]
14. Zinder, Y.; Su, B.; Singh, G.; Sorli, R. Scheduling UET-UCT tasks: Branch-and-bound search in the priority space. *Optim. Eng.* **2010**, *11*, 627–646. [CrossRef]
15. Tang, N. Calculation of Latency of Real-Time System and Fixed-Parameter Tractibility of UET-UCT Scheduling Problems. Ph.D. Thesis, Sorbonne Universitè, Paris, France, 2022.
16. Giroudeau, R.; König, J.-C.; Valery, B. Scheduling UET-tasks on a star network: Complexity and approximation. *4OR* **2011**, *9*, 29–48. [CrossRef]
17. Su, Y.; Vardi, S.; Ren, X.; Wierman, A. Communication-aware scheduling of precedence-constrained tasks on related machines. *Oper. Res. Lett.* **2023**, *51*, 709–716. [CrossRef]
18. Maiti, B.; Rajaraman, R.; Stalfa, D.; Svitkina, Z.; Vijayaraghavan, A. Scheduling precedence-constrained jobs on related machines with communication delay. In Proceedings of the IEEE 61st Annual Symposium on Foundations of Computer Science (FOCS), Durham, NC, USA, 16–19 November 2020; pp. 834–845.
19. Graham, R.I. The combinatorial mathematics of scheduling. *Sci. Am.* **1978**, *238*, 124–133. [CrossRef]
20. Lee, C.-Y. Machine scheduling with an availability constraint. *J. Glob. Optim.* **1996**, *9*, 395–416. [CrossRef]
21. Lee, C.-Y. Two-machine flowshop scheduling with availability constraints. *Eur. J. Oper. Res.* **1999**, *114*, 420–429. [CrossRef]

https://doi.org/10.3390/sym18010103

22. Canon, L.-C.; Essafi, A.; Trystram, D. A proactive approach for coping with uncertain resource availabilities on desktop grids. In Proceedings of the 21st International Conference on High Performance Computing (HiPC), Goa, India, 17–20 December 2014; pp. 1–9.
23. Jaykrishnan, G.; Levin, A. Scheduling with cardinality dependent unavailability periods. *Eur. J. Oper. Res.* **2024**, *316*, 443–458. [CrossRef]
24. Shabtay, D. Single-machine scheduling with machine unavailability periods and resource dependent processing times. *Eur. J. Oper. Res.* **2022**, *296*, 423–439. [CrossRef]
25. Ait Aba, M.; Zaourar, L.; Munier, A. Efficient algorithm for scheduling parallel applications on hybrid multicore machines with communications delays and energy constraint. *Concurr. Comput. Pract. Exp.* **2020**, *32*, e5573. [CrossRef]
26. Amiri, M.M.; Gündüz, D. Computation scheduling for distributed machine learning with straggling workers. *IEEE Trans. Signal Process.* **2019**, *67*, 6270–6284. [CrossRef]
27. Trystram, D.; Guinand, F. Scheduling UET Trees with communication delays on two processors. *RAIRO Oper. Res.* **2000**, *34*, 131–144.
28. Ben Abdellafou, K.; Hadda, H.; Korbaa, O. Heuristic algorithms for scheduling intrees on m machines with non-availability constraints. *Oper. Res.* **2021**, *21*, 55–71. [CrossRef]

https://doi.org/10.3390/sym18010103

symmetry

MDPI

Article

Symmetry-Aware Superpixel-Enhanced Few-Shot Semantic Segmentation

Lan Guo [1,†], Xuyang Li [1,†], Jinqiang Wang [1], Yuqi Tong [1], Jie Xiao [1], Rui Zhou [1], Ling-Huey Li [2], Qingguo Zhou [1,*] and Kuan-Ching Li [2,*]

[1] School of Information Science and Engineering, Lanzhou University, Lanzhou 730000, China; guol2023@lzu.edu.cn (L.G.); lxuyang2023@lzu.edu.cn (X.L.); jqwang16@lzu.edu.cn (J.W.); tongyq2024@lzu.edu.cn (Y.T.); xiaoj2024@lzu.edu.cn (J.X.); zr@lzu.edu.cn (R.Z.)

[2] Department of Computer Science and Information Engineering, Providence University, Taichung 43301, Taiwan; s1091858@gm.pu.edu.tw

[*] Correspondence: zhouqg@lzu.edu.cn (Q.Z.); kuancli@pu.edu.tw (K.-C.L.)

[†] These authors contributed equally to this work.

Abstract: Few-Shot Semantic Segmentation (FSS) faces significant challenges in modeling complex backgrounds and maintaining prediction consistency due to limited training samples. Existing methods oversimplify backgrounds as single negative classes and rely solely on pixel-level alignments. To address these issues, we propose a symmetry-aware superpixel-enhanced FSS framework with a symmetric dual-branch architecture that explicitly models the superpixel region-graph in both the support and query branches. First, top–down cross-layer fusion injects low-level edge and texture cues into high-level semantics to build a more complete representation of complex backgrounds, improving foreground–background separability and boundary quality. Second, images are partitioned into superpixels and aggregated into "superpixel tokens" to construct a Region Adjacency Graph (RAG). Support-set prototypes are used to initialize query-pixel predictions, which are then projected into the superpixel space for cross-image prototype alignment with support superpixels. We further perform message passing/energy minimization on the RAG to enhance intra-region consistency and boundary adherence, and finally back-project the predictions to the pixel space. Lastly, by aggregating homogeneous semantic information, we construct robust foreground and background prototype representations, enhancing the model's ability to perceive both seen and novel targets. Extensive experiments on the PASCAL-5^i and COCO-20^i benchmarks demonstrate that our proposed model achieves superior segmentation performance over the baseline and remains competitive with existing FSS methods.

Keywords: few-shot learning; semantic segmentation; cross-layer feature fusion; symmetry-aware superpixels

1. Introduction

Semantic segmentation, a core task in computer vision, has broad applicability across medical image analysis, autonomous driving, robotic vision, and remote sensing image interpretation [1,2]. However, the stringent demand for large-scale, pixel-level annotations in conventional segmentation methods makes data collection and labeling prohibitively expensive, substantially limiting their practicality in real-world scenarios. To alleviate this issue, few-shot semantic segmentation (FSS) has emerged, which aims to achieve rapid adaptation and accurate segmentation of novel classes under conditions of extreme annotation scarcity.

Few-shot segmentation (FSS) typically uses a dual-branch architecture (support and query). The goal is to learn generalizable representations from the support set and quickly adapt them for segmenting the query image. Prototype learning, a common approach, extracts class prototypes from the support set and uses pixel–prototype matching on the query image for fast adaptation. However, FSS faces challenges due to limited supervision, distribution shifts, and noise in pixel-level decisions, leading to issues such as foreground–background confusion, inconsistent intra-region predictions, and inaccurate boundaries, especially in complex scenes with varying object scales [3–5].

Most existing prototype-based methods rely on pixel-level prototype alignment. These approaches tend to oversimplify the background into a single negative prototype, leading to foreground–background confusion. This practice can induce foreground–background confusion and biased matching in complex scenes. Simultaneously, the absence of explicit regional topological constraints in pixel-level decisions often results in discontinuities within objects and boundary bleeding. To mitigate these limitations, recent studies have approached the problem from multiple angles: for example, cross-domain FSS explores automatically generated prompts and interactions with large models to boost generalization and transferability; intrinsic feature enhancement and consistency modeling strive to extract more discriminative and alignable semantic representations from limited samples, thereby stabilizing pixel-level decisions [6]; in addition, boundary- and structure-aware enhancements have been shown to significantly reduce misclassification and omission around object edges [7]. Despite these efforts, several critical gaps remain insufficiently addressed in current few-shot semantic segmentation research. First, background oversimplification persists, as most existing methods treat diverse backgrounds as a uniform negative class, failing to capture the inherent complexity and heterogeneity of real-world background distributions. This oversimplification introduces systematic bias during prototype matching and undermines the model's ability to distinguish subtle foreground–background boundaries. Second, representations of complex backgrounds remain incomplete—relying solely on high-level semantics may overlook fine-grained low-level cues such as edges and textures, which are crucial for accurate boundary localization and foreground–background separability. Third, a lack of region-level consistency and boundary handling arises from purely pixel-level prototype alignment, which lacks explicit constraints on regional topology and adjacency, making it difficult to guarantee intra-region consistency and precise boundary alignment. Finally, the need for multi-prototype alignment becomes evident, as single-prototype strategies fail to capture intra-class variation and cannot adequately handle diverse object appearances within the same semantic category.

To this end, we propose a symmetry-aware superpixel-enhanced few-shot semantic segmentation method. The core idea is to explicitly perform symmetric superpixel region-graph modeling in both the support and query branches. First, through top–down cross-layer fusion, we inject fine-grained low-level cues (e.g., edges and textures) into high-level semantics to build a more complete representation of complex backgrounds, thereby improving foreground–background separability and boundary quality. At the structural level, we partition the query image into superpixels and construct a Region Adjacency Graph (RAG): we initialize query-pixel predictions using support prototypes, project them into the superpixel space for cross-image prototype alignment with support superpixels, and then perform message passing and energy minimization on the RAG to enhance intra-region consistency and boundary adherence; finally, we back-project the predictions to the pixel space. At the representational level, we aggregate homogeneous semantic information to construct robust foreground and background prototype representations, compensating for the mismatch caused by oversimplifying the negative class.

Our contributions are as follows:

1. We design a top–down cross-layer fusion strategy that effectively injects low-level edge and texture cues into high-level semantics, yielding a more complete and separable representation in complex backgrounds. This alleviates the foreground–background confusion caused by oversimplifying the negative class and enhances the model's sensitivity to seen and unseen targets.

2. We propose a symmetry-aware framework that explicitly performs region-graph modeling and cross-image prototype alignment in both the support and query branches. This design systematically improves intra-region consistency and boundary quality.

3. On the PASCAL-5^i and COCO-20^i benchmarks, our method surpasses the baseline in segmentation accuracy and delivers competitive results compared with the existing FSS approaches, validating its effectiveness and generalizability.

2. Related Work

2.1. Few-Shot Learning

Few-shot learning (FSL) aims to build machine learning systems that can learn new tasks from very limited labeled samples, and has become a key route to addressing data scarcity [8–10]. Research in this area largely follows two directions: optimization-based meta-learning and non-parametric metric learning. Meta-learning approaches learn favorable model initializations or optimization strategies so that the model can quickly adapt to new tasks with few samples [11–13]. These methods typically optimize model parameters via meta-learning and often require fine-tuning during testing. In contrast, metric-learning methods keep parameters fixed at test time and perform inference by computing similarities between query and support samples, offering fast inference and obviating parameter updates [14–19]. Concretely, the mean of support features serves as a class-specific representation, and distance-based matching is used to classify the query set.

The rise of vision–language models has opened new opportunities for FSL: recent work explores leveraging pre-trained vision–language models to enhance tasks such as few-shot object detection [20–22]. In addition, cross-domain few-shot learning employs techniques such as adaptive transformer networks to bridge distribution gaps between the source and target domains [23,24]. These advances suggest that FSL is progressing toward more practical and versatile solutions.

2.2. Semantic Segmentation

Semantic segmentation assigns a semantic label to every pixel in an image and has wide applications in autonomous driving, medical image analysis, and remote sensing image understanding [25,26]. Inspired by the success of fully convolutional networks (FCNs), numerous FCN-based architectures have been proposed for semantic segmentation, such as UNet [27], DeepLab [28], SegNet [29], and PSPNet [30]. Traditional methods typically adopt an encoder–decoder design to support end-to-end learning from feature extraction to dense prediction. Over time, the field has evolved from conventional FCNs to architectures that integrate multiple advanced mechanisms. Current research hotspots focus on effectively incorporating attention mechanisms and multi-scale feature fusion strategies into FCN backbones [31–34]. Notably, despite the strong performance of deep learning under full supervision, the heavy reliance on large-scale labeled datasets limits applicability in label-scarce scenarios—motivating the rise of few-shot semantic segmentation research.

2.3. Few-Shot Semantic Segmentation

Few-shot semantic segmentation (FSS) combines the strengths of FSL and semantic segmentation, aiming to achieve accurate pixel-level segmentation of novel classes with only a few labeled examples [35,36]. Distinct from image classification, which emphasizes global feature matching, FSS requires dense, pixel-level prediction—making learning under few-shot conditions particularly challenging.

Shaban et al. [37] first proposed an FSS model based on a dual-branch architecture. Subsequent works have introduced many deep learning-based FSS methods [13,31,38–40]. Recent surveys indicate that existing methods can be broadly grouped into three categories: prototype metric-based, meta-learning-based, and conditional parameterization-based approaches [41]. In recent studies [42–46], the averaged deep features extracted by a backbone are used as class-specific representations—an archetypal use of metric learning. Prototype metric-based methods, which extract class prototypes from the support set and perform similarity matching to segment the query image, have become mainstream. However, these methods typically focus on foreground regions in the current support images and seldom exploit background regions; moreover, because each class representation is learned independently per support set, substantial contextual information is lost. Some meta-learning approaches [47–50] have shown promising results in FSS, but they often introduce many hyperparameters and face optimization challenges [6,19]. Subsequent research [51–53] has enhanced prototype representations by incorporating deep descriptors and pixel-level metric learning, leveraging richer, transferable semantics in fine-grained features [54,55]. Furthermore, Vision Transformers (ViTs) have demonstrated exceptional performance in the field of few-shot semantic segmentation. Dos Santos et al. [56] utilized Vision Transformers for multi-scale feature fusion and enhanced few-shot segmentation effectiveness through self-attention mechanisms. This study indicates that ViTs possess strong feature learning capabilities under few-sample conditions. MSDNet [57] incorporates a multi-scale decoder and transformer-guided prototyping approach to improve few-shot semantic segmentation performance, further confirming the potential of ViTs in this task.

Nonetheless, purely pixel-based prototype alignment generally lacks explicit constraints on regional topology and adjacency, making it difficult to guarantee intra-region consistency and precise boundary alignment. Furthermore, existing methods often model the background coarsely as a "single negative class", which mismatches the diverse and structurally complex background distributions in real scenes and thus induces systematic bias during prototype matching. Consequently, under few-shot settings, jointly addressing the coupled challenges of complex background modeling, robust cross-image matching, and regional structural consistency remains central to advancing FSS performance.

To mitigate these issues, we adopt a dual-branch design. Even under limited samples, we posit that background regions may still contain valuable class cues or structural information. Accordingly, we propose a symmetry-aware superpixel-enhanced FSS method. The core idea is to explicitly construct symmetric superpixel region graphs in both the support and query branches: via top–down cross-hierarchical feature fusion, we inject fine-grained low-level cues (edges and textures) into high-level semantic representations to strengthen the modeling of complex backgrounds, thereby improving the foreground–background separability and boundary quality. Structurally, we first partition the query image into superpixels and build a Region Adjacency Graph (RAG); initialize query predictions at the pixel level using support prototypes and project them into the superpixel space to achieve cross-image prototype alignment between support and query; then perform message passing and energy minimization on the RAG to optimize regional consistency and boundary alignment; and finally, map the optimized results back to the pixel space. At the representational level, we aggregate semantically consistent regional information to construct robust foreground and background prototypes, alleviating the mismatch induced by oversimplifying the negative class.

3. Task Definition

With the rapid development of deep learning, semantic segmentation has achieved remarkable progress in computer vision; however, much of this success hinges on large-scale, pixel-level annotated datasets [6,55]. Acquiring dense pixel annotations is both time consuming and costly, and is even infeasible in many real-world scenarios [50]. Therefore, we aim to train a model that can learn from a tiny number of samples and accurately segment unseen categories using only a few annotated examples. More formally, the task can be cast as a (C)-way (K)-shot segmentation problem, where there are (C) different categories and only (K) labeled images per category available as guidance [58]. In line with prior work, we primarily focus on the 1-way 1-shot and 1-way 5-shot settings.

In few-shot semantic segmentation, the base set $\mathcal{D}_{\text{base}}$ and the novel set $\mathcal{D}_{\text{novel}}$ are drawn from two disjoint label spaces $\mathcal{C}_{\text{base}}$ and $\mathcal{C}_{\text{novel}}$, i.e.,

$$\mathcal{C}_{\text{base}} \cap \mathcal{C}_{\text{novel}} = \varnothing. \tag{1}$$

Following the standard episodic protocol, multiple episodes are sampled from $\mathcal{D}_{\text{base}}$ and $\mathcal{D}_{\text{novel}}$, namely

$$\begin{aligned} \mathcal{D}_{\text{base}} &= \{(\mathcal{S}_i, \mathcal{Q}_i)\}_{i=1}^{N_{\text{base}}}, \\ \mathcal{D}_{\text{novel}} &= \{(\mathcal{S}_i, \mathcal{Q}_i)\}_{i=1}^{N_{\text{novel}}}, \end{aligned} \tag{2}$$

where N_{base} and N_{novel} denote the numbers of episodes for base and novel classes, respectively.

Each training or testing episode e_i consists of a support set $\mathcal{S}_i$ and a query set $\mathcal{Q}_i$, i.e.,

$$e_i = (\mathcal{S}_i, \mathcal{Q}_i). \tag{3}$$

Concretely, the support set $\mathcal{S}_i$ contains several semantic classes. For each class $c \in \mathcal{C}$, there are K distinct image–mask pairs:

$$\mathcal{S}_i^c = \left\{ \left(I_{c,s}^j, M_{c,s}^j\right) \right\}_{j=1}^{K}, \quad I_{c,s}^j \in \mathbb{R}^{3\times H\times W}, \; M_{c,s}^j \in \{0,1\}^{H\times W} \tag{4}$$

where, $I_{c,s}^j$ represents the feature map at channel c in spatial position s of the j-th layer, and $M_{c,s}^j$ represents the corresponding mask encoding at the same position.

Similarly, the query set $\mathcal{Q}_i$ contains l_i images from the same classes as the support set:

$$\mathcal{Q}_i^c = \left\{ \left(I_{c,q}^j, M_{c,q}^j\right) \right\}_{j=1}^{l_i}, \tag{5}$$

where $I_{c,q}^j$ denotes the j-th query RGB image and $M_{c,q}^j$ is its corresponding ground-truth binary mask. Note that the query masks $M_{c,q}^j$ are used only for evaluation during testing and are not involved in the model's inference. Throughout, $I \in \mathbb{R}^{3\times H\times W}$ represents an RGB image, and $M \in \{0,1\}^{H\times W}$ is a binary segmentation mask, with 1 indicating foreground pixels and 0 indicating background pixels.

4. Methodology

4.1. Overview

We propose a symmetry-aware superpixel-enhanced framework for few-shot semantic segmentation, as illustrated in Figure 1, and the algorithm pseudocode of the model is presented in Algorithm 1. The model adopts a symmetric dual-branch architecture that inputs a support image and a query image. The backbone and the Cross-Layer Feature Fusion (CFF) module share weights across branches, enforcing consistent "symmetry awareness". CFF adaptively fuses high-level semantics with low-level details to produce feature maps Fs and Fq that encode semantic cues and boundary information.

Algorithm 1: Prototype-guided few-shot image segmentation via cross-layer fusion and superpixel-relational matching

Input : support image $\mathbf{X}_s$, support mask $\mathbf{Y}_s$; query set $\mathbf{X}_q$; network $\Theta = \{\phi, \mathcal{F}, \mathcal{R}\}$; fusion levels L; superpixels N; temperature τ; binarization threshold δ; epochs E; batch size B.
Output: predicted query masks $\hat{\mathbf{M}}_q$; trained network Θ.

Initialize backbone ϕ, fusion module $\mathcal{F}$, relation module $\mathcal{R}$, and optimizer
`// Stage 1.  Prototype construction from the support set`
Extract multi-level support features: $\{\mathbf{F}_s^{(l)}\}_{l=1}^{L} \leftarrow \{\phi^{(l)}(\mathbf{X}_s)\}_{l=1}^{L}$
Fuse support features: $\tilde{\mathbf{F}}_s \leftarrow \mathcal{F}(\{\mathbf{F}_s^{(l)}\}_{l=1}^{L})$
Resize mask to the feature resolution: $\tilde{\mathbf{Y}}_s \leftarrow \mathrm{Resize}(\mathbf{Y}_s, \mathrm{size}(\tilde{\mathbf{F}}_s))$
Compute class prototype by masked average pooling and normalization: $\mathbf{p} \leftarrow \mathrm{Normalize}(\mathrm{MAP}(\tilde{\mathbf{F}}_s, \tilde{\mathbf{Y}}_s))$
`// Stage 2.  Main learning/inference loop`
$t \leftarrow 0$
repeat `// stop at` $t \geq E$ `or early convergence`
  Sample a mini-batch of queries (with masks if training): $(\mathbf{X}_q^{(b)}, \mathbf{M}_q^{(b)})$ of size B
  Extract multi-level query features: $\{\mathbf{F}_q^{(l)}\}_{l=1}^{L} \leftarrow \{\phi^{(l)}(\mathbf{X}_q^{(b)})\}_{l=1}^{L}$
  Fuse query features: $\tilde{\mathbf{F}}_q \leftarrow \mathcal{F}(\{\mathbf{F}_q^{(l)}\}_{l=1}^{L})$
  Generate superpixels: $\mathcal{S}_s \leftarrow \mathrm{SLIC}(\tilde{\mathbf{F}}_s, N)$, $\mathcal{S}_q \leftarrow \mathrm{SLIC}(\tilde{\mathbf{F}}_q, N)$
  Superpixel pooling: $\mathbf{Z}_s \leftarrow \mathrm{SPPool}(\tilde{\mathbf{F}}_s, \mathcal{S}_s)$, $\mathbf{Z}_q \leftarrow \mathrm{SPPool}(\tilde{\mathbf{F}}_q, \mathcal{S}_q)$
  Relational matching to the prototype: $\mathbf{r}_s \leftarrow \mathcal{R}(\mathbf{Z}_s, \mathbf{p})$, $\mathbf{r}_q \leftarrow \mathcal{R}(\mathbf{Z}_q, \mathbf{p})$
  Scatter weights and enhance features: $\bar{\mathbf{F}}_s \leftarrow \mathrm{Enhance}(\tilde{\mathbf{F}}_s, \mathcal{S}_s, \mathbf{r}_s)$, $\bar{\mathbf{F}}_q \leftarrow \mathrm{Enhance}(\tilde{\mathbf{F}}_q, \mathcal{S}_q, \mathbf{r}_q)$
  Non-parametric matching (cosine similarity): $\mathbf{S} \leftarrow \mathrm{CosSim}(\bar{\mathbf{F}}_q, \mathbf{p})$
  Probabilistic mask and upsampling: $\hat{\mathbf{M}}_q^{(b)} \leftarrow \sigma(\mathbf{S}/\tau)$, $\hat{\mathbf{M}}_q^{(b)} \leftarrow \mathrm{Resize}(\hat{\mathbf{M}}_q^{(b)}, \mathrm{size}(\mathbf{X}_q^{(b)}))$
  if *training labels* $\mathbf{M}_q^{(b)}$ *are available* **then**
    Compute loss: $\mathcal{L} \leftarrow \mathrm{BCE}(\hat{\mathbf{M}}_q^{(b)}, \mathbf{M}_q^{(b)}) + \lambda\,\mathrm{Dice}(\hat{\mathbf{M}}_q^{(b)}, \mathbf{M}_q^{(b)})$
    Update Θ via backpropagation
  else
    `// inference only`
  Binarize masks for reporting: $\hat{\mathbf{M}}_q^{(b)} \leftarrow \mathbb{I}[\hat{\mathbf{M}}_q^{(b)} \geq \delta]$
  $t \leftarrow t + 1$
until $t \geq E$

To further structure the representation, we introduce a Superpixel–Prototype Relational Matching (SPRM) module. First, superpixels are generated on both the support and query sides, and their internal features are aggregated to obtain structured region representations. Using the support annotations as priors, we then perform relation modeling and noise suppression between regions inside/outside the mask and the class prototypes, strengthening intra-class consistency while mitigating inter-class confusion. After SPRM, the support image undergoes mask-guided aggregation and prototype refinement to produce a set of diverse, boundary-sensitive class prototypes (Prototype Generation) that explicitly capture intra-class multimodality in appearance and deformation. Finally, non-parametric matching measures the similarity between the query features Fq and the refined prototypes, yielding a pixel-wise probability map from which the query mask is predicted. The entire pipeline is trained end-to-end under an episodic setting: symmetry awareness ensures representational consistency across branches, superpixels enhance boundary and region consistency, and the prototype set models intra-class diversity, enabling more accurate and robust segmentation under minimal supervision.

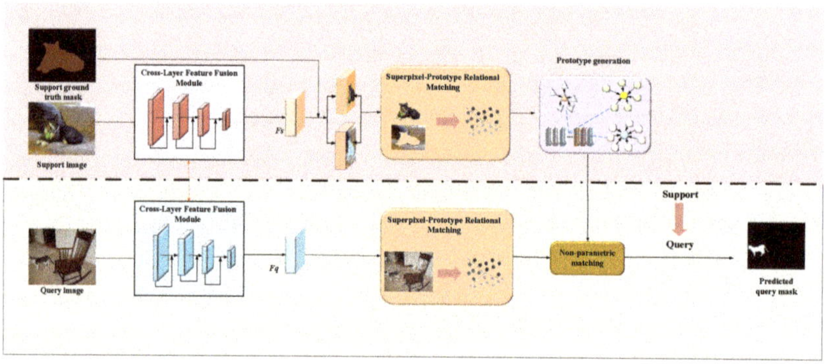

Figure 1. Overall architecture of the Symmetry-Aware Superpixel-Enhanced Model for few-shot semantic segmentation in a 1-way 1-shot setting.

4.2. Cross-Layer Feature Fusion

In few-shot semantic segmentation, many existing methods treat the background as a single monolithic class, overlooking its rich hierarchical structure and fine-grained details. This simplification hinders the model's ability to fully understand complex and variable background content, thereby degrading the accuracy of foreground segmentation. As illustrated in Figure 2, a visualization of features from different backbone layers reveals that shallow features retain more detailed edge and texture cues but lack semantic consistency, whereas deep features possess intense semantic expressiveness yet lose spatial details critical to segmentation. This representational mismatch and information gap lead to suboptimal performance when the model encounters backgrounds with diverse appearances and complex structures.

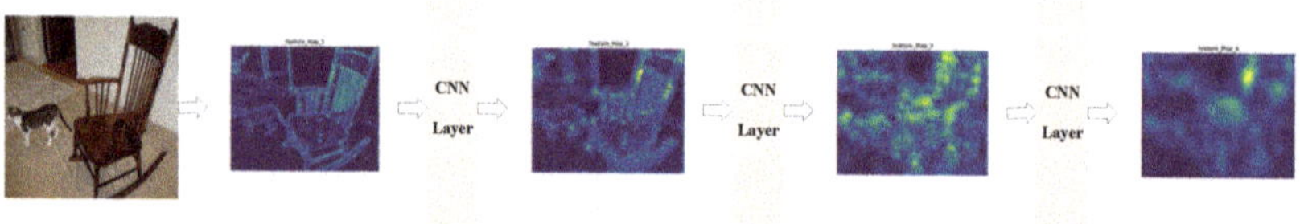

Figure 2. Cross-Layer Feature Visualization. From left to right, the figure shows feature heatmaps from different layers of the backbone network: shallow layers highlight edges and texture details, while deeper layers produce responses that progressively focus on semantic regions and become more abstract. This visualization indicates that cross-layer features are complementary.

To address these issues, we propose a top–down Cross-Layer Fusion (CLF) mechanism. CLF selectively injects fine-grained cues—such as edges and textures—from low-level features into high-level semantic features, yielding fused representations that combine semantic consistency with spatial detail. This fusion strategy produces a more complete and discriminative multi-level characterization of complex backgrounds, which not only markedly improves the separability between foreground and background regions but also enhances the boundary localization and overall segmentation quality. To effectively integrate multi-scale features, we formulate our cross-layer fusion mechanism, where X_q^l

denotes the query feature representation extracted from the l-th layer, and X_s^l represents the corresponding support features from the same layer level.

In the query branch, given a query image I_q, we extract multi-level features using the backbone shared with the support branch:

$$\{X_q^2, X_q^3, X_q^4, X_q^5\}. \tag{6}$$

A 1×1 convolution is applied for channel alignment and normalization. Starting from the deepest stage, we perform top–down fusion: the high-level feature is upsampled to provide semantic guidance, while the corresponding low-level feature is selectively injected via a gating mechanism, forming

$$P_q^l = \mathrm{Up}\left(P_q^{l+1}\right) + G_q^l \odot \hat{X}_q^l, \tag{7}$$

where $\mathrm{Up}(\cdot)$ denotes upsampling and $\odot$ is element-wise multiplication.

Finally, features from all levels are converted to a high-resolution scale, concatenated, and compressed to obtain the fused representation:

$$F_q = \psi\left(\mathrm{Concat}(P_q^2, \mathrm{Up}(P_q^3), \mathrm{Up}^2(P_q^4), \mathrm{Up}^3(P_q^5))\right). \tag{8}$$

This fused feature retains both semantic consistency and boundary details, and is subsequently used to compute similarity with support prototypes for segmentation. The entire procedure shares weights with the support branch and does not rely on class masks.

In the support branch, we utilize image masks to obtain the background region of the original image. Given an RGB input image $I \in \mathbb{R}^{3 \times w \times h}$ and a background mask $M \in \{0,1\}^{w \times h}$, where w and h are the image width and height, the background image is computed according to the following equation:

$$I^{BM_0} = I \odot M \tag{9}$$

where $\odot$ denotes the Hadamard product. As shown in Figure 3, the image I and the obtained background image I^{BM_0} are fed into the backbone network for feature extraction. Cross-layer background feature fusion is performed at the first two layers and the final output layer of the network. For simplicity, we describe the feature fusion process for the first layer output of the feature extraction network. After passing through the first layer of the backbone, I and I^{BM_0} yield feature maps $F^I \in \mathbb{R}^{c \times w' \times h'}$ and $F^{BM_0} \in \mathbb{R}^{c \times w' \times h'}$, respectively, where c is the number of channels, and w' and h' are the width and height of the feature maps. Using bilinear interpolation to match the mask M with the obtained feature dimensions, denoted by function $\tau(\cdot) : \mathbb{R}^{w \times h} \rightarrow \mathbb{R}^{c \times w' \times h'}$, we then perform feature masking on F^I according to Equation to obtain the first-layer background features:

$$F^{BM_1} = F^I \odot \tau(M) \tag{10}$$

Finally, fine-grained information from F^{BM_0} is supplemented into F^{BM_1} to obtain the final background feature F^{BM_0-1}. As illustrated in Figure 4, to better fuse the feature information of F^{BM_1} and F^{BM_0}, we introduce the masking method proposed in [59] within the Hybrid Background Module (HBM). Specifically, inactive values in the high-level background feature F^{BM_1} are replaced by corresponding values from the low-level background feature F^{BM_0}, while other activated values remain unchanged to preserve semantic information. We then input F^{BM_0-1} and F^I to the second layer of the backbone network and repeat the above operations.

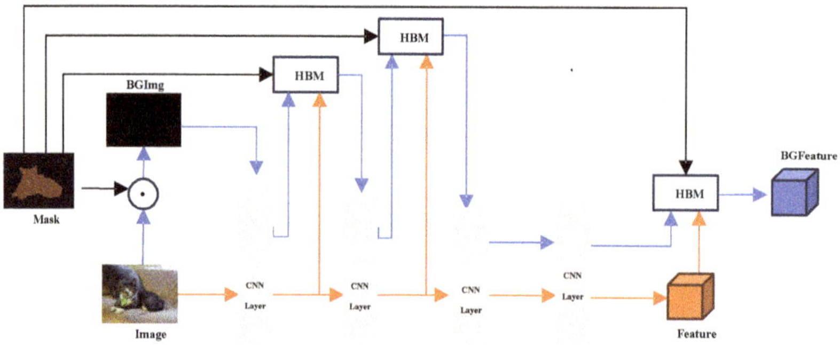

Figure 3. Cross-Layer Feature Fusion. Through a cross-hierarchical feature integration mechanism, fine-grained low-level cues are injected into high-level semantics, yielding optimized background representations in complex scenes.

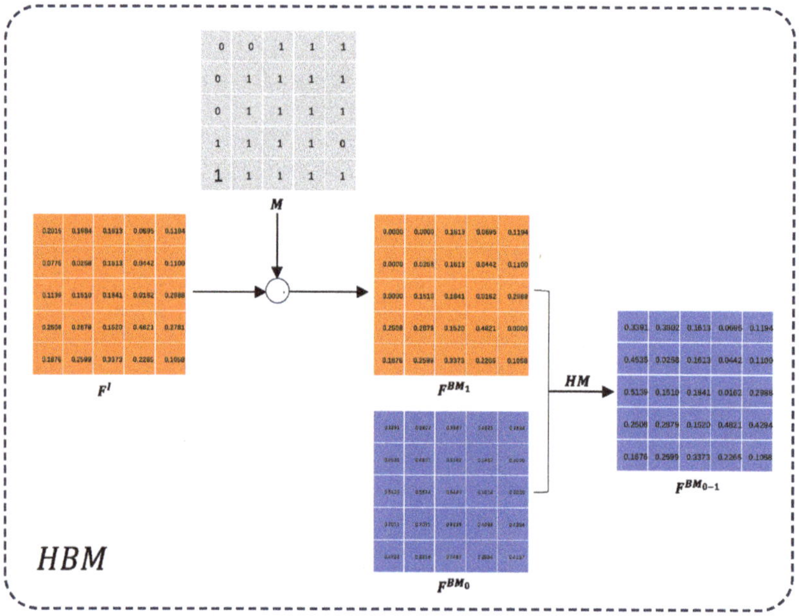

Figure 4. Hybrid Background Feature Module (HBM). The input feature F^{l} is masked by the background mask M to obtain the background feature F^{BM_1}. Then, F^{BM_1} is combined with the background feature F^{BM_0} extracted from the previous convolutional layer to produce the hybrid background feature $F^{\mathrm{BM}_{0-1}}$.

4.3. Superpixel–Prototype Relational Matching

Few-shot semantic segmentation suffers from unstable prototypes and imprecise boundaries. Pixel-wise dense matching is highly susceptible to noise; therefore, we propose a Superpixel–Prototype Relational Matching (SPRM) module. Pixel-level features are aggregated into superpixel-level tokens to construct a region graph, upon which cross-image prototype alignment and message passing are performed at the regional level. The refined representations are then projected back to the pixel space for fine-grained prediction. As illustrated in Figure 5, this design ensures cross-image semantic alignment while leveraging the boundary-awareness of superpixels to enhance regional consistency and boundary adherence. Superpixel segmentation adaptively partitions the image into regions according to visual cues; consistency clustering enforces intra-token feature homogeneity, and, when combined with hierarchical feature fusion, it preserves fine details and edge information more effectively.

Figure 5. Superpixel–Prototype Relational Matching. The image feature map is fed into a superpixel segmentation module, which groups spatially adjacent and visually similar pixels into superpixels. For each superpixel, mean pooling is performed in the feature space to obtain its feature centroid, which serves as a fine-grained pseudo-prototype. The collection of these pseudo-prototypes compactly yet sufficiently characterizes the semantic distribution of the entire query image.

Given a query image I_q and its deep feature map $F \in R^{H \times W \times C}$, we apply SLIC/SEEDS to partition the image domain $\Omega = \{1, \ldots, H\} \times \{1, \ldots, W\}$ into a set of superpixels $S = \{S_k\}_{k=1}^{k}$ that are pairwise disjoint and whose union covers the whole image, i.e., $S_i \cap S_j = \varnothing$ for $i \neq j$, and $\bigcup_{k=1}^{K} S_k = \Omega$. Within each superpixel, mean pooling is performed to obtain a region token:

$$\mathbf{p}_k = \frac{1}{|S_k|} \sum_{x \in S_k} F(x) \in \mathbb{R}^C, \quad k = 1, \ldots, K. \tag{11}$$

where $F(x)$ denotes the C-dimensional feature vector at pixel x. The resulting token set can be written as

$$P = [\mathbf{p}_1, \ldots, \mathbf{p}_K]^\top \in \mathbb{R}^{K \times C}. \tag{12}$$

We further construct a Region Adjacency Graph $G = (V, E)$ where $V = \{1, \ldots, N\}$. An undirected edge $(i, j) \in E$ is created if the superpixels S_i and S_j are spatially adjacent (touch each other). The edge weight integrates color, spatial, and boundary-strength cues via a weighted combination:

$$w_{ij} = \exp\Big(-\alpha \|\mu_i - \mu_j\|_2^2 - \beta \|c_i - c_j\|_2^2 \Big) \cdot (1 + \gamma b_{ij}), \tag{13}$$

where μ_i denotes the centroid coordinates, c_i the average color, and b_{ij} the boundary confidence score.

To capture multi-modal semantics within each category, we introduce K_c prototype centers $\{p_{c,k}\}_{k=1}^{K_c}$ for each class c. The region–prototype relationship is modeled via a soft assignment as follows:

$$q_{i,k}^c = \frac{\exp\big(\kappa \langle \hat{f}_i, \hat{p}_{c,k} \rangle\big)}{\sum_{m=1}^{K_c} \exp\big(\kappa \langle \hat{f}_i, \hat{p}_{c,m} \rangle\big)}, \qquad \sum_k q_{i,k}^c = 1. \tag{14}$$

Building on this, the prototypes are updated via weighted aggregation:

$$p_{c,k} = \frac{\sum_{i=1}^{N} q_{i,k}^c t_i}{\sum_{i=1}^{N} q_{i,k}^c}. \tag{15}$$

After obtaining the multi-prototypes for each class, we define a region-level class distribution $z_i \in \Delta^{|c|} Z_i \in \Delta^{|C|}$ (where Δ denotes the probability simplex). Its energy function consists of a unary term (prototype similarity) and a pairwise term (graph smoothness/boundary alignment) as given by the equation

$$\min_{\mathbf{z},\{\hat{\mathbf{p}}_{c,k}\}} E(\mathbf{z},\{\hat{\mathbf{p}}_{c,k}\}) = \sum_{i=1}^{N} \mathrm{CE}(z_i, \sigma(\max_k \langle \{t_i, \hat{p}_{c,k}\} \rangle)_{c\in\mathcal{C}}) + \lambda \sum_{(i,j)\in\mathcal{E}} w_{ij} \|z_i - z_j\|_2^2 \quad (16)$$

where $\sigma(\cdot)$ denotes the *softmax* operator. The energy is minimized via a few iterations of message passing with Laplacian regularization to obtain $\hat{z}_i$. The region-level predictions are then back-projected to the pixel domain to produce a fine-grained mask, which is fused with the pixel-level logits as shown in the equation:

$$\ell(x,c) = \beta\, T(F(x), p_c^{(0)}) + (1-\beta)\, \hat{z}_{s(x)}(c), \quad (17)$$

where the second term represents pixel-class similarity. Here, $s(x)$ returns the superpixel index to which pixel x belongs, and $\beta \in [0,1]$ controls the fusion weight.

4.4. Non-Parametric Metric Learning

The semantic segmentation task aims to learn target object segmentation patterns from support images and generalize them to corresponding targets in query images. Specifically, this task can be formulated as a pixel-wise category inference problem in the spatial domain. As illustrated in Figure 6, this work leverages a non-parametric metric learning mechanism to compute the semantic similarity $\beta_{c,q}^{(x,y)}$ between the feature vector $F_q \in \mathbb{R}^{d\times h\times w}$ at each spatial location (x,y) of the deep features $F_q^{(x,y)}$ obtained from encoding the query image and each class prototype $p_c \in \mathbb{R}^{d\times 1\times 1}$, thereby accomplishing the segmentation of unknown categories based on this similarity, and the similarity computation is defined as

$$\beta_{c,q}^{(x,y)} = \frac{\mathbf{F}_q^{(x,y)} \cdot \mathbf{p}_c}{\|\mathbf{F}_q^{(x,y)}\|\, \|\mathbf{p}_c\|}, \qquad p_c \in \mathcal{P},\, c \in \mathcal{C} \quad (18)$$

where $\mathcal{P} \in \mathbb{R}^{2\times d\times 1\times 1}$ encompasses all class prototypes for both foreground and background. Subsequently, the class prototype index $\ell_{c,q}^{(x,y)}$ that best matches the feature vector at each location is obtained through the argmax$(\cdot)$ operation as shown in the following equation:

$$\ell_{c,q}^{(x,y)} = \arg\max\left(\beta_{c,q}^{(x,y)}\right) \quad (19)$$

Based on this, the class prototypes corresponding to all spatial locations are integrated to generate a semantic response map $G \in \mathbb{R}^{h'\times w'}$. Subsequently, bilinear interpolation is employed to resize G to the original image dimensions, yielding $G' \in \mathbb{R}^{h\times w}$ which is concatenated with the query features E_Q along the channel dimension to construct an enhanced support branch for the better transfer of segmentation information from the support set. Finally, the model performs pixel-wise classification to determine whether each pixel belongs to the target class or background in the support image. The overall pipeline structure is illustrated in Figure 6. During training, a cross-entropy loss function is utilized to optimize the prototype representations in an end-to-end manner according to the equation

$$\mathcal{L}_{s\to q} = -\frac{1}{hw} \sum_{x,y} \sum_{P_c} \varpi \left[M_{c,q}^{(x,y)} = c \right] \log Z_{c,q}^{(x,y)} \quad (20)$$

where $M_{c,q}^{(x,y)}$ is the ground truth mask of the query image. Optimizing the $\mathcal{L}_{q\to q}$ will derive a suitable class-specific prototype for each class. Specifically, $M_{c,q}^{(x,y)}$ is only used in the testing stage.

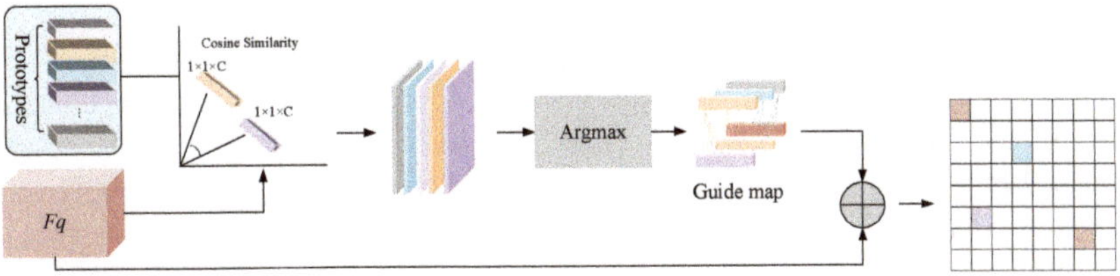

Figure 6. Illustration of non-parametric metric learning framework. The pipeline begins with prototypes extracted from support images, which are compared with query features Fq using cosine similarity computation (1 × 1 × C). The argmax operation selects the most similar prototype to generate a guide map at each spatial location. This guide map is concatenated with the original query features Fq along the channel dimension (denoted by ⊕) to produce enhanced features for final segmentation prediction. The framework enables effective knowledge transfer from support samples to query images through prototype-based similarity matching.

5. Experimental Design

5.1. Datasets and Evaluation Protocol

Datasets: We assess our method on two canonical few-shot semantic segmentation benchmarks, PASCAL-5^i and COCO-20^i.

PASCAL-5^i is constructed from PASCAL VOC 2012 [60] and the SBD dataset [61], covering 20 object categories. It uses 10,582 training and 1449 validation images as the base and novel pools, respectively.

COCO-20^i [62], derived from COCO-2014, is larger and more challenging, spanning 80 categories with 82,783 training and 40,504 validation images serving as base and novel pools. For both datasets, we follow the four-fold protocol in [37]: the categories are split evenly into four folds; in each run, three folds are used for training, and the remaining fold is reserved for testing.

Evaluation metrics: Following common practice [37,47], we report the mean Intersection over Union (mIoU) and foreground–background IoU (FB-IoU). For class c, the IoU is

$$\mathrm{IoU}_c = \frac{\mathrm{tp}_c}{\mathrm{tp}_c + \mathrm{fp}_c + \mathrm{fn}_c}, \tag{21}$$

where tp_c, fp_c, and fn_c denote the counts of true-positive, false-positive, and false-negative pixels for that class. The mean over the C foreground classes gives

$$\mathrm{mIoU} = \frac{1}{C}\sum_{c=1}^{C} \mathrm{IoU}_c \tag{22}$$

with $C = 5$ for $PASCAL - 5^i$ and $C = 20$ for $COCO - 20^i$. FB-IoU disregards class labels and averages IoU over foreground and background, i.e., $C = 2$. All numbers are averaged across four trials.

Test protocol: Because randomly sampled test episodes can vary in difficulty, we evaluate the baseline and our method on the same test episodes to ensure fair comparison.

Baseline: As our approach is grounded in metric learning, we adopt PANet [39] as the baseline, consistent with prior work [63], and denote it as PANet. For fairness, both our method and the baseline share the same backbone feature extractor.

5.2. Implementation Details

We adopt ResNet [64] and VGG [65] as our backbone networks, pre-trained on ImageNet, including ResNet-50 and ResNet-101. We discard the last backbone stage and the final ReLU to achieve better generalization when using the backbone network. We use

SGD to optimize our model with a momentum of 0.9, an initial learning rate of 1×10^{-4}, and decay by a factor of 2 every 2000 iterations. The model is trained for 24,000 iterations. The batch size is set to 4 for training, limited by GPU memory constraints when processing 473×473 resolution images with superpixel computation. During evaluation, we use a batch size of 1 following standard FSS protocols. Both images and masks are resized and cropped to (473×473) and augmented with random horizontal flipping. Evaluation is performed on original images.

To balance region-level semantic coherence and computational efficiency, we set the number of superpixels to 300 for all query images by default. For datasets with significantly different image resolutions, we further adjust the superpixel count according to the image area as $N = \left\lfloor \frac{H \times W}{600} \right\rfloor$, where H and W denote the height and width, respectively. We use the SLIC algorithm with a compactness parameter set to 10 to generate superpixels, ensuring each superpixel conveys sufficient local context without sacrificing boundary precision. The number of support branch multi-prototypes per class is set to 3, empirically determined to balance alignment robustness and computational efficiency. The loss function comprises a binary cross-entropy loss and a Dice loss with weights of 1.0 and 1.0 respectively, and the region consistency term is weighted by 0.5.

For evaluation, we conduct 1000 episodes per class per fold, with each episode randomly sampling one support–query pair, ensuring statistical significance of the reported mIoU and FB-IoU metrics. Regarding seed policy, we employ a fixed random seed (seed = 1234) for dataset splitting and episode sampling to ensure reproducible results. All experiments are implemented on PyTorch 1.13.1 and conducted on a server composed of one Intel(R) Xeon(R) Gold 6242 CPU with 256 GB memory and one NVIDIA A100 40 GB GPU accelerator card.

5.3. Experimental Results

We benchmark our approach against state-of-the-art methods on PASCAL-5^i and COCO-20^i using two evaluation metrics. Experiments cover the 1-way 1-shot and 1-way 5-shot settings with three backbones—VGG-16, ResNet-50, and ResNet-101—and we report both mIoU and FB-IoU.

$PASCAL-5^i$. From Table 1, we can observe that our SSENet method demonstrates consistent superiority across different backbone networks. For VGG-16, our method achieves 65.4 mIoU and 77.2 FB-IoU in 1-shot segmentation task, outperforming the previous best method DCP by 4.47% and 2.12%, respectively. In the 5-shot task, our method obtains 68.3 mIoU and 81.3 FB-IoU, which surpasses DCP by 0.74% and 0.74%, respectively, demonstrating the effectiveness of our approach even with limited backbone capacity. For ResNet-50, our method achieves 67.4 mIoU and 78.9 FB-IoU in the 1-shot segmentation task, which outperforms the state-of-the-art method DCP by 1.97% and 1.68% respectively. In the 5-shot task, our method reaches 71.0 mIoU and 81.3 FB-IoU, exceeding DCP by 1.00% and 3.57%, respectively. Furthermore, our method significantly outperforms PANet by 38.4% and 28.6% mIoU under 1-shot and 5-shot segmentation tasks, respectively, along with 17.9% and 13.9% higher FB-IoU performance, demonstrating the effectiveness of our approach in leveraging support features for enhanced segmentation. For ResNet-101, our method achieves 68.2 mIoU and 78.3 FB-IoU in the 1-shot task, outperforming the previous best method DCP by 1.34% mIoU while showing a slight decrease of 0.25% in FB-IoU. In the 5-shot task, our method obtains 72.5 mIoU and 81.6 FB-IoU, which surpasses DCP by 1.40% mIoU while showing a decrease of 1.33% in FB-IoU. Compared with PANet*, our method shows substantial improvements of 33.2% and 26.1% mIoU under 1-shot and 5-shot segmentation tasks respectively, along with 11.4% and 13.3% higher FB-IoU performance. MSDNet achieves a marginally higher FB-IoU in the ResNet-101 configuration (e.g., 85.0 vs. 81.6 in the 5-shot setting), as our model prioritizes semantic accuracy through region-level consistency enforcement rather than aggressive binary foreground–background separation. Overall, our SSENet consistently delivers superior segmentation performance across different experimental settings, validating the robustness and effectiveness of our proposed approach.

To further verify the segmentation effectiveness of our proposed method, we evaluate our method and PANet on 2-way 1-shot and 5-shot segmentation performance as shown in Table 2. We observe that our method also performs favorably in both metrics across all backbone networks. Specifically, in the 1-shot setting, our method obtains 62.7, 63.2, and 67.9 mIoU and 73.8, 74.1, and 77.5 FB-IoU with VGG-16, ResNet-50 and ResNet-101, respectively, which significantly outperforms PANet by 39.0%, 39.5%, and 36.3% mIoU and 15.0%, 15.1%, and 13.0% FB-IoU, respectively. In the 5-shot setting, our method achieves 59.4, 60.2, and 65.3 mIoU and 78.2, 79.5, and 80.9 FB-IoU with VGG-16, ResNet-50, and ResNet-101 respectively, surpassing PANet by 23.2%, 23.4%, and 20.0% mIoU and 16.0%, 15.6%, and 10.7% FB-IoU, respectively. These substantial improvements across different backbone architectures demonstrate that the proposed method has superior generalization performance and robustness in more challenging 2-way segmentation scenarios.

Regarding COCO-20^i dataset analysis, from Table 3, we can observe that our SSENet method achieves state-of-the-art performance across different backbone networks on the more challenging COCO-20^i dataset. For VGG-16, our method achieves 43.1 mIoU and 65.8 FB-IoU in the 1-shot segmentation task, outperforming the previous best method SAGNN by 15.5% and 7.5%, respectively. In the 5-shot task, our method obtains 45.6 mIoU and 66.8 FB-IoU, which surpasses SAGNN by 12.0% and 5.9%, respectively, demonstrating significant improvements even with limited backbone capacity. For ResNet-50, our method achieves 47.0 mIoU and 70.1 FB-IoU in the 1-shot segmentation task, outperforming the state-of-the-art method DCP by 3.3% mIoU. Notably, our FB-IoU performance substantially exceeds other methods, with a remarkable improvement of 11.3% over ASGNet. In the 5-shot task, our method reaches 53.8 mIoU and 73.9 FB-IoU, exceeding DCP by 5.7% mIoU and surpassing ASGNet by 26.6% mIoU and 10.1% FB-IoU, respectively. These results demonstrate the effectiveness of our approach in leveraging multiple support examples for enhanced performance. For ResNet-101, our method achieves 47.2 mIoU and 68.9 FB-IoU in the 1-shot task, outperforming the previous best method DCP by 5.8% mIoU and exceeding NTRENet by 20.7% mIoU and 2.1% FB-IoU. In the 5-shot task, our method obtains 53.6 mIoU and 72.4 FB-IoU, which surpasses DCP by 8.5% mIoU and outperforms NTRENet by 24.1% mIoU and 4.0% FB-IoU. The consistent improvements across different backbone architectures validate that our method can effectively handle the increased complexity and diversity of the COCO-20^i dataset. Overall, our SSENet demonstrates superior segmentation performance and excellent generalization capability on this challenging dataset.

Table 1. Results of 1-way 1-shot and 5-shot segmentation on *PASCAL-5^i^* dataset using mIoU and FB-IoU metric. The best results are in bold. * indicates the results we replicated ourselves.

Methods	Backbone	1-Shot		5-Shot	
		mIoU	FB-IoU	mIoU	FB-IoU
OSLSM [37]	VGG-16	40.8	61.3	44.0	61.5
co-FCN [44]		41.1	60.1	41.4	60.2
PL [42]		42.7	61.2	43.7	62.3
AMP [45]		43.4	62.2	46.9	63.8
PANet [39]		48.1	66.5	55.7	68.4
SG-One [18]		46.3	63.1	47.1	65.9
JGLNet [66]		49.3	68.3	55.6	70.6
DRNet [67]		52.4	67.5	55.2	70.0
PFENet [68]		58.0	–	59.0	–
MGNet [69]		43.9	67.8	50.3	50.3
LSTNet [70]		58.5	–	60.4	–
DCP [71]		62.6	75.6	67.8	80.6
SSENet (Ours)		**65.4**	**77.2**	**68.3**	**81.3**
PANet * [39]	ResNet-50	48.7	66.9	55.6	71.4
CGNet [72]		47.6	64.1	49.5	66.2
PPNet [52]		52.9	–	63.0	–
SML [47]		51.3	67.1	60.0	72.2
PFENet [68]		60.8	73.3	61.9	73.9
ASGNet [51]		59.3	69.2	63.9	74.2
DRNet [67]		58.6	71.4	61.7	73.7
DGPNet [6]		63.2	–	73.1	–
MSDNet [57]		64.3	77.1	68.7	**82.1**
DCP [71]		66.1	77.6	70.3	78.5
SSENet (Ours)		**67.4**	**78.9**	**71.0**	81.3
PANet * [39]	ResNet-101	51.2	70.3	57.5	72.0
A-MCG [73]		–	61.2	–	62.2
PPNet [52]		55.2	70.9	65.1	77.5
FWB [74]		56.2	–	59.9	–
DAN [75]		58.2	71.9	60.5	72.3
VPI [76]		57.3	–	60.4	–
ASGNet [51]		59.3	71.7	64.4	75.2
LSTNet [70]		61.8	–	64.2	–
PRMG [77]		62.6	–	65.7	–
PFENet+ [78]		62.6	75.1	64.0	76.6
MSDNet [57]		64.7	77.3	70.8	**85.0**
DCP [71]		67.3	**78.5**	71.5	82.7
SSENet (Ours)		**68.2**	78.3	**72.5**	81.6

Table 2. Results of 2-way 1-shot and 5-shot tasks on PASCAL-5^i dataset.

Methods	Task	mIoU			FB-IoU		
		VGG-16	ResNet-50	ResNet-101	VGG-16	ResNet-50	ResNet-101
PANet (Baseline)	1-shot	45.1	45.3	49.8	64.2	64.4	68.6
SSENet (Ours)		62.7	63.2	67.9	73.8	74.1	77.5
PANet (Baseline)	5-shot	48.2	48.8	54.4	67.4	68.6	73.1
SSENet (Ours)		59.4	60.2	65.3	78.2	79.5	80.9

Table 3. Results of 1-way 1-shot and 5-shot segmentation on *COCO-20^i* dataset. * denotes the results implemented by ourselves. The best results are in bold.

Methods	Backbone	1-Shot		5-Shot	
		mIoU	FB-IoU	mIoU	FB-IoU
PANet [39]	VGG-16	20.9	59.2	29.7	63.5
DRNet [67]		18.5	58.3	25.2	62.6
MGNet [69]		27.8	61.1	35.6	63.8
JGLNet [66]		25.3	61.8	34.7	63.6
LSTNet [70]		35.8	–	37.5	–
PFENet [68]		34.1	60.0	37.7	61.6
SML [47]		22.6	59.3	–	–
SAGNN [79]		37.3	61.2	40.7	63.1
SSENet (Ours)		**43.1**	**65.8**	**45.6**	**66.8**
RPMM [49]	ResNet-50	30.6	60.4	42.5	67.0
PANet * [39]		23.6	63.0	34.2	64.1
PPNet [52]		29.0	–	38.5	–
SML [47]		23.3	59.5	–	–
ASR [80]		33.8	–	36.7	–
MLC [63]		33.9	–	40.6	–
ASGNet [51]		34.6	60.4	42.5	67.1
CWT [50]		32.9	–	41.3	–
DRNet [67]		23.3	61.4	32.2	64.8
SSP [81]		33.6	–	41.3	–
QSCMNet [58]		36.4	60.7	42.8	64.8
LSTNet [70]		36.6	–	38.0	–
PFENet + QSR [82]		35.1	–	38.2	–
DCP [71]		45.5	–	50.9	–
SSENet (Ours)		**47.0**	**70.1**	**53.8**	**73.9**
FWB [74]	ResNet-101	21.2	–	23.7	–
A-MCG [73]		–	52.0	–	64.7
PANet * [39]		35.1	63.7	41.4	66.5
PMMs [49]		29.6	–	34.3	–
DAN [75]		24.4	62.3	29.6	63.9
PFENet [68]		38.5	63.0	42.7	65.8
VPI [76]		23.4	–	27.8	–
SAGNN [79]		37.2	60.9	42.7	63.4
CWT [50]		32.4	–	42.0	–
NTRENet [83]		39.1	67.5	43.2	69.6
PFENet+ [78]		38.2	61.8	39.9	63.4
LSTNet [70]		38.2	–	38.2	–
PFENet + QSR [82]		36.9	–	41.2	–
DCP [71]		44.6	–	49.4	–
SSENet (Ours)		**47.2**	**68.9**	**53.6**	**72.4**

To further verify the segmentation effectiveness of our method, we evaluate and compare our proposed method and PANet on 2-way 1-shot and 5-shot segmentation performance on the COCO-20^i dataset as shown in Table 4. Additionally, our method also performs favorably in both metrics across all backbone networks. Specifically, in the 1-shot setting, our method obtains 39.7, 41.0, and 45.8 mIoU and 64.3, 69.2, and 64.9 FB-IoU with VGG-16, ResNet-50 and ResNet-101, respectively, which significantly outperforms PANet by 93.7%, 83.9%, and 33.9% mIoU and 9.5%, 16.1%, and 2.4% FB-IoU, respectively. In the 5-shot setting, our method achieves 48.2, 46.9, and 51.2 mIoU and 66.0, 71.4, and 70.6 FB-IoU with VGG-16, ResNet-50, and ResNet-101 respectively, surpassing PANet by 47.4%, 44.3%, and 27.7% mIoU and 7.8%, 14.8%, and 7.3% FB-IoU, respectively. These substantial improvements across different backbone architectures demonstrate that the proposed method has superior generalization performance and robustness in more challenging 2-way segmentation scenarios on the COCO-20^i dataset.

Table 4. Results of 2-way 1-shot and 5-shot tasks using ResNet-50 backbone on COCO-20^i dataset.

Methods	Task	mIoU			FB-IoU		
		VGG-16	ResNet-50	ResNet-101	VGG-16	ResNet-50	ResNet-101
PANet (Baseline)	1-shot	20.5	22.3	34.2	58.7	59.6	63.4
SSENet (Ours)		39.7	41.0	45.8	64.3	69.2	64.9
PANet (Baseline)	5-shot	32.7	32.5	40.1	61.2	62.2	65.8
SSENet (Ours)		48.2	46.9	51.2	66.0	71.4	70.6

5.4. Ablation Studies

Here, we conduct ablation studies on PASCAL-5^i and COCO-20^i datasets using ResNet-50, and report the average performance of all results on mIoU and FB-mIoU. The quantitative results are shown in Table 5, and the qualitative results are shown in Figure 7.

Effect of different components. In this section, we analyze the impact of different components on the performance of our method with ResNet-50 in the 1-way 1-shot setting as shown in Table 5. Fs+Fq&CLF represents a variant that uses the CLF module to obtain fine-grained foreground regions (Fs) and query-specific features (Fq) based on extracted features, while excluding other components. Similarly, Fs&CLF+Fq&CLF represents our design where both support and query features are processed through the CLF module to enhance feature fusion. Fs&CLF+Fq&CLF+FG+BG&SPRM denotes a variant of our method where SPRM is used in conjunction with all other components to extract the fine-grained relational features of background and foreground regions.

Table 5. Ablation studies on the effect of different components. F: Foreground, B: Background, C: CLF Module, S: SPRM Module.

Variants	PASCAL-5^i		COCO-20^i		Speed (FPS)
	mIoU	FB-mIoU	mIoU	FB-mIoU	
F + B (Baseline)	48.7	66.9	23.6	63.0	17.4
F_s + F_qC	50.3	67.8	25.8	63.7	17.2
F_sC + F_qC	52.1	68.6	28.2	64.3	17.2
F_sC + F_qC + F + B	54.2	69.5	33.8	64.9	17.2
F_s + F_qC + FS + B	56.0	70.3	35.1	65.6	16.8
F_s + F_qC + F + BS	57.8	71.2	36.4	66.2	16.8
F_sC + F_q + FS + B	59.4	72.0	38.6	66.8	16.8
F_sC + F_q + F + BS	61.1	72.9	40.7	67.4	16.7
F_sC + F_qC + F + BS	62.6	73.7	42.8	68.1	16.7
F_sC + F_qC + FS + B	64.2	74.6	44.7	68.7	16.5
F_sC + F_qC + F + BS	65.8	75.9	46.2	69.3	16.5
F_sC + F_qC + FS + BS (Ours)	**67.4**	**78.9**	**47.0**	**70.1**	16.1

In Table 5, we first analyze the impact of the main components of our method, namely the fine-grained feature extraction modules (Fs, Fq), Cross-Layer Feature Fusion (CLF), and the Superpixel–Prototype Relational Matching (SPRM) module. We can see that each component plays a vital role in performance improvement. Starting from the baseline FG + BG (48.7% mIoU), the introduction of Fs + Fq&CLF improves the performance to 50.3%, demonstrating the effectiveness of fine-grained feature learning. Furthermore, we observe that when CLF is applied to both support and query features simultaneously

(Fs&CLF + Fq&CLF), the performance further improves to 52.1%, which provides better feature alignment and fusion effects. Moreover, the integration of another module, SPRM, has also brought significant improvements. For example, Fs + Fq&CLF + FG&SPRM + BG achieves 56.0%, while our complete model Fs&CLF + Fq&CLF + FG&SPRM + BG&SPRM reaches the best performance of 67.4% mIoU on PASCAL-5^i and 47.0% on COCO-20^i. This further confirms the aforementioned hypothesis that relational matching between superpixels and prototypes can effectively capture fine-grained spatial correspondences, and explicit relational modeling can enhance feature discrimination capability.

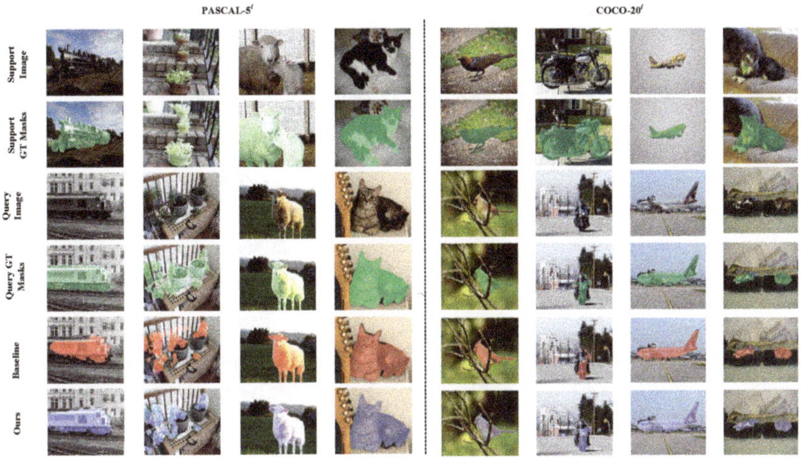

Figure 7. Qualitative results of 1-way 1-shot setting on PASCAL-5^i.

Visualization analysis. Figure 7 shows our method with the baseline method on 1-way 1-shot qualitative results. We observe that our method can give satisfying segmentation results on unseen classes from the background with only the guidance of the support images, even if some support images and query images do not share much appearance similarities.

Compared to the baseline, our SSENet demonstrates significant improvements in background consistency, with the most notable enhancements evident in boundary quality and object completeness. In the PASCAL-5^i examples shown in Figure 7, specifically in the train scene (leftmost), our method produces more accurate and complete segmentation of the red locomotive, while the baseline shows fragmented predictions with missing regions in the central part of the train. Similarly, in the construction equipment scene (second from left), our approach achieves better boundary adherence and reduces the obvious false negative regions present in the baseline results. The animal segmentation examples (sheep and cat in columns 3–4) particularly highlight our method's superior capability in capturing fine-grained details and maintaining object completeness, whereas the baseline exhibits incomplete segmentations with significant missing portions of the target objects.

This demonstrates that our method effectively suppresses background noise through the Cross-Layer Feature Fusion (CLF) module, which integrates fine-grained edge and texture information with high-level semantics, resulting in cleaner and more coherent background predictions. The most striking improvement lies in boundary precision, where our Superpixel–Prototype Relational Matching (SPRM) module enforces regional consistency by operating on superpixel-level tokens rather than individual pixels, leading to markedly sharper and more accurate object boundaries. In challenging scenarios involving objects at different scales or with varying contextual backgrounds, our method demonstrates enhanced robustness through the CLF module's ability to inject low-level cues into high-level representations, enabling the better handling of fine-grained details while maintaining semantic understanding for larger structures.

6. Conclusions and Future Work

In this work, we propose a symmetry-aware superpixel-enhanced few-shot semantic segmentation method that effectively addresses critical limitations in existing approaches, namely insufficient complex background modeling and poor regional prediction consistency through explicit superpixel region graph modeling. Our main contributions include three aspects: first, we design a symmetric dual-branch architecture that leverages explicit superpixel region graph modeling to enhance background representation and prediction consistency; second, we propose a top–down cross-layer fusion mechanism that effectively integrates fine-grained edge and texture information into high-level semantic features; finally, we construct a cross-image prototype alignment strategy based on Region Adjacency Graphs (RAG) with message passing optimization to obtain more robust foreground and background prototype representations. Extensive experiments and ablation studies on PASCAL-5^i and COCO-20^i benchmarks demonstrate the effectiveness and superiority of our proposed method, achieving consistent improvements across multiple backbone architectures. Despite achieving good results, our framework still has certain limitations. The method exhibits superpixel granularity sensitivity, where inappropriate superpixel counts can affect segmentation quality, and shows cross-domain generalization challenges when substantial domain gaps exist between training and testing scenarios. While these limitations do not undermine the core contributions, they highlight important areas for future improvement and represent valuable directions for advancing few-shot semantic segmentation research.

Adaptive superpixel optimization represents a key direction, and we will explore dynamic superpixel granularity selection mechanisms and learnable superpixel generation networks to automatically adapt to different scene complexities and object scales. We plan to investigate methods for predicting optimal superpixel parameters based on image characteristics and object complexity, potentially through reinforcement learning or adaptive sampling strategies. We will pursue enhanced cross-domain generalization capabilities by incorporating domain adaptation techniques into our cross-layer fusion mechanism and exploring meta-learning approaches to improve adaptation to new domains with minimal fine-tuning. We will develop domain-aware feature alignment strategies and investigate adversarial training methods to learn domain-invariant representations that maintain segmentation accuracy across diverse visual contexts.

Author Contributions: Conceptualization, Q.Z.; Methodology, L.G. and K.-C.L.; Software, J.W.; Validation, J.W. and J.X.; Formal analysis, X.L.; Investigation, Y.T.; Resources, X.L., R.Z. and Q.Z.; Data curation, L.-H.L.; Writing—original draft, L.G.; Writing—review & editing, K.-C.L. All authors have read and agreed to the published version of the manuscript.

Funding: This research was funded by the National Key R&D Program of China, under Grant Nos. 2023YFB4503903 and 2020YFC0832500; the National Natural Science Foundation of China, under Grant Nos. U22A20261 and 61402210; the Gansu Province Science and Technology Major Project—Industrial Project, under Grant Nos. 22ZD6GA048 and 23ZDGA006; the HY-Project, under Grant No. 4E49EFF3; the Gansu Province Key Research and Development Plan—Industrial Project, under Grant No. 22YF7GA004; the Gansu Provincial Science and Technology Major Special Innovation Consortium Project, under Grant No. 21ZD3GA002; the Fundamental Research Funds for the Central Universities, under Grant Nos. lzujbky-2024-jdzx15, lzujbky-2022-kb12, lzujbky-2021-sp43, lzujbky-2020-sp02, and lzujbky-2019-kb51; the Open Project of Gansu Provincial Key Laboratory of Intelligent Transportation, under Grant No. GJJ-ZH-2024-002; the Science and Technology Plan of Qinghai Province, under Grant No. 2020-GX-164; 2023 China Higher Education Institutions

Industry-Academia-Research Innovation Fund for Digital Intelligence and Educational Projects No. 2023RY020.

Data Availability Statement: The raw data supporting the conclusions of this article will be made available by the authors on request.

Conflicts of Interest: The authors declare no conflicts of interest.

References

1. Han, D.; Shi, J.; Zhao, J.; Wu, H.; Zhou, Y.; Li, L.H.; Khan, M.K.; Li, K.C. LRCN: Layer-residual Co-Attention Networks for visual question answering. *Expert Syst. Appl.* **2025**, *263*, 125658. [CrossRef]
2. Xia, C.; Li, X.; Gao, X.; Ge, B.; Li, K.C.; Fang, X.; Zhang, Y.; Yang, K. PCDR-DFF: Multi-modal 3D object detection based on point cloud diversity representation and dual feature fusion. *Neural Comput. Appl.* **2024**, *36*, 9329–9346. [CrossRef]
3. He, W.; Zhang, Y.; Zhuo, W.; Shen, L.; Yang, J.; Deng, S.; Sun, L. APSeg: Auto-Prompt Network for Cross-Domain Few-Shot Semantic Segmentation. In Proceedings of the IEEE/CVF Conference on Computer Vision and Pattern Recognition (CVPR), Seattle, WA, USA, 16–22 June 2024; pp. 23762–23772.
4. Jin, K.; Du, W.; Tang, M.; Liang, W.; Li, K.; Pathan, A.S.K. LSODNet: A Lightweight and Efficient Detector for Small Object Detection in Remote Sensing Images. *IEEE J. Sel. Top. Appl. Earth Obs. Remote. Sens.* **2025**, *18*, 24816–24828. [CrossRef]
5. Shen, W.; Ma, A.; Wang, J.; Zheng, Z.; Zhong, Y. Adaptive Self-Supporting Prototype Learning for Remote Sensing Few-Shot Semantic Segmentation. *IEEE Trans. Geosci. Remote. Sens.* **2024**, *62*, 5634116. [CrossRef]
6. Johnander, J.; Edstedt, J.; Felsberg, M.; Khan, F.S.; Danelljan, M. Dense Gaussian Processes for Few-Shot Segmentation. In *Lecture Notes in Computer Science, Proceedings of the Computer Vision, ECCV 2022, PT XXIX, 17th European Conference on Computer Vision (ECCV), Tel Aviv, Israel, 23–27 October 2022*; Avidan, S., Brostow, G., Cisse, M., Farinella, G., Hassner, T., Eds.; Springer Nature: Cham, Switzerland, 2022; Volume 13689, pp. 217–234. [CrossRef]
7. Ma, J.; Bai, S.; Pan, W. Boosting Few-Shot Semantic Segmentation with Prior-Driven Edge Feature Enhancement Network. *IEEE Trans. Artif. Intell.* **2025**, *6*, 211–220. [CrossRef]
8. Zhang, H.; Xu, J.; Jiang, S.; He, Z. Simple Semantic-Aided Few-Shot Learning. In Proceedings of the 2024 IEEE/CVF Conference on Computer Vision and Pattern Recognition (CVPR), Seattle, WA, USA, 16–22 June 2024; pp. 28588–28597. [CrossRef]
9. McCall, A. Few-Shot Learning in Computer Vision: Overcoming Data Scarcity. *ResearchGate* **2022**. Available online: https://www.researchgate.net/publication/390542684_Few-Shot_Learning_in_Computer_Vision_Overcoming_Data_Scarcity (accessed on 8 October 2025).
10. Zhao, J.; Kong, L.; Lv, J. An Overview of Deep Neural Networks for Few-Shot Learning. *Big Data Min. Anal.* **2025**, *8*, 145–188. [CrossRef]
11. Zhang, J.; Zhao, C.; Ni, B.; Xu, M.; Yang, X. Variational Few-Shot Learning. In Proceedings of the IEEE/CVF International Conference on Computer Vision (ICCV), Seoul, Republic of Korea, 27 October–2 November 2019.
12. Dvornik, N.; Schmid, C.; Mairal, J. Diversity with Cooperation: Ensemble Methods for Few-Shot Classification. In Proceedings of the 2019 IEEE/CVF International Conference on Computer Vision (ICCV 2019), Seoul, Republic of Korea, 27 October–2 November 2019; pp. 3722–3730. [CrossRef]
13. Schwartz, E.; Karlinsky, L.; Shtok, J.; Harary, S.; Marder, M.; Kumar, A.; Feris, R.; Giryes, R.; Bronstein, A. Delta-encoder: An effective sample synthesis method for few-shot object recognition. In *Advances in Neural Information Processing Systems*; Bengio, S., Wallach, H., Larochelle, H., Grauman, K., Cesa-Bianchi, N., Garnett, R., Eds.; Curran Associates, Inc.: Red Hook, NY, USA, 2018; Volume 31.
14. Snell, J.; Swersky, K.; Zemel, R. Prototypical Networks for Few-shot Learning. In *Advances in Neural Information Processing Systems*; Curran Associates, Inc.: Red Hook, NY, USA, 2017; Volume 30. [CrossRef]
15. Sung, F.; Yang, Y.; Zhang, L.; Xiang, T.; Torr, P.H.S.; Hospedales, T.M. Learning to Compare: Relation Network for Few-Shot Learning. In Proceedings of the 2018 IEEE/CVF Conference on Computer Vision and Pattern Recognition (CVPR), Salt Lake City, UT, USA, 18–23 June 2018; pp. 1199–1208. [CrossRef]
16. Guo, Y.; Codella, N.C.; Karlinsky, L.; Codella, J.V.; Smith, J.R.; Saenko, K.; Rosing, T.; Feris, R. A Broader Study of Cross-Domain Few-Shot Learning. In *Image Processing Computer Vision Pattern Recognition and Graphics, Proceedings of the 16th European Conference on Computer Vision-ECCV-Biennial, Electrical Network, Glasgow, UK, 23–28 August 2020*; Vedaldi, A., Bischof, H., Brox, T., Frahm, J., Eds.; PT XXVII; Springer International Publishing: Cham, Switzerland, 2020; Volume 12372, pp. 124–141. [CrossRef]
17. Wang, Y.; Lee, D.; Heo, J.; Park, J. One-Shot Summary Prototypical Network Toward Accurate Unpaved Road Semantic Segmentation. *IEEE Signal Process. Lett.* **2021**, *28*, 1200–1204. [CrossRef]
18. Zhang, X.; Wei, Y.; Yang, Y.; Huang, T.S. SG-One: Similarity Guidance Network for One-Shot Semantic Segmentation. *IEEE Trans. Cybern.* **2020**, *50*, 3855–3865. [CrossRef]

19. Tian, P.; Wu, Z.; Qi, L.; Wang, L.; Shi, Y.; Gao, Y. Differentiable meta-learning model for few-shot semantic segmentation. In Proceedings of the AAAI Conference on Artificial Intelligence, New York, NY, USA, 7–12 February 2020; Volume 34, pp. 12087–12094.
20. Askari, F.; Fateh, A.; Mohammadi, M.R. Enhancing few-shot image classification through learnable multi-scale embedding and attention mechanisms. *Neural Netw.* **2025**, *187*, 107339. [CrossRef]
21. Ren, G.; Liu, J.; Wang, M.; Guan, P.; Cao, Z.; Yu, J. Few-Shot Object Detection via Dual-Domain Feature Fusion and Patch-Level Attention. *Tsinghua Sci. Technol.* **2025**, *30*, 1237–1250. [CrossRef]
22. Liu, T.; Sun, F. Self-Aligning Multi-Modal Transformer for Oropharyngeal Swab Point Localization. *Tsinghua Sci. Technol.* **2024**, *29*, 1082–1091. [CrossRef]
23. Paeedeh, N.; Pratama, M.; Ma'sum, M.A.; Mayer, W.; Cao, Z.; Kowlczyk, R. Cross-domain few-shot learning via adaptive transformer networks. *Knowl.-Based Syst.* **2024**, *288*, 111458. [CrossRef]
24. Liu, Y.; Sun, Y.; Chen, Z.; Feng, C.; Zhu, K. Global Spatial-Temporal Information Encoder-Decoder Based Action Segmentation in Untrimmed Video. *Tsinghua Sci. Technol.* **2025**, *30*, 290–302. [CrossRef]
25. Zhang, J.; Chen, X.; Yang, B.; Guan, Q.; Chen, Q.; Chen, J.; Wu, Q.; Xie, Y.; Xia, Y. Advances in attention mechanisms for medical image segmentation. *Comput. Sci. Rev.* **2025**, *56*, 100721. [CrossRef]
26. Zhi, P.; Jiang, L.; Yang, X.; Wang, X.; Li, H.W.; Zhou, Q.; Li, K.C.; Ivanović, M. Cross-Domain Generalization for LiDAR-Based 3D Object Detection in Infrastructure and Vehicle Environments. *Sensors* **2025**, *25*, 767. [CrossRef]
27. Ronneberger, O.; Fischer, P.; Brox, T. U-Net: Convolutional Networks for Biomedical Image Segmentation. In *Lecture Notes in Computer Science, Proceedings of the 18th International Conference on Medical Image Computing and Computer-Assisted Intervention (MICCAI), Munich, Germany, 5–9 October 2015*; Navab, N., Hornegger, J., Wells, W., Frangi, A., Eds.; PT III; Tech Univ Munich: Munich, Germany; Friedrich Alexander Univ Erlangen Nuremberg: Erlangen, Germany, 2015; Volume 9351, pp. 234–241. [CrossRef]
28. Chen, L.C.; Papandreou, G.; Kokkinos, I.; Murphy, K.; Yuille, A.L. DeepLab: Semantic Image Segmentation with Deep Convolutional Nets, Atrous Convolution, and Fully Connected CRFs. *IEEE Trans. Pattern Anal. Mach. Intell.* **2018**, *40*, 834–848. [CrossRef]
29. Badrinarayanan, V.; Kendall, A.; Cipolla, R. SegNet: A Deep Convolutional Encoder-Decoder Architecture for Image Segmentation. *IEEE Trans. Pattern Anal. Mach. Intell.* **2017**, *39*, 2481–2495. [CrossRef]
30. Zhao, H.; Shi, J.; Qi, X.; Wang, X.; Jia, J. Pyramid Scene Parsing Network. In Proceedings of the IEEE Conference on Computer Vision and Pattern Recognition (CVPR), Honolulu, HI, USA, 21–26 July 2017.
31. He, J.; Deng, Z.; Zhou, L.; Wang, Y.; Qiao, Y. Adaptive Pyramid Context Network for Semantic Segmentation. In Proceedings of the IEEE/CVF Conference on Computer Vision and Pattern Recognition (CVPR), Long Beach, CA, USA, 15–20 June 2019.
32. Choi, S.; Kim, J.T.; Choo, J. Cars Can't Fly Up in the Sky: Improving Urban-Scene Segmentation via Height-Driven Attention Networks. In Proceedings of the IEEE/CVF Conference on Computer Vision and Pattern Recognition (CVPR), Seattle, WA, USA, 14–19 June 2020.
33. Elhassan, M.A.; Huang, C.; Yang, C.; Munea, T.L. DSANet: Dilated spatial attention for real-time semantic segmentation in urban street scenes. *Expert Syst. Appl.* **2021**, *183*, 115090. [CrossRef]
34. Guo, L.; Li, X.; Wang, J.; Xiao, J.; Hou, Y.; Zhi, P.; Yong, B.; Li, L.; Zhou, Q.; Li, K. EdgeVidCap: A Channel-Spatial Dual-Branch Lightweight Video Captioning Model for IoT Edge Cameras. *Sensors* **2025**, *25*, 4897. [CrossRef]
35. Catalano, N.; Matteucci, M. Few Shot Semantic Segmentation: A review of methodologies, benchmarks, and open challenges. *arXiv* **2024**, arXiv:2304.05832. . [CrossRef]
36. Tang, S.; Yan, S.; Qi, X.; Gao, J.; Ye, M.; Zhang, J.; Zhu, X. Few-shot medical image segmentation with high-fidelity prototypes. *Med. Image Anal.* **2025**, *100*, 103412. [CrossRef]
37. Shaban, A.; Bansal, S.; Liu, Z.; Essa, I.; Boots, B. One-Shot Learning for Semantic Segmentation. *arXiv* **2017**, arXiv:1709.03410. . [CrossRef]
38. Li, A.; Luo, T.; Xiang, T.; Huang, W.; Wang, L. Few-Shot Learning with Global Class Representations. In Proceedings of the IEEE/CVF International Conference on Computer Vision (ICCV), Seoul, Republic of Korea, 27 October–2 November 2019.
39. Wang, K.; Liew, J.H.; Zou, Y.; Zhou, D.; Feng, J. PANet: Few-Shot Image Semantic Segmentation with Prototype Alignment. In Proceedings of the IEEE/CVF International Conference on Computer Vision (ICCV), Seoul, Republic of Korea, 27 October–2 November 2019.
40. Luo, X.; Wu, H.; Zhang, J.; Gao, L.; Xu, J.; Song, J. A Closer Look at Few-shot Classification Again. In Proceedings of the 40th International Conference on Machine Learning, Honolulu, HI, USA, 23–29 July 2023; Krause, A., Brunskill, E., Cho, K., Engelhardt, B., Sabato, S., Scarlett, J., Eds.; Proceedings of Machine Learning Research; PMLR: Cambridge, MA, USA, 2023; Volume 202, pp. 23103–23123.
41. Liu, Y.; Zhu, Y.; Chong, H.; Yu, M. Few-shot image semantic segmentation based on meta-learning: A review. *J. Intell. Fuzzy Syst.* **2024**, *47*, 351–367. [CrossRef]

42. Dong, N.; Xing, E.P. Few-shot semantic segmentation with prototype learning. In Proceedings of the BMVC, Newcastle, UK, 3–6 September 2018; Volume 3, p. 4.
43. Zhang, C.; Lin, G.; Liu, F.; Yao, R.; Shen, C. CANet: Class-Agnostic Segmentation Networks with Iterative Refinement and Attentive Few-Shot Learning. In Proceedings of the IEEE/CVF Conference on Computer Vision and Pattern Recognition (CVPR), Long Beach, CA, USA, 15–20 June 2019.
44. Rakelly, K.; Shelhamer, E.; Darrell, T. Conditional Networks for Few-Shot Semantic Segmentation. ICLR Workshop. 2018. Available online: https://openreview.net/forum?id=SkMjFKJwG (accessed on 8 October 2025).
45. Siam, M.; Oreshkin, B.N.; Jagersand, M. AMP: Adaptive Masked Proxies for Few-Shot Segmentation. In Proceedings of the IEEE/CVF International Conference on Computer Vision (ICCV), Seoul, Republic of Korea, 27 October–2 November 2019.
46. He, Z.; Li, L.; Wang, H. Symmetry-Guided Dual-Branch Network with Adaptive Feature Fusion and Edge-Aware Attention for Image Tampering Localization. *Symmetry* **2025**, *17*, 1150. [CrossRef]
47. Pambala, A.K.; Dutta, T.; Biswas, S. SML: Semantic meta-learning for few-shot semantic segmentation⋆. *Pattern Recognit. Lett.* **2021**, *147*, 93–99. [CrossRef]
48. Zhang, B.; Xiao, J.; Qin, T. Self-Guided and Cross-Guided Learning for Few-Shot Segmentation. In Proceedings of the IEEE/CVF Conference on Computer Vision and Pattern Recognition (CVPR), Virtual, 19–25 June 2021; pp. 8312–8321.
49. Yang, B.; Liu, C.; Li, B.; Jiao, J.; Ye, Q. Prototype Mixture Models for Few-Shot Semantic Segmentation. In *Image Processing Computer Vision Pattern Recognition and Graphics, Proceedings of the 16th European Conference on Computer Vision-ECCV-Biennial, Electrical Network, Glasgow, UK, 23–28 August 2020*; Vedaldi, A., Bischof, H., Brox, T., Frahm, J., Eds.; PT VIII; Springer International Publishing: Cham, Switzerland, 2020; Volume 12353, pp. 763–778. [CrossRef]
50. Lu, Z.; He, S.; Zhu, X.; Zhang, L.; Song, Y.Z.; Xiang, T. Simpler Is Better: Few-Shot Semantic Segmentation with Classifier Weight Transformer. In Proceedings of the IEEE/CVF International Conference on Computer Vision (ICCV), Virtual, 11–17 October 2021; pp. 8741–8750.
51. Li, G.; Jampani, V.; Sevilla-Lara, L.; Sun, D.; Kim, J.; Kim, J. Adaptive Prototype Learning and Allocation for Few-Shot Segmentation. In Proceedings of the IEEE/CVF Conference on Computer Vision and Pattern Recognition (CVPR), Virtual, 19–25 June 2021; pp. 8334–8343.
52. Liu, Y.; Zhang, X.; Zhang, S.; He, X. Part-Aware Prototype Network for Few-Shot Semantic Segmentation. In *Image Processing Computer Vision Pattern Recognition and Graphics, Proceedings of the 16th European Conference on Computer Vision-ECCV-Biennial, Electrical Network, Glasgow, UK, 23–28 August 2020*; Vedaldi, A., Bischof, H., Brox, T., Frahm, J., Eds.; PT IX; Springer International Publishing: Cham, Switzerland, 2020; Volume 12354, pp. 142–158. [CrossRef]
53. Li, W.; Xu, J.; Huo, J.; Wang, L.; Gao, Y.; Luo, J. Distribution consistency based covariance metric networks for few-shot learning. In Proceedings of the AAAI Conference on Artificial Intelligence, Honolulu, HI, USA, 27 January–1 February 2019; Volume 33, pp. 8642–8649.
54. Strudel, R.; Garcia, R.; Laptev, I.; Schmid, C. Segmenter: Transformer for Semantic Segmentation. In Proceedings of the IEEE/CVF International Conference on Computer Vision (ICCV), Virtual, 11–17 October 2021; pp. 7262–7272.
55. Chen, H.; Li, H.; Li, Y.; Chen, C. Sparse spatial transformers for few-shot learning. *Sci.-China-Inf. Sci.* **2023**, *66*, 210102. [CrossRef]
56. Dos Santos, M.E.; Guimarães, S.J.F.; Patrocínio, Z.K.G. Cross-Attention Vision Transformer for Few-Shot Semantic Segmentation. In Proceedings of the 2023 IEEE Ninth Multimedia Big Data (BigMM), Laguna Hills, CA, USA, 11–13 December 2023; pp. 64–71. [CrossRef]
57. Fateh, A.; Mohammadi, M.R.; Jahed-Motlagh, M.R. MSDNet: Multi-scale decoder for few-shot semantic segmentation via transformer-guided prototyping. *Image Vis. Comput.* **2025**, *162*, 105672. [CrossRef]
58. Shao, J.; Gong, B.; Dai, K.; Li, D.; Jing, L.; Chen, Y. Query-support semantic correlation mining for few-shot segmentation. *Eng. Appl. Artif. Intell.* **2023**, *126*, 106797. [CrossRef]
59. Moon, S.; Sohn, S.S.; Zhou, H.; Yoon, S.; Pavlovic, V.; Khan, M.H.; Kapadia, M. HM: Hybrid Masking for Few-Shot Segmentation. In Proceedings of the Computer Vision–ECCV 2022: 17th European Conference, Tel Aviv, Israel, 23–27 October 2022; Springer Nature: Cham, Switzerland, 2022; pp. 506–523. [CrossRef]
60. Everingham, M.; Van Gool, L.; Williams, C.K.I.; Winn, J.; Zisserman, A. The Pascal Visual Object Classes (VOC) Challenge. *Int. J. Comput. Vis.* **2010**, *88*, 303–338. [CrossRef]
61. Hariharan, B.; Arbeláez, P.; Bourdev, L.; Maji, S.; Malik, J. Semantic contours from inverse detectors. In Proceedings of the 2011 International Conference on Computer Vision, Barcelona, Spain, 6–13 November 2011; pp. 991–998. [CrossRef]
62. Lin, T.Y.; Maire, M.; Belongie, S.; Hays, J.; Perona, P.; Ramanan, D.; Dollar, P.; Zitnick, C.L. Microsoft COCO: Common Objects in Context. In *Lecture Notes in Computer Science, Proceedings of the 13th European Conference on Computer Vision (ECCV), Zurich, Switzerland, 6–12 September 2014*; Fleet, D., Pajdla, T., Schiele, B., Tuytelaars, T., Eds.; PT V; Springer International Publishing: Cham, Switzerland, 2014; Volume 8693, pp. 740–755. [CrossRef]
63. Yang, L.; Zhuo, W.; Qi, L.; Shi, Y.; Gao, Y. Mining Latent Classes for Few-Shot Segmentation. In Proceedings of the IEEE/CVF International Conference on Computer Vision (ICCV), Virtual, 11–17 October 2021; pp. 8721–8730.

64. He, K.; Zhang, X.; Ren, S.; Sun, J. Deep Residual Learning for Image Recognition. In Proceedings of the IEEE Conference on Computer Vision and Pattern Recognition (CVPR), Las Vegas, NV, USA, 27–30 June 2016.
65. Simonyan, K.; Zisserman, A. Very Deep Convolutional Networks for Large-Scale Image Recognition. *arXiv* **2015**, arXiv:1409.1556. [CrossRef]
66. Chang, Z.; Lu, Y.; Ran, X.; Gao, X.; Zhao, H. Simple yet effective joint guidance learning for few-shot semantic segmentation. *Appl. Intell.* **2023**, *53*, 26603–26621. [CrossRef]
67. Gao, G.; Fang, Z.; Han, C.; Wei, Y.; Liu, C.H.; Yan, S. DRNet: Double Recalibration Network for Few-Shot Semantic Segmentation. *IEEE Trans. Image Process.* **2022**, *31*, 6733–6746. [CrossRef]
68. Tian, Z.; Zhao, H.; Shu, M.; Yang, Z.; Li, R.; Jia, J. Prior Guided Feature Enrichment Network for Few-Shot Segmentation. *IEEE Trans. Pattern Anal. Mach. Intell.* **2022**, *44*, 1050–1065. [CrossRef]
69. Chang, Z.; Lu, Y.; Wang, X.; Ran, X. MGNet: Mutual-guidance network for few-shot semantic segmentation. *Eng. Appl. Artif. Intell.* **2022**, *116*, 105431. [CrossRef]
70. Chen, Y.; Chen, S.; Yang, Z.X.; Wu, E. Learning self-target knowledge for few-shot segmentation. *Pattern Recognit.* **2024**, *149*, 110266. [CrossRef]
71. Lang, C.; Cheng, G.; Tu, B.; Han, J. Few-Shot Segmentation via Divide-and-Conquer Proxies. *Int. J. Comput. Vis.* **2024**, *132*, 261–283. [CrossRef]
72. Wang, H.; Yang, Y.; Jiang, X.; Cao, X.; Zhen, X. You only need the image: Unsupervised few-shot semantic segmentation with co-guidance network. In Proceedings of the 2020 IEEE International Conference on Image Processing (ICIP), Virtual, 25–28 September 2020; IEEE: Piscataway, NJ, USA, 2020; pp. 1496–1500.
73. Hu, T.; Yang, P.; Zhang, C.; Yu, G.; Mu, Y.; Snoek, C.G. Attention-based multi-context guiding for few-shot semantic segmentation. In Proceedings of the AAAI Conference on Artificial Intelligence, Honolulu, HI, USA, 27 January–1 February 2019; Volume 33, pp. 8441–8448.
74. Nguyen, K.; Todorovic, S. Feature Weighting and Boosting for Few-Shot Segmentation. In Proceedings of the 2019 IEEE/CVF International Conference on Computer Vision (ICCV), Seoul, Republic of Korea, 27 October–2 November 2019; pp. 622–631. [CrossRef]
75. Wang, H.; Zhang, X.; Hu, Y.; Yang, Y.; Cao, X.; Zhen, X. Few-Shot Semantic Segmentation with Democratic Attention Networks. In *Image Processing Computer Vision Pattern Recognition and Graphics, Proceedings of the 16th European Conference on Computer Vision-ECCV-Biennial, Electrical Network, Glasgow, UK, 23–28 August 2020*; Vedaldi, A., Bischof, H., Brox, T., Frahm, J., Eds.; PT XIII; Springer International Publishing: Cham, Switzerland, 2020; Volume 12358, pp. 730–746. [CrossRef]
76. Wang, H.; Yang, Y.; Cao, X.; Zhen, X.; Snoek, C.; Shao, L. Variational Prototype Inference for Few-Shot Semantic Segmentation. In Proceedings of the 2021 IEEE Winter Conference on Applications of Computer Vision (WACV), Electrical Network, Virtual, 5–9 January 2021; pp. 525–534. [CrossRef]
77. Zhang, L.; Zhang, X.; Wang, Q.; Wu, W.; Chang, X.; Liu, J. RPMG-FSS: Robust Prior Mask Guided Few-Shot Semantic Segmentation. *IEEE Trans. Circuits Syst. Video Technol.* **2023**, *33*, 6609–6621. [CrossRef]
78. Hu, Y.; Huang, X.; Luo, X.; Han, J.; Cao, X.; Zhang, J. Learning Foreground Information Bottleneck for few-shot semantic segmentation. *Pattern Recognit.* **2024**, *146*, 109993. [CrossRef]
79. Xie, G.S.; Liu, J.; Xiong, H.; Shao, L. Scale-Aware Graph Neural Network for Few-Shot Semantic Segmentation. In Proceedings of the IEEE/CVF Conference on Computer Vision and Pattern Recognition (CVPR), Virtual, 19–25 June 2021; pp. 5475–5484.
80. Liu, B.; Ding, Y.; Jiao, J.; Ji, X.; Ye, Q. Anti-Aliasing Semantic Reconstruction for Few-Shot Semantic Segmentation. In Proceedings of the IEEE/CVF Conference on Computer Vision and Pattern Recognition (CVPR), Virtual, 19–25 June 2021; pp. 9747–9756.
81. Fan, Q.; Pei, W.; Tai, Y.W.; Tang, C.K. Self-support Few-Shot Semantic Segmentation. In *Lecture Notes in Computer Science, Proceedings of the 17th European Conference on Computer Vision (ECCV), Tel Aviv, Israel, 23–27 October 2022*; Avidan, S., Brostow, G., Cisse, M., Farinella, G., Hassner, T., Eds.; PT XIX; Springer Nature: Cham, Switzerland, 2022; Volume 13679, pp. 701–719. [CrossRef]
82. Guan, H.; Spratling, M. Query semantic reconstruction for background in few-shot segmentation. *Vis. Comput.* **2024**, *40*, 799–810. [CrossRef]
83. Liu, Y.; Liu, N.; Cao, Q.; Yao, X.; Han, J.; Shao, L. Learning Non-Target Knowledge for Few-Shot Semantic Segmentation. In Proceedings of the IEEE/CVF Conference on Computer Vision and Pattern Recognition (CVPR), New Orleans, LA, USA, 18–24 June 2022; pp. 11573–11582.

symmetry

MDPI

Article

A Novel Approach in 3D Model Reconstruction from Engineering Drawings Based on Symmetric Adjacency Matrices Using DXF Files and Genetic Algorithm

Predrag Mitić [1], Vladimir Kočović [1], Milan Mišić [2], Miladin Stefanović [1], Aleksandar Đorđević [1,*], Marko Pantić [3] and Damir Projović [4]

1 Faculty of Engineering, University of Kragujevac, 34000 Kragujevac, Serbia; predrag2904@gmail.com (P.M.); vladimir.kocovic@kg.ac.rs (V.K.); miladin@kg.ac.rs (M.S.)
2 Kosovo and Metohija Academy of Applied Studies, 38218 Leposavić, Serbia; milan.misic@pr.ac.rs
3 Department of Production Engineering, Faculty of Technical Sciences, University of Priština in Kosovska Mitrovica, 38220 Kosovska Mitrovica, Serbia; marko.pantic@pr.ac.rs
4 Department of Management, Military Academy, The University of Defence in Belgrade, 11000 Belgrade, Serbia; damirpro@yahoo.com
* Correspondence: adjordjevic@kg.ac.rs

Abstract: The application of CAD/CAM technologies in modern production has revolutionized manufacturing processes, leading to significant improvements in precision, efficiency, and flexibility. These technologies enable the design and manufacturing of complex geometries with high accuracy, reducing errors and material waste. CAD/CAM integration streamlines workflows, enhances productivity, and facilitates rapid prototyping, accelerating the time-to-market for new products. Additionally, it supports customization and scalability in production, allowing for cost-effective small-batch and large-scale manufacturing. Without a 3D model of the product, it is not possible to use the advantages of applying advanced CAD/CAM technologies. Recognizing 3D models from engineering drawings is essential for modern production, especially for outsourcing companies in fluctuating market conditions, where the production process is organized with 2D workshop drawings on paper. This paper proposes a novel methodology for reconstructing 3D models from 2D engineering drawings, specifically those in DXF file format, leveraging a genetic algorithm. A core component of this approach is the representation of the 2D drawing as a symmetric adjacency matrix. This matrix serves as the foundational data structure for the genetic algorithm, enabling the evolutionary process to effectively optimize the 3D reconstruction. The experimental evaluation, conducted on multiple engineering drawing test cases (including both polyhedral and cylindrical geometries), demonstrated consistent convergence of the proposed GA-based method toward topologically valid and geometrically accurate 3D wireframe models. The approach achieved successful reconstruction in all cases, with fitness scores ranging from 1.1 to 112.2 depending on model complexity, and average execution times from 2 to 100 s. These results confirm the method's robustness, scalability, and applicability in real-world CAD environments, while establishing a new direction for topology-driven 3D reconstruction using evolutionary computation.

Keywords: symmetric adjacency matrices; 3D model reconstruction; genetic algorithm; engineering drawings; DXF file

1. Introduction

The integration of computer-aided design and computer-aided manufacturing (CAD/CAM) technologies has profoundly transformed modern manufacturing by enabling rapid prototyping, design precision, and flexible production. However, in many industrial environments, particularly those relying on legacy documentation, two-dimensional (2D) workshop drawings remain the predominant format for technical communication. These drawings are often the only documentation available, especially in subcontracting or archival scenarios, making the automatic reconstruction of three-dimensional (3D) models from 2D sources a critical challenge.

The reconstruction of 3D models from 2D technical drawings is a key problem in CAD, reverse engineering, and model understanding. Orthographic projections, as standardized 2D representations, encode critical geometric and topological information of an object, yet lack depth and perspective, making the reconstruction process inherently underdetermined and often ambiguous.

Despite decades of research, the fully automated reconstruction of 3D models from 2D orthographic drawings remains a technically demanding problem. The majority of existing approaches are either limited to specific object categories (e.g., polyhedral shapes), require supervised learning with annotated datasets, or rely heavily on manually defined features and heuristics. One critical limitation is the absence of topological data in standard formats such as Drawing Exchange Format (DXF), which only contain isolated geometric entities (lines, arcs, circles) without information on how these entities are connected across views. This is particularly evident in the case of the DXF. Developed by Autodesk, DXF is an open, CAD-native file format originally created to enable interoperability between different CAD systems. In a DXF file, each geometric entity is represented by a structured ASCII or binary record, which facilitates programmatic extraction of coordinates and primitive types but does not include explicit topological connectivity.

Moreover, many methods do not generalize well to complex industrial parts that include curved surfaces, intersecting features, or non-standard projection layouts. Computational complexity is another barrier, as approaches based on exhaustive geometric matching or volumetric reconstruction often become infeasible for drawings with a high number of elements. Consequently, there is a clear need for reconstruction methods that can operate without prior knowledge of shape classes, while remaining computationally tractable and tolerant to incomplete or ambiguous input data.

Automated 3D reconstruction from 2D orthographic projections has become increasingly important due to its role in streamlining digital manufacturing workflows. Since 3D models serve as the foundation for CAM (such as AutoCAD Mechanical v24.0) software and the generation of CNC programs, their availability is essential for modern production systems. Manual reconstruction is time-consuming, error-prone, and incompatible with the demands of scalable, automated manufacturing environments.

Recent studies have attempted to address these limitations through machine learning models, rule-based extraction, and graph-based interpretations. For example, Furferi et al. [1] employed a set of geometric rules for feature recognition, while Zhang et al. [2] proposed a method based on shape matching and solid feature extraction. However, these approaches typically depend on either specific geometric constraints or extensive domain knowledge, which limits their flexibility. CNN-based techniques [3,4] have shown promise in object classification tasks but are not easily adaptable to wireframe reconstruction without labeled training datasets.

Furthermore, although some researchers have explored the use of genetic algorithms (GA) for reconstruction tasks [5], these efforts are often restricted to prismatic objects or simplified scenarios with predefined projections. To the best of our knowledge, no existing study has formulated the reconstruction task using a symmetric topological representation that abstracts the geometry into a generalized graph structure. This gap highlights the need for a new approach that combines topological abstraction and evolutionary optimization to address the limitations of current methods in terms of generality, scalability, and independence from geometric priors.

The primary purpose of this study is to develop a robust and generalizable methodology for reconstructing 3D wireframe models from 2D orthographic engineering drawings in DXF format. Unlike existing methods that rely on geometry-specific rules or extensive training datasets, our approach seeks to abstract the reconstruction process by modeling the structural relationships within the drawing. This enables the proposed method to function independently of specific shape types and to be applicable to a broad range of industrial components, including those with curved or hybrid geometries.

To address these challenges, this paper proposes a novel method that integrates geometric reasoning with a topological representation based on symmetric adjacency matrices. This representation compactly encodes the relationships between vertices and edges, supporting efficient detection of geometric consistencies and inconsistencies across projections. The proposed method extracts geometric entities directly from DXF files and constructs a connectivity matrix that forms the basis for identifying spatial relations. A GA is then employed to search the solution space for a plausible 3D reconstruction that satisfies geometric constraints while aligning projections from multiple views. This hybrid strategy enhances automation and robustness, particularly in reconstructing wireframe models from standard 2D technical drawings.

The proposed approach is expected to achieve accurate and consistent reconstruction of 3D wireframe models from 2D technical drawings, even in cases where traditional methods fail due to geometric ambiguity or incomplete data. Through extensive testing on real-world engineering examples—including both polyhedral and cylindrical components—the method is designed to demonstrate strong generalization capabilities, low computational overhead, and high structural fidelity. These outcomes would confirm the practical potential of the approach for integration into CAD/CAM workflows and digital twin environments.

The remainder of this paper is organized as follows. Section 2 reviews the background and related work in 3D reconstruction from 2D drawings, focusing on existing methodologies and identifying research gaps. Section 3 presents the theoretical model, outlining the assumptions, mathematical formulation, and the complete workflow for wireframe reconstruction using symmetric adjacency matrices. Section 4 introduces the genetic algorithm developed for optimization, including chromosome representation, fitness evaluation, and evolutionary operators. Section 5 discusses the experimental setup and presents results obtained on several real-world test cases, including polyhedral and cylindrical geometries. Section 6 concludes the paper with a summary of findings, identified limitations, and future research directions.

2. Background and Related Work

The reconstruction of 3D models from 2D technical drawings has been explored since the 1970s, primarily through two fundamental approaches: Boundary Representation (B-Rep) and Constructive Solid Geometry (CSG). B-Rep describes objects by their boundaries (vertices, edges, and surfaces), while CSG relies on Boolean operations over basic geometric primitives. The first known algorithm for generating 3D models from orthographic projections was introduced in 1973 [2] and later formalized in subsequent works [3,4]. These early methods mainly focused on polyhedral object reconstruction, with a more efficient algorithm proposed in [5].

Previous studies on 3D model reconstruction from 2D drawings have explored a range of methodologies, including rule-based systems, graph-based representations, and evolutionary computation. Zhang et al. [2] classify existing methods into three main groups: wireframe reconstruction, direct solid reconstruction, and machine learning-based methods. This classification can be extended to include metaheuristic approaches such as GAs, which, despite their potential, remain relatively underexplored. A comprehensive review of modern methods is provided in [2].

Within the wireframe domain, Furferi et al. [1] developed a MATLAB v7. 10 algorithm that utilizes vector drawings and vertex connectivity to construct 3D models. The authors in [6] applied fuzzy logic to analyze surface connectivity, while [7] addressed the construction of conic curves using Bézier interpolation. However, most methods struggle with curved edges and complex shapes. A decision tree approach is used in [8] to recognize surfaces from all three projections, though the algorithm is complex due to multiple parallel analyses.

Further developments include [9–12], which introduce a hybrid model linking vertices, edges, and surfaces, later converted into B-Rep. Although informative, this method requires high computational resources due to surface relation identification in each view. Varley [12] applied shortest path algorithms on graphs to detect loops corresponding to surfaces. Others, such as [13,14], rely on extrusion and knowledge bases but are limited to simple forms and predefined geometries.

Machine learning approaches—particularly convolutional and transformer neural networks—are becoming more prominent, yet a functional model for direct 3D reconstruction from 2D drawings is still lacking [9], and thus this work does not explore that domain further.

Among metaheuristic strategies, GAs show promise. Chen and Feng [15] were the first to apply GAs for reconstructing 3D models from imprecise 2D contours. Similar concepts have been explored in [16–18], although these are largely limited to prismatic shapes and do not handle more complex surfaces.

Based on the literature, three main challenges can be identified: high computational complexity, limited applicability to drawings with mixed geometries, and underutilization of genetic algorithms. This paper introduces a novel method based on symmetric connectivity matrices, which efficiently encodes the topology of 2D entities extracted from DXF files and serves as the foundation for GA-based optimization. Our approach enables wireframe model reconstruction through graph-based traversal, independent of shape complexity, including lines, arcs, and curves.

Unlike existing GA approaches that operate on contours or raster images, our method uses a graph-based representation with clearly defined topology. To the best of our knowledge, this is the first work to formulate wireframe reconstruction as a graph optimization problem addressed via evolutionary algorithms. The method demonstrates good performance and opens promising directions for further research. The proposed method not only enhances the efficiency of shape reconstruction but also emphasizes the inherent symmetry in structural representations of engineering geometries.

3. Model Elements and Workflow for 3D Model Reconstruction from 2D Engineering Drawings

3.1. Initial Hypotheses and Assumptions

This paper hypothesizes that representing 2D orthographic projections using symmetric adjacency matrices enables efficient, scalable, and accurate reconstruction of 3D wireframe models through evolutionary optimization. The central assumption is that the topological and geometric relationships inherent in 2D technical drawings can be compactly encoded in symmetric matrices and interpreted as graph structures, forming a consistent foundation for reconstructing 3D geometry.

The main contributions of this paper are:

- A novel representation of 2D engineering drawings using symmetric adjacency matrices.
- A mathematical model that formalizes the 3D wireframe reconstruction problem as a binary integer optimization task.
- Development and implementation of a customized genetic algorithm for solving this optimization problem
- Experimental validation across both polyhedral and cylindrical geometries, demonstrating the method's generality and robustness, including cases with curved edges and varying levels of drawing complexity.

Figure 1 shows a 3D model of a typical industrial machine part, designed in one of the software packages.

Figure 1. Typical industrial machine part.

For drawing creation, including the method of marking individual components of the drawing, certain conventions have been adopted over the past decades and regulated by appropriate standards [19]. The goal of adopting these conventions is to ensure that drawings provide unambiguous instructions for the manufacture of the depicted parts. These standards, whether international ISO standards or national standards, are integrated into commercial software packages and offer multiple options for representing individual elements of machine parts in technical or workshop drawings. These options provide designers with some freedom when creating workshop drawings, making it practically impossible to incorporate all possibilities into an algorithm for identifying geometric information. Therefore, this research is based on the following assumptions:

It is assumed that the 2D workshop drawing is complete and contains three orthographic projections made according to ISO-E or European projection layout: front view, top view, and left view, as shown in Figure 2.

It is assumed that the 2D workshop drawing contains all the necessary information that clearly and unambiguously defines the shape of the machine part. Sections, details, partial views, etc., are not considered, meaning all edges, vertices, and hidden lines are shown in the corresponding projections (Figure 2).

The dimensions of the 3D model can be directly obtained from the vertex coordinates, assuming they can be corrected with an appropriate scaling factor. For simplicity, this research assumes that the orthographic projections are created at a scale of 1:1.

It is assumed that all three orthographic projections are created in accordance with the dimensional and geometric tolerances previously embedded in the 3D model.

DXF files, due to their binary or ASCII format, offer a significant advantage in entity recognition tasks, as highlighted in [20,21]. This format simplifies the identification of geometric entities such as lines, circles, points, and polylines within engineering drawings. When an object is provided with three projections in the DXF format, identifying the individual components (such as lines, circles, etc.) is a relatively straightforward process. However, the DXF format lacks topological data, meaning the file contains no logical sequence for the entities and no explicit information about their connectivity. In simpler terms, details about the spatial arrangement of projections and the edges associated with them are absent. Due to this limitation, a method to separate the drawing into three distinct views is required before proceeding with further analysis [6].

These assumptions simplify the input data for the process of the identification and conversion of geometric information, enabling its practical implementation. Without these assumptions, the process of identifying and recognizing geometric information would significantly exceed the scope of this research.

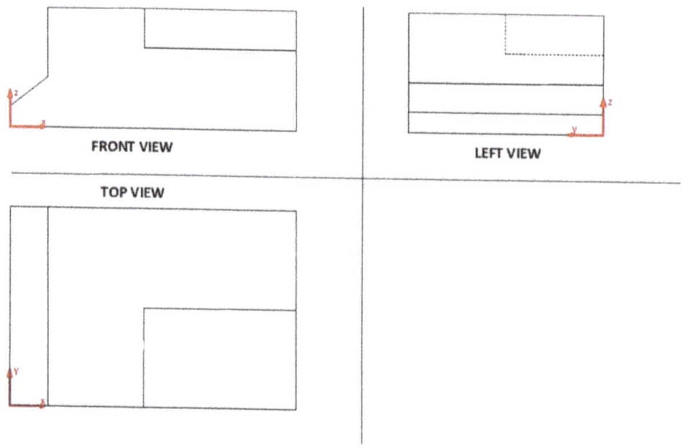

Figure 2. Orthographic projections—engineering drawing of an industrial part.

3.2. *Workflow of 3D Reconstruction Process*

The flowchart presented in Figure 3 outlines the overall workflow of the proposed methodology, beginning with the parsing of DXF projections and culminating in the reconstruction process based on a GA. Each element of the flowchart corresponds to a specific sub-procedure, the details of which are elaborated in the subsequent sections. This modular structure ensures clarity and reproducibility, reflecting the systematic integration of geometric data processing and evolutionary optimization.

The orthographic projections shown in Figure 4, which are analogous to the example found in [16] consist of different flat geometric shapes. These shapes can be lines, circular arcs and circles. Those geometric shapes represent entities that form contours as shown in Figure 4. Also, it should be noted that entities are defined by their starting and ending points and some other characteristics that depend on the type of the entity.

In the example shown in Figure 4, which represents the front view of the part shown in Figure 1, there are a total of 9 points that form line entities. A line is an entity determined with the starting point (X_1, Y_1) and the ending point (X_2, Y_2), i.e., the coordinates of the starting and ending points in the Cartesian coordinate system.

In addition to line entities, there are also entity circle, determined by the coordinate of the center (X, Y) in the Cartesian coordinate system, and the radius R and an Arc or circular arc, determined by the coordinate of the center (X, Y) in the Cartesian coordinate system and the radius R, as well as the initial and final angle of the circular arc expressed in degrees.

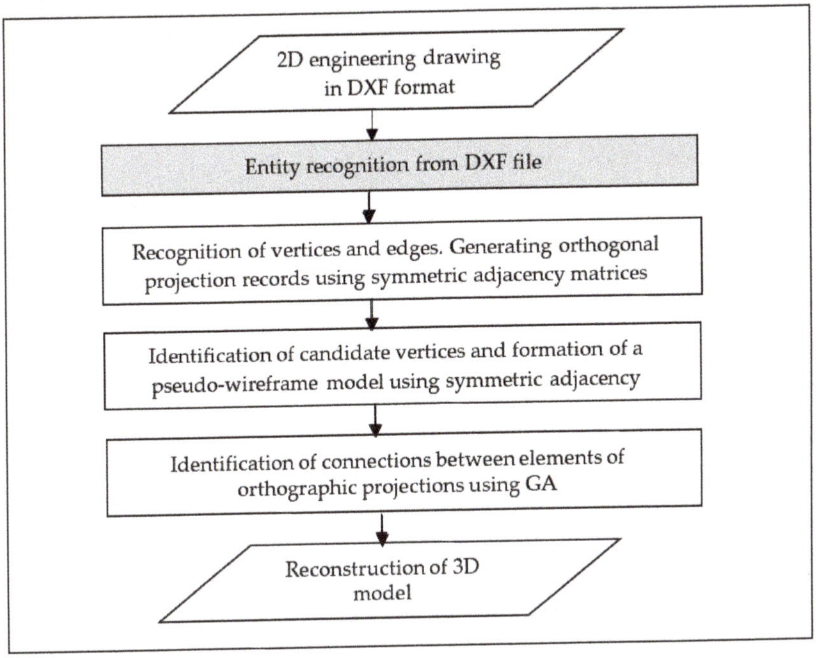

Figure 3. Flow diagram of 3D model reconstruction process.

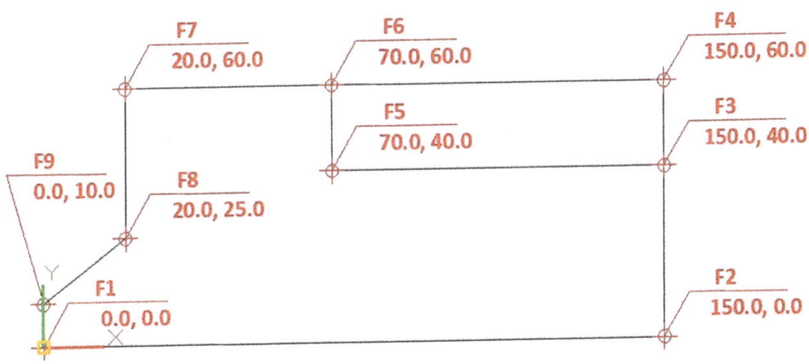

Figure 4. Entities of orthographic projection.

Recognizing lines, circles, points, and polylines is fundamental to automated 3D model recognition, as they define surface boundaries. While entities recognition and positioning in DXF files are relatively simple and well documented in [16], our research addresses the more complex challenge of automatically establishing topological relationships between vertices and edges. The following presents the structured pseudocode for the extraction of line entities from the entities section of a DXF file. A similar approach is used for processing circular arcs and other entity types (Algorithm 1).

The procedure is organized into five key stages:

- File selection: User selects a DXF file from disk.
- Data initialization: The file is loaded and the ENTITIES section is located.
- Parsing logic: LINE entities are scanned and decomposed into vertex coordinate pairs.
- Edge creation: Edges are constructed by linking each vertex pair.

- Post-processing: Duplicate vertices are removed and the final vertex and edge arrays are produced.

Algorithm 1 Extraction of line entities and graph construction from a DXF file.

```
PROCEDURE ExtractLineEntities
    INPUT: FilePath (string)–dxf file path
    OUTPUT: VertexList (list of unique vertices), EdgeList (list of edges)
    // 1. File selection
    Open DXF file at FilePath
    IF file cannot be opened THEN
        RETURN error
    // 2. Data initialization
    Locate "ENTITIES" section in file
    IF "ENTITIES" section not found THEN
        RETURN error
    Initialize empty list RawVertices
    Initialize empty list EdgeList
    // 3. Parsing logic
    FOR each entity in "ENTITIES" section DO
        IF entity type is "LINE" THEN
            Read start point (X1, Y1)
            Read end point (X2, Y2)
    // 4. Edge creation
            Add (X1, Y1) to RawVertices
            Add (X2, Y2) to RawVertices
            Add edge: ( (X1, Y1), (X2, Y2) ) to EdgeList
        END FOR
    // 5. Post-processing
    VertexList ← Remove duplicate points from RawVertices
    FOR each edge in EdgeList DO
        Replace (X1, Y1) and (X2, Y2) with corresponding indices in VertexList
    END FOR
    RETURN VertexList, EdgeList
END PROCEDURE
```

3.3. Creating Orthographic Projection Matrices

This section expands on how edges are formed from vertices based on their coordinates, and how this relationship is mathematically represented to construct the adjacency matrix AdjA for the front view (Figure 4).

Definition 1. *Let:*

$P = \{p_1, p_2, \ldots, p_3\}$: *A set VA of n vertices in the front orthographic projection. Each vertex is represented as:* $p_i = \{x_i, y_j\}, i, j \in \{1, 2, \ldots, n\}$

$E = \{e_1, e_2, \ldots, e_3\}$: *A set EA of m edges, where each edge* e_k *connects two vertices* p_i *and* p_j*. Each edge is represented as:* $e_k = \{p_i, p_j\}, i, j \in \{1, 2, \ldots, n\}, i \neq j$

Each entity is defined by a start point $(x_s,\ y_s)$*, and an endpoint* $(x_k,\ y_k)$*.*

Edge is defined by start and end points.

$$p_i = (x_s, y_s),\ p_j = (x_e, y_e)\ e_k = (p_i, p_j).$$

If the start or end point does not exactly match a vertex in P, a proximity threshold $\epsilon > 0$ *to account for numerical inaccuracies can be applied:* $p_i - (x_s, y_s)\| \le \epsilon$ *and* $\|p_j - (x_e, y_e)\| \le \epsilon$

The adjacency matrix is defined as:

$$AdjA \in \mathbb{R}^{n \times n},\ AdjA[i,j] = \begin{cases} 1, & \text{if } (p_i, p_j) \in E \\ 0, & \text{otherwise.} \end{cases}$$

where indicates that an edge exists between vertices. It is important to notice that orthogonal projection can be represented as an undirected graph [16] and then the matrix $AdjA$ *is symmetric:*

$$AdjA[i,j] = AdjA[j,i], \forall i,j.$$

Diagonal elements $AdjA[i,i] = 0$*-no self-loops are considered as:* $AdjA[i,i] = 0, \forall i.$

The adoption of symmetric adjacency matrices is driven by their capacity to compactly encode topological relationships among vertices in a standardized and computationally efficient format. In contrast to edge lists or conventional graph-based representations, symmetric matrices inherently minimize redundancy—owing to their structural symmetry—and support efficient matrix operations, such as the computation of the Frobenius norm, which plays a critical role in the iterative optimization process governed by GA. Furthermore, this representation naturally corresponds to the undirected nature of edge relationships in engineering drawings, thereby preserving consistent connectivity across multiple orthographic projections. By abstracting geometric entities into binary topological relations, the proposed approach achieves a high level of generality, effectively handling both linear and curved elements without introducing additional algorithmic complexity.

The preceding definitions lay the groundwork for constructing the adjacency matrix representing the orthogonal projection. The construction of an adjacency matrix is a simple algorithm and for verifying the consistency of the matrix two important rules should be checked as follows:

- Edge count: The total number of edges, i.e., 1's in $AdjA$ (excluding diagonal elements) should be equal $2m$ for m edges: $\sum_{i,j} AdjA_{ij} - \sum_i AdjA_{ii} = 2m$;
- Symmetry: For undirected graph: $AdjA = AdjA^T$.

However, there is one difference in this study that is very important for the research presented.

Figure 5 presents the orthogonal projection matrix for the front view shown in Figure 4. As can be seen, vertices F_4–F_6 form an edge, but so do vertices F_4–F_7. The same applies to vertices F_4–F_2 and F_4–F_3. The formula for the number of edges would hold if vertices F_4–F_3 and F_4–F_6 formed edges but F_4–F_7 and F_4–F_6 did not, and then it would be an undirected graph. However, the 3D model is unknown, and whether there is, for example, an edge F_4–F_7 can only be determined by considering hidden edges and a series of vertex relationship tests and calculations, which is difficult to perform for more complex models. Therefore, the assumption is introduced that the orthogonal projection matrix must include projections of all possible surfaces that the 3D model can have in a direction normal to the projection plane, which are defined for the example in Figure 4 by vertices 1-2-4-6-7-8-9, 1-2-3-5-6-7-8-9, and 3-4-6-5.

Following the previous discussion, new rules were introduced into the model. These rules establish a new coordinate, denoted as $c \in x, y, z,$ that find all points $V_i \in S$ such that : $c_i = C,\ \forall i \in I$, which states that if there are three or more points where one specific coordinate remains constant, then any pair of these points can be connected by a valid edge, as follows:

1. Let $S = V_1, V_2, \ldots, V_n$, where $V_i = (x_i, y_i, z_i)$ for $i = 1, 2, \ldots, n$.
2. For a specific coordinate $c \in x, y, z$, find all points $V_i \in S$ such that : $c_i = C, \forall i \in I$, where C is a constant. $I \subseteq \{1, 2, \ldots, n\}$
3. If $|I| \geq 3$ then all points in the subset: $Sc = Vi : i \in I$ can form valid edges E.

	F1	F2	F3	F4	F5	F6	F7	F8	F9
F1	0	1	0	0	0	0	0	0	1
F2	1	0	1	1	0	0	0	0	0
F3	0	1	0	1	1	0	0	0	0
F4	0	1	1	0	0	1	1	0	0
F5	0	0	1	0	0	1	0	0	0
F6	0	0	0	1	1	0	1	0	0
F7	0	0	0	1	0	1	0	1	0
F8	0	0	0	0	0	0	1	0	1
F9	1	0	0	0	0	0	0	1	0

Figure 5. Front orthogonal projection matrix.

The number of valid edges now can be calculated using the formula for the binomial coefficient

$$E = \binom{|I|}{2} = \frac{|I|(|I|-1)}{2}, \quad \text{if } |I| \geq 3,$$

where each edge corresponds to a pair of points., i.e., representing several ways to select a pair of points from $|I|$. Now, a completely defined way of forming a matrix of orthogonal projections is given. In addition to the matrix shown in Figure 5, for each projection, a sequence of vertex coordinates is defined and shown in Table 1 for the example of the projection from Figure 4. In the same way, projection matrices and vertex coordinate arrays are formed for the other two orthogonal projections.

Table 1. Vertex coordinate array for front projection.

	X	Z
F1	X_1	Z_1
F2	X_2	Z_2
F3	X_3	Z_3
F4	X_4	Z_4
F5	X_5	Z_5
F6	X_6	Z_6
F7	X_7	Z_7
F8	X_8	Z_8
F9	X_9	Z_9

Now, three square adjacency matrices are defined, representing orthogonal projections $AdjA$ is an $n_A \times n_A$ matrix, $AdjB$ is an $n_B \times n_B$ matrix, $AdjC$ is an $n_C \times n_C$ matrix. Each matrix corresponding to the to the number of vertices in the respective projection.

For each orthogonal projection, a coordinate array is associated: $V_A = V_{A1}, V_{A2}, \ldots, V_{A_{n_A}}$, $V_B = V_{B1}, V_{B2}, \ldots, V_{B_{n_B}}$, $V_C = V_{C1}, V_{C2}, \ldots, V_{C_{n_C}}$ where the length of each array $(|V_A| = n_A, \ |V_B| = n_B, \ |V_C| = n_C)$ corresponds to the dimension of the associated adjacency matrix. With these definitions, the symmetric adjacency matrix describes the connectivity (edges) of vertices in each projection and coordinate arrays provide the spatial locations of the vertices in their respective views. Now, a 3D model is given with:

$$M = \{AdjA, VA, AdjB, VB, AdjC, VC\}$$

This formulation sufficiently describes each orthogonal projection to proceed with the identification of candidate vertices and the formation of a pseudo-wireframe model.

Table 2 provides a comparative overview of commonly used topology representations in 3D model reconstruction. This highlights the advantages of the proposed method over traditional edge-based, raster, and graph-matching approaches.

Table 2. Comparative overview of topology representations in 3D reconstruction methods.

Representation Method	Input Structure	Geometry Independence	Supports Curved edges	Suitability for GA	Complexity Level
Edge list	List of connected points	✕ Limited	No	Medium	Medium
B-Rep/CSG	Surfaces and operations	No	Partial	No	High
Image-based/Raster methods	Pixel-based shape data	No	No	No	Medium/High
Graph matching	Labeled graphs	Partial	With conditions	Yes	High
Symmetric adjacency matrix (This paper)	Binary vertex–vertex topology	Yes	Partial, to be tested for complex curves	Optimized	Low/Structured

As seen in Table 2, the symmetric adjacency matrix offers an optimal balance of generality, simplicity, and GA compatibility, making it a robust foundation for 3D reconstruction from engineering drawings.

The following pseudocode presents the process of converting a DXF file into a symmetric adjacency matrix, encapsulating the previously described methodology in a clear, step-by-step format (Algorithm 2).

Algorithm 2 Generation of a symmetric adjacency matrix from DXF orthographic pro-jections.

Pipeline for converting DXF data into a symmetric adjacency matrix
Input: DXF file containing 2D orthographic projections (front, top, left)
Output: Symmetric adjacency matrices for each projection
Import and parse the DXF file (ASCII format)
Segment the drawing into three orthographic views based on spatial grouping
For each view:

1. dentify geometric entities: LINE, ARC, CIRCLE
2. Extract start and end points for each entity
3. Create vertex list by grouping nearby points (with tolerance ε)
4. Generate edge list by mapping entities to vertex pairs
5. Build adjacency matrix: set $Adj[i][j] = 1$ if an edge connects vertex i and j

Ensure symmetry: enforce $Adj[i][j] = Adj[j][i]$
Validate: check consistency rules (number of edges, symmetry, no self-loops)

3.4. Generation of Candidate Vertices and a Pseudo Wireframe Model

The formation of a pseudo-wireframe model was initially described and formalized in [3,4], with an additional method presented in [5]. In this paper, a new method for forming a pseudo wireframe model will be presented. The initial step involves defining all potential vertices for the pseudo-wireframe model, which entails several sub steps. The goal is to identify all potential 3D vertices $V_i^{3D} = (x_i, y_i, z_i)$ that are consistent across all three orthogonal projections. This is achieved by verifying compatibility between the projection based on the given coordinates. Based on the discussions in Section 3.3, a step-by-step procedure for generating candidate vertices is provided:

1. Iterate over all combinations: For each combination of indices $(i, j, k), i \in 1, 2, \ldots, n_A$, $j \in 1, 2, \ldots, n_B, \quad k \in 1, 2, \ldots, n_C$ evaluates the following condition:
2. Compatibility check: A vertex (x, y, z)) is a candidate if the following conditions are met:

$$\begin{aligned} |x_{Ai} - x_{Bj}| &= 0 \\ |y_{Bj} - x_{Ck}| &= 0 \\ |y_{Ai} - y_{Ck}| &= 0 \end{aligned}$$

3. Generate candidate vertex: If the conditions hold, compute the candidate vertex as $x = x_{Ai}, y = y_{Bj}, z = y_{Ck}$.
4. Store candidate: Add the candidate vertex $V^{3D} = (x, y, z)$ to the result set: $V^{3D}_{\text{candidates}}$
5. Output: The final result is the set of all valid candidate vertices: $V^{3D}_{\text{candidates}} = V_1^{3D}, V_2^{3D}, \ldots, V_m^{3D}$, where $m \leq n_A \cdot n_B \cdot n_C$ depends on the number of valid combinations.

Following the logic that an orthogonal projection is represented by a symmetric adjacency matrix and a set of vertex coordinates, the same applies to the pseudo-wireframe 3D model. Therefore, it is necessary to define the matrix *Adj* as the symmetric adjacency matrix of edges in the 3D model. The procedure is relatively simple and evaluates whether an edge exists between two vertices in a 3D model based on their adjacency in the spatial symmetric adjacency matrix and their projections in the three orthogonal views. An edge is considered to exist within a 3D model if and only if its representation is present in all orthogonal projections. The visual representation of an edge in these projections can vary, appearing as either a line or a point. This variability is determined by the edge's spatial orientation relative to the coordinate planes—specifically, whether it is orthogonal or parallel to them. Generally, if an edge is neither orthogonal nor parallel to any coordinate plane, it will manifest as a line in all three projections.

For each pair of candidate vertices (v_i, v_j), their corresponding *Adj*[*i*][*j*] is determined as follows:

1. Map Vertices to Projections: Project vertices v_i and v_j onto the orthogonal planes:

$$\begin{aligned} P_1 = (x_i, z_i) \wedge P_2 = (x_j, z_j) \text{ for } xz \text{ plane} \\ P_3 = (x_i, y_i) \wedge P_4 = (x_j, y_j) \text{ for } xy \text{ plane} \\ P_5 = (y_i, z_i) \wedge P_6 = (y_j, z_j) \text{ for } yz \text{ plane} \end{aligned}$$

   Using these projections, locate the corresponding indices in the projection vertex arrays:

$$\begin{aligned} I_1 = IndexOf(P_1, VA),\ I_2 = IndexOf(P_2, VA) \\ I_3 = IndexOf(P_3, VB),\ I_4 = IndexOf(P_4, VB) \\ I_5 = IndexOf(P_5, VB),\ I_6 = IndexOf(P_6, VB) \end{aligned}$$

2. Edge existence check in projections: Evaluate whether edges exist between the projected vertices in their respective adjacency matrices:

$$E_A = (AdjA[I_1][I_2] > 0) \vee ((I_1 = I_2) \wedge (AdjA[I_1][I_2] = 0))$$
$$E_B = (AdjB[I_3][I_4] > 0) \vee ((I_3 = I_4) \wedge (AdjB[I_3][I_4] = 0))$$
$$E_C = (AdjC[I_5][I_6] > 0) \vee ((I_5 = I_6) \wedge (AdjC[I_5][I_6] = 0))$$

3. Spatial edge update: Update the spatial symmetric adjacency matrix *Adj* for the edge *[i][j]*

$$E_A \wedge E_B \wedge E_C \Rightarrow Adj[i][j] = 1 \neg(E_A \wedge E_B \wedge E_C) \Rightarrow Adj[i][j] = 0$$

The 3D model is now represented by $M = \{Adj, V^{3D}_{candidates}\}$, which defines all possible solutions of the pseudo-wireframe model. Figures 6 and 7 illustrate the reconstruction process for the part shown in Figure 1. Figure 6 presents the symmetric adjacency matrix AdjA, while Figure 7 shows all possible 3D models generated from this matrix and the corresponding candidate vertices. Figure 7a shows a pseudo-wireframe 3D model that encompasses three valid reconstruction candidates, as their geometries are consistent with the input projections. Among them, the model in Figure 7d is the one intended for reconstruction, while the models shown in Figure 7b,c are also geometrically valid solutions; however, they do not represent the target 3D reconstruction and must therefore be discarded during the process.

	T_1	T_2	T_3	T_4	T_5	T_6	T_7	T_8	T_9	T_{10}	T_{11}	T_{12}	T_{13}	T_{14}	T_{15}	T_{16}	T_{17}	T_{18}	T_{19}
T_1	0	1	1	0	0	0	0	0	0	0	0	0	0	0	0	0	0	1	0
T_2	1	0	0	1	0	0	0	0	0	0	0	0	0	0	0	0	0	0	1
T_3	1	0	0	1	1	0	1	0	0	0	0	0	0	0	0	0	0	0	0
T_4	0	1	1	0	0	0	0	0	1	0	0	0	0	0	0	0	0	0	0
T_5	0	0	1	0	0	1	1	0	0	1	0	0	0	0	0	0	0	0	0
T_6	0	0	0	0	1	0	0	1	0	0	1	0	0	0	0	0	0	0	0
T_7	0	0	1	0	1	0	0	1	1	0	0	1	0	1	0	0	0	0	0
T_8	0	0	0	0	0	1	1	0	1	0	0	0	1	0	0	0	0	0	0
T_9	0	0	0	1	0	0	1	1	0	0	0	0	0	0	1	0	0	0	0
T_{10}	0	0	0	0	1	0	0	0	0	0	1	1	0	0	0	0	0	0	0
T_{11}	0	0	0	0	0	1	0	0	0	1	0	0	1	0	0	0	0	0	0
T_{12}	0	0	0	0	0	0	1	0	0	1	0	0	1	1	0	0	0	0	0
T_{13}	0	0	0	0	0	0	0	1	0	0	1	1	0	0	0	0	0	0	0
T_{14}	0	0	0	0	0	0	1	0	0	0	0	1	0	0	1	1	0	0	0
T_{15}	0	0	0	0	0	0	0	0	1	0	0	0	0	1	0	0	1	0	0
T_{16}	0	0	0	0	0	0	0	0	0	0	0	0	0	1	0	0	1	1	0
T_{17}	0	0	0	0	0	0	0	0	0	0	0	0	0	0	1	1	0	0	1
T_{18}	1	0	0	0	0	0	0	0	0	0	0	0	0	0	0	1	0	0	1
T_{19}	0	1	0	0	0	0	0	0	0	0	0	0	0	0	0	0	1	1	0

Figure 6. Example of adjacency matrix of pseudo-wireframe mode.

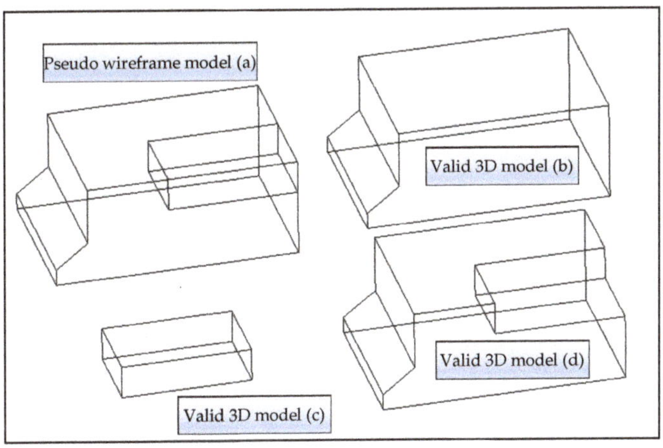

Figure 7. Example of pseudo wireframe model with all possible 3D models: (**a**) pseudo-wireframe model with ambiguous geometry; (**b–d**) represent different valid interpretations of the 3D model reconstructed from the same projection data.

Human designers often approach engineering drawings by attempting to mentally reconstruct the 3D object through identification of geometric relationships across multiple views. This process typically involves a sequence of intuitive evaluations and repeated adjustments, which continues until a coherent 3D representation is formed in their minds [6].

The process of 3D wireframe model reconstruction can be defined as a process of adding or removing candidate vertices and their corresponding edges while respecting constraints related to geometric consistency until a solution is obtained that satisfies predefined criteria. This defined process of 3D wireframe model reconstruction represents a standard optimization problem, for the realization of which it is necessary to define a mathematical model that should be independent of the optimization method.

3.5. Mathematical Formulation of the Proposed Model

Input variables

1. Orthogonal projection symmetric adjacency matrices and their dimensions:

- $AdjA \in \{0,1\}^{n_A x n_A}$ adjacency matrix for the front projection;
- $AdjB \in \{0,1\}^{n_B x n_B}$ adjacency matrix for the top projection;
- $AdjC \in \{0,1\}^{n_C x n_C}$ adjacency matrix for the left projection.

2. Vertex coordinates of projections:

- $V_A = \{(x_i^A, z_i^A)\}_{i=1}^{n_A}$ coordinates of vertices in front projection;
- $V_B = \{(x_i^B, y_i^B)\}_{i=1}^{n_B}$ coordinates of vertices in top projection;
- $V_C = \{(y_i^C, z_i^C)\}_{i=1}^{n_C}$ coordinates of vertices in left projection.

1. Coordinate vertex set and connectivity:

- $V_K = \{(x_i^K, y_i^K, z_i^K)\}_{i=1}^{N_K}$ 3D candidate vertex coordinates;
- $Adj \in \{0,1\}^{N_K x N_K}$ symmetric adjacency matrix for pseudo-wireframe model.

2. Bounds on the number of vertices:

- $n \leq N \leq NK$, $n = max(n_A, n_B, n_C)$.

3. Target number of edges:

- Marked as T where T is derived from Adj.

Control variables of the mathematical model

In addition to the observed model's input variables, it is necessary to define a vector of control variables, that is, variables that describe the optimization objectives stated.

$$x_i \in \{0,\ 1\},\ i = 1, 2,\ \ldots,\ N_K \tag{1}$$

where x_i—vertex inclusion indicator is a binary variable indicating whether vertex i is included in the 3D model

$$e_{ij} \in \{0,\ 1\},\ i, j = 1, 2,\ \ldots,\ N_K \tag{2}$$

where e_{ij}—edge inclusion indicator is a binary variable indicating whether edge (i, j) is included in the 3D model

$$Adj^{curr}(x_i, e_{ij}) \in \{0,\ 1\},\ i, j = 1, 2,\ \ldots,\ N_K \tag{3}$$

where Adj^{curr}—reduced symmetric adjacency matrix is a binary variable representing the current 3D model using x_i and e_{ij}.

The objective function

The objective function of the mathematical model represents the criteria of optimization. As mentioned earlier the goal is to measure the difference between current 3D model and the target 3D model where target 3D model is represented with orthogonal projections. However, determining this difference is not sufficient, and even has a smaller impact on the optimization result, because orthogonal projections encompass all possible model solutions that are geometrically consistent. Therefore, in addition to measuring the difference between projections, it is necessary to introduce an additional parameter into the objective function. Figure 7 clearly shows that the solutions differ in the number of edges, although all edges are displayed in a pseudo-wireframe model. The target number of edges cannot be the number of edges of the pseudo-wireframe model because valid models have fewer edges. It is necessary to determine the difference between the number of edges of $Adj^{curr}(x_i, e_{ij})$ and the target number of edges that the model to be recognized has. This can be achieved with the following procedure:

1. Identify the vertex with the highest weight (most edges) in *Adj*;
2. Set all entries in the corresponding row and column of that vertex 0 in *Adj*;
3. $Adj = Adj^{curr}(x_i, e_{ij})$;
4. Repeat steps 1–3 until each row and column in *Adj* has either 0 or 3 non-zero entries but without violating geometric consistency;
5. The sum off all 1-values in *Adj* after processing is the target number of edges *T*.

When there is more than one goal to achieve during the optimization process, there are several ways to define an objective function [21] without entering in space of multi-objective optimization. Finally, objective function $F(x,e)$ can be written as:

$$min(F(x,e)) = min(\omega_1 \cdot F_N(x,e) + \omega_2 \cdot (F_T(x,e) \times p)) \tag{4}$$

$$F_N(x,\ e) = \|AdjA - ProjA(x,\ e)\|_F^2 + \|AdjB - ProjB(x,\ e)\|_F^2 + \|AdjC - ProjC(x,\ e)\|_F^2 \tag{5}$$

$$F_T(x,e) = (E(x,e) - T)^2 \tag{6}$$

where $F_N(x,\ e)$ is the Frobenius norm between goal projections adjacency matrices and projection adjacency matrices of orthogonal projections of current 3D model *ProjA*, *ProjB*, *ProjC*. $F_T(x,e)$ is the difference between the total number of edges of a current 3D model and the target number of edges, ω_1, and ω_2 are weighting coefficients that determine weights for the two objectives in the overall objective function. Vector $\vec{p}$ is a penalty vector and will be explained later.

Constraints of a mathematical model

The vertex–edge consistency constraint ensures that an edge e_{ij} can only exist if both of its corresponding vertices *i* and *j* are included in the model. This is critical for maintaining logical consistency in the graph structure of the 3D model.

$$e_{ij} \leq x_i, e_{ij} \leq x_j, \forall i, j. \tag{7}$$

This constraint ensures that edges cannot "float" without being connected to valid vertices. In other words, if a vertex is excluded from the model, all edges connected to that vertex must also be excluded. This maintains the integrity of the graph structure during the iterative procedure.

The geometric consistency constraint prevents the removal of vertices and their associated edges if the result violates the required geometric structure during the iterative procedure. Specifically, it is required that the symmetric adjacency matrix $Adj^{curr}(x_i, e_{ij})$

after removing a vertex (and its corresponding edges) must have a non-zero-sum, ensuring that at least some connections remain.

$$\sum_{i,j} e_{ij} \cdot x_i \cdot x_j \neq 0 \tag{8}$$

The minimum and maximum vertices constraint ensures that the reconstructed 3D model contains only vertices within the permissible range defined by the input data. This constraint is expressed as:

$$n \leq \sum_{i=1}^{K} x_i \leq N_K \tag{9}$$

The edge connectivity constraint ensures that if an edge $(e_{ij} = 1)$ exists, then both vertices x_i and x_j are present. This adds a lower bound on the sum $x_i + x_j$, reinforcing that both vertices must exist for the edge to be valid.

$$x_i + x_j \geq 2 \cdot e_{ij}, \quad \forall i, j. \tag{10}$$

3.6. Introduction to the Proposed GA for 3D Wireframe Model Reconstruction

An acceptable 3D wireframe model can be defined as a selected subset of vertices derived from a larger set, structured to represent a 3D object while adhering to the constraints specified in a corresponding integer programming formulation. Genetic algorithms (GAs), as modern metaheuristic optimization techniques, are particularly well suited for addressing such problems due to their strong capability to converge toward a global optimum with high probability in most cases [22].

It is important to emphasize that the performance of a GA is significantly influenced by the choice of crossover and mutation operators [23]. However, for the model under consideration, the most critical component is the penalization of candidate solutions based on their validity. Only feasible solutions, as defined by the problem's constraints, are accepted in the model, and further explanation will be provided in subsequent sections.

Numerous variants of genetic operators exist in the literature, many of which can be tailored to accommodate specific characteristics of the problem at hand, thereby enhancing the adaptability of the GA. Since the general functioning of GAs is well established and extensively documented, this work provides only brief definitions of the fundamental GA components, contextualized within the proposed model.

In this model, a gene corresponds to a vertex (denoted as xix_ixi) and serves as the basic unit of encoded information. An individual or chromosome is a combination of such genes, representing a candidate 3D wireframe model. A population refers to the collection of all such individuals, i.e., the full set of acceptable 3D wireframe configurations.

Parents are two feasible 3D wireframe models that participate in reproduction to generate new candidate models. The fitness function evaluates the quality of each model; in this context, it is based on the discrepancy between the orthogonal projections derived from the engineering drawing and those generated from the candidate model, along with the difference in the number of edges. This is formally defined in Equation (4) of the mathematical model.

The crossover operator is responsible for combining two parent solutions (analogous to tool paths) to produce a new offspring. The mutation operator, on the other hand, modifies one or more genes within a single individual with the aim of introducing variability and potentially discovering superior solutions. The specific implementation of these genetic operators, as applied in the proposed model, will be detailed in later sections.

3.7. Chromosome Representation and Decoding: Initial Population

The initial phase of any genetic algorithm involves selecting a suitable encoding scheme to represent candidate solutions. Choosing the right representation is paramount, as it impacts every subsequent stage of the GA's execution. In our framework, this entails encoding each chromosome as a binary vector, with the specifics dictated by the underlying model. The approach is based on a binary chromosome representation where each gene corresponds to a vertex in the model, and the total number of genes equals the dimension of the symmetric adjacency matrix. A gene's value indicates the inclusion (1) or exclusion (0) of a vertex in the reconstructed model. Each vertex is assigned a weight based on the number of edges connected to it. Typically, vertices in most mechanical parts have a maximum of three edges, but the pseudo-wireframe model may include vertices with higher connectivity (e.g., four, five, or more edges).

The reconstruction process differentiates between acceptable and valid individuals. Acceptable individuals are those maintaining geometric consistency, making them suitable for the initial population. Valid individuals are obtained through the evolutionary process, where crossover and mutation operators improve the population by refining geometric and structural consistency. Geometric consistency is maintained by ensuring that the sum of all elements in the symmetric adjacency matrix is not zero after the removal of any vertex or its edges.

The chromosome is decoded into the current symmetric adjacency matrix, reflecting the connectivity of the vertices included in the current individual. This matrix is compared with the original adjacency matrix to measure projection consistency and edge count.

The initial population includes chromosomes that do not violate geometric consistency. During the evolutionary process, vertices with higher weights are more likely to be excluded, provided their removal does not disrupt the model's structural integrity. The optimization ensures convergence to a valid model. For a model with 19 vertices (as shown in Figure 7), the chromosome is represented as a binary vector (11).

$$x = [1, 0, 1, 1, 0, 1, 1, 1, 0, 0, 1, 1, 1, 1, 0, 0, 1, 1, 0] \tag{11}$$

$$w = [3, 3, 4, 3, 4, 4, 3, 6, 4, 4, 3, 3, 4, 3, 4, 3, 3, 3, 3] \tag{12}$$

The weights are calculated based on the adjacency matrix *Adj* (Figure 6), resulting in the weight vector $\vec{\omega}$ (12). Each gene is not only defined by its binary value but also by its position within the chromosome and its associated entry in the adjacency matrix. Beyond its value, a gene is further specified by an index denoting its position within the chromosome and its corresponding entry in the connectivity matrix. Gene selection, for creating a chromosome, specifically the inclusion of vertex ij in the model, is entirely stochastic taking into account only the constraint given in (9), rendering the example provided in (11) incompatible with any valid solution in the beginning of the evolution process. The initial population is formed as an array of chromosomes, without the implementation of other constraints except (9).

3.8. Fitness Calculation: Penalization of Acceptable Chromosomes

The fitness function plays a central role in steering the GA toward geometrically valid and topologically optimal 3D reconstructions. It integrates a projection consistency component—quantified using the Frobenius norm—with a penalty term that accounts for deviations from the expected number of edges. Each chromosome is assessed according to these dual criteria, and only individuals that satisfy predefined geometric constraints are retained as valid solutions. This fitness evaluation framework promotes convergence toward a unique, structurally coherent configuration, thereby ensuring topological consistency across projections within a finite number of evolutionary iterations.

The fitness function evaluates the quality of a chromosome in the GA, guiding the evolutionary process toward reconstructing the 3D wireframe model. It is defined with Equation (4), where:

- $F_N(x, e)$: Frobenius norm-based projection consistency measure, evaluating how well the reconstructed model matches the initial orthogonal projections.
- $F_T(x, e)$: Edge count consistency measure, assessing the difference between the current number of edges and the target edge count.
- ω_1 and ω_2: Weighting coefficients balancing the importance of F_N and F_T. In the context of the observed model $\omega_1 = 0.3$ and $\omega_2 = 0.7$.
- $\vec{p}$: Penalty vector, calculated as the product of the binary chromosome x and the weight vector $\vec{\omega}$, which represents the number of edges connected to each vertex.

The penalty mechanism is implemented through the penalty vector $\vec{p}$ discourages chromosomes with vertices that have excessive edge weights ($w > 3$). Each gene x_i is penalized with a factor proportional $10 \cdot w_i$ if $w_i > 3$. This ensures that vertices with high connectivity do not dominate the solution, as they often represent unrealistic or invalid structures in the context of the model. A lower fitness value indicates a better individual. Poorly penalized chromosomes are less likely to be selected as parents, preventing them from evolving further. This introduces a sort of genetic engineering into the algorithm by focusing the evolutionary process on improving acceptable solutions into valid ones.

Example of fitness evaluation:

$$x = [1, 0, 1, 1, 0, 1, 1, 1, 0, 0, 1, 1, 1, 1, 0, 0, 1, 1, 0]$$

$$w = [3, 3, 4, 3, 4, 4, 3, 6, 4, 4, 3, 3, 4, 3, 4, 3, 3, 3, 3]$$

The penalty vector $\vec{p}$ is computed by multiplying x and ω followed by penalizing genes with $w_i > 3$

$$p = [3, 0, 40, 3, 0, 40, 3, 60, 0, 0, 3, 3, 40, 3, 0, 0, 3, 3, 0]$$

- $F_N(x, e) = 0.2$ (normalized projection consistency for example);
- $F_T(x, e) = 0.1$ (normalized edge count difference for example);
- $\omega_1 = 0.5$ and $\omega_2 = 0.5$.

$$F(x, e) = 0.5 \cdot 0.2 + 0.5 \cdot 20.2 = 10.2$$

Computing and summing elements of p gives up $p \cdot F_T(x, e) = 20.2$

Final fitness: $F(x, e) = 0.5 \cdot 0.2 + 0.5 \cdot 20.2 = 10.2$

Chromosomes with penalized vertices (e.g., w_3, w_5, w_6, w_8) contribute to higher fitness values. The algorithm favors chromosomes with lower weights, as they are closer to valid configurations.

3.9. Selection of Parents, Crossover, and Mutation Operator

In our GA framework, a pair of feasible 3D wireframe models ("parents") is chosen to generate a new candidate solution. Parent selection is achieved by ranking models according to their fitness values; those with the lowest fitness scores are marked as parents and advanced to the crossover pool. This selection cycle repeats until the predefined number of parent pairs—determined by the algorithm's population size—has been reached.

Crossover then combines genetic information from two parent chromosomes to produce offspring. Each child inherits a mixture of binary-encoded genes from both parents, and specialized crossover operators (e.g., one-point, two-point, uniform) appropriate for binary strings are applied to effect this exchange. A concise review of the most widely used crossover techniques can be found in [23–25]. For the observed model, single-point crossover is chosen. The operation of single-point crossover is illustrated by the following example:

- Parent 1: x^1= [1, 0, 1, 1, 0, 1, 1, 0, 0, 1];
- Parent 2: x^2= [0, 1, 0, 0, 1, 0, 1, 1, 1, 0].

A random crossover point is selected. For this example, let the crossover point be after the 5th gene (index 5). The chromosomes are split into two segments:

- Parent 1: [1, 0, 1, 1, 0]||[1, 1, 0, 0, 1];
- Parent 2: [0, 1, 0, 0, 1]||[0, 1, 1, 1, 0].

The offspring are generated by swapping the segments:

- Offspring 1: [1, 0, 1, 1, 0] + [0, 1, 1, 1, 0] = [1, 0, 1, 1, 0, 0, 1, 1, 1, 0];
- Offspring 2: [0, 1, 0, 0, 1] + [1, 1, 0, 0, 1] = [0, 1, 0, 0, 1, 1, 1, 0, 0, 1].

Each gene in the chromosome corresponds to a vertex in the model. The value 11 means the vertex is included, and 0 means it is excluded. The crossover combines the structural characteristics of both parents. For instance:

- Offspring 1 inherits the first half of Parent 1 and the second half of Parent 2.
- Offspring 2 inherits the first half of Parent 2 and the second half of Parent 1.

After generating offspring, their fitness is evaluated using the fitness function, where penalties $\vec{p}$ are applied if vertices with high edge weights are included. Single-point crossover creates new combinations of genes, promoting diversity in the population. In the 3D model reconstruction problem, Parent 1 and Parent 2 might represent partial solutions that preserve different structural features of the model. By combining their chromosomes, offspring may inherit valid structural properties from both, leading to improved fitness and closer approximations to the target model.

The mutation operator chosen is an inversion operator. It is a mutation mechanism used in GA to introduce variability into the population. It works by flipping the value of a randomly selected gene in a chromosome.

- If the gene's value is 1, it is changed to 0, and vice versa.
- The operation is triggered based on a predefined mutation rate, ensuring controlled and rare alterations to preserve promising solutions while exploring new ones.

This operator prevents premature convergence by injecting diversity into the population and helps the algorithm explore new areas of the solution space. In the context of 3D model reconstruction, inversion can add or remove vertices from the model, refining the population towards geometrically consistent and valid solutions.

A known limitation of GA is its tendency to converge toward a local optimum, which may not necessarily yield a valid 3D model reconstruction. This is compounded by the fact that the GA's execution is typically constrained by a predefined number of generations. Furthermore, given that the symmetric adjacency matrix encoding the 3D model's edges encompasses all potentially valid solutions, it becomes imperative to establish supplementary termination criteria for the recognition process. Specifically, the reconstructed 3D model must exhibit geometric consistency, ensuring the absence of edge overlaps and the uniqueness of the solution. Consequently, an iterative GA execution is required until a single, geometrically sound solution is achieved, devoid of any edge ambiguities.

3.10. Pseudo Code of Proposed GA

The genetic algorithm implementation requires four primary configuration parameters: (1) population cardinality, (2) quantity of parent individuals selected for reproduction, (3) probability of genetic mutation, and (4) maximum evolutionary cycles. The computational process begins by instantiating the initial population and evaluating each candidate solution's fitness. Through iterative generational advancement, the algorithm performs selective breeding using single-point crossover operations, introduces random mutations, and continuously monitors for topological validity until convergence criteria are satisfied (Algorithm 3).

Algorithm 3 Evolutionary reconstruction framework.

```
PseudoCode Evolutionary Reconstruction Framework
Parameters:
  - POP_SIZE: Integer (Population cardinality)
  - NUM_PARENTS: Integer (Reproductive pool size)
  - MUT_RATE: Float ∈ [0, 1] (Variation probability)
  - MAX_GEN: Integer (Termination condition)
1. INITIALIZATION:
   population = GENERATE_RANDOM_POPULATION(POP_SIZE)
   EVALUATE_FITNESS(population)
   current_gen = 1
2. GENERATIONAL LOOP:
   WHILE current_gen ≤ MAX_GEN:
       selected_parents = BestFitness(population, NUM_PARENTS)
       offspring = EMPTY_SET()
       WHILE SIZE(offspring) < (POP_SIZE-NUM_PARENTS):
          parent1, parent2 = SELECT_PAIR(selected_parents)
          child = SINGLE_POINT_RECOMBINATION(parent1, parent2)
          IF RANDOM() < MUT_RATE:
              child = APPLY_MUTATION(child)
          ADD_TO_SET(offspring, child)
       population = COMBINE(selected_parents, offspring)
       EVALUATE_FITNESS(population)
       current_gen += 1
       IF VALID_SOLUTION_EXISTS(population) AND
          NOT HAS_EDGE_CONFLICTS(population):
          BREAK
3. TERMINATION:
   RETURN BEST_SOLUTION(population)
```

4. Experimental Results

The mathematical model provided in Section 2 is realized through application in which the previously presented GA is implemented and is written in the object-oriented programming language Delphi. It is independent executable software platform and in the following paragraph, a brief overview of the main screen and the functionality of the application is provided.

4.1. Brief Overview of the Software Platform

Figure 8 presents the application's initial screen. In the middle of the main form there are command buttons for the following:

- Data entry (loading orthogonal symmetric projection matrices and vertex arrays);
- Executing the GA;
- Closing the application.

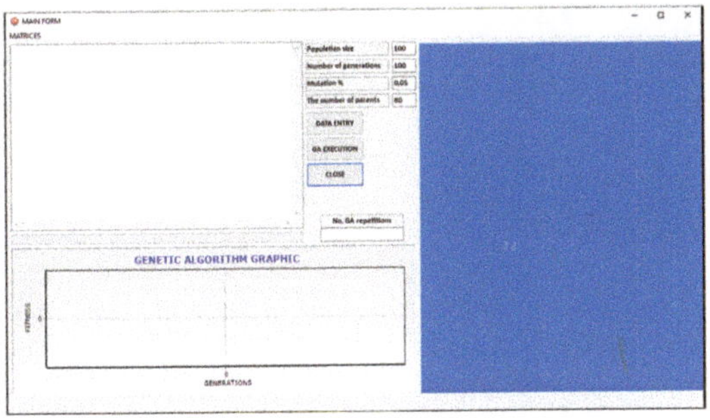

Figure 8. The main form of application for 3D reconstruction.

The left side of the input form displays the GA execution results, while the bottom half visualizes the GA process. The left half of the main form displays the results of the GA execution, the initial symmetric adjacency matrix of the pseudo-wireframe model, the fitness of each best individual in the generation, and the symmetric adjacency matrix of the best solution obtained at the end of the GA execution. In the middle of the main form, there is information about the number of GA executions up to the moment of obtaining the best solution, as well as the GA parameters that can be changed. In the right part of the main form, there is a window with a 3D graphical representation of the GA execution, while at the bottom, there is a diagram of the GA execution The application begins by loading orthogonal projections, i.e., DXF files for each view, and forming symmetric adjacency matrices for each projection.

4.2. The Structure and Loading Process of Input Data

The input data consist of pre-generated matrices of orthogonal projections and arrays of vertex coordinates for each projection. The data are stored in *.txt files for each projection, as shown in Table 3.

The first line contains the name of the projection (e.g., Front), followed by the dimension of the matrix AdjA in the format $n_A \times n_A$, and then the adjacency matrix of the front orthogonal projection. Next comes the array of vertex coordinates, and at the end, there is an empty line. This pattern is repeated for the subsequent projections, i.e., AdjB, VB, AdjC and VA, VB and VC.

Table 3. Sample input structure of projection data stored in plain text files.

Section	Example Content
Projection name	Front
Adjacency matrix size	9 × 9
Adjacency matrix (AdjA)	0 1 0 0 0 0 0 0 1 1 0 1 1 0 0 0 0 0 0 1 1 1 0 0 0 0 0 0 1 1 0 1 1 0 0 0 0 0 0 1 0 1 0 0 0 0 0 0 1 1 0 1 0 0 0 0 0 0 0 1 0 1 0 0 0 0 0 0 0 1 0 1 1 0 0 0 0 0 0 1 0

Table 3. *Cont.*

Section	Example Content
Vertex coordinates (VA)	0 0 150 0 150 40 150 60 70 40 70 60 20 60 20 25 0 10

4.3. Testing Parameters

The proposed solution has been tested on several real models, four of which will be presented here.

The first, which is simpler, is shown as an example throughout this paper. The second, more complex part, with 40 vertices and 168 edges in the pseudo-wireframe model, is shown in Figure 9 as a solid model and in Figure 10 as a wireframe model. The edges marked in red represent those that do not belong to the real model but to the set of all valid solutions. Also, vertices marked in red are vertices that belong to the candidate set but that do not belong to the vertices of a real 3D model. In Table 4, the geometric characteristics of both models are provided.

Figure 9. Solid model of PR0004 test model.

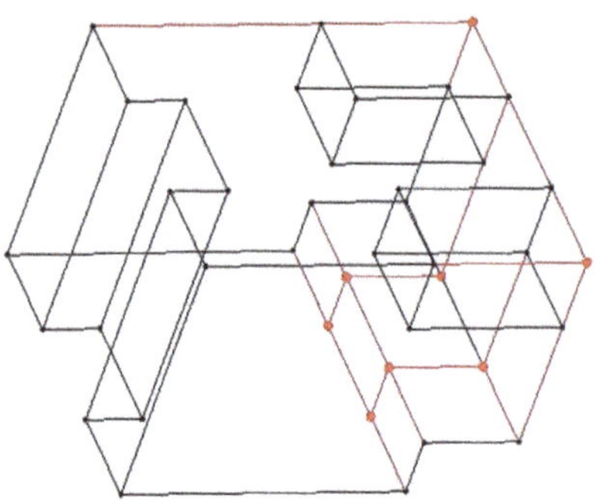

Figure 10. Three-dimensional pseudo-wireframe model of PR0004 test model.

Table 4. The geometric characteristics of tested models.

Model Name	No. Edges 3D Wireframe	No. Vertices 3D Wireframe	No. Edges 3D Real Model	No. Vertices 3D Real Model
PR0003	66	19	27	18
PR0004	168	40	60	32

Given that GA results can vary based on input parameters, five GA runs were conducted with different parameter sets. Table 5 presents the parameter values for each run, while Tables 6 and 7 lists the names of the output parameters with experimental results for PR0003 and PR0004, respectively.

Table 5. The parameters for the execution of GA.

Name of Parameter	I	II	II	IV	V
Population size	100	200	300	400	500
Number of parents	80	80	240	320	420
Mutation in %	1	1	1	1	1
Number of generations	100	100	100	100	100

Table 6. Test output parameter list with obtained values for PR0003.

Name of Parameter	I	II	II	IV	V
Fitness	1.1	1.1	1.1	1.1	/
Execution time/computational complexity in sec	2	2	3	4	/
Valid solution obtained (Yes/No)	Yes	Yes	Yes	Yes	/
Solution with double edges	No	No	No	No	/
No. of double edges	/	/	/	/	/
No. of GA repetitions	1	1	1	1	/

Table 7. Test output parameter list with obtained values for PR0004.

Name of Parameter	I	II	II	IV	V
Fitness	10.3	10.3	10.3	10.3	10.3
Execution time/computational complexity in sec	60	54	90	94	100
Valid solution obtained (Yes/No)	Yes	Yes	Yes	Yes	Yes
Solution with double edges	No	No	No	No	No
No. of double edges	/	/	/	/	/
No. of GA repetitions	6	4	4	3	3

To evaluate the impact of different parameter settings, the GA was run with four (PR0003) and five (PR0004) parameter configurations. The results are tabulated in Tables 6 and 7, and visualized in Figures 11–20. The primary objective was to assess the GA's ability to converge to valid solutions for complex shapes like PR0004, while restricting the analysis to polyhedral shapes.

The second objective of the experimental testing of the proposed GA was to examine its convergence capability toward valid solutions for geometric solids with cylindrical surfaces. This presents a greater challenge, particularly for GAs [19]. Figure 21 illustrates an example of a 3D solid model of PR0007 with cylindrical surfaces, while Figure 22 shows the experimental results for I parameter group. The testing was conducted using the first four configurations of GA parameters, and the results are presented in Table 8. Figure 23 illustrates a more complex, typical industrial part with cylindrical surfaces part tested with the first three configurations of GA parameters, while Figure 24 shows the experimental results for I parameter group. The testing results are presented in Table 9.

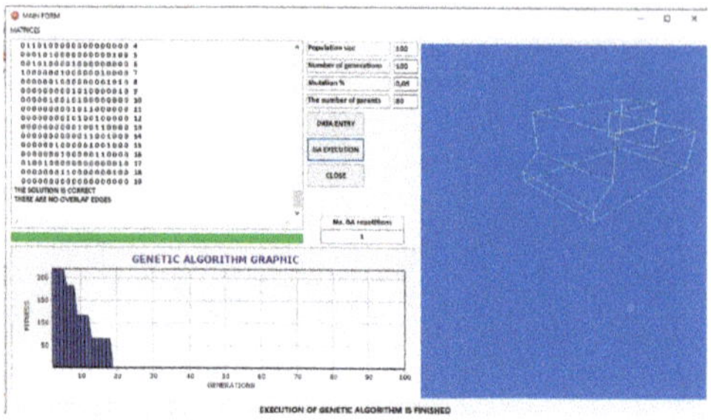

Figure 11. GA execution-PR0003 I group.

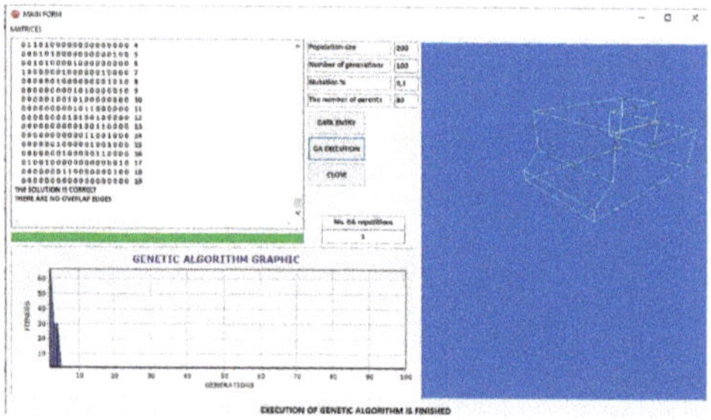

Figure 12. GA execution-PR0003 II group.

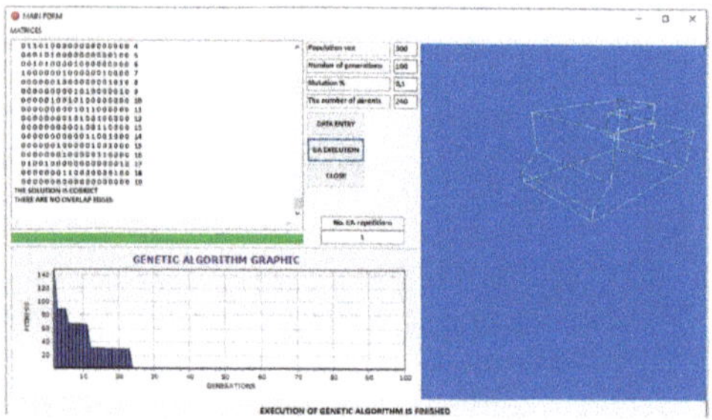

Figure 13. GA execution-PR0003 III group.

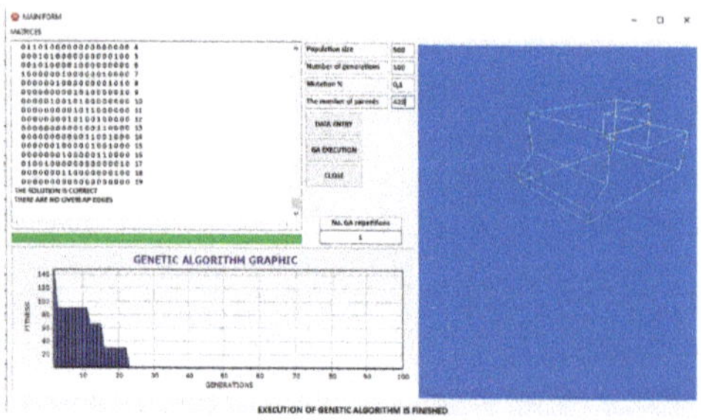

Figure 14. GA execution-PR0003 IV group.

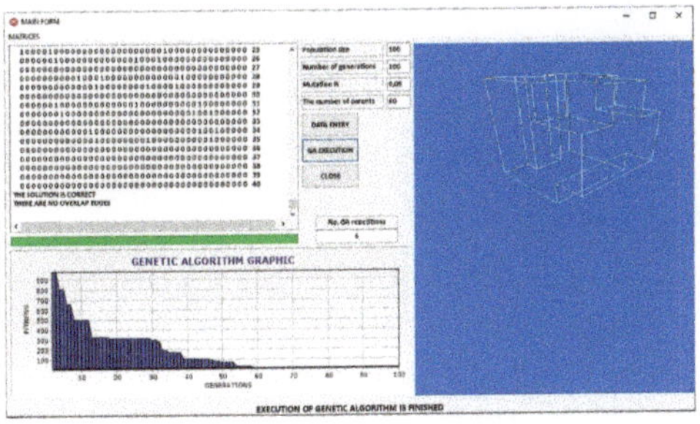

Figure 15. GA execution-PR0004 I group.

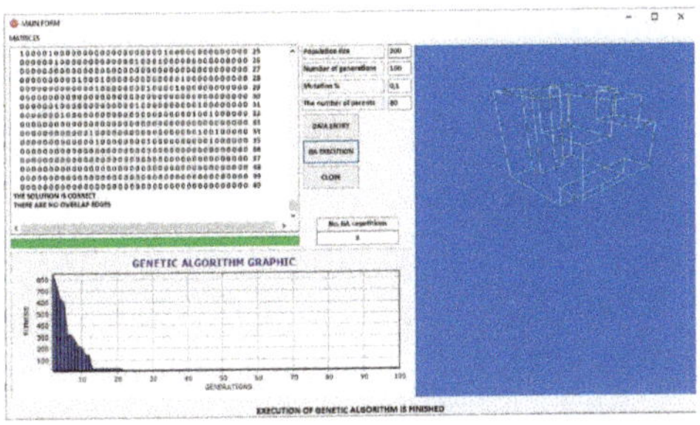

Figure 16. GA execution-PR0004 II group.

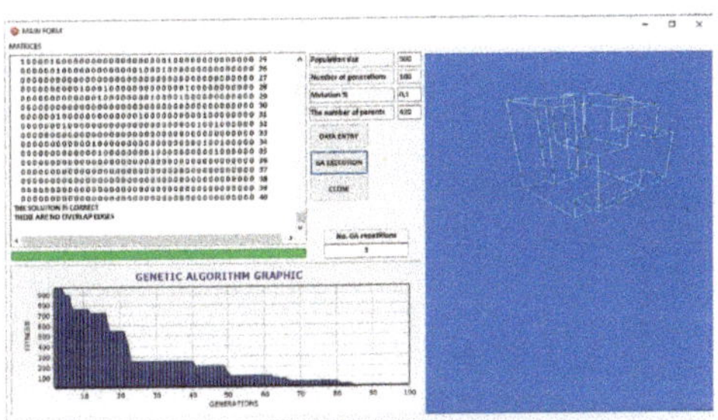

Figure 17. GA execution-PR0004 III group.

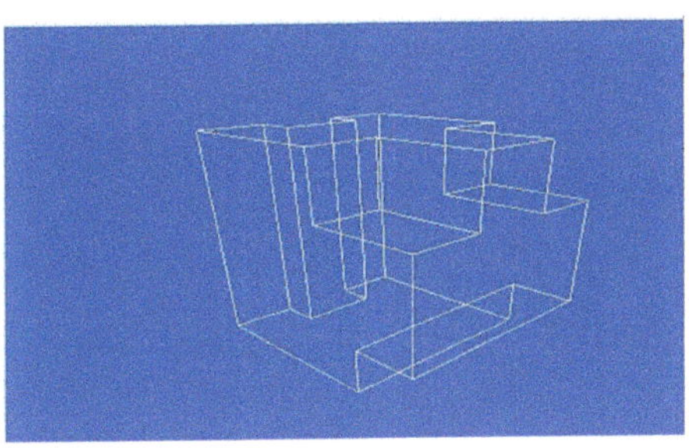

Figure 18. GA execution-PR0004 IV group.

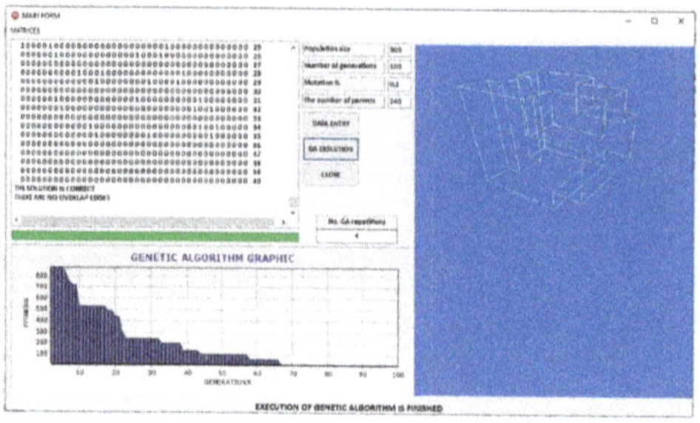

Figure 19. GA execution-PR0004 V group.

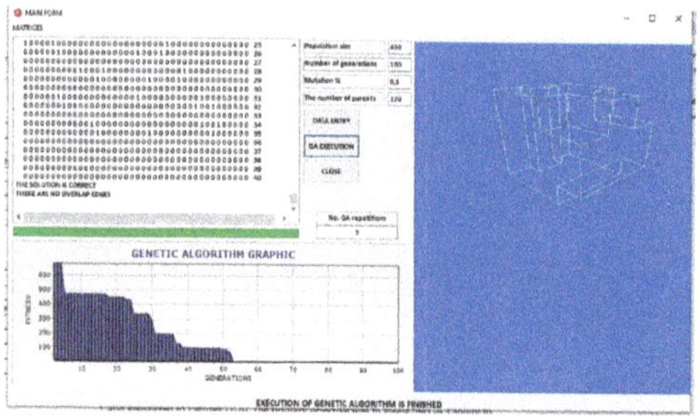

Figure 20. PR0004 after execution of GA.

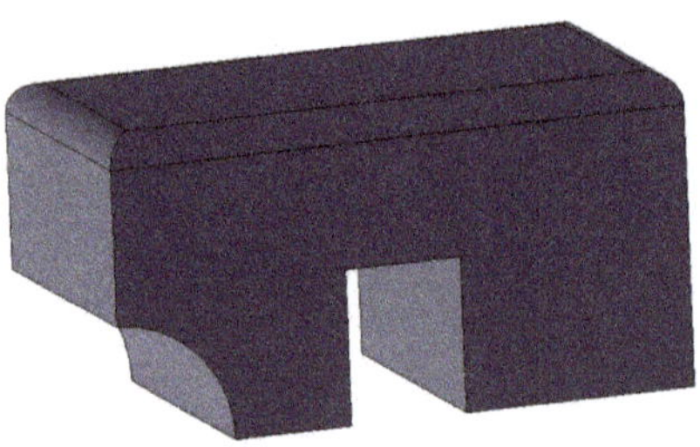

Figure 21. PR0007 3D solid model.

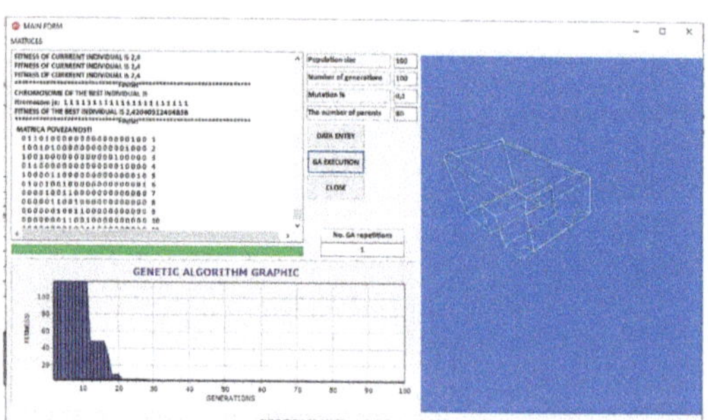

Figure 22. PR0007 results after execution of GA.

To examine the behavior of the proposed genetic algorithm (GA) under different evolutionary parameter settings, a series of experimental runs was performed on two test cases of increasing complexity—PR0003 and PR0004. Figures 11–20 provide a detailed visualization of the algorithm's execution across five parameter groups for each model, with particular focus on convergence characteristics, solution accuracy, and structural validity of the reconstructed wireframe models.

Table 8. Test output parameter list with obtained values for PR0007.

Name of Parameter	I	II	II	IV	V
Fitness	2.4	2.4	2.4	2.4	/
Execution time/computational complexity in sec	2	2	3	4	/
Valid solution obtained (Yes/No)	Yes	Yes	Yes	Yes	/
Solution with double edges	No	No	No	No	/
No. of double edges	/	/	/	/	/
No. of GA repetitions	1	1	1	1	/

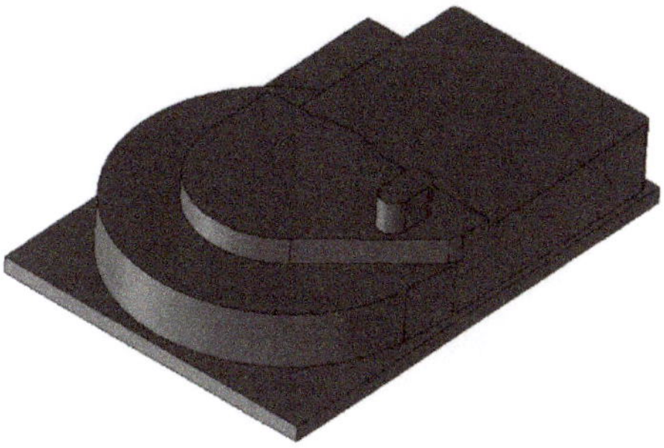

Figure 23. PR0005 3D solid model.

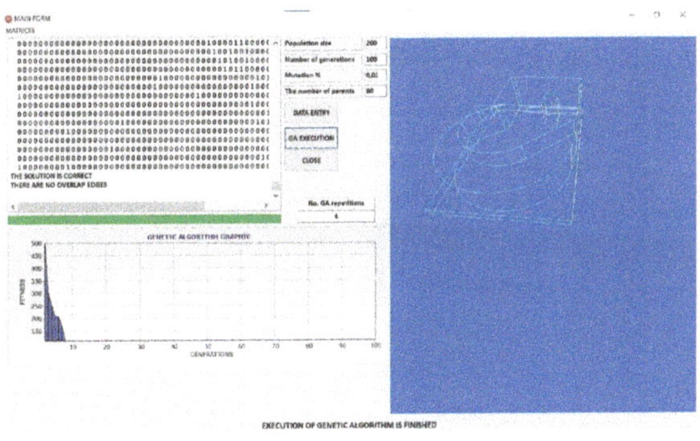

Figure 24. PR0005 results after execution of GA.

Table 9. Test output parameter list with obtained values for PR0005.

Name of Parameter	I	II	II	IV	V
Fitness	112.20	112.20	112.20	/	/
Execution time/computational complexity in sec	60	86	94	/	/
Valid solution obtained (Yes/No)	Yes	Yes	Yes	/	/
Solution with double edges	No	No	No	/	/
No. of double edges	/	/	/	/	/
No. of GA repetitions	6	4	5	/	/

For the simpler polyhedral model PR0003, Figures 11 and 12 depict the GA performance under parameter Groups I and II, respectively. In Figure 11, a steady convergence trend is observed, with gradual fitness improvements stabilizing after approximately 50 generations. The resulting wireframe model adheres to the expected topological structure, demonstrating that even conservative parameter settings can yield valid results. In contrast, Figure 12 reveals a steeper initial drop in fitness values under Group II, indicating faster convergence. Despite the more aggressive parameter configuration, the final model remains both geometrically and topologically consistent, confirming the robustness of the GA framework in lower-complexity scenarios.

Further testing with Groups III and IV for PR0003, shown in Figures 13 and 14, reveals subtle yet meaningful differences in convergence dynamics. Figure 13 demonstrates that Group III supports rapid early-stage exploration followed by stable convergence, producing a structurally correct wireframe representation. Figure 14, using Group IV, leads to slightly faster convergence, suggesting that fine-tuned parameter values can improve efficiency without compromising solution quality. These results emphasize the importance of parameter calibration, even when dealing with relatively simple geometric forms.

The evaluation is extended to the more complex polyhedral model PR0004, where the algorithm's scalability is tested against increased topological density and geometric intricacy. In Figure 15, which corresponds to Group I, the convergence curve progresses more gradually, with fitness values improving steadily over time. The adjacency matrix and final model visualization confirm the algorithm's ability to resolve denser connectivity patterns. Figure 16, representing Group II, shows a more aggressive convergence profile, with earlier stabilization of fitness values and successful reconstruction of the intended 3D geometry, underscoring the algorithm's adaptability to different optimization pressures.

Figures 17 and 18 offer insight into the GA's behavior under Groups III and IV for the PR0004 case. Figure 17 illustrates a longer convergence trajectory, with fitness improvements extending across 80 generations, a reflection of the search space complexity. Nonetheless, the final model is both topologically complete and geometrically accurate. Figure 18 isolates the final reconstruction obtained with Group IV and clearly displays the fidelity of the solution, even without the accompanying convergence plot. The preservation of structural proportions across all model layers attests to the reliability of the topological encoding and optimization procedure.

Finally, the outcomes associated with Group V and the fully reconstructed model are presented in Figures 19 and 20. As shown in Figure 19, the algorithm exhibits continued fitness refinement across an extended number of generations, suggesting a broader exploration phase. Despite the higher number of iterations, the resulting solution remains robust, validating the algorithm's effectiveness even under more exhaustive parameter regimes. Figure 20 displays the final reconstructed geometry in isolation, emphasizing the GA's capacity to capture the full complexity of the PR0004 model and maintain structural integrity throughout the optimization process.

Collectively, these figures provide strong empirical evidence of the proposed method's generalizability and resilience across a wide range of parameter settings and model complexities. The consistent convergence behavior and reliable reconstruction outcomes reinforce the applicability of the GA framework to real-world CAD and reverse engineering tasks involving polyhedral geometry.

In the subsequent phase of the experimental evaluation, the focus shifts toward more complex models that incorporate curved surfaces and a combination of cylindrical and rectangular geometries. The objective of this testing stage was to assess the genetic algorithm's (GA) ability to reconstruct 3D wireframe models for shapes that deviate significantly from purely polyhedral forms. These cases increase the reconstruction challenge and provide insight into the algorithm's suitability for real-world industrial applications.

Figure 21 presents the 3D solid model of the PR0007 test case, which features a blend of straight edges, rounded transitions, and a characteristic cutout at the base. This geometry introduces a reconstruction challenge due to the need to preserve topological consistency in the presence of local curvature and interrupted surfaces.

The execution of the GA for PR0007 is shown in Figure 22, where the convergence curve demonstrates rapid early-stage fitness improvement, followed by stabilization. The reconstructed wireframe model faithfully reproduces the primary geometric and topological features of the target object, confirming that the proposed algorithm can handle curved features without relying on additional heuristics.

Moving forward, Figure 23 depicts a more demanding 3D solid model, designated PR0005, which includes complex curved contours, multi-layered structures, and non-rotational symmetries. This model was specifically chosen for its resemblance to real-world components commonly found in mechatronic and precision mechanical assemblies.

The results of applying the GA to PR0005 are illustrated in Figure 24, where the algorithm successfully identifies key edge connections and generates a valid topological mesh. Despite the model's intricate morphology, the reconstruction maintains geometric consistency, and the convergence curve indicates that the solution is reached within a reasonable number of generations. This confirms the method's applicability to technically challenging components within engineering environments.

Overall, the visual and quantitative results presented in Figures 11–24 confirm the effectiveness and versatility of the proposed GA-based reconstruction framework across a wide spectrum of geometric complexities. The method consistently produced topologically valid and geometrically accurate wireframe models, demonstrating strong potential for integration into automated CAD pipelines and reverse engineering workflows in both academic and industrial contexts.

5. Discussion

The experimental results demonstrate that the GA is highly effective in solving problems involving simple geometries such as PR0003 and also PR0007 with cylindrical surfaces. Even under the most constrained parameter settings, the algorithm consistently converged to the correct solution within a few iterations. For instance, for the PR0003 model, the GA found the exact solution in just two seconds. The same applies to PR0007, which is a part with relatively simple cylindrical surface geometry.

During the testing of other models, it was noticed that this GA is very effective for the models with a number of vertices between 15 and 25 and with a number of edges between 20 and 35. In these intervals, the GA converges to the accurate solution in a single run. During testing mutation was always at 10% rate. Since the results for PR0003 did not change, testing with parameter group V was deemed unnecessary. For more complex parts, such as PR0004, it is clear that an accurate solution is always obtained, but across several runs, which leads to an increased runtime.

The execution time of the GA for complex parts is longer, which also depends on the amount of computation, but this is not a problem regarding the characteristics of modern computers. For example, for PR0004, the ADj matrix is 40×40, and intensive calculations are performed on it at all times. In this case, as well as in other more complex parts that were tested, for the number of l vertices greater than 25, solutions are always obtained where the geometric consistency is not violated and the solution does not go beyond the set of solutions represented by the pseudo-wireframe model. Also, no new surfaces are created, and there is no edge overlapping, meaning that individual candidate vertices remain in the solution because all constraints are satisfied and they do not create new shapes in the model.

For typical industrial parts with cylindrical shape, such as the component shown in Figure 23, the execution time is observed to be longer. However, the correct solution is obtained after several GA iterations. This demonstrates that the proposed method effectively handles both simpler and more complex models with cylindrical surfaces.

It should be noted that even the variation of mutation did not lead to convergence to the exact solution, which is also the nature of GA, while for simpler models it converges very quickly to the exact solution because the search space is smaller.

Considering the test results presented in Tables 5–7, and the relationship between the complexity of the part being reconstructed and the GA's execution time, where this time encompasses all GA executions until a valid solution is obtained, it is clear that the proposed GA is most efficient with the second group of parameters for simple and moderately complex geometry parts. During intensive testing of the proposed algorithm, it was also shown that for highly complex geometry parts, the best parameters are from groups IV and V. In all tests conducted to date, the geometry of the part has been consistently and accurately recognized, even for complex components; however, the number of GA executions reached up to eight times, with execution times extending up to 180 s. Given that an accurate solution was consistently obtained, this represents an exceptionally favorable final testing outcome.

In contrast to previous GA-based approaches—which typically rely on raster preprocessing or predefined libraries of geometric primitives—the proposed method employs a mathematically rigorous topological framework that supports the reconstruction of a broader range of 3D models, including those containing curved and free-form elements. By leveraging a connectivity-based representation rather than heuristic feature extraction, the approach enhances model generality and eliminates dependence on prior shape classification. As summarized in Table 10, this results in improved scalability, increased robustness across diverse input data, and a significant reduction in preprocessing complexity.

Table 10. Comparison with GA-based 3D reconstruction methods.

Study	Input Type	Shape Support	Method Basis	Optimization Target	Geometry Type Independence	DXF (Vector) Support	Topological Model
Chen & Feng [15]	Raster image	Prismatic + curved	Contour extraction	Projection consistency	✓ Yes	No	Full
Gorgani & Pak [6]	2D drawings	Only prismatic shapes	B-Rep reconstruction	Face alignment	No	No	Partial
Siddique & Zakaria [17]	Raster image	Simple shapes	Shape features	Edge position, face equalization	No	No	No
This paper	DXF (vector)	Prismatic + Curved	Symmetric matrices	Vertex to Vertex–edge topology	Yes	Yes	Full

Although some of the limitations of the proposed methodology were briefly outlined in Section 3.1, they are revisited and elaborated here to ensure clarity and completeness. This dedicated discussion aims to contextualize the current scope of the model and highlight avenues for future enhancement.

First, the method assumes that the input 2D engineering drawing is complete and composed of exactly three orthographic projections—front, top, and left—conforming to the ISO-E (European) projection standard, as illustrated in Figure 2. These views are expected to encapsulate all essential geometric information, including both visible and hidden edges. At the present stage, the framework does not support sectional views, auxiliary projections, or drawings that are incomplete.

Second, the approach presumes that all orthographic views are rendered at a consistent 1:1 scale, thereby enabling the direct use of vertex coordinates for 3D reconstruction. A global scaling factor may be optionally applied, but the model does not yet incorporate dimensioning metadata or tolerancing information embedded in annotations.

Third, although DXF files are advantageous for extracting basic geometric entities such as lines and arcs, they lack topological information—i.e., they do not provide an explicit mapping of entity connectivity or view separation. Therefore, a custom segmentation procedure is required to distinguish between projections and reconstruct their internal structure.

Additionally, the method relies on the recognition of basic geometric primitives (e.g., LINE, ARC) to infer edge shapes. In its current form, the model does not support complex freeform surfaces or non-cylindrical geometries. Interpretation of such features would require integrating advanced geometric representations and curvature analysis tools and mathematical tools for curvature and surface analysis.

It is important to emphasize that these constraints do not compromise the core of the methodology, which is fundamentally based on a binary vertex-to-vertex topological model. The approach remains general and extensible, and these limitations may be addressed through future enhancements, such as the incorporation of geometric reasoning modules or hybrid shape descriptors. Therefore, the challenges identified here also represent promising directions for future research and model refinement.

6. Conclusions

In this paper, a method for encoding 2D engineering drawings using symmetric connectivity matrices is presented. These matrices significantly facilitate the formation of a mathematical model and enable the problem of recognizing 3D models from 2D engineering drawings to be reduced to an integer linear programming problem. A GA has been developed, successfully recognizing 3D models of both polyhedral shapes and models with cylindrical surfaces. For testing purposes, a fully independent software platform was created, covering the entire process from generating symmetric adjacency matrices from orthogonal projections to part recognition. This platform includes real-time graphical visualization of the recognition process and allows testing of parts with various geometric shapes without additional adjustments.

The advantage of the proposed model lies in its simplicity, as the problem of recognizing a 3D wireframe model is reduced to the problem of linear integer programming. The model does not necessarily require a DXF format as a starting point, as it is designed to accept, with minor modifications, any other vector format used for engineering drawings. So far, it has only been tested on polyhedral shapes, and on simpler cylindrical ones, although theoretically, it should also work with all shapes since it is based on edges, including curved edges that are not straight lines.

To the best of our knowledge, no previous work in the available literature has introduced a 3D reconstruction model that combines symmetric connectivity matrices with GA. Furthermore, studies [16–19] that utilize GA for geometry recognition generally achieve lower success rates in 3D reconstruction and are predominantly limited to polyhedral shapes.

However, one of its shortcomings is that it does not recognize surfaces but only the wireframe model, and has not yet been tested on parts with highly complex geometry, which, in addition to polyhedral shapes and cylindrical surfaces, also include other types of surfaces.

Future research directions involve improving the GA process, potentially selecting other crossover and mutation operators, redefining weight coefficients and methods for penalizing poor individuals, and possibly hybridizing GA with other optimization algorithms to achieve even better results with polyhedral shapes and cylindrical surfaces. Additionally, intensive testing and possible modifications are required to recognize other non-cylindrical surfaces.

This solution, as conceived, can serve as a foundation for the complete automation of the 3D model recognition process from engineering drawings, or as an initial phase toward the full integration of CAD/CAM activities.

In future work, we aim to expand the proposed methodology beyond wireframe reconstruction, with the goal of achieving fully automated generation of solid models directly from standard technical documentation. This advancement would facilitate the practical integration of the method into industrial CAD environments, thereby enhancing its applicability in real-world engineering workflows.

Moreover, the utilization of symmetric adjacency matrices establishes a geometry-independent framework that enables the method to process both linear and nonlinear edges with equal robustness. By prioritizing topological relationships over explicit surface definitions, the approach circumvents limitations commonly associated with specific part geometries. This abstraction not only improves the generalizability of the system but also creates opportunities for further extension into complex design domains, including freeform surfaces and non-standard projection views. Such developments would significantly broaden the scope of the method and reinforce its relevance in advanced CAD and reverse engineering applications.

Author Contributions: Conceptualization, P.M. and V.K.; methodology, A.Đ.; software, P.M. and M.S.; validation, M.M., M.P. and D.P.; formal analysis, P.M.; investigation, V.K.; resources, M.M. and M.P.; data curation, D.P.; writing—original draft preparation, P.M. and M.S.; writing—review and editing, A.Đ.; visualization, M.P.; supervision, M.S.; project administration, D.P.; funding acquisition, M.M. All authors have read and agreed to the published version of the manuscript.

Funding: This research received no external funding.

Data Availability Statement: The data are available upon reasonable request from the authors.

Conflicts of Interest: The authors declare no conflicts of interest.

References

1. Furferi, R.; Governi, L.; Palai, M.; Volpe, Y. From 2D Orthographic views to 3D Pseudo-Wireframe: An Automatic Procedure. *Int. J. Comput. Appl.* **2010**, *5*, 18–24. [CrossRef]
2. Zhang, C.; Pinquié, R.; Polette, A.; Carasi, G.; De Charnace, H.; Pernot, J.P. Automatic 3D CAD models reconstruction from 2D orthographic drawings. *Comput. Graph.* **2023**, *114*, 179–189, ISSN 0097-8493. [CrossRef]
3. Idesawa, M. A system to generate a solid figure from three view. *Bull. JSME* **1973**, *16*, 216–225. [CrossRef]
4. Wesley, M.A.; Markowsky, G. Fleshing out projections. *IBM J. Res. Dev.* **1981**, *25*, 934–954. [CrossRef]
5. Yan, Q.; Chen, C.L.P.; Tang, Z. Efficient algorithm for the reconstruction of 3D objects from orthographic projections. *Comput. Aided Des./Comput.-Aided Des.* **1994**, *26*, 699–717. [CrossRef]
6. Gorgani, H.H.; Pak, A.J.; Sadeghi, S. 3D Model Reconstruction from Two Orthographic Views using Fuzzy Surface Analysis. *Eur. J. Sustain. Dev. Res.* **2019**, *3*, em0081. [CrossRef]
7. Zhang, A.; Xue, Y.; Sun, X.; Hu, Y.; Luo, Y.; Yan-Guang, W.; Zhong, S.; Wang, J.; Tang, J.; Cai, G. Reconstruction of 3D Curvilinear Wireframe Model from 2D Orthographic Views. In *Computational Science—ICCS 2004*; Lecture Notes in Computer Science; Springer: Berlin/Heidelberg, Germany, 2004; pp. 404–411. [CrossRef]
8. Gong, J.; Zhang, G.; Zhang, H.; Sun, J. Reconstruction of 3D curvilinear wire-frame from three orthographic views. *Comput. Graph.* **2006**, *30*, 213–224. [CrossRef]
9. Lu, Z.; Guo, J.; Xiao, J.; Wang, Y.; Zhang, X.; Yan, D. Extracting Cycle-aware Feature Curve Networks from 3D Models. *Comput. Aided Des./Comput.-Aided Des.* **2021**, *131*, 102949. [CrossRef]
10. Gong, J.; Zhang, H.; Zhang, G.; Sun, J. Solid reconstruction using recognition of quadric surfaces from orthographic views. *Comput. Aided Des./Comput.-Aided Des.* **2006**, *38*, 821–835. [CrossRef]

11. Gong, J.; Zhang, H.; Zhang, Y.; Sun, J. Converting hybrid wire-frames to B-rep models. In Proceedings of the 2007 ACM Symposium on Solid and Physical Modeling, Beijing, China, 4–6 June 2007. [CrossRef]
12. Varley, P. A new algorithm for finding faces in wireframes. *Comput. Aided Des./Comput.-Aided Des.* **2010**, *42*, 279–309. [CrossRef]
13. Çıçek, A.; Gülesın, M. Reconstruction of 3D models from 2D orthographic views using solid extrusion and revolution. *J. Mater. Process. Technol.* **2004**, *152*, 291–298. [CrossRef]
14. Cohen, M. 3D Reconstruction of Solid Models from Engineering Orthographic Views using Variational Geometry and Composite Graphs. *Comput.-Aided Des. Appl.* **2007**, *4*, 159–167. [CrossRef]
15. Chen, K.; Feng, X. Solid model reconstruction from engineering paper drawings using Genetic Algorithms. *Comput. Aided Des./Comput.-Aided Des.* **2003**, *35*, 1235–1248. [CrossRef]
16. Bebis, G.; Louis, S.J.; Varol, Y.; Yfantis, A. Genetic object recognition using combinations of views. *IEEE Trans. Evol. Comput.* **2002**, *6*, 132–146. [CrossRef]
17. Siddique, M.T.; Zakaria, M. 3D Reconstruction of geometry from 2D image using Genetic Algorithm. In *Proceeding of the 2010 International Symposium on Information Technology, Kuala Lumpur, Malaysia, 15–17 June 2010*; IEEE: New York, NY, USA, 2010; pp. 1–5. [CrossRef]
18. Gorgani, H.H.; Pak, A.J. A Genetic Algorithm based Optimization Method in 3D Solid Reconstruction from 2D Multi-View Engineering Drawings. *Appl. Comput. Mech.* **2018**, *49*, 161–170. [CrossRef]
19. *Autocad Online Help 2018*; Autodesk Inc.: San Francisco, CA, USA, 2018.
20. *Autocad 2018, DXF Reference*; Autodesk Inc.: San Francisco, CA, USA, 2018.
21. Singiresu, S.R. *Engineering Optimisation-Theory and Practice*, 4th ed.; John Wiley & Sons, Inc.: Hoboken, NJ, USA, 2009.
22. Umbarkar, A.J.; Sheth, P.D. Crossover operators in genetic algorithms: A review. *ICTACT J. Soft Comput.* **2015**, *6*, 1083–1092.
23. Ngyen, H.D.; Yoshikara, I.; Yamamori, K.; Yasunaga, M. Greedy genetic algorithms for symmetric and assymetric TSP. *IPSJ Trans. Math. Model. Its Appl.* **2002**, *43*, 165–175.
24. Wei, J.-D. *Approaches to the Travelling Salesman Problem Using Evolutionary Computing Algorithms*; InTech: Houston, TX, USA, 2006. [CrossRef]
25. Mitic, P.; Nedic, B. Multi-Hole Drilling Tool Path Optimization Using Genetic Algorithm. *Int. J. Qual. Res.* **2022**, *16*, 417–428. [CrossRef]

symmetry

MDPI

Article

Measuring Device for More Precise Mistuning Identification of Integrated Bladed Discs

Ondřej Kučera [1], Václav Píštěk [1,*], Oleksij Fomin [2], Pavel Kučera [1] and Sergii Sagin [3]

1 Institute of Automotive Engineering, Brno University of Technology, Technická 2896/2, 616-69 Brno, Czech Republic; 192222@vutbr.cz (O.K.); kucera@fme.vutbr.cz (P.K.)
2 Department of Cars and Carriage Facilities, State University of Infrastructure and Technologies, Kyrylivska Street, 9, 04071 Kyiv, Ukraine; fomin_ov@gsuite.duit.edu.ua
3 Department of Ship's Power Plant, National University "Odessa Maritime Academy", 8, Didrikhson Street, 65052 Odessa, Ukraine; saginsergii@gmail.com
* Correspondence: pistek.v@fme.vutbr.cz; Tel.: +420-541-142-271

Abstract: In integrated turbine wheel designs, small deviations, known as mistuning, often occur in the modal properties of individual blades due to manufacturing tolerances and material inhomogeneity. During operation, this mistuning can cause some rotor blades to be subjected to significantly higher loads than predicted for an ideal rotor. The degree of rotor mistuning can only be determined using methods of experimental modal analysis. However, the manual use of the modal hammer cannot ensure precise repeatability of the force impulse's location and timing, leading to inaccuracies. This article introduces a mechanism that replaces manual modal hammer operations, guaranteeing consistent impact location and timing while eliminating double strikes. The device was verified on bladed discs of various sizes, and its usability is demonstrated in this article on a turbine wheel of a marine engine turbocharger. The developed mechanism automates modal hammer strikes, ensuring precisely repeatable force courses and positioning for each impact. This automation reduces the measurement time and significantly improves the accuracy. The results of this research showed that even with careful manual operation of the modal hammer by an experienced operator, statistically significant differences arise in the repeated measurements of a bladed disc mistuning, whereas with the use of the presented measuring device, the results of the repeated measurements are practically identical.

Keywords: bladed disc; mistuning; measuring device; turbocharger; marine engine

1. Introduction

The issue of structural vibrations poses a significant challenge in the design of new devices across a wide range of engineering products. This challenge spans various applications, including combustion engine components, turbines, vehicle parts, and even large-scale structures, such as buildings and bridges, where structural integrity is paramount and precise knowledge of dynamic characteristics is essential. Addressing dynamic stress in these applications is, therefore, crucial [1]. This article primarily focuses on machines and their components, where understanding dynamic behaviour is vital to prevent failure or damage during operation. Excessive machine vibrations are closely linked to performance and may cause malfunctions due to the risk of increased mechanical stress. For instance, in the case of a turbine wheel from a marine engine turbocharger, higher mechanical stress can accelerate wear or lead to cracks, culminating in the breakage of blade tips or entire blades. Another notable effect of machine vibrations is increased noise during operation [2],

https://doi.org/10.3390/sym17050717

which creates an uncomfortable working environment and reduces operator satisfaction. Reducing machine vibrations remains a pressing issue in the field, drawing the attention of numerous researchers and experts [3–12].

Vibration measurements can be categorised into two approaches based on their objectives. The first approach involves measuring vibration responses during the operation of a machine in its natural working environment and is referred to as the field of vibrodiagnostics [13]. The second approach, which holds greater relevance to the topic discussed here [14], involves inducing oscillations in the component or machine through known excitation and measuring the response, as illustrated in Figure 1. This method is often carried out in more controlled laboratory conditions outside of the machine's working environment, enabling more precise response measurements. Structural excitation can be implemented in various ways, with the simplest being impact excitation using a modal impact hammer. Alternatively, shakers—connecting devices designed for this purpose—can be employed. For modal testing of small- to medium-sized structures, excitation with a modal impact hammer is typically sufficient. The procedure involves identifying specific points or a network of points on the structure, depending on the component's scope, where hammer strikes are executed. The response at these points is recorded by a sensor fixed at a designated reference point, which remains stationary during excitation. Dynamic responses can be detected using accelerometers or optical instruments, such as laser vibrometers. The measured values at individual points form the matrix elements of the frequency response function $H(\Omega)$ [1], as defined in Equation (1) below.

$$H(\Omega) = \frac{output}{input} = \frac{motion}{force} = \frac{response}{excitation} \tag{1}$$

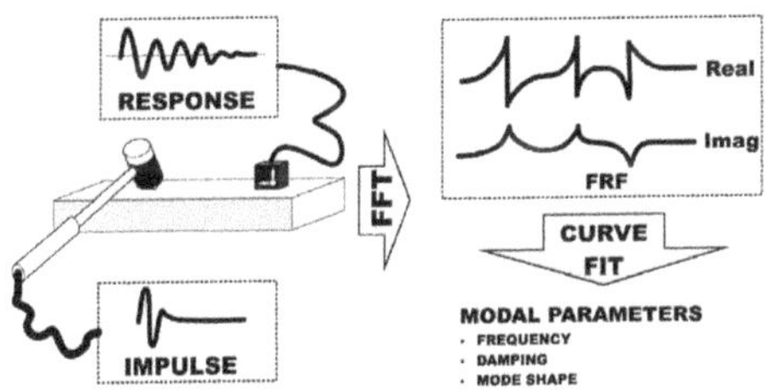

Figure 1. Principle of the experimental modal analysis.

The measured data are processed using the fast Fourier transformation (FFT), which converts it from the time domain to the frequency domain. Before this conversion, a weighting function is often applied to minimise the impact of slightly attenuated signals in the measured data. Following this, the converted data are interpolated with a curve, enabling the determination of the frequency response function and the extraction of desired modal parameters.

This method is referred to as modal testing [15]. An example of its application under real-world conditions is demonstrated in Figure 2, featuring a turbine wheel from a marine engine turbocharger.

Modal testing, also known as modal analysis, is a critical and robust tool in machinery design, providing insights into how a structure's design responds to various dynamic loads. It involves studying the dynamic properties of structures through structural testing or simulations based on a finite element analysis. These properties include resonance frequencies, also referred to as natural frequencies, and structural modes. The dynamic behaviour of a structure under operational loads is determined by its mass M, stiffness K, and damping distribution B. Understanding these properties enables designers to modify or optimise the structural designs to enhance their dynamic performance [16].

The vibration behaviour of any component, such as a turbocharger turbine wheel, is governed by the differential equation of motion.

$$M\ddot{q} + B\dot{q} + Kq = F(t). \tag{2}$$

Here, q represents the vector of generalised coordinates, F denotes the vector of forces, and t stands for time, with the continuous structure being discretised into a finite number of degrees of freedom [17].

Experimental modal tests on turbine wheels with integrated blades have been performed in the past using a manually controlled excitation of a modal hammer, as described in [17] and shown in Figure 2. During testing, the turbine wheel is positioned on a highly flexible pad to minimise the influence of boundary conditions.

Figure 2. Experimental modal analysis of a turbine wheel using hand-guided modal hammer excitation.

The modal hammer is used to excite individual rotor blades at an appropriate location, typically near the blade tip. The resulting blade vibrations are measured contactless using a laser Doppler vibrometer. However, in experiments involving manual guidance of the modal hammer, certain inaccuracies can occur due to the inherent variability of manual operations [18–22].

Some of these inaccuracies include the following:

- Variability of strike force. Manual control of the modal hammer can cause variability in the strike force between individual measurements. If the strike force is not constant, it can affect the results of the analysis, especially in terms of accurate measurements of amplitudes and frequencies of the structure's response.
- Incorrect strike angle. It is difficult to ensure that the strike is always performed at the required angle during manual operations. Changes in the angle can alter the excitation characteristics and lead to errors in the data, which may impact the accuracy of mode identification.
- Lack of repeatability. Manual control can lead to repeatability issues, meaning that each strike may not be exactly the same. Even small differences in position, angle, and strike force can cause changes in the dynamic responses of the measured structure.
- Introduction of unwanted influences. In addition to the strike force, manual operation may transfer vibrations from the hand or arm to the hammer. These transfers can

affect the results of the analysis, as unwanted interferences may be recorded in the data instead of a pure structural response.

- Limited positioning accuracy. The placement of the hammer at different points on the structure (depending on the manual handling) can influence the characteristics of the excitation. Different areas of the structure may have different dynamic properties, resulting in varying responses to the same strike.

When evaluating the results of the experimental modal analysis with the manual control of the modal hammer (see Figure 2), the authors have long observed that the results of repeated measurements of the same bladed discs show significant statistical dispersion in the degree of mistuning of individual blades. Therefore, the intention arose to control the modal hammer with a suitable mechanism instead of a human hand, which would ensure the repeatability of the location and timing of force impulses on all blades.

2. Materials and Methods

2.1. Inaccuracies in Manual Control of the Modal Hammer

The first type of inaccuracy mentioned above can be observed in Figure 3, which illustrates the force generated by the hammer's force sensor during individual blade strikes. At a glance, variations in the strength of each strike are clearly noticeable. Additionally, some strikes exhibit double impacts, visible even without zooming in on the time axis. Achieving consistent, high-quality hammer strikes suitable for a modal analysis demands significant practice in manually controlling the modal impact hammer.

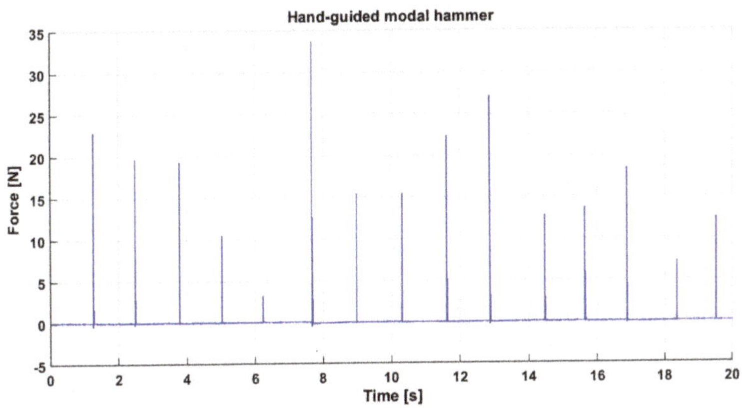

Figure 3. Signal measured by a force sensor at the tip of a modal hammer during multiple hand-guided strikes on a single turbine wheel blade.

While these factors—aside from double strikes—may theoretically have a minimal impact on the evaluation of transfer functions, practical experience reveals that they exert a non-negligible influence. This makes data evaluation cumbersome, increases testing time, and, above all, the aforementioned large statistical deviations arise when evaluating the degree of mistuning.

2.2. Measuring Device Replacing the Human Hand

To address these challenges, a concept was developed for a measuring device capable of conducting experimental modal tests on integrated bladed discs—specifically turbine wheels of various sizes and blade counts—while simultaneously mitigating these shortcomings. Ideally, such a device would be fully automatic and remotely controlled via a computer. However, before developing a more advanced fully automatic system, it was necessary to validate the functionality of a simpler, semi-automatic device. This device replaces the manual guidance of the modal hammer with a controlled mechanism, though it is still manually operated.

The core of the device consists of a hammer holder mounted on an axis supported by two radial ball bearings, which facilitate the primary measuring motion—the hammer strike. Additionally, the device allows for secondary movements, including displacements and rotations, essential for accurately aligning the hammer perpendicular to the analysed blade during measurements on turbine wheels of varying sizes.

To conduct the initial tests, the prototype shown in Figure 4 was assembled. This prototype enables the primary hammer movement as well as secondary adjustments, thanks to its aluminium adjustable console on which the device is mounted. The hammer is manually cocked, with its impact and subsequent return to the starting position ensured by a system of tension springs. The alignment and rotation of the hammer perpendicular to the blade's measured location were achieved by adjusting the console to the appropriate position.

Figure 4. First assembled prototype of the measuring device.

The principle behind the hammer's impact on the turbine blade involves setting its equilibrium position to maintain a gap of several millimetres between the hammer tip and the blade surface. This gap depends on the desired impact force, the stiffness, and the number of tension springs. When the hammer is extended to its designated stop, an over-oscillation occurs upon release, causing it to strike the blade as it moves beyond the equilibrium position. The system of tension springs ensures that the hammer gradually returns to its equilibrium without causing any further impacts.

To evaluate the device's functionality, particularly with regard to double strikes of the hammer, it is sufficient to analyse the force impulse recorded by the hammer's force sensor. A series of hammer strikes was conducted to confirm the device's operational accuracy. Data collection was performed at 20 s intervals with a sampling rate of 50 kHz, facilitated by the NI cDAQ-9179 measurement card. The data were recorded using the LabView software (version 2024) and subsequently exported to MatLab (version 2024) for processing and visualisation, with the results displayed in Figure 5.

At first glance, the results demonstrate that the measuring device fulfils the defined requirements. The location and force of individual strikes remain consistent across all instances, indicating that the device provides reliable hammer guidance. Consequently, all test measurements are suitable for experimental modal testing and, importantly, do not exhibit the previously mentioned errors, particularly double strikes. In Figure 6, there are examples of incorrect strikes when manually operating the modal hammer. This does not occur when using the measuring device; Figure 7 shows examples of hammer strikes, which are practically identical.

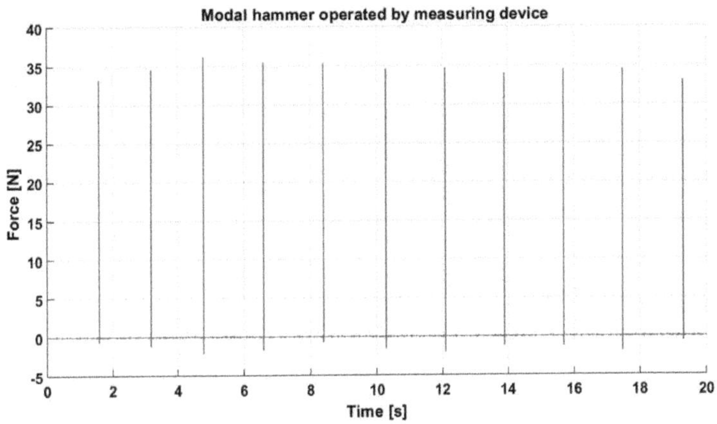

Figure 5. Force waveforms recorded during the operation of the modal hammer by the measuring device.

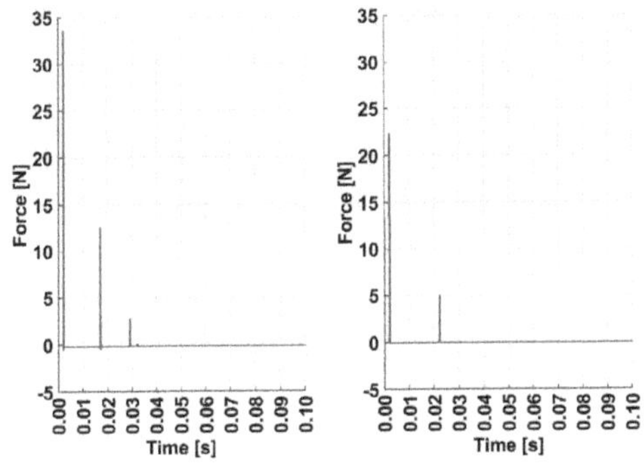

Figure 6. Incorrect triple and double strikes when manually operating the modal hammer.

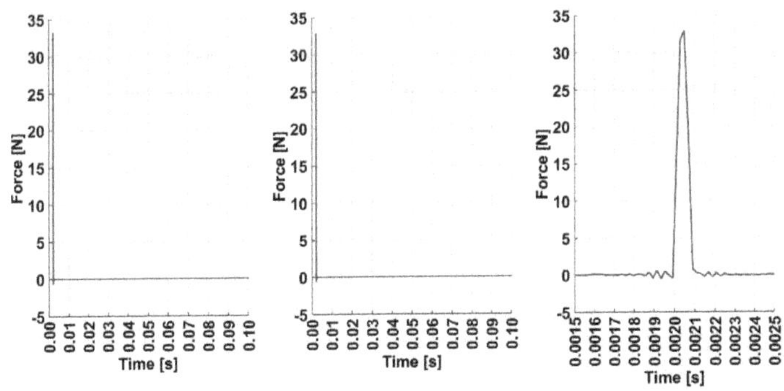

Figure 7. Examples of force impulses of the modal hammer when using the measuring device (the figure on the right is a zoom of the figure on the left).

As observed, each strike involves only a single hammer impact on the turbine blade. This confirms that the concept of designing a measuring device is validated through the successful practical testing of the prototype, paving the way for further development of the device.

The next stage of development focuses on automating the hammer's cocking mechanism and ensuring consistent striking force. To achieve this, a stepper motor was selected, as shown in Figure 8. The motor operates in one full revolution, during which it cocks and releases the hammer. This design allows the hammer sufficient time to stabilise in its equilibrium position after each strike before the motor returns to its starting position. Consequently, strikes can be performed consecutively, reducing the measurement time while eliminating the need to account for hammer settling, thereby preventing deviations in the measurements.

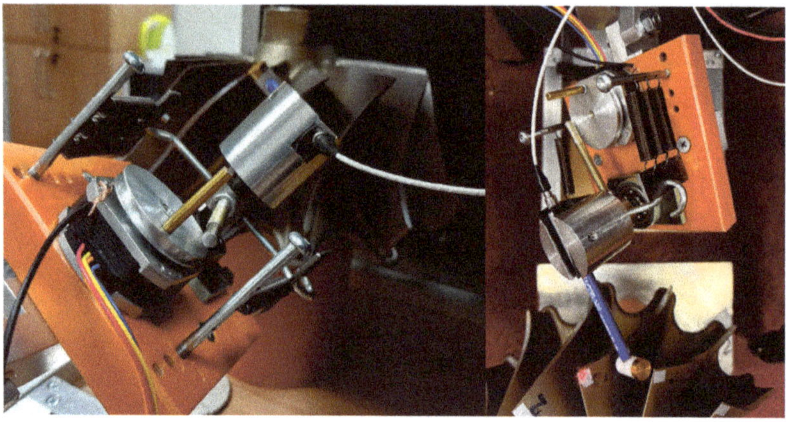

Figure 8. Details of the measuring device enhanced with a stepper motor for automated functionality.

3. Results

To verify the full functionality of the improved measuring mechanism, an experimental modal analysis was conducted on a real turbine wheel from a marine engine turbocharger. Utilising a single laser vibrometer in combination with a computational FE model offers several advantages over scanning vibrometers in turbine wheel analyses. A simple laser vibrometer is significantly more economical, reducing laboratory equipment costs. Additionally, the measurement process is less time-intensive, as scanning the entire turbine wheel surface is unnecessary—measuring a single point on each blade suffices when natural frequencies are accurately matched to mode shapes derived from the computational model. This method can also be automated with relative ease, enabling efficient processing and evaluation of the acquired data. As a result, the turbine manufacturer gains comprehensive statistical insights into blade parameters, addressing mistuning influenced by various factors in the production process.

3.1. Computational Model of Tuned Turbine Wheel

The computational finite element model of the tuned turbine wheel was developed using the ANSA software (version 2024). Leveraging the turbine wheel's cyclic symmetry, the analysis focused on a single sector without any loss of information, as all sectors were considered identical. This approach significantly reduced the model's degrees of freedom. Element size and type were carefully optimised through a series of sensitivity analyses to ensure both accuracy and computational efficiency. A fine, structured mesh was employed for the blade surface to capture detailed stress distributions and geometric features, while larger elements were utilised for the disc body and shaft, where stress gradients were less pronounced. This combination ensured optimal balance between precision and computational cost.

To validate the robustness of the results, mesh independence was demonstrated by performing analyses with multiple mesh resolutions. The results showed consistent outcomes, indicating that further refinement of the mesh would not significantly alter the conclusions of the analysis.

To generate the complete rotational model, the mesh of one sector underwent periodic expansion and merging of sector boundaries, as illustrated in Figure 9. For optimal correlation with the real turbine wheel mounted in plain bearings, no boundary conditions were applied during the computational modal analysis.

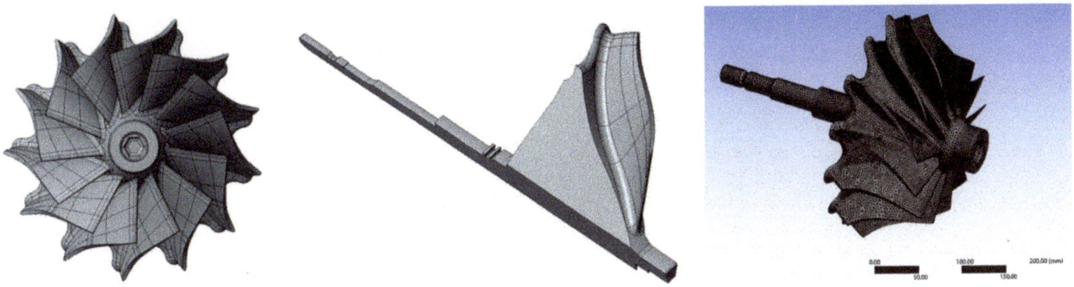

Figure 9. Finite element model of the turbine wheel.

The computed natural frequencies of the blade are presented in Table 1. These frequencies, covering the range up to 18,000 Hz, include the first seven modes. The calculated values offer an approximation of the blade-dominant mode shapes within the rotationally symmetric turbine wheel.

Table 1. Computed natural frequencies of the turbine wheel blade section.

Mode [-]	Frequency [Hz]
1	4075.7
2	7020.7
3	8556.3
4	10,664.0
5	11,831.0
6	14,548.0
7	16,108.0

3.2. Measurement and Processing of Measured Data

The measuring chain comprises a Dytran modal hammer (Dytran Instruments Inc., Chatsworth, CA, USA), which generates excitation impulses that are subsequently captured by a POLYTEC Sensor Head OFV-505 (Polytec GmbH, Waldbronn, Germany) laser vibrometer. The vibrometer is connected via an OFV-5000 vibrometer (Polytec GmbH, Waldbronn, Germany) controller to an NI cDAQ-9179 (National Instruments, Austin, TX, USA) measurement centre, equipped with NI-9229 and NI-9234 modules. The measurement centre is linked to the computer through a USB interface. Generally, the device can record data with a high sampling rate. In the case of this measurement, the sampling rate was set to 50,000 Hz. In terms of the accuracy of the individual modules, the values for calibration every year at temperatures of 23 °C ± 5 °C for NI-9232 are "Percent of Reading (Gain Error)" 0.1% and "Offset (Percent of Range)" 0.023%, and for NI-9229 are "Percent of Reading (Gain Error)" 0.03% and "Offset (Percent of Range)" 0.008%. The Doppler laser vibrometer head was configured as per the data sheet instructions, with the laser beam precisely aimed at the blade tip, where reflective tape was applied. The vibrometer lens was positioned perpendicular to the blade surface at the prescribed distance.

The experiment was carried out as a standard experimental modal analysis, with the only distinction being the placement of the modal hammer within the aforementioned measuring device. This setup allowed for the automation of hammer strikes, as illustrated in Figure 10.

Figure 10. Experimental modal analysis of the turbine wheel performed using the measuring device (The turbine wheel blades are numbered).

During the measurement process, the turbine rotor was positioned on a soft plastic tube with rubber ends. To ensure the response of the measured blade was not influenced by the oscillation of other blades, all blades were intentionally detuned by attaching weights of reasonable size [23]. These weights were glued to the tip of each blade using an adhesive with a consistency similar to beeswax.

Data collection was conducted using the LabView software (version 2024), with a specially compiled program for recording measurements. Once activated, the program facilitated the collection and storage of a 20 s measurement segment, during which multiple strikes with a modal hammer were made at the same blade location. The program was configured with a maximum sampling rate of 50 kHz, simultaneously recording the measured response from the laser vibrometer and the excitation pulse from the modal hammer sensor. This process was repeated for all turbine blades.

The data obtained were processed using the MATLAB software (version 2024). Initially, data from the LabView program were loaded and subsequently divided into individual quantities for plotting and further processing. A critical step before converting the data from the time domain to the frequency domain involved applying a weighting function in the time domain, specifically an exponential window (Figure 11).

As defined in the following equation:

$$y_i = e^{\frac{\ln f}{n-1}i},\ i = 1\ldots n, \tag{3}$$

the exponential window is characterised by the parameters f (the final value of the window), n (the sample count), and i (the function index).

In lightly damped blade systems, the structural response often extends beyond the data collection period, as illustrated in Figure 12 (TOP). Since the response does not diminish to near zero by the end of the time record, an exponential window is employed. This technique attenuates the signal towards the record's conclusion, reducing it to approximately 1%. The resulting signal, as depicted in Figure 12 (BOTTOM), offers a more accurate representation of a transient event.

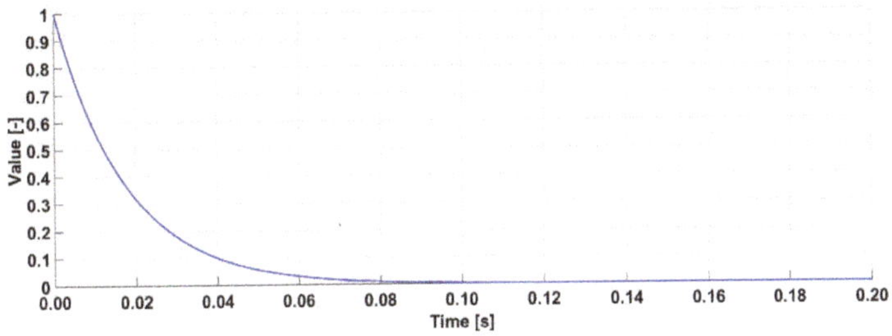

Figure 11. Weighting function of the exponential window type.

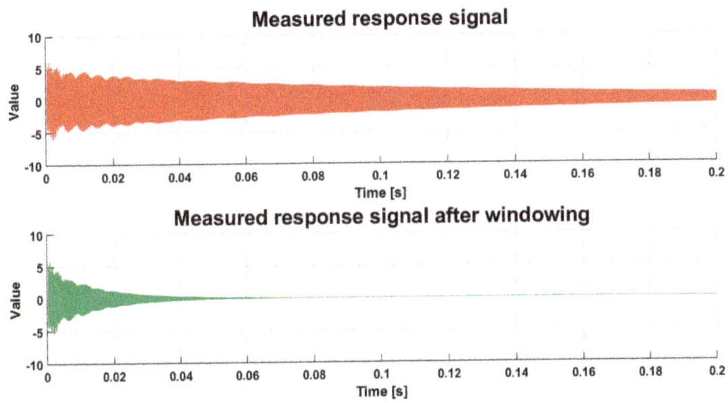

Figure 12. Measured response signal of a lightly damped turbine blade under impact excitations, (**TOP**) original and (**BOTTOM**) modified, using the exponential window.

The data were analysed using a fast Fourier transform (FFT) algorithm in its complex form to determine the system's transfer function. Specifically, an FFT analysis was applied to the impact force and its corresponding measured response. The transfer function was then derived by calculating the ratio of the system's output to its input:

$$Y_i = ABS\left(\frac{FFT_{out}}{FFT_{force}}\right),\ i = 1 \ldots n, \tag{4}$$

The resulting FFT analysis produced complex vectors, namely FFT_{out} from the response data and FFT_{force} from the force pulse data. These calculations were performed using complex arithmetic. Each turbocharger blade was measured five times to minimise potential errors. The data from these measurements were processed, resulting in five FFT spectra that were subsequently averaged. With a time window of 0.2 s, the FFT offered a frequency resolution of 5 Hz, ensuring an uncertainty of 2.5 Hz per spectral component, an accuracy entirely suitable for assessing turbine wheel mistuning.

For illustration, Figure 13 shows the transfer function of blade No. 1, where the mentioned appropriate weights were not placed on the other blades during the measurement. It is evident that, due to mistuning of the other blades, the natural frequency of the measured blade cannot be reliably evaluated. A significant difference occurs when suitable weights are applied to the unmeasured blades (Figure 14), making it possible to clearly associate individual peaks with the corresponding modal shapes of the blades.

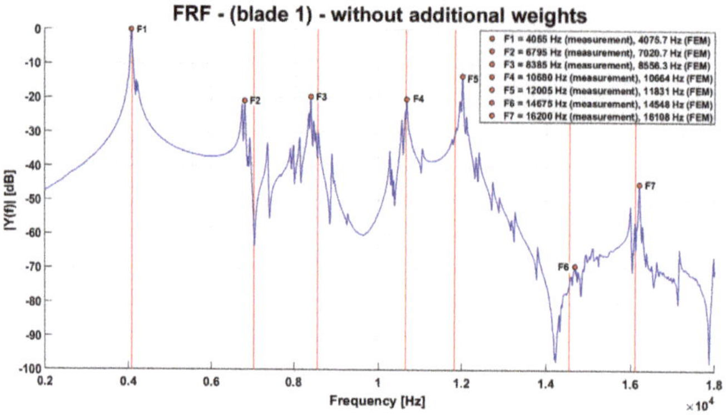

Figure 13. Natural frequencies from the FE model and the transfer function without additional weights.

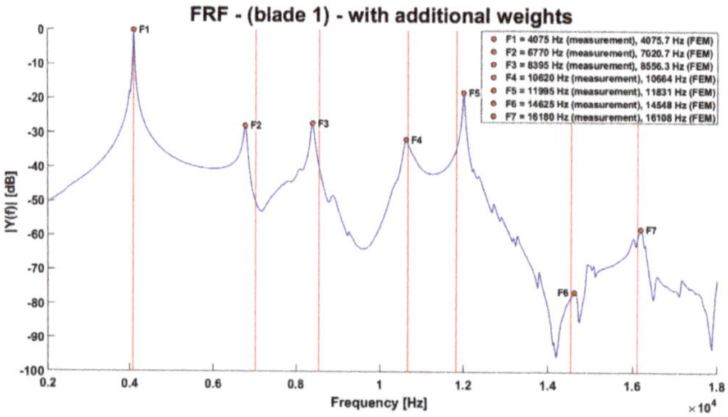

Figure 14. Natural frequencies from the FE model and the transfer function with additional weights.

The same process, i.e., a measurement with additional weights on the unmeasured blades, was repeated for all blades. The individual peaks in the transfer functions, as plotted in Figure 15, represent the natural frequencies of the respective blades.

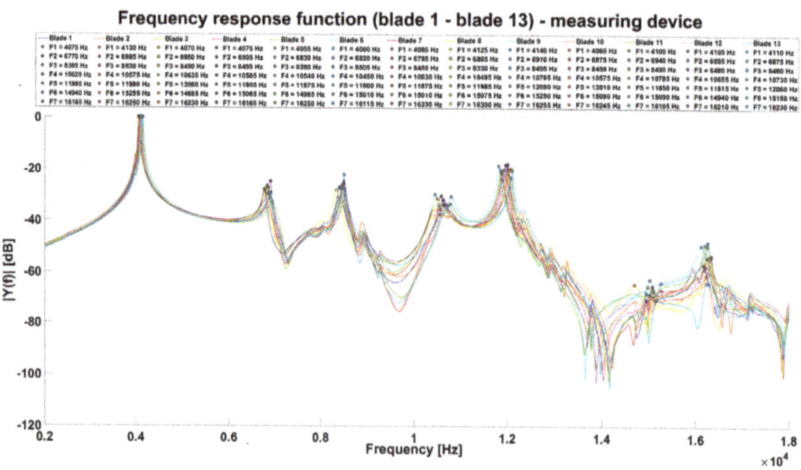

Figure 15. Comparison of measured transfer functions of individual turbine blades measured by the presented measuring device.

Similarly, the results of the modal analysis of the same turbine wheel were evaluated using manual control of the modal hammer, as shown in Figure 16.

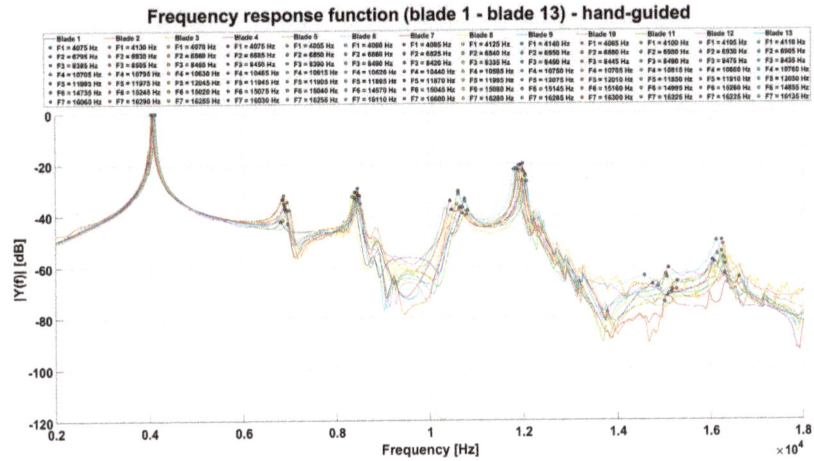

Figure 16. Comparison of measured transfer functions of individual turbine blades measured by a hand-guided modal hammer.

4. Discussion

Slight deviations in the transfer functions of individual blades can be observed. These discrepancies stem from minor variations in material and geometric properties, which arise due to manufacturing tolerances and material inhomogeneity. In real turbine wheels with an integrated design, such differences lead to small deviations in the modal properties of individual blades from their nominal values, commonly referred to as mistuning.

As a result, certain blades may experience significantly higher stress levels during operation than those calculated for an ideal rotor. Determining the extent of turbine wheel mistuning is only possible through an experimental modal analysis. This challenge inspired the improvement and acceleration of modal testing for rotors with an integrated design by developing and manufacturing a measuring device to guide a modal hammer, replacing manual hammer strikes.

The results of the turbine wheel experimental modal analysis show that the designed measuring device meets the set requirements for the accuracy and repeatability of the modal hammer strikes. The mistuning of adjacent blades is represented by the relative deviations in eigenfrequencies among all of the blades.

$$\Delta f_i = \frac{f_i - f_0}{f_0},\ f_0 = \frac{1}{N}\sum_{j=1}^{N} f_j \tag{5}$$

The blade mistuning results for the measured turbine wheel, obtained using the measuring device, are depicted in Figure 17, while those derived from a manual operation with a modal hammer are shown in Figure 18.

From the comparison of these two figures, noticeable differences are evident, with the only variation in the conducted measurements being the method of modal hammer operation. The processing and evaluation of the measured signals remained entirely consistent. The repeated measurements of the same turbine wheel using the measuring device yielded results that closely matched those shown in Figure 17. In contrast, the manual operation of the modal hammer resulted in statistically significant deviations compared to the results depicted in Figure 18. Similar findings were observed during measurements of various other turbine wheels of different sizes and designs, conducted using both methods. These results underscore that the manual operation of the modal hammer introduces significant inaccuracies in the modal analysis of turbine wheels. Consequently, replacing manual handling with an appropriate mechanical device is strongly recommended to ensure the repeatability of force impulses in both their timing and point of application.

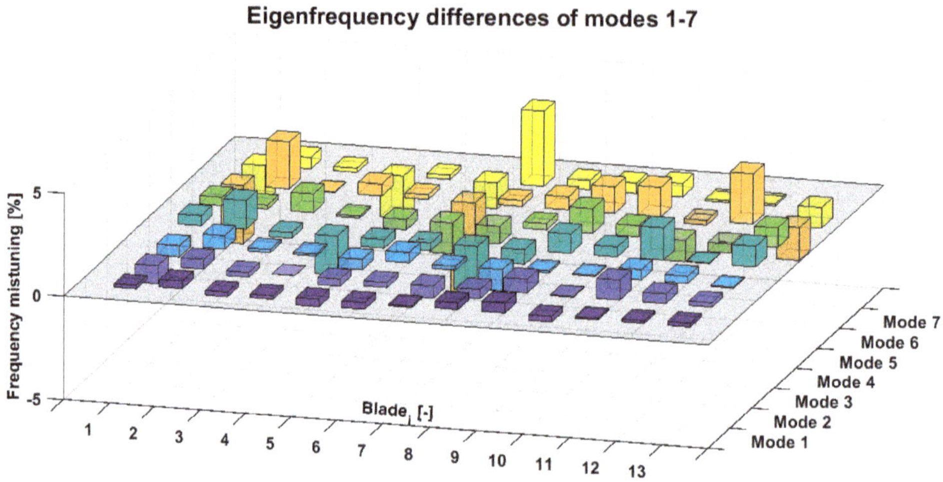

Figure 17. Eigenfrequency differences of modes 1–7 measured using the presented device.

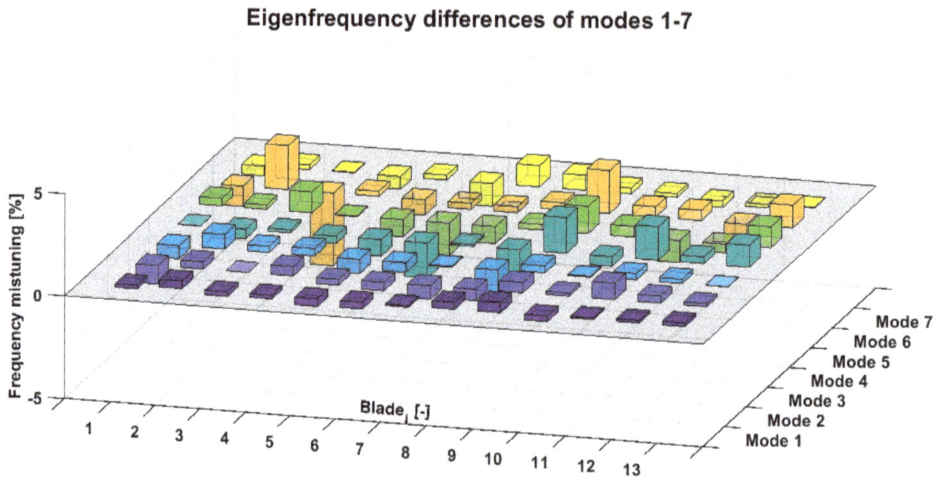

Figure 18. Eigenfrequency differences of modes 1–7 measured with a hand-guided modal hammer.

The developed measuring device successfully automates the process of modal hammer strikes, ensuring consistent force and precise positioning for each impact. This automation not only significantly reduces the measurement time but also improves the accuracy of the results. With its ability to deliver reliable and repeatable excitation impulses, the device proves to be a valuable tool for analysing the dynamic properties and mistuning of turbocharger blade wheels.

The successful prototype testing highlights its potential for broader applications in industrial practice. Future enhancements should focus on optimising the design and integrating the device into comprehensive measurement systems. Moreover, exploring additional automation possibilities could further boost the efficiency and precision of the measurement process.

Author Contributions: Conceptualisation, O.K., V.P. and O.F.; methodology, O.K., S.S. and P.K.; software, P.K.; validation, V.P., P.K. and O.F.; formal analysis, S.S.; investigation, O.K. and P.K.; resources, O.F.; data curation, O.F.; writing—original draft preparation, O.K., P.K., O.F. and V.P.; writing—review and editing, P.K.; visualisation, S.S. and O.K.; supervision, V.P.; project administration, V.P. and S.S.; funding acquisition, V.P. All authors have read and agreed to the published version of the manuscript.

Funding: This publication was supported by the project "Innovative Technologies for Smart Low Emission Mobilities", funded as project No. CZ.02.01.01/00/23_020/0008528 by the Programme Johannes Amos Comenius, call Intersectoral cooperation.

Data Availability Statement: Data available on request.

Acknowledgments: The authors thank Brno University of Technology for the support.

Conflicts of Interest: The authors declare no conflicts of interest.

Abbreviations

The following abbreviations are used in this manuscript:

FFT	Fast Fourier Transform
FRF	Frequency Response Function

References

1. Ewins, D.J. *Modal Testing: Theory, Practice and Application*, 2nd ed.; Wiley: Hoboken, NJ, USA, 2000; ISBN 978-0-863-80218-8.
2. Zhao, J.; Experimental Modal Analysis Overview. Crystal Instruments. 2017. Available online: https://www.crystalinstruments.com/blog/2017/8/28/experimental-modal-analysis-overview (accessed on 28 January 2025).
3. Feng, K.; Ji, J.C.; Ni, Q.; Beer, M. A review of vibration-based gear wear monitoring and prediction techniques. *Mech. Syst. Signal Process.* **2023**, *182*, 109605. [CrossRef]
4. Qin, Y.; Tang, X.; Jia, T.; Duan, Z.; Zhang, J. Noise and vibration suppression in hybrid electric vehicles: State of the art and challenges. *Renew. Sustain. Energy Rev.* **2020**, *124*, 109782. [CrossRef]
5. Moon, B.Y.; Cho, D.S. A study on vibration reduction by heat deformation of casting frame motor. *J. Mech. Sci. Technol.* **2022**, *36*, 1621–1630. [CrossRef]
6. Qiang, L.; Jingxin, L.; Jing, M.; Dayong, G.; Jiaming, H. Structure design and vibration control of vibration reduction boring bar with variable damping. *Int. J. Adv. Manuf. Technol.* **2024**, *134*, 5301–5319. [CrossRef]
7. You, X.; Feng, H.; Zhang, H.; Liu, P. Optimization analysis of vibration reduction for aeroengine multistage blade-disk system. *J. Vibroeng.* **2024**, *26*, 1547–1566. [CrossRef]
8. Park, M.-H.; Yeo, S.; Choi, J.-H.; Lee, W.-J. Review of noise and vibration reduction technologies in marine machinery: Operational insights and engineering experience. *Appl. Ocean Res.* **2024**, *152*, 104195. [CrossRef]
9. Haywood-Alexander, M.; Mills, R.S.; Champneys, M.D.; Jones, M.R.; Bonney, M.S. Full-scale modal testing of a Hawk T1A aircraft for benchmarking vibration-based methods. *J. Sound Vib.* **2024**, *576*, 118295. [CrossRef]
10. Pais, T.; Silvestri, P. Full scale cruise ship dynamic identification using operational modal analysis on sea trial data measurements. *Ocean Eng.* **2024**, *311*, 118931. [CrossRef]
11. Cai, J.; Ding, S.; Zhang, Q.; Liu, R.; Zeng, D.; Zhou, L. Broken Ice Circumferential Crack Estimation via Image Techniques. *Ocean Engineering* **2022**, *259*, 111735. [CrossRef]
12. Zhi, S.; Wu, H.; Shen, H.; Wang, T.; Fu, H. Entropy-Aided Meshing-Order Modulation Analysis for Wind Turbine Planetary Gear Weak Fault Detection under Variable Rotational Speed. *Entropy* **2024**, *26*, 409. [CrossRef] [PubMed]
13. Monka, P.; Monkova, K.; Uban, M.; Hruzik, L.; Vasina, M. Vibrodiagnostics as the tool of a tap wear monitoring. *Procedia Struct. Integr.* **2018**, *13*, 959–964. [CrossRef]
14. Gatti, P.L. Experimental modal analysis. In *Applied Structural and Mechanical Vibrations;* CRC Press: London, UK, 1999.
15. He, J.; Fu, Z.-F. *Modal Analysis;* Butterworth-Heinemann: Oxford, UK, 2001; ISBN 978-0-7506-5079-3. [CrossRef]
16. Siemens. Modal Analysis: What Is Modal Analysis? 2025. Available online: https://www.sw.siemens.com/en-US/technology/modal-analysis/ (accessed on 21 February 2025).

17. Píštěk, V.; Kučera, P.; Fomin, O.V.; Lovska, A. Effective Mistuning Identification Method of Integrated Bladed Discs of Marine Engine Turbochargers. *J. Mar. Sci. Eng.* **2020**, *8*, 379. [CrossRef]
18. Ewins, D.J. *Experimental Modal Analysis*; Springer: London, UK, 2000; ISBN 978-1852334236.
19. Blevins, R.D. *Modal Testing: Theory, Practise and Application*; Prentice Hall: Upper Saddle River, NJ, USA, 2001; ISBN 978-0750675991.
20. Statham, G.E.M. *Introduction to Experimental Modal Analysis and Testing*; Prentice Hall: Upper Saddle River, NJ, USA, 2000; ISBN 978-0131048536.
21. Shapiro, M.H. *Vibration Testing: Theory and Practice*; Wiley-Interscience: New York, NY, USA, 1993; ISBN 978-0471047890.
22. Schenck, W.C.; Driscoll, G.B. *Handbook of Experimental Structural Dynamics*; ASME Press: New York, NY, USA, 1997; ISBN 978-0791802099.
23. Kühhorn, A.; Beirow, B. Method for Determining Blade Mistuning on Integrally Manufactured Rotor Wheels. U.S. Patent 20,100,286,934 A1, 11 November 2010.

symmetry

MDPI

Article

Optimization of Qualitative Indicators of the Machined Surface in Symmetrical Machining of TS by WEDM Technology

Ľuboslav Straka

Department of Automobile and Manufacturing Technologies, Faculty of Manufacturing Technologies with the Seat in Presov, Technical University of Kosice, Sturova 31, 080 01 Presov, Slovakia; luboslav.straka@tuke.sk; Tel.: +421-55-602-6365

Abstract: Current approaches in the process of evaluating the quality of the machined surface during wire electrical discharge machining (WEDM) generally do not include the assessment of micro- and macro-geometric indicators of both parts of the cut. In practice, however, there are specific cases when it is necessary to use both halves of the cut. In such cases, it is necessary to choose a special approach not only in the machining process but also when evaluating the quality indicators of the machined surface. Therefore, experimental measurements were aimed at the identification of these micro- and macro-geometrical indicators in symmetrical WEDM. Within them, qualitative indicators of flat and curved surfaces were assessed. The identification of individual characteristics was carried out using Suftes, Roundtest Mitutoyo, and a 3D coordinate measuring device. The design of the experiment followed the full DoE factorial design method, and the obtained results were processed using the Taguchi method. Based on the obtained results, the response of macro and micro-geometric parameters was characterized by means of multiple regression models (MRM) in symmetrically machined surfaces of tool steel EN X37CrMoV5-1 (Bohdan Bolzano, Kladno, ČR) by WEDM technology. They revealed the mutual dependence of the output qualitative indicators of the eroded area on the input variables' main technological parameters (MTP). Subsequent multi-parameter optimization resulted in a suitable level of setting of the MTP input variable parameters I, t_{on}, U, and t_{off} (9 A, 32 μs, 15 μs, and 70 V), through which the greatest agreement of macro and micro-geometric output indicators of symmetrically machined surfaces can be achieved. By applying the optimized levels of MTP settings for symmetrical WEDM of tool steel EN X37CrMoV5-1, their agreement was achieved at the level of 95%.

Keywords: optimization; surface quality; symmetry cut (SC); tool steel (TS); wire electrical discharge machining (WEDM)

1. Introduction

In the wire electrical discharge machining (WEDM) process, it would be most appropriate for the cut to have zero width, the same dimensional parameters, the same quality of the machined surface, and no residual stress acting in the subsurface layers. Since it is not possible to achieve this 100%, it is necessary to try to at least minimize these shortcomings in the WEDM process. This is because any deviation of the actually achieved quality of the machined surface from the ideal state can cause serious problems. Another problem in the WEDM process is symmetrical machining. Although symmetrical machining in many classical machining technologies is well mastered, the situation is different in the WEDM process. This is due to the fact that with this technology, machining is carried out by spark erosion during the mutual movement of the tool and the workpiece. At the same time, the electric potential of the spark can cause the instability of the electro-erosive process on the individual sides of the cut, which results in a different achieved quality of the machined surface.

Based on the analysis performed in the given area, it can be concluded that the potential of electrical discharge has a direct impact on the quality of the machined surface during WEDM. At the same time, on the basis of a wide range of experiments, it is evident that it depends on a large number of factors. The experiments carried out so far were partially focused on the identification of the influence of selected input factors on the evaluated output qualitative indicators of the machined area. A partial contribution to the issue was the result of experimental research conducted by Gong et al. [1]. As part of the conducted experimental research, they dealt with the accuracy and surface quality of the cut. They found that as the duration of the pause between discharges increased, the consistency of the notch width improved. They also observed that smaller craters, fragments, cracks, cavities, and spherical drops on the eroded surface can be achieved with a lower intensity of electrical discharges during offset cuts. At the same time, they observed that the size of the convex top of the machined surface decreases, and the peaks and valleys of the waves are more concentrated. Paulo et al. focused their research in even greater depth [2]. As part of their research, they dealt with the symmetry of the crater itself. They found that the aspect ratio of individual craters depends on the pulse energy. With low-energy pulses, rounder craters are created, while with high-energy pulses, elongated craters are formed. These craters then have an impact on the final quality of the eroded surface. A different approach to solving this problem was provided by Pradhan et al. [3], who, as part of their experimental research, chose the response method of selected input parameters on the output quality of the machined surface. They identified parameters that significantly contribute to the resulting quality of the machined surface. Researchers Rees et al. [4] performed a comparative study in which they described the effects of material microstructure refinement on the resulting surface quality of the machined surface during WEDM. They found that the choice of the electrode material used in the application of the electro-erosive process has a significant impact on the achievable aspect ratio of the machined surface and its roughness. In addition to the mentioned authors, many others have described the effects of various input factors and their levels on the output quality parameters of the machined surface. However, their research was limited to the selected type of machined material in connection with the selected parameters of the machined surface.

Although assessing the quality of the machined surface in WEDM from the point of view of micro-geometry parameters is undeniably important, its assessment from the point of view of macro-geometry parameters is no less important. Errors in the macro geometry of the eroded surface affect its future functionality to the same extent. In this direction, new knowledge was brought by Naveed [5], who, as part of his research, devoted himself to deformations of the contour of the machined position. The aim of his research was to identify the extent, nature, and causes of the undesirable effects of the EDM process of EN3B steel and, at the same time, to identify important parameters that can be used to demonstrate the quality of the contour cut. He found that a thinner wire diameter provides a better surface layer quality in terms of its roughness but causes larger contour errors. In his article [6], he describes the findings regarding the WEDM cutting surfaces of samples on which the contour method of residual stress measurement was applied. The results of the research provided detailed information on the effects of the cutting process on the quality of the machined surface in terms of the contour profile at the beginning, in the middle, and at the end of the cut. Precise electrical discharge machining of profiles with a small radius of rounding was dealt with by Abyar et al. [7]. They theoretically analyzed the causes of first and second finishing-stage machining errors on arc paths, developing a mathematical methodology to predict these errors with 78% to 83% accuracy. Authors Zahoor et al. [8] conducted an experimental study to investigate the effect of galvanized copper wire and main technological parameters (MTP) in the machining of a complex profile from an IN718 superalloy. They found that galvanized copper wire is suitable for machining complex curved geometric profiles such as convex, concave, straight, and inclined. At the same time, the best results in terms of geometric accuracy were recorded with concave geometric elements. The problem associated with the deviation of the wire guidance in the corner parts, which causes the profile error, was dealt with by Selvakumar et al. [9]. As part of their experimental research, they found a way to minimize the corner error by adjustment, which improved the geometric accuracy of the profile in the corners by 25%. The accuracy of machined convex and concave profiles through WEDM was addressed by Farooq et al. [10]. They comprehensively investigated the effect of MTP on the geometric accuracy of convex and concave profiles, including corner radii, during WEDM of a Ti6Al4V alloy. Through SEM, they found that the discharge energy significantly affects the profile accuracy and surface integrity. Researchers Firouzabadi et al. [11] focused on improving the accuracy of concave corners with a small radius in the finishing stage. They found that to achieve accurate corner radii, it was necessary to increase the length of the corner arc traveled by the wire in a concave corner with a small radius. Ahmad et al. [12] focused their research on identifying the influence of residual stress on the errors of the machined profile by WEDM technology. As part of the experimental research, they found that the duration of the spark pulse is a critical parameter in improving the quality of the machined profile. From the analysis carried out in the area of the influence of selected input factors on the macro geometry of the machined surface in WEDM, it can be concluded that their research, as in the case of micro geometry, was only carried out to a limited extent. At the same time, not one of the conducted research studies was concerned with assessing the quality of symmetrically machined surfaces during WEDM. Therefore, based on the analysis of the current state in the area of micro- and macro-geometry assessment in the symmetrical machining of materials by WEDM technology, a research gap was identified. These reasons led us to carry out experimental research, the aim of which was to optimize processes in symmetrical machining of materials using WEDM technology. At the same time, the conducted research contributes to the database of already existing knowledge in the given area. The inspiration for the multi-parametric optimization process was the method proposed by Wang et al. [13]. They proposed an optimization method through which it is possible to improve the accuracy of the machined surface in WEDM. Their system can also predict corner errors as well as recommend optimal machining parameters for smaller corner errors and higher machining speed. Optimization in the WEDM process was also addressed by researchers Divya et al. [14]. As part of the conducted research, they analyzed the possibilities of using multi-objective optimization in the WEDM process. To optimize the parameters of the electro-erosive process with one goal, they recommend applying the Taguchi method.

As already mentioned above, in the process of symmetrical machining by WEDM technology, a significant problem is the different achieved quality of the machined surface [15]. Since this problem has not yet been solved based on the analysis of the current state, an experiment was proposed. The proposed experiment to solve the given problem was oriented with the aim of minimizing micro- and macro-geometric deviations of symmetrically machined surfaces by WEDM technology. The experiment followed the method of full DoE factorial design [16–19]. Significant input variable parameters related to the MTP and their influence on the monitored output qualitative micro and macro indicators of the machined surface were identified. In terms of input-independent parameters of the electro-erosive process, peak current I, pulse on-time duration t_{on}, pulse off-time duration t_{off}, and voltage of discharge U were assessed at three levels. From the point of view of the output-dependent qualitative micro- and macro-geometric indicators of the machined surface, the parameters of roughness Ra and Rz and deviations of flatness Δz_f and cylindricity Δy_C were assessed. The obtained results of experimental measurements were processed by the Taguchi method [20–23]. Subsequently, based on the processed results of the experimental measurements, the response of the input variable parameters of the electro-erosive process to the assessed output-dependent micro- and macro-geometric indicators during symmetrical WEDM was identified by means of multiple regression models (MRM) [24–26]. At the same time, the multi-parametric optimization was carried out to identify suitable levels of MTP input variable parameters of the electro-erosive process, through which the greatest agreement of macro- and micro-geometric output indicators of symmetrically machined surfaces can be achieved [27–31]. Experimental research was carried out on samples that were made by WEDM technology with a brass wire electrode. It is a type of wire tool electrode, which, based on previous experiments, demonstrates the achievement of the best qualitative results of the machined surface in terms of the assessed quality indicators of the machined surface. For that reason, it was assumed that even with symmetrical machining, this type of electrode would show the smallest deviations of the output micro- and macro-geometric indicators of the machined surfaces.

2. Materials and Methods

2.1. *Theoretical Starting Points for the Research of Micro- and Macro-Geometric Indicators of the Machined Surface in the Process of Symmetrical WEDM*

As is clear from the performed analysis, there has been only minimal interest in the dimensional accuracy of symmetrically machined surfaces by WEDM technology within the research community. At the same time, the reported studies regarding the quality of the machined surface during WEDM in terms of micro- and macro-geometric accuracy in most cases focused only on assessing the quality indicators of the machined surface of only one part of the section. In addition, in many cases, research has focused only on the characteristics of one qualitative indicator. In doing so, researchers did not take into account mutual combinations of the effects of several output qualitative indicators of the machined area. Therefore, the aim of the conducted experimental research was to investigate the mutual effects of the combination of four key qualitative indicators of the machined surface during symmetrical machining of surfaces by WEDM technology and, at the same time, find the optimal combination of the main controllable input-independent parameters for the four output-monitored quality indicators of the eroded area. This problem was solved in the form of mathematical modeling with subsequent optimization [32–35].

The task of modeling the quality of the machined surface in the WEDM process is to transform the mechanisms taking place on the machined surface into a mathematical formula. The latter should accordingly describe the achieved qualitative results of the machined surface based on a detailed definition of the input variables of the process parameters. Defining the mathematical function is the first step required in the optimization process. Its definition requires extensive knowledge of the interrelationships of input-independent MTP and output-dependent indicators of the machined surface in WEDM. After defining them, it is possible to select a suitable optimization criterion with subsequent implementation of the algorithm in a suitable software environment [36,37]. Based on the analysis of the current state in the field of process optimization in WEDM, it can be concluded that the optimization of the response of the machined surface, based on the analysis of the variability of input factors, is a suitable technique for finding optimal machining conditions in WEDM [38–41]. For the given case, the minimal deviation of the assessed micro- and macro-geometric indicators of the eroded area appears to be a suitable optimization criterion. As part of the experimental measurements, deviations of the micro-geometric indicators of the eroded surface were assessed in terms of roughness Ra and Ra. The micro-geometric indicators of the machined surface Ra and Ra are defined by the standard [42]. The roughness of the machined surface after WEDM is comparable to the quality of finely ground surfaces. Although ground surfaces are generally characterized by a high gloss of the machined surface, in many cases, they show higher values of the mean arithmetic deviation of the roughness profile Ra, or the maximum height of the roughness profile Rz, than matte eroded surfaces. The parameter Rz characterizes the largest height of the unevenness of the profile without any averaged values, while the mean arithmetic deviation of the roughness profile Ra exceeds by 3 to 5 times (Figure 1).

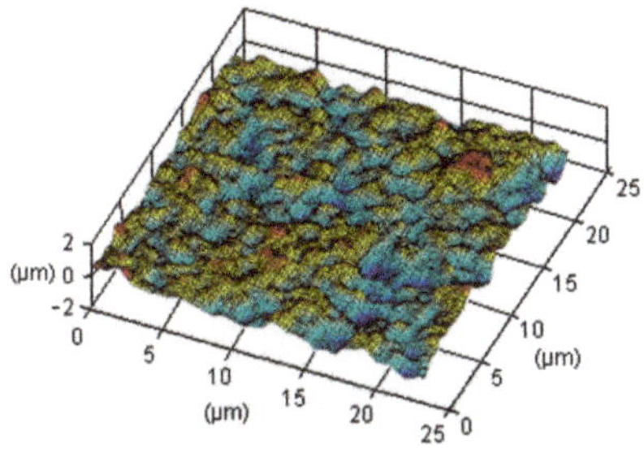

Figure 1. Micro geometry of the eroded surface.

From the performed analysis, it is clear that the macro-geometric indicators of the machined surface represent a separate group of significant geometric deviations of the machined surface after WEDM. Oniszczuk-Swiercz et al. [43], Narendranath et al. [44], and Kadam et al. [45] claim that in order to maintain the required quality of the machined surface after WEDM, deviations in the flatness and circularity of the eroded profile are significant. Therefore, within the assessment of the macro-geometric accuracy of the eroded surface, the deviations of the flatness indicator Δz_f were taken into account in accordance with the applicable standard [46]. In practice, these deviations are evaluated quantitatively as the largest distance between the points of the given profile in the normal direction or as the sum of the absolute values of the largest distances of the points of the given profile on both sides of the middle element. The real eroded surface is then represented by the surface that is separated from the surrounding environment by an ideal flat surface (Figure 2).

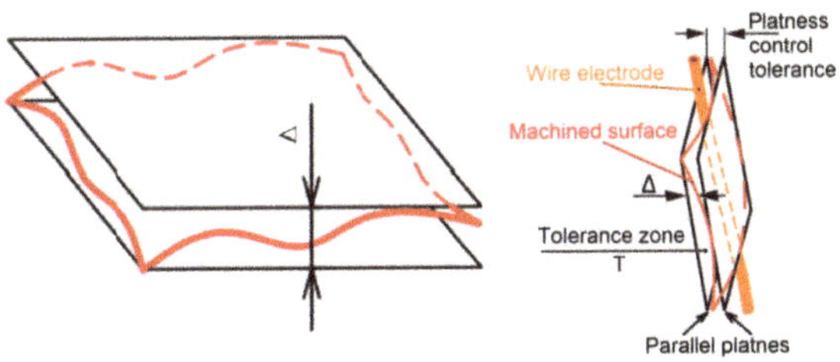

Figure 2. Macro geometry of the eroded surface.

In addition to flatness deviations Δz_f, the circularity deviations of the profile Δy_C were also taken into account when assessing the macro-geometric accuracy of the eroded surface. Their identification was carried out in accordance with the measurement method according to the standard [47]. The basic condition for the correct evaluation of the roundness deviation was in compliance with the standard [48]. At the same time, for the correct evaluation of the roundness deviations of the profile Δy_C, data on the actual profile with the filtered-out roughness and waviness component were required on the nominal surface. The profile of the circular surface was obtained in the form of a polar diagram. It is about recording the values of the measured deviations so that it is possible to easily create a replacement element. The replacement element can be an envelope or a central circle, while the roundness deviation is evaluated using its center.

On the basis of the detailed identification of all four output qualitative indicators of the machined surface during symmetrical machining of surfaces by WEDM technology, it was possible to design mathematical regression models. Through them, using the optimization method, we subsequently determined a suitable combination of output-independent parameters of the WEDM process to the required level of combinations of output-dependent qualitative indicators of the machined surface [49–51]. Additionally, the optimization of the output-dependent qualitative indicators of the machined area Ra, Rz, Δz_f, and Δy_C must primarily respect their minimum deviation. At the same time, the experimental research carried out was designed with an emphasis on an organized approach to obtaining optimal output-dependent qualitative parameters of the machined surface during WEDM and suitable values of important MTP settings [52,53]. Thus, the optimization criterion was the minimization of the deviation of the parameters Ra, Rz, Δz_f, and Δy_C, while the predicted response was x, and the desired function was Ra, Rz, Δz_f, and Δy_C. The suitability value varied from 0 to 1. If the suitability value was 0, it meant that the predicted value was completely undesirable. If the suitability value was equal to 1, the predicted value was idle. The corresponding response requirement increased with the value of the parameters Ra, Rz, Δz_f, and Δy_C. Formula (1) describes the function of minimizing the one-sided transformation of the deviations of parameters Ra, Rz, Δz_f, and Δy_C.

$$\mathrm{Ra}, \mathrm{Rz}, \Delta z_f, \Delta y_c = \left\{ \left(\frac{x - x_{max}}{x_{min} - y x_{max}} \right)^{vol} \begin{cases} 0 \to x \leq x_{min} \\ x_{min} \leq x \leq x_{max} \\ 1 \to x \leq x_{max} \end{cases} \right. \tag{1}$$

Ra, Rz, Δz_f, and Δy_C are a function of the desired value of x, and the parameters $x_{min/max}$ are the lower/upper limit values of the x response. *Vol* is a volume that can be varied from 0.01 to 10 to adjust the shape of the desired function. The overall desired function D ($0 \leq D \leq 1$) is then defined as the geometric mean of the individual desired functions. The multi--objective function is consequently the geometric mean of all the transformed responses of one objective problem shown in Equation (2). The higher the value of D, the better the response of the combined levels.

$$D = \left(\mathrm{Ra} \times \mathrm{Rz} \times \Delta z_f \times \Delta y_c \right)^{\frac{1}{n}} \tag{2}$$

Multi-parameter optimization with multi-response can be performed using a demand function in conjunction with WEDM symmetrically machined surface response methodology. The input-independent parameters of the electro-erosive process are then peak current I, pulse on-time duration t_{on}, pulse off-time duration t_{off}, and voltage of discharge U.

2.2. Material of Experimental Samples and Used Technological Devices

As part of the application experiment, low-alloy tool steel marked EN X37CrMoV5-1 (W.-Nr. 1.2343) was used to make the samples. It is a chromium–molybdenum–silicon–vanadium tool steel, which has a high hot strength of Rm $\geq$ 900 N·mm^{-2} and a high resistance to tempering. In a wide temperature range, it has good toughness and plastic properties, with good resistance to the formation of cracks. From the point of view of chemical composition, the carbides in a given tool steel are very small and evenly distributed. This property gives this tool steel excellent cold and hot fatigue resistance and corrosion resistance. In terms of physical properties, it shows good oxidation resistance, as well as high toughness and wear resistance at medium temperature. These properties allow the given tool steel to maintain stable performance in various demanding environments. Table 1 shows selected chemical, mechanical, and physical properties of tool steel EN X37CrMoV5-1.

Table 1. Chemical, mechanical, and physical properties of tool steel EN X37CrMoV5-1.

Chemical Composition (wt %)	Mechanical Properties	Physical Properties
0.32–0.42 C	Tensile strength R_m 950 MPa	Specific heat capacity 460 J·kg^{-1}·K^{-1}
0.20–0.50 Mn	Yield strength $Rp_{0,2}$ 600 MPa	Thermal expansion coefficient 11.5 × 10^{-6} m·m^{-1}·K^{-1}
0.80–1.20 Si	Hardness in the annealed state 225 HB_{max}	Thermal conductivity 25 W·m^{-1}·K^{-1}
4.50–5.50 Cr	Achievable hardness after refining 56 HRC	Electrical conductivity 1.92 Siemens·m·mm^{-2}
1.10–1.50 Mo	Machinability 75.0–80.0%	Specific electrical resistance 0.52 Ω·mm^{2}·m^{-1}
0.30–0.50 V	Poisson's ratio 0.27–0.30	Density 7.8 kg·dm^{-3}
0.030 P_{max}	Elongation 6–16%	Hot forming temperature 900–1100 °C
0.030 S_{max}	Reduction area 42–58%	Exposure temperature 540 °C

The experimental samples were made on an AgieCharmilles CUT E 350 electrical discharge machine. It is a compact electro-erosive device of the Swiss manufacturer GF that enables the cutting of metallic electrically conductive materials. The AgieCharmilles CUT E 350 electrical discharge machine has an ergonomic AC CUT HMI interface with a 19″ touch screen, a wire preparation system using the Thermocut module, automatic wire threading, the possibility of bevel cutting, and other progressive functions.

Demineralized water treated with deionization resin to an electrical conductivity of about 10 μS·cm^{-1} was used as a dielectric.

The experimental samples were made with a wire tool electrode Ø 0.25 mm labeled AC Brass LP 1000. It is a standard brass wire electrode in the ratio 63%Cu/37%Zn. It is designed for a wide range of operations performed on modern electrical discharge machines. It is particularly suitable for precise machining with acceptable performance, which puts it in the category of universal wire electrodes.

As already mentioned in the introduction, the output indicators of micro- and macro-geometric accuracy of the machined surface during symmetrical machining of tool steels by WEDM technology are largely dependent on the combination of input-independent MTP settings. At the same time, on the basis of the performed analysis, it can be assumed that peak current I(A), pulse on-time duration t_{on}(μs), pulse off-time duration t_{off}(μs), and voltage of discharge U(V) have a significant influence on the assessed output-dependent indicators of the eroded area Ra, Rz, Δz_f, and Δy_C. Table 2 shows the lower, middle, and upper values of the MTP settings during symmetrical machining of tool steel EN X37CrMoV5-1 by WEDM technology with a Ø 0.25 mm wire tool electrode marked AC Brass LP 1000.

Mitutoyo Surftest SJ 400 (Mitutoyo, Kawasaki, Japan) contact roughness meter with automatic radius and slope compensation with an accuracy of 0.001 μm was used to measure the micro-geometric indicators Ra and Rz of symmetrically machined surfaces using WEDM technology. Figure 3 shows the measurement of the micro-geometric indicators Ra and Rz of symmetrically machined surfaces from tool steel EN X37CrMoV5-1 by WEDM technology.

Table 2. Lower, middle, and upper values of MTP settings for symmetrical machining of tool steel with WEDM technology.

Setting Value	MTP			
	Peak Current I (A)	Pulse On-Time Duration t_{on} (μs)	Pulse Off-Time Duration t_{off} (μs)	Voltage of Discharge U (V)
Low	9	20	10	70
Middle	14	26	15	80
High	19	32	20	90

Figure 3. Measurement of micro-geometric indicators of the eroded surface Ra and Rz of symmetrically machined surfaces of experimental samples with the Mitutoyo Surftest SJ 400 device (Mitutoyo, Kawasaki, Japan).

Contact 3D CNC coordinate machine Rapid-Plus (Thome Präzision, GmbH, Messel, Germany) with a measuring range of 1500 mm × 800 mm × 700 mm and a measurement accuracy of 0.01 μm was used to measure the macro-geometric indicator of the eroded surface Δz_f of symmetrically machined surfaces using WEDM technology. Figure 4 shows the measurement of macro-geometric deviations of the flatness of the eroded surface Δz_f of symmetrically machined surfaces made of tool steel EN X37CrMoV5-1 by WEDM technology.

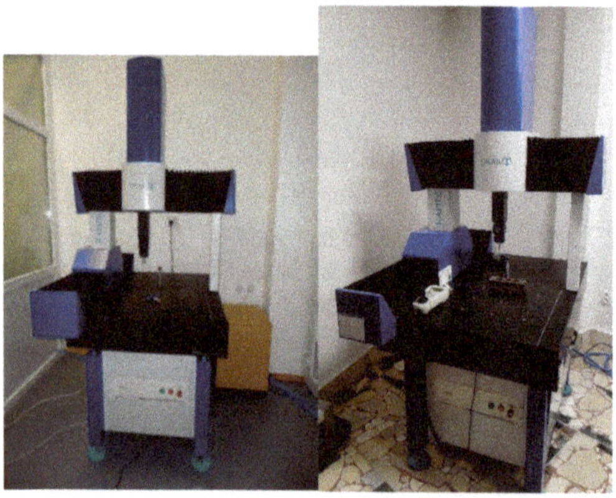

Figure 4. Measurement of macro-geometric deviations of the flatness of the eroded surface Δz_f of symmetrically machined surfaces of experimental samples by a 3D CNC coordinate machine Rapid-Plus.

A compact measuring device, Roundtest RA-120 (Mitutoyo, Kawasaki, Japan), was used to measure the macro-geometric indicator of the eroded surface Δy_C of symmetrically machined surfaces by WEDM technology in accordance with the valid standards [46,47]. Figure 5 shows the measurement of the macro-geometric deviations of the circularity of the eroded surface Δy_C of symmetrically machined surfaces from tool steel EN X37CrMoV5-1 by WEDM technology.

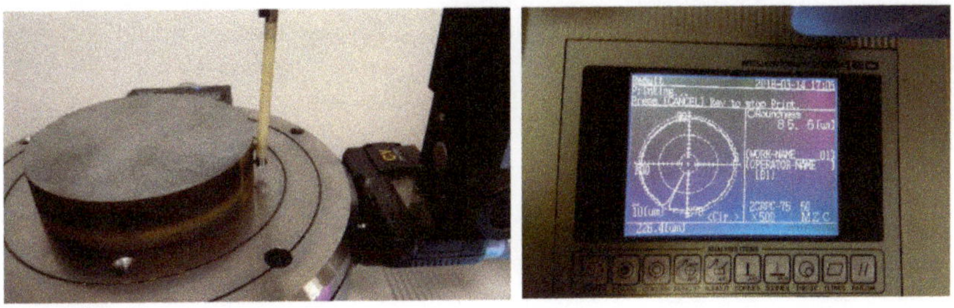

Figure 5. Measurement of macro-geometric deviations of circularity Δy_C of the eroded surface of symmetrically machined surfaces of experimental samples by the Roundtest RA-120 measuring device.

2.3. Design of Experiment Plan

Based on the analysis of methods suitable for the design of the plan of experiments in the production of samples through WEDM technology, the Taguchi method was chosen. It is a very effective tool for investigating the response of the output-dependent quality indicator of the machined area to several input-independent variables of the MTP. In addition, it allows us to summarize the condition of minimizing the influence of the causes of variations with relatively little sensitivity to uncontrollable factors. The advantage of applying this method compared to traditional fully factorial designs of experiments is that it allows for reducing the scale of the set of experiments. This is particularly beneficial in the production of experimental samples by WEDM technology, which is characterized by an extremely time-consuming nature.

As part of the design of the experiment, the application of a two-level setting of specific MTPs was considered, while the set would represent 64 samples. However, there was a risk that in the case of a non-linear dependence of input/output values, the measured results would be burdened with a disproportionately large error. In the case of the application of a 4-level setting of specific MTP, the recorded results would be somewhat more accurate, but the set would represent 128 experimental samples, which is twice the number of samples. Therefore, due to the effectiveness of the conducted research, the design of the experiment was based on a four-factor analysis of 3 levels of setting the input-independent variables of the MTP in WEDM, namely peak current I(A), pulse on-time duration t_{on}(μs), pulse off-time duration t_{off}(μs), and voltage of discharge U(V). This represents a set of 9 levels (L9) of combinations of MTP settings for each type of cut and height of the material being machined. In doing so, 2 types of cuts were applied with a material thickness of 30.0 mm and 130.0 mm. At the same time, with each symmetrical cut, 2 machined surfaces of the samples were created, which represents a total of 72 experimental samples. The results of experimental measurements of output qualitative indicators of the machined surface Ra and Rz after WEDM of tool steel EN X37CrMoV5-1 with brass wire electrode AC Brass LP 1000 are shown in Tables 3 and 4.

From the results of experimental measurements listed in Table 3, it can be observed that the lowest value of the quality indicator of the micro geometry of the machined surface Ra was recorded for the sample with a material thickness of 130.0 mm and the MTP setting at the L1 level (I 9 A, t_{on} 20 μs, t_{off} 10 μs, and U 70 V). The highest Ra value was recorded when machining material with a material thickness of 30.0 mm and MTP setting at L9 level (I 19 A, t_{on} 32 μs, t_{off} 15 μs, and U 70 V). It was found that the opposite sides of the eroded surface show deviations ΔRa in the range of 0.025 μm to 0.050 μm.

At the same time, the smallest deviation ΔRa was recorded when machining samples with a thickness of H = 130.0 mm at the L1 level of the MTP setting, and conversely, the highest when machining samples with a thickness of H = 30.0 mm at the L9 level. It follows that, in addition to the MTP, the micro geometry of the machined surface in WEDM is also influenced by the thickness of the machined material H, while the value of the Ra indicator decreases with the increasing thickness of the machined material at an identical MTP setting.

Table 3. Measured values of the micro geometry output indicator of the machined surface Ra according to the four-factor three-level plan of experiments.

Run No.	MTP				Experimental Results							
	I (I)	t_{on} (μs)	t_{off} (μs)	U (V)	Ra (μm) for Adjacent Side of the Cut		Ra (μm) for Opposite Side of the Cut		Maximum Deviation ΔRa (μm)		Percentage (%)	
					H = 30 mm	H = 130 mm	H = 30 mm	H = 130 mm	H = 30 mm	H = 130 mm	H = 30 mm	H = 130 mm
1	9	20	10	70	1.04	0.98	1.1	1.03	0.030	0.025	5.45	4.85
2	9	26	15	80	1.37	1.29	1.43	1.35	0.030	0.030	4.20	4.44
3	9	32	20	90	1.72	1.63	1.8	1.69	0.040	0.030	4.44	3.55
4	14	20	15	90	2.06	1.94	2.14	2.01	0.040	0.035	3.74	3.48
5	14	26	20	70	2.39	2.27	2.48	2.34	0.045	0.035	3.63	2.99
6	14	32	10	80	2.65	2.52	2.74	2.59	0.045	0.035	3.28	2.70
7	19	20	20	80	2.84	2.69	2.93	2.77	0.045	0.040	3.07	2.89
8	19	26	10	90	2.98	2.83	3.08	2.91	0.050	0.040	3.25	2.75
9	19	32	15	70	3.08	2.92	3.18	3.01	0.050	0.045	3.14	2.99

Table 4. Measured values of the micro geometry output indicator of the machined surface Rz according to the four-factor three-level plan of experiments.

Run No.	MTP				Experimental Results							
	I (I)	t_{on} (μs)	t_{off} (μs)	U (V)	Rz (Mm) for Adjacent Side of the Cut		Rz (μm) for Opposite Side of the Cut		Maximum Deviation ΔRz (μm)		Percentage (%)	
					H = 30 mm	H = 130 mm	H = 30 mm	H = 130 mm	H = 30 mm	H = 130 mm	H = 30 mm	H = 130 mm
1	9	20	10	70	4.75	4.52	5.04	4.73	0.15	0.11	5.75	4.44
2	9	26	15	80	6.32	5.94	6.63	6.19	0.16	0.13	4.68	4.04
3	9	32	20	90	7.94	7.51	8.29	7.78	0.17	0.14	4.22	3.47
4	14	20	15	90	9.47	8.93	9.85	9.24	0.19	0.16	3.86	3.35
5	14	26	20	70	10.98	10.41	11.42	10.77	0.22	0.18	3.85	3.34
6	14	32	10	80	12.17	11.58	12.63	11.97	0.23	0.20	3.64	3.26
7	19	20	20	80	13.05	12.38	13.53	12.78	0.24	0.20	3.55	3.13
8	19	26	10	90	13.73	13.02	14.24	13.45	0.26	0.22	3.58	3.20
9	19	32	15	70	14.16	13.42	14.69	13.87	0.27	0.23	3.61	3.24

Based on the measured data in Table 4, it can be concluded that the highest value of the qualitative indicator of the micro geometry of the machined surface Rz was recorded when machining material with a material thickness of 30.0 mm and the MTP setting at the L9 level (I 19 A, t_{on} 32 μs, t_{off} 15 μs, and U 70 V). The lowest value of Rz was recorded for the sample with a material thickness of 130.0 mm and MTP setting at L1 level (I 9 A, t_{on} 20 μs, t_{off} 10 μs, and U 70 V). In addition, the results showed that the opposite sides of the eroded surface show deviations of ΔRz in the range of 0.11 μm to 0.27 μm. At the same time, the smallest deviation ΔRz was recorded when machining samples with a thickness of H = 130.0 mm at the L1 level of the MTP setting. Conversely, the highest when machining samples with a thickness of H = 30.0 mm at the L9 level of the MTP setting. It follows that as the thickness of the machined material increases with the identical MTP setting, the value of the Rz indicator decreases.

The results of experimental measurements of the output qualitative indicators of the macro geometry of the machined surface Δz_f and Δy_C of symmetrically machined surfaces of tool steel EN X37CrMoV5-1 with material thickness H = 30.0 and 130.0 mm using WEDM technology with a brass wire electrode AC Brass LP 1000 are shown in Tables 5 and 6.

Table 5. Measured values of the output indicator of the macro geometry of the machined surface Δz_f according to the four-factor three-level plan of experiments.

Run No.	MTP				Experimental Results							
	I (I)	t_{on} (μs)	t_{off} (μs)	U (V)	z_f (μm) for Adjacent Side of the Cut		z_f (μm) for Opposite Side of the Cut		Maximum Deviation Δz_f (μm)		Percentage (%)	
					H = 30 mm	H = 130 mm	H = 30 mm	H = 130 mm	H = 30 mm	H = 130 mm	H = 30 mm	H = 130 mm
1	9	20	10	70	8.2	16.8	7.8	16.1	0.2	0.35	4.88	4.17
2	9	26	15	80	8.7	18.1	8.1	17.2	0.3	0.45	6.90	4.97
3	9	32	20	90	9.1	19.3	8.4	18.2	0.35	0.55	7.69	5.70
4	14	20	15	90	9.6	20.5	8.8	19.1	0.4	0.7	8.33	6.83
5	14	26	20	70	10.1	21.9	9.1	20.4	0.5	0.75	9.90	6.85
6	14	32	10	80	10.4	23.4	9.3	21.7	0.55	0.85	10.58	7.26
7	19	20	20	80	10.9	24.8	9.7	22.8	0.6	1	11.01	8.06
8	19	26	10	90	11.2	26.5	9.9	24.2	0.65	1.15	11.61	8.68
9	19	32	15	70	11.5	28.3	10.1	25.7	0.7	1.3	12.17	9.19

Table 6. Measured values of the macro geometry output indicator of the machined surface Δy_C according to the four-factor three-level plan of experiments.

Run No.	MTP				Experimental Results							
	I (I)	t_{on} (μs)	t_{off} (μs)	U (V)	Y_c (Mm) for Adjacent Side of the Cut		y_C (μm) for Opposite Side of the Cut		Maximum Deviation Δy_C (μm)		Percentage (%)	
					Ø 30 mm	Ø 130 mm	Ø 30 mm	Ø 130 mm	Ø 30 mm	Ø 130 mm	Ø 30 mm	Ø 130 mm
1	9	20	10	70	120.7	65.3	118.1	64.1	1.3	0.6	2.15	1.84
2	9	26	15	80	121.8	66.1	118.9	64.7	1.5	0.7	2.38	2.12
3	9	32	20	90	124.1	66.9	120.7	65.2	1.7	0.9	2.74	2.54
4	14	20	15	90	125.7	69.2	121.9	67.3	1.9	1.0	3.02	2.75
5	14	26	20	70	128.1	69.8	124.1	67.8	2.0	1.0	3.12	2.87
6	14	32	10	80	129.9	70.2	125.5	68.1	2.2	1.1	3.39	2.99
7	19	20	20	80	131.4	71.1	126.7	68.9	2.4	1.1	3.58	3.09
8	19	26	10	90	133.8	71.9	128.9	69.6	2.5	1.2	3.66	3.20
9	19	32	15	70	136.5	74.2	131.4	71.7	2.6	1.3	3.74	3.37

The range of measured data of the parameter z_f in Table 5 ranges from 7.8 μm to 28.3 μm. The lowest z_f value was recorded at a thickness of 30.0 mm and the MTP setting at the L1 level (I 9 A, t_{on} 20 μs, t_{off} 10 μs, and U 70 V) and the highest at 130.0 mm thickness and the MTP setting at L9 level (I 19 A, t_{on} 32 μs, t_{off} 15 μs, and U 70 V). Based on the measured data, it can also be concluded that the opposite sides of the eroded surface show deviations Δz_f in the range of 0.2 μm to 1.3 μm. At the same time, the smallest deviation Δz_f was recorded when machining samples with a thickness of H = 30.0 mm at the L1 level of the MTP setting and the largest when machining samples with a thickness of H = 130.0 mm at the L9 level of the MTP setting. It follows that, in addition to MTP, the thickness of the machined material H has an influence on the macro geometry of the machined surface in WEDM, while the value of the Δz_f indicator increases with the increasing thickness of the machined material.

Based on experimental measurements (Table 6), the y_C parameter was found to be in the range of 64.1 µm to 136.5 µm. At the same time, the lowest y_C value was recorded for the sample with Ø 130.0 mm and an MTP setting at L1 level (I 9 A, t_{on} 20 µs, t_{off} 10 µs, and U 70 V). On the contrary, the highest value of the qualitative indicator of the macro geometry of the machined surface y_C was recorded when machining the sample with Ø 30.0 mm and setting the MTP at the L9 level (I 19 A, t_{on} 32 µs, t_{off} 15 µs, and U 70 V). It was also found that the opposite sides of the eroded surface showed deviations Δy_C in the range of 0.6 µm to 2.6 µm. The lowest value of deviation Δy_C was recorded when machining samples with Ø 130.0 mm at the L1 level, with the highest at Ø 30.0 mm at the L9 level. Therefore, it can be concluded that, in addition to MTP, the macro geometry of the machined surface during WEDM is also influenced by Ø, while as its value increases, the deviation Δy_C decreases.

3. Results

3.1. Four-Factor Analysis of the Influence of Selected MTP on Micro- and Macro-Geometric Indicators of Symmetrically Machined Surfaces by WEDM Technology

Based on the average values of the micro-geometry output indicators of the machined surface Ra and Rz of symmetrically machined surfaces of tool steel EN X37CrMoV5-1 using WEDM technology with a brass wire electrode AC Brass LP 1000 recorded in Tables 3 and 5, a four-factor analysis of the influence of selected MTP was performed using the Taguchi method. The results of the performed four-factor analysis on the three-level MTP settings are presented in the graphs in Figures 6 and 7.

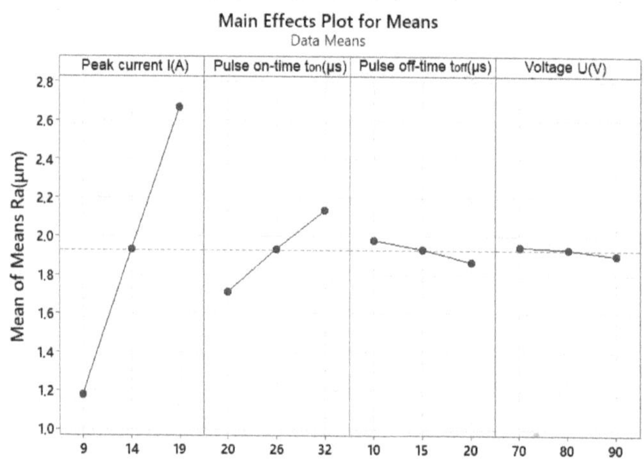

Figure 6. Four-factor analysis of the main effect of MTP with three-level settings on the output indicator of micro geometry of the machined surface Ra of symmetrically machined surfaces by WEDM technology.

From the performed four-factor analysis of the main effect of MTP with four-level settings on the output indicators of micro geometry of the machined surface Ra and Rz of symmetrically machined surfaces by WEDM technology, the following facts were found. It was found that parameter I has the greatest influence on the indicator of the micro geometry of the machined surface Ra and Rz, followed by t_{on}. U and t_{off} have the smallest influence of the considered parameters. At the same time, it was found that the best and better quality of the machined surface in terms of Ra and Rz indicators can be achieved with the combination of MTP with the minimum value of the parameters I and t_{on} and, at the same time, with the maximum value of the parameters U and t_{off}.

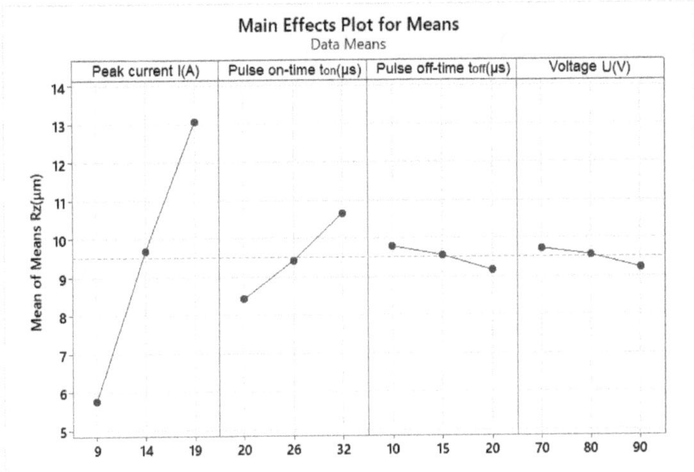

Figure 7. Four-factor analysis of the main effect of MTP with three-level settings on the output indicator of micro geometry of machined surface Rz of symmetrically machined surfaces by WEDM technology.

Based on the average values of the output indicators of the macro geometry of the machined surface z_f and y_C of symmetrically machined surfaces of tool steel EN X37CrMoV5-1 using WEDM technology with a brass wire electrode AC Brass LP 1000 recorded in Tables 5 and 6, a four-factor analysis of the influence of selected MTP was performed using the Taguchi method. The results of the performed four-factor analysis on the three-level MTP settings are presented in the graphs in Figures 8 and 9.

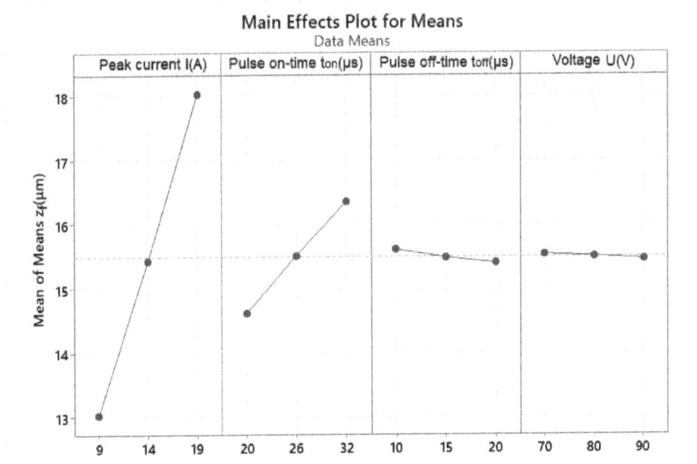

Figure 8. Four-factor analysis of the main effect of MTP with three-level settings on the output indicator of macro geometry z_f of the machined surface of symmetrically machined surfaces by WEDM technology.

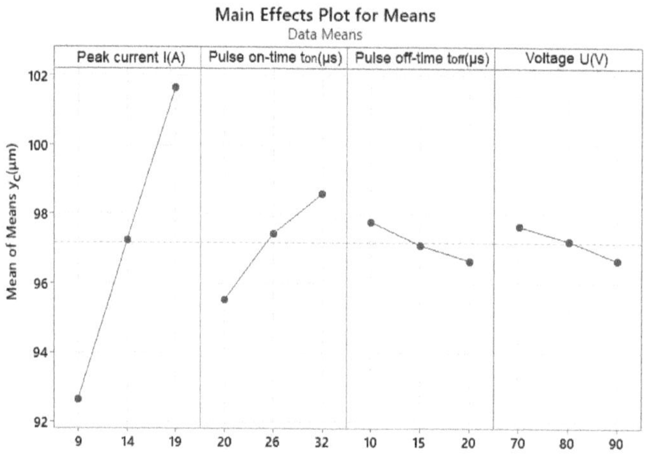

Figure 9. Four-factor analysis of the main effect of MTP with three-level settings on the output indicator of macro geometry of the machined surface y_C of symmetrically machined surfaces by WEDM technology.

From the performed four-factor analysis of the main effect of MTP with three-level settings on the output indicators of the machined surface macro geometry z_f and y_C of symmetrically machined surfaces by WEDM technology, the following facts were found. It was found that parameter I has the greatest influence on the indicator of the macro geometry of the machined surface z_f and y_C, followed by t_{on}. U and t_{off} have the smallest influence of the assessed parameters. At the same time, the parameters U and t_{off} have an almost negligible influence on the z_f indicator. At the same time, it was found that the best and better quality of the machined surface in terms of z_f and y_C indicators can be achieved with the combination of MTP with the minimum value of the parameters I and t_{on} and, at the same time, with the maximum value of the parameters U and t_{off}.

3.2. Modeling and Simulation of Macro-Geometric Indicators of the Machined Surface During Symmetrical WEDM of Tool Steel

In order to mathematically model the output micro- and macro-geometric indicators of symmetrically machined surfaces by WEDM technology, multiple regression models (MRM) were compiled at the 95% confidence level. The proposed MRMs apply to the machining of tool steel EN X37CrMoV5-1 through WEDM technology with brass wire electrodes Ø 0.25 mm. They are applicable for a wide spectrum of material thickness H. The input parameters of MRM are the independent variables of MTP (I, t_{on}, t_{off}, and U). The output parameters of MRM are dependent micro- and macro-geometric indicators of the eroded area (Ra, Rz, Δz_f, and Δy_C). The higher validity of the proposed MRM is represented by the value of determination coefficients (R^2), which is close to the value of 1. The MRM, which is represented by Equation (3), was compiled on the basis of experimentally measured values recorded in Table 3 with regard to the minimization of the Ra indicator.

$$Ra = -0.7158+0.14875 \cdot I+0.03507 \cdot t_{on} - 0.01125 \cdot \mathrm{t_{off}} - 0.002292 \cdot \mathrm{U} \quad (3)$$

Figure 10 shows the MRM for the micro geometry output indicator Ra of symmetrically machined surfaces of EN X37CrMoV5-1 tool steel using WEDM technology with brass wire electrode Ø 0.25 mm, including model building sequence and incremental impact of variables. Multiple regression of the Ra indicator depending on the input MTP was performed with regard to its minimization.

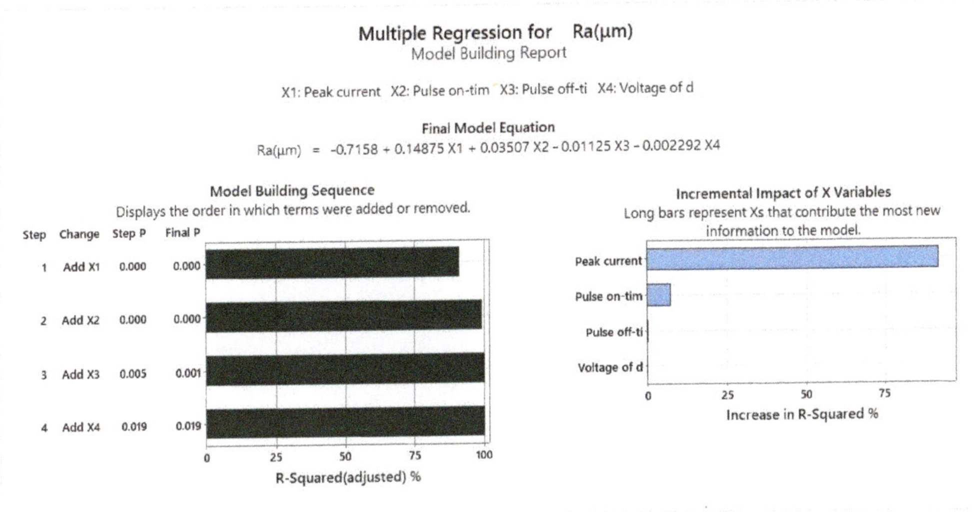

Figure 10. The protocol of the performed multiple regression for the output indicator of micro geometry Ra of symmetrically machined surfaces of tool steel EN X37CrMoV5-1 by WEDM technology.

In an identical way, on the basis of the experimentally measured values recorded in Table 4, the compiled MRM output indicator of micro geometry Rz of symmetrically machined surfaces of tool steel EN X37CrMoV5-1 by WEDM technology is represented by Equation (4):

$$Rz = -2.53 + 0.7537 \cdot I + 0.1806 \cdot t_{on} - 0.0337 \cdot t_{off} - 0.0265 \cdot U \quad (4)$$

Figure 11 shows the result of the performed multiple regression, which describes the dependence of the micro-geometry output indicator Rz of symmetrically machined surfaces of tool steel EN X37CrMoV5-1 by WEDM technology on input-independent MTP. At the same time, it presents the model building sequence and incremental impact of variables within the multiple regression of the Rz indicator with regard to its minimization.

Equation (5) represents the MRM, which was compiled on the basis of experimentally measured values of the macro-geometry output indicator Δz_f of symmetrically machined surfaces of tool steel EN X37CrMoV5-1 by WEDM technology recorded in Table 5:

$$\Delta z_f = 5.058 + 0.49917 \cdot I + 0.14444 \cdot t_{on} - 0.02083 \cdot t_{off} - 0.00375 \cdot U \quad (5)$$

Figure 12 shows the result of the performed multiple regression, which describes the dependence of the macro geometry output indicator Δz_f of symmetrically machined surfaces of tool steel EN X37CrMoV5-1 by WEDM technology on input-independent MTP. At the same time, it presents the model building sequence and incremental impact of variables within the performed multiple regression of the Δz_f indicator with regard to its minimization.

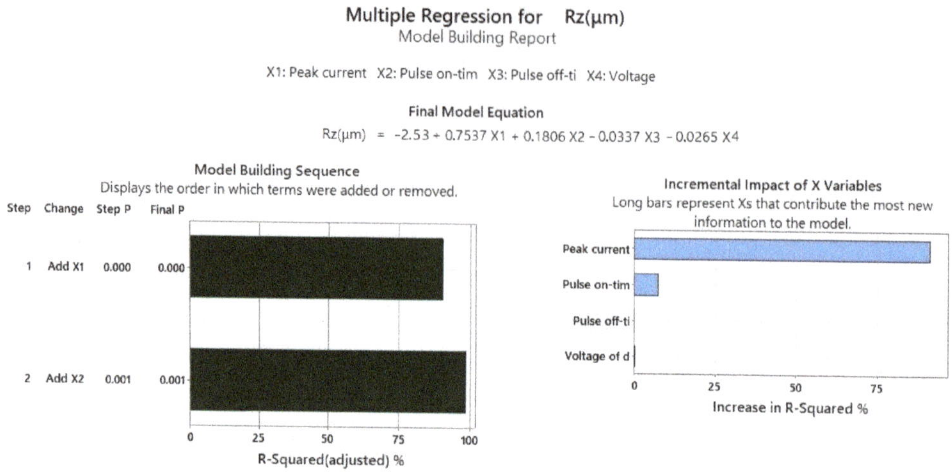

Figure 11. The protocol of the performed multiple regression for the output indicator of the Rz micro geometry of symmetrically machined surfaces of tool steel EN X37CrMoV5-1 by WEDM technology.

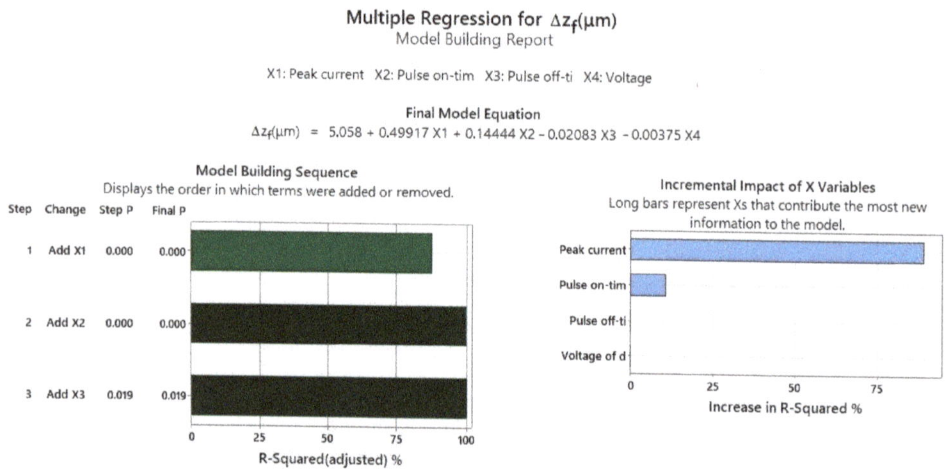

Figure 12. The protocol of the performed multiple regression for the macro geometry output indicator Δz_f of symmetrically machined surfaces of tool steel EN X37CrMoV5-1 by WEDM technology.

Equation (6) represents the MRM, which was compiled on the basis of experimentally measured values of the macro geometry output indicator Δy_C of symmetrically machined surfaces of tool steel EN X37CrMoV5-1 by WEDM technology recorded in Table 6:

$$\Delta y_C = 83.55 + 0.9017 \cdot I + 0.2549 \cdot t_{on} - 0.1125 \cdot t_{off} - 0.0492 \cdot U \tag{6}$$

Figure 13 shows the result of the performed multiple regression, which describes the dependence of the macro geometry output indicator Δy_C of symmetrically machined surfaces of tool steel EN X37CrMoV5-1 by WEDM technology on input-independent MTPs. At the same time, it presents the model building sequence and incremental impact of variables within the performed multiple regression of the Δy_C indicator with regard to its minimization.

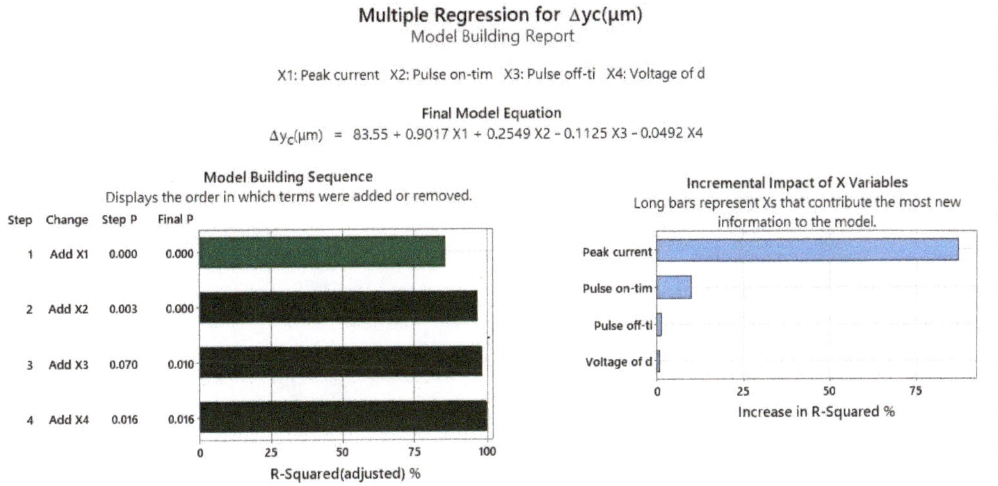

Figure 13. The protocol of the performed multiple regression for the macro geometry output indicator Δy_C of symmetrically machined surfaces of tool steel EN X37CrMoV5-1 by WEDM technology.

On the basis of the performed multiple regression, which is described by the compiled MRM (3) to (6), a simulation of the monitored micro- and macro-geometric indicators (Ra, Rz, Δz_f, and Δy_C) was performed for WEDM tool steel EN X37CrMoV5-1 with brass wire electrode. All indicators were simulated with regard to their minimization depending on the input MTP (I, t_{on}, t_{off}, and U) for a wide spectrum of the parameter H. Simulation of the output indicator of the macro geometry Δz_f of symmetrically machined surfaces of tool steel EN X37CrMoV5-1 by WEDM technology depending on the indicators Ra, Rzm and H parameters is described by Regression Equation (7):

$$\Delta \text{zf} \; = 14.69 \; - \; 0.0043 \cdot \text{H} \; - \; 8.04 \cdot Ra + 0.000179 \cdot H^2 + 1.848 \cdot Ra^2 + 0.04502 \cdot H \cdot Ra \quad (7)$$

$$\Delta \text{zf} \; = 7.203 \; + \; 0.0019 \cdot \text{H} \; + 0.0091 \cdot Rz + 0.000249 \cdot H^2 + 0.008888 \cdot H \cdot Rz \quad (8)$$

Subsequently, 3D dependences (Figure 14) were constructed, which graphically show the simulation of the output macro-geometric indicator of the eroded surface Δz_f during symmetrical WEDM of tool steel EN X37CrMoV5-1 with brass wire electrode AC Brass LP 1000 in the range of thicknesses H = 10.0 mm to 360.0 mm.

From the performed prediction shown in Figure 14 it can be observed that with the increasing value of the index Ra and Rz of the eroded surface and at the same time with the increasing value of the parameter H for WEDM tool steel EN X37CrMoV5-1, the simulated value of the output macro-geometric indicator of the eroded surface Δz_f also increases. With the thickness of the machined material H = 10.0 mm and a constant value of Ra = 0.20 μm, the simulated value of the indicator Δz_f = 7.3 μm. At a constant value of Ra = 3.80 μm and thickness H = 10.0 mm, the simulated value of the indicator Δz_f = 12.50 μm. With the thickness of the machined material H = 360.0 mm and the value Ra = 0.20 μm, the predicted value of the indicator Δz_f = 36.70 μm. At the value Ra = 3.80 μm and the thickness H = 360.0 mm, the predicted value of the indicator Δz_f = 91.1 μm. From the simulated values of the output macro-geometric indicator of the eroded surface Δz_f for symmetrical WEDM of tool steel EN X37CrMoV5-1, it can be concluded that the lowest value is possible with the smallest thickness of the machined material H, and at the same time the lowest value of the Ra and Rz indicators.

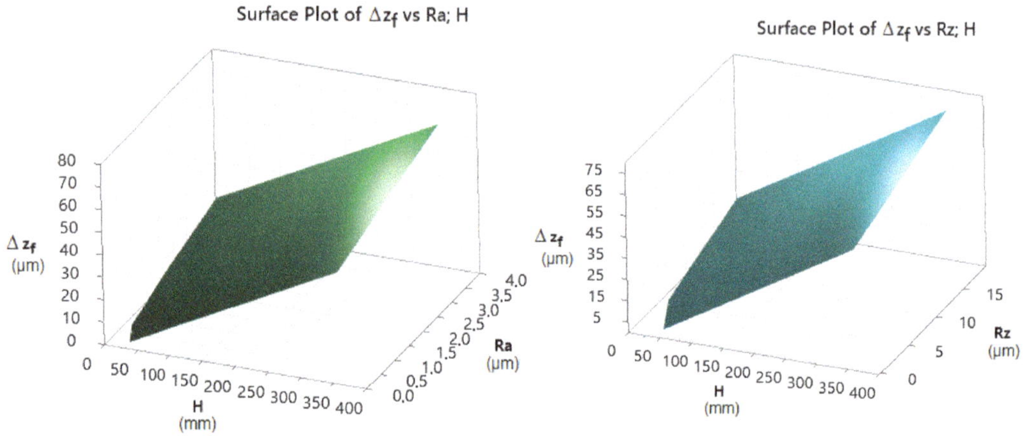

Figure 14. Simulation of the output macro-geometric indicator of the eroded surface Δz_f during symmetrical WEDM of tool steel EN X37CrMoV5-1.

In the same way, the simulation of the output macro-geometric indicator of the eroded area Δy_C was performed in the case of symmetrical WEDM of tool steel EN X37CrMoV5-1. This prediction is described by the following Regression Equations (8):

$$\Delta yc = 135.24 - 0.5031 \cdot D - 1.189 \cdot Ra - 0.000131 \cdot D^2 + 2.248 \cdot Ra^2 - 0.02404 \cdot H \cdot Ra \quad (9)$$

$$\Delta yc = 124.963 - 0.54610 \cdot D + 2.977 \cdot Rz + 0.000151 \cdot D^2 - 0.05599 \cdot Rz^2 - 0.006798 \cdot H \cdot Rz \quad (10)$$

Three-dimensional graphical dependence in Figure 15 shows the performed simulation of the output macro-geometric indicator of the eroded area Δy_C during symmetrical WEDM of tool steel EN X37CrMoV5-1 with a brass wire electrode based on Regression Equations (9) and (10).

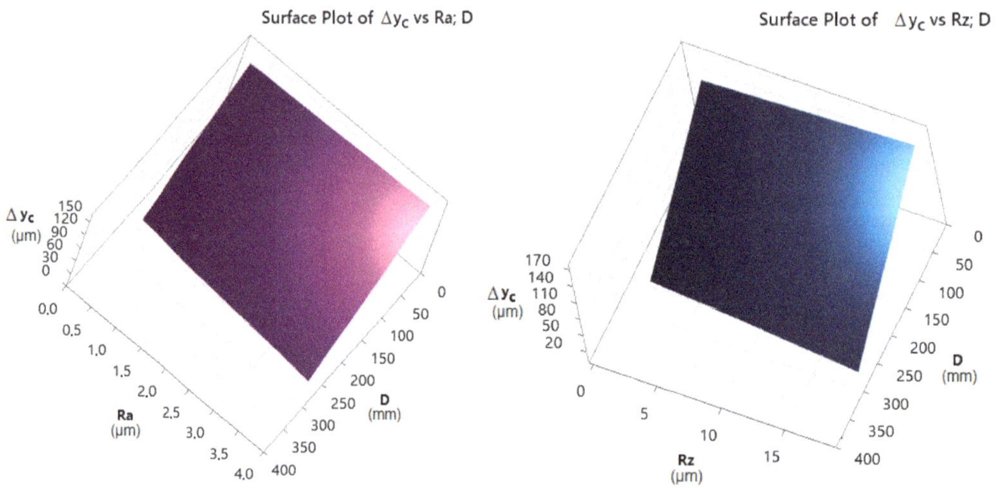

Figure 15. Simulation of the output macro-geometric indicator of the eroded surface Δy_C during symmetrical WEDM of tool steel EN X37CrMoV5-1.

From the graphs in Figure 15, it is evident that with increasing Ø of the machined surface of tool steel EN X37CrMoV5-1 and with a constant value of the Ra and Rz indicators, there is a decrease in the predicted value of the output macro-geometric indicator of the eroded surface Δy_C. With a Ø of the machined material of 10.0 mm and a constant value of Ra = 0.20 μm, the simulated value of the indicator Δy_C = 129.80 μm. With roughness Ra = 3.80 μm and Ø 10.0 mm, the simulated value of the indicator Δy_C = 157.20 μm. At Ø 220.0 mm and a constant value of Ra = 0.20 μm, the predicted value of the indicator Δy_C = 17.50 μm. With roughness Ra = 3.80 μm and Ø 220.0 mm, the predicted value of the indicator Δy_C = 26.40 μm. From the simulated values of the output macro-geometric indicator of the eroded surface Δy_C for symmetrical WEDM tool steel EN X37CrMoV5-1, it can be concluded that the lowest value is possible at the largest Ø and, at the same time, lower value of the Ra and Rz indicators.

3.3. *Optimization of Micro- and Macro-Geometric Indicators of the Machined Surface During Symmetrical WEDM of Tool Steel*

Based on the obtained multiple regression reports for the optimization of the output micro- and macro-geometric indicators of the machined surface Ra, Rz, Δz_f, and Δy_C for WEDM tool steel with regard to their minimization and MTP setting I, t_{on}, t_{off} a U, several facts can be observed. First of all, it can be observed that with the increasing value of the parameters I and t_{on}, and at the same time with the decreasing value of the parameter t_{off} and U for WEDM tool steel, there is a significant increase in the output micro-geometric indicators Ra and Rz. At the same time, the most favorable value of the parameter Ra = 0.98 μm and Rz = 4.52 μm was achieved at the L1 level with the setting of MTP (I 9 A, t_{on} 20 μs, t_{off} 10 μs and U 70 V. On the contrary, their highest value Ra = 3.18 μm and Rz = 14.69 μm was achieved at the L9 level with the MTP setting I 19 A, t_{on} 32 μs, t_{off} 15 μs, and U 70 V. At the same time, with this MTP setting, there is a significant increase in the output macro-geometric indicators of the machined surface Δz_f and Δy_C.

For a more detailed identification of the change in the assessed output micro- and macro-geometric indicators of the machined surface Ra, Rz, Δz_f, and Δy_C after WEDM of tool steels depending on H and Ø, their mutual optimization was subsequently performed. Figure 16 shows the graphical optimization of the output micro- and macro-geometric indicators of the machined area Ra, Rz, and Δz_f with regard to their minimization based on their predicted values, which were obtained through MRM defined by Formulas (7) and (8).

From the graphical dependencies shown in Figure 16, it can be observed that with the increasing thickness of the machined material H and the increasing value of the output micro-geometric indicators of the machined surface Ra and Rz for WEDM tool steel, the value of the output macro-geometric indicator of the machined surface Δz_f also increases significantly. With the thickness of the machined material H = 10.0 mm and the value Ra = 0.2 μm, the predicted value of the macro-geometric indicator of the machined surface Δz_f = 13.2 μm. With the thickness of the machined material H = 360.0 mm and the value Ra = 3.8 μm, the predicted value of the macro-geometric indicator of the machined surface Δz_f = 94.1 μm.

Based on the performed graphic optimization of WEDM tool steel, it can be concluded that a favorable value of the output macro-geometric indicator of the machined surface Δz_f is achieved when machining material with a thickness H in the range of 100.0 mm to 150.0 mm. At the same time, this favorable value can be achieved with MTP settings, which correspond to the values of the micro-geometric indicators of the machined surface Ra = 0.4 μm to 0.6 μm and Rz = 2.0 μm to 3.0 μm.

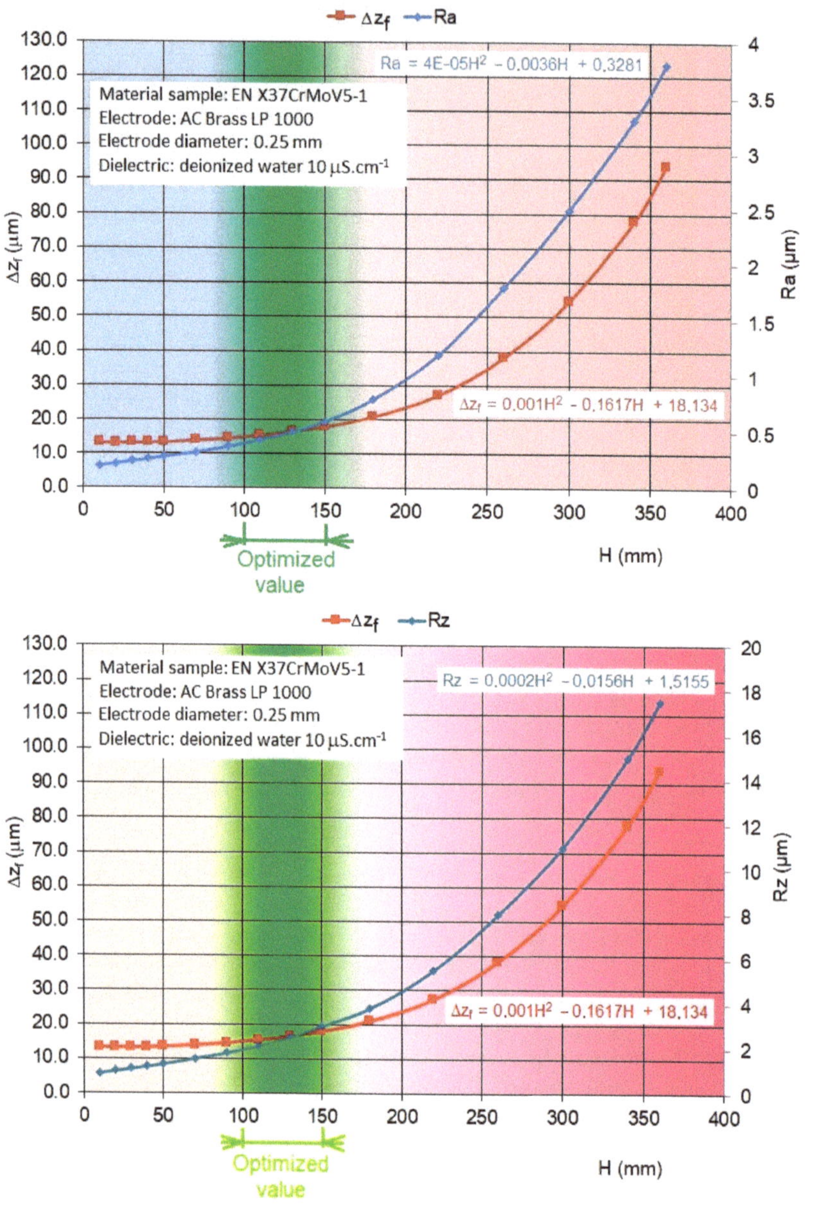

Figure 16. Optimization of the output micro- and macro-geometric indicators of the machined surface Ra, Rz, and Δz_f during WEDM of tool steel with thickness H with regard to their maximization.

Subsequently, graphic optimization (Figure 17) of the output micro- and macro-geometric indicators of the machined surface Ra, Rz, and Δy_C was performed with regard to their minimization based on their predicted values, which were obtained through MRM defined by Formulas (9) and (10).

From the graphical dependencies shown in Figure 17, it can be observed that with the increasing Ø of the machined material D for WEDM tool steel, the value of the output macro-geometric indicator of the machined surface Δy_C decreases. However, with the increasing value of the D parameter, the value of the output micro-geometric indicators of the machined surface, Ra and Rz, increases. With the Ø of the machined material $D = 10.0$ mm and the value of Ra = 0.2 μm, the predicted value of the macro-geometric indicator of the machined surface $\Delta y_C = 130.1$ μm. With the Ø of the machined material $D = 220.0$ mm and the value of Ra = 1.2 μm, the predicted value of the macro-geometric indicator of the machined surface $\Delta y_C = 13.2$ μm.

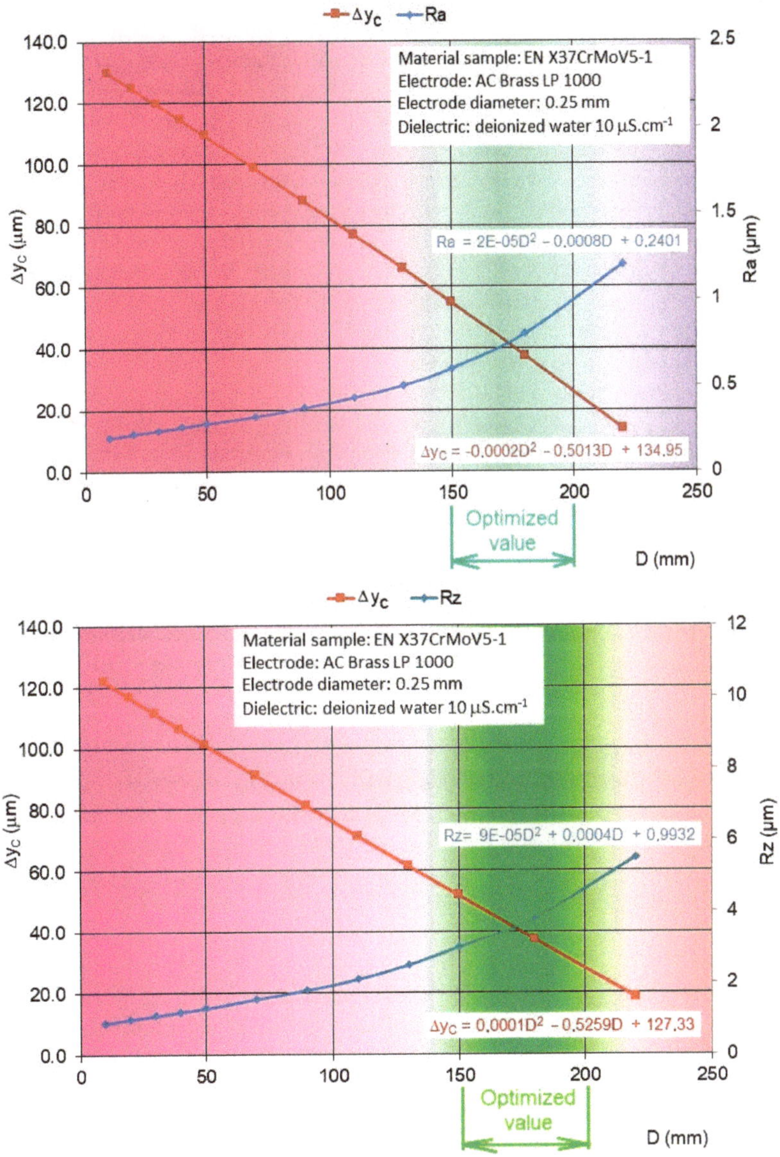

Figure 17. Optimization of the output micro- and macro-geometric indicators of the machined surface Ra, Rz, and Δy_C during WEDM of tool steel with D with regard to their maximization.

4. Discussion

Based on the obtained results of experimental measurements of output micro- and macro-geometric indicators of symmetrically machined surfaces of tool steel EN X37CrMoV5-1 with a brass wire electrode by WEDM technology, the following facts were found. First of all, through a four-factor analysis of the main effect of MTP with three levels of output micro- and macro-geometry settings of the machined surface indicators Ra, Rz, z_f, and y_C, it was found that parameter I has the greatest influence on these indicators, followed by t_{on}. Furthermore, it was found that the lowest value of the indicators Ra, Rz, z_f, and y_C can be achieved at the lowest value of input-independent MTP (I, t_{on}) and, at the same time, the highest value of MTP (t_{off}, U). This is because the potential of the electrical discharge is primarily formed by the intensity of the current and the length of its duration. At the same time, the lower electrical discharge potential has a positive effect on the quality of the machined surface. However, on the other hand, it negatively affects the overall productivity of the electro-erosive process. The voltage parameters and the duration of the break between discharges are only filler parameters to maintain the stability of the electro-erosive process. Additionally, in cooperation with the dielectric liquid, they help to effectively remove eroded material particles from the erosion site, which has a positive impact on improving the quality of the machined surface, both in terms of roughness parameters and geometric accuracy.

At the same time, it was found that the parameters of micro geometry Ra and Rz and macro geometry z_f and y_C influence each other. This means that at a constant thickness H of the machined material, respectively Ø, when the value of the Ra and Rz indicators decreases, the values of the z_f and y_C indicators also decrease. Additionally, the lowest predicted value of the z_f indicator can be achieved with the thickness of the machined material H = 10.0 mm and the roughness of the eroded surface Ra = 0.20 μm. The lowest predicted value of the y_C indicator can be achieved at Ø 220.0 mm and roughness of the eroded surface Ra = 0.20 μm.

In addition, based on the results of the WEDM tool steel graphic optimization, it can be concluded that a favorable value of the output macro-geometric indicator of the machined surface Δy_C is achieved when machining material with the range Ø of 150.0 to 200.0 mm. At the same time, this favorable value can be achieved with MTP settings, which correspond to the values of the micro-geometric indicators of the machined surface Ra = 0.6 to 0.9 μm and Rz = 3.1 to 4.6 μm. Given the MPT setting and the optimized parameters of the machined surface, the minimum deviation of the monitored quality indicators of symmetrically machined surfaces with WEDM technology is achieved. This will increase the efficiency of the electro-erosion process by eliminating the need to apply another additional cut to eliminate the resulting deviation.

5. Conclusions

As mentioned in the introduction, the differences in the quality of symmetrically machined surfaces by WEDM technology are a serious problem that has not been solved so far. Therefore, the aim of the conducted experimental research was to minimize the differences in output micro- and macro-geometric indicators of symmetrically machined surfaces by WEDM technology. From the point of view of the micro-geometric indicators of the machined surface, the parameters Ra and Rz were taken into account, and from the point of view of macro-geometric indicators, parameters z_f and y_C. The design and evaluation of the experimental results were carried out with the application of Taguchi's method. Based on the analysis of the current state, the input variable parameters of the electro-erosive process I, t_{on}, t_{off}, and U were identified. Subsequently, based on the experimental measurements, their influence on the output-dependent indicators of the micro geometry of the eroded surface was identified Ra in the range of 0.98 µm to 3.18 µm and Rz in the range 4.52 µm to 13.53 µm, as well as for macro-geometry output indicators of the eroded surface Δz_f in the range of 7.80 µm to 28.30 µm and Δy_C in the range of 64.10 µm to 136.50 µm. It was found that peak current I and pulse on-time duration have the greatest influence on the given output qualitative indicators of the eroded area. On the contrary, pulse off-time duration t_{off} and voltage of discharge U have the smallest influence. The results of experimental measurements also showed that lower values of indicators Ra, Rz, and Δz_f with identical MTP settings were recorded when machining samples had smaller thicknesses. On the contrary, lower values of Δy_C indicators at identical MTP settings were recorded when machining samples had a larger Ø. The differences with respect to the thickness and diameter of the machined samples ranged in the case of Ra at the level of 4.85% to 3.14%, in the case of Rz at the level of 4.44 to 3.61%, in the case of Δz_f at the level of 4.17% to 12.17%, and in the case of Δy_C at the level of 1.84% to 3.74%. Subsequently, on the basis of the obtained and numerically processed results, MRMs were compiled, which enable the prediction of the given output indicators of the eroded surface of tool steel EN X37CrMoV5-1 for material thickness in the range of 10.0 mm to 360.0 mm and Ø in the range of 10.0 mm to 220.0 mm. Based on them, the value of Δz_f was predicted in the range of 7.3 µm to 96.3 µm and the value of Δy_C in the range of 13.70 µm to 129.80 µm with the corresponding value of the Ra indicator 0.20 µm to 3.80 µm and the Rz indicator 0.90 µm to 17.50 µm. It follows that the lowest values of the micro- and macro-geometric indicators of the machined surface Ra, Rz, z_f, and y_C can be achieved by optimal MTP settings when machining materials with a smaller height and larger profile diameter. By adopting the given recommendations, identical quality in symmetrically machined surfaces can be obtained by WEDM technology. This eliminates the need for another additional cut to achieve identical quality in the giant cutting surfaces.

Funding: This research was funded by the Scientific Grant Agency of the Ministry of Education, Science, Research, and Sport of the Slovak Republic, grant number VEGA 1/0371/23.

Data Availability Statement: All data are published within the paper.

Acknowledgments: The author would like to thank the grant agency for supporting research work by the project VEGA 1/0371/23.

Conflicts of Interest: The author declares no conflicts of interest.

Nomenclature

H	thickness (mm)
TS	tool steels
I	peak current (A)
MRM	multiple regression models
MTP	main technological parameters
Ra	micro-geometric indicator (µm)
Rz	micro-geometric indicator (µm)
D	profile diameter (mm)
t_{on}	pulse on-time duration (µs)
t_{off}	pulse off-time duration (µs)
U	voltage of discharge (V)
WEDM	wire electrical discharge machining
Δz_f	flatness deviation (µm)
Δy_C	roundness deviation (µm)

References

1. Gong, Y.D.; Sun, Y.; Wen, X.L.; Zhou, Y.G.; Liu, Y. Experimental study on accuracy and surface quality of TC2 in LS-WEDM multiple cuts. *J. Braz. Soc. Mech. Sci. Eng.* **2016**, *38*, 2421–2433. [CrossRef]
2. Paulo, E.; Moritz, W.; VMR, C.J.; Sikora, M.; Konrad, W. WEDM single crater asymmetry. *Int. J. Adv. Manuf. Technol.* **2021**, *117*, 2421–2427.
3. Pradhan, B.B.; Masanta, M.; Sarkar, B.R.; Bhattacharyya, B. Investigation of electro-discharge micro-machining of titanium super alloy. *Int. J. Adv. Manuf. Technol.* **2009**, *41*, 1094–1106. [CrossRef]
4. Rees, A. Micro Electrical Discharge Machining: Axis-Symmetric Component Manufacture and Surface Integrity. Ph.D. Thesis, Cardiff University, Cardiff, UK, 2011. Available online: https://orca.cardiff.ac.uk/id/eprint/55139/1/U585528.pdf (accessed on 3 February 2025).
5. Naveed, N. Deformation Characterisations for the WEDM Contour Cut Surfaces. *Int. J. Robot. Mechatron.* **2017**, *4*, 22–32. [CrossRef]
6. Naveed, N. Experimental study of the effects of wire EDM on the characteristics of ferritic steel, at a micro-scale on the contour cut surface. *Metall. Res. Technol.* **2018**, *115*, 413. [CrossRef]
7. Abyar, H.; Abdullah, A.; Shafaroud, A.A. Theoretical and experimental analysis of machining errors on small arced corners during WEDM finishing stages. *Mach. Sci. Technol.* **2019**, *23*, 734–757. [CrossRef]
8. Zahoor, S.; Azam, H.A.; Mughal, M.P.; Ahmed, N.; Rehman, M.; Hussain, A. WEDM of complex profile of IN718: Multi-objective GA-based optimization of surface roughness, dimensional deviation, and cutting speed. *Int. J. Adv. Manuf. Technol.* **2021**, *114*, 2289–2307. [CrossRef]
9. Selvakumar, G.; Balasubramanian, V.; Lenin, N. Investigation on corner accuracy in wire cut EDM of AISI D3 tool steel. *Int. J. Rapid Manuf.* **2020**, *9*, 58–70. [CrossRef]
10. Farooq, M.U.; Ali, M.A.; He, Y.; Khan, A.M.; Pruncu, C.I.; Kashif, M.; Ahmed, N.; Asif, N. Curved profiles machining of Ti6Al4V alloy through WEDM: Investigations on geometrical errors. *J. Mater. Res. Technol.* **2020**, *9*, 16186–16201. [CrossRef]
11. Abyar Firouzabadi, H.; Parvizian, J.; Abdullah, A. Improving accuracy of curved corners in wire EDM successive cutting. *Int. J. Adv. Manuf. Technol.* **2015**, *76*, 447–459. [CrossRef]
12. Ahmad, B.; Fitzpatrick, M.E. Minimization and mitigation of wire EDM cutting errors in the application of the contour method of residual stress measurement. *Metall. Mater. Trans. A* **2016**, *47*, 301–313. [CrossRef]
13. Wang, S.M.; Wu, J.X.; Gunawan, H.; Tu, R.Q. Optimization of machining parameters for corner accuracy improvement for WEDM processing. *Appl. Sci.* **2022**, *12*, 10324. [CrossRef]
14. Divya, M.; Sateesh, N.; Subbiah, R. Review on multi objective optimization of wire cut EDM process parameters using grey relational analysis. *Mater. Today Proceed.* **2020**, *26*, 3124–3130. [CrossRef]
15. Dzionk, S.; Siemiatkowski, M.S. Studying the effect of working conditions on WEDM machining performance of super alloy Inconel 617. *Machines* **2020**, *8*, 54. [CrossRef]
16. Demircioglu, P.; Bogrekci, I.; Eris, Y.; Ozkan, S.C. Optimization of cutting die life cycle and investigation of parameters affecting die life cycle. *Eng. Rev.* **2024**, *44*, 50–64. [CrossRef]
17. Evin, E.; Tomáš, M.; Kmec, J. Optimization of electro-discharge texturing parameters for steel sheets' finishing rollers. *Materials* **2020**, *13*, 1223. [CrossRef]
18. Gorgani, H.H.; Jahazi, A.; Pak, A.J.; Shabani, S. A hybrid algorithm for adjusting the input parameters of the wirecut EDM machine in order to obtain maximum customer satisfaction. *SN Appl. Sci.* **2023**, *5*, 37. [CrossRef]
19. Panda, A.; Nahornyi, V. Predicting the service life of mechanical systems considering their blow-up mode operation. *MM Sci. J.* **2024**, *11*, 7436–7441. [CrossRef]
20. Pi, V.N.; Tam, D.T.; Cuong, N.M.; Tran, T.H. Multi-objective optimization of PMEDM process parameters for processing cylindrical shaped parts using taguchi method and grey relational analysis. *Int. J. Mech. Prod. Eng. Res. Dev.* **2020**, *10*, 669–678.
21. Kiyak, M. Investigation of effects of cutting parameters on surface quality and hardness in the wire-EDM process. *Int. J. Adv. Manuf. Technol.* **2021**, *119*, 647–655. [CrossRef]
22. Hašová, S.; Straka, Ľ. Design and verification of software for simulation of selected quality indicators of machined surface after WEDM. *Acad. J. Manuf. Eng.* **2016**, *14*, 13–20.
23. Hegde, A.; Shetty, R.; Nayak, R.; Shetty, S. Design of experiments integrated with neural networks for optimization and predictive modelling of electrode wear of novel Ti-6Al-4V-SiCp composites during die sinking electric discharge machining. *Mater. Res. Express* **2024**, *11*, 056522. [CrossRef]
24. Dodun, O.; Slătineanu, L.; Nagîț, G.; Hrițuc, A.; Mihalache, A.M.; Beșliu-Băncescu, I. WEDM-generated slot width variation modelling. *Micromachines* **2022**, *13*, 1231. [CrossRef] [PubMed]
25. Mouralova, K.; Bednar, J.; Benes, L.; Prokes, T.; Zahradnicek, R.; Fries, J. Mathematical models for machining optimization of Ampcoloy 35 with different thicknesses using WEDM to improve the surface properties of mold parts. *Materials* **2023**, *16*, 100. [CrossRef]

26. Vagaská, A.; Gombár, M.; Straka, Ľ. Selected Mathematical optimization methods for solving problems of engineering practice. *Energies* **2022**, *15*, 2205. [CrossRef]
27. Straka, L.; Corny, I. Prediction and Multiparametric Optimization of the Machined Surface Quality of Tool Steels in Precise Wire Electrical Discharge Machining. *Machines* **2024**, *12*, 248. [CrossRef]
28. Kosaraju, S.; Bobba, B.P.; Salkuti, S.R. Optimization and microstructural studies on the machining of Inconel 600 in WEDM using untreated and cryogenically treated zinc electrodes. *Materials* **2023**, *16*, 3181. [CrossRef] [PubMed]
29. Rimár, M.; Abraham, M.; Fedák, M.; Kulikov, A.; Oravec, P.; Váhovský, J. Methods of increasing the efficiency of cogeneration based energy equipment. *MM Sci. J.* **2019**, *6*, 2935–2938. [CrossRef]
30. Kopytowski, A.; Świercz, R.; Oniszczuk-Świercz, D.; Zawora, J.; Kuczak, J.; Żrodowski, Ł. Effects of a New Type of Grinding Wheel with Multi-Granular Abrasive Grains on Surface Topography Properties after Grinding of Inconel 625. *Materials* **2023**, *16*, 716. [CrossRef]
31. Kalita, K.; Chakraborty, S.; Ghadai, R.K.; Chakraborty, S. Parametric optimization of non-traditional machining processes using multi-criteria decision making techniques: Literature review and future directions. *Multiscale Multidiscip. Model. Exp. Des.* **2023**, *6*, 1–40. [CrossRef]
32. Kumar, P.V.; Manikandan, V.; Manavaalan, G.; Elango, S. Optimization of automated anodizing plant efficiency and process prediction using Random Forest based Levy flight method. *Chem. Eng. Sci.* **2024**, *300*, 120512. [CrossRef]
33. Panda, A.; Anisimov, V.M.; Anisimov, V.V.; Diadiura, K.O.; Pandova, I. Increasing of wear resistance of linear block-polyurethanes by thermal processing methods. *MM Sci. J.* **2021**, *10*, 4731–4735. [CrossRef]
34. Zhu, Z.; Guo, D.; Xu, J.; Lin, J.; Lei, J.; Xu, B.; Wu, X.; Wang, X. Processing Characteristics of Micro Electrical Discharge Machining for Surface Modification of TiNi Shape Memory Alloys Using a TiC Powder Dielectric. *Micromachines* **2020**, *11*, 1018. [CrossRef] [PubMed]
35. Ragauskas, P.; Jasevičius, R. Objective Function Distortion Reduction in Identification Technique of Composite Material Elastic Properties. *Vibration* **2024**, *7*, 177–195. [CrossRef]
36. Mohanraj, T.; Sakthivel, G.; Pramanik, A. Use of RSM desirability approach to optimize WEDM of mild steel. *Phys. Scr.* **2024**, *99*, 105976.
37. Straka, L.; Pitel, J.; Corny, I. Influence of the main technological parameters and material properties of the workpiece on the geometrical accuracy of the machined surface at WEDM. *Int. J. Adv. Manuf. Technol.* **2021**, *115*, 3065–3087. [CrossRef]
38. Świercz, R.; Oniszczuk-Świercz, D.; Zawora, J.; Marczak, M. Investigation of the Influence of Process Parameters on Shape Deviation after Wire Electrical Discharge Machining. *Arch. Metall. Mater.* **2019**, *64*, 1457–1462. [CrossRef]
39. Lee, S.; Lee, Y.; Park, B.; Lee, C. Structural Optimization of Scarfing Machine with Acceleration Profile and Multi-Objective Genetic Algorithm Approach. *Machines* **2024**, *12*, 398. [CrossRef]
40. Mahanti, R.; Das, M. Sustainable EDM production of micro-textured die-surfaces: Modeling and optimizing the process using machine learning techniques. *Measurement* **2024**, *242*, 115775. [CrossRef]
41. Ming, W.; Guo, X.; Zhang, G.; Hu, S.; Liu, Z.; Xie, Z.; Zhang, S.; Duan, L. Optimization of process parameters and performance for machining Inconel 718 in renewable dielectrics. *Alex. Eng. J.* **2023**, *79*, 164–179. [CrossRef]
42. *STN EN ISO 21920-2:2021*; Geometrical Product Specifications (GPS)—Surface Texture: Profile. Part 2: Terms, Definitions and Surface Texture Parameters. Available online: https://www.iso.org/standard/72226.html (accessed on 3 February 2025).
43. Oniszczuk-Swiercz, D.; Swiercz, R.; Chmielewski, T.; Salacinski, T. Experimental investigation of influence WEDM parameters on surface roughness and flatness deviation. *Metal* **2020**, *29*, 611–617.
44. Narendranath, G.; Prakash, J.U. Optimization of circularity error with Taguchi for SAE-4130 considering surface responses in Wire-EDM machining. *J. Basic Sci. Eng.* **2024**, *21*, 532–545.
45. Kadam, T.; Abdul, R.M.; Yelamasetti, B. An experimental study on roundness error in wire EDM for ferro materials. *Mater. Today Proc.* **2021**, *46*, 843–848. [CrossRef]
46. *STN EN ISO 12781-2:2011-08 (01 4408)*; Geometrical Product Specifications (GPS)—Flatness-Rectangular Grid Extraction Strategy. Available online: https://www.iso.org/standard/53625.html (accessed on 3 February 2025).
47. *STN EN ISO 12181-1:2011*; Geometrical Product Specifications (GPS)—Roundness. Part 1: Vocabulary and Parameters of Roundness. Available online: https://www.iso.org/standard/53620.html (accessed on 3 February 2025).
48. *STN EN ISO 4291:1985*; Methods for the Assessement of Departure from Roundness—Measurement of Variations in Radius. Available online: https://www.iso.org/standard/10135.html (accessed on 3 February 2025).
49. Nowicki, R.; Oniszczuk-Świercz, D.; Świercz, R. Experimental Investigation on the Impact of Graphite Electrodes Grain Size on Technological Parameters and Surface Texture of Hastelloy C-22 after Electrical Discharge Machining with Negative Polarity. *Materials* **2024**, *17*, 2257. [CrossRef]
50. Straka, L.; Corny, I. Simulation and Optimization of Surface Roughness and Process Performance during Machining of HSS by Micro-WEDM Technology. *Micromachines* **2024**, *15*, 372. [CrossRef]

51. Rani, S.S.; Sundari, V.K.; Jose, P.S.H.; Sivaranjani, S.; Stalin, B.; Pritima, D. Enrichment of material subtraction rate on Eglin steel using electrical discharge machining process through modification of electrical circuits. *Mater. Today* **2020**, *33*, 4428–4430. [CrossRef]
52. Singh, V.; Sharma, A.K.; Goyal, A.; Saxena, K.K.; Negi, P.; Rao, P.C.S. Electric discharge machining performance measures and optimisation: A review. *Adv. Mater. Process. Technol.* **2024**, *10*, 517–530. [CrossRef]
53. Singh, D.P.; Mishra, S. Effect of different reinforcements in wire electric discharge machining of various geometrical profiles in metal matrix composites. *Int. J. Interact. Des. Manuf.* **2024**, *18*, 351–373. [CrossRef]

symmetry

Article

Topology Optimization, Part Orientation, and Symmetry Operations as Elements of a Framework for Design and Production Planning Process in Additive Manufacturing L-PBF Technology

Slobodan Malbašić [1,*], Aleksandar Đorđević [2,*], Srđan Živković [3], Dragan Džunić [2] and Vlada Soković [4]

1 Department for Defence Technologies, 11000 Belgrade, Serbia
2 Faculty of Engineering, University of Kragujevac, 34000 Kragujevac, Serbia; dzuna@kg.ac.rs
3 Military Technical Institute, 11000 Belgrade, Serbia; srdjan.zivkovic@mod.gov.rs
4 Military Academy, University of Defence, 11000 Belgrade, Serbia; vlada.sokolovic@va.mod.gov.rs
* Correspondence: slobodan.malbasic@mod.gov.rs (S.M.); adjordjevic@kg.ac.rs (A.Đ.)

Abstract: This paper investigates the possibility of the application of different optimization techniques in the design and production planning phase in the metal additive manufacturing process, specifically laser powder bed fusion (L-PBF) additive technology. This technology has a significant market share and belongs to the group of mature additive technology for the production of end-use metal parts. In the application of this technology, there is a space for additional cost/time reduction by simultaneously optimizing topology structure and part orientations. Simultaneous optimization reduces the production time and, indirectly, the cost of parts production, which is the goal of effective process planning. The novelty in this paper is the comparison of the part orientation solutions defined by the software algorithm and the experienced operator, where the optimal result was selected from the aspect of time and production costs. A feature recognition method together with symmetry operations in the part orientation process were also examined. A framework for the optimal additive manufacturing planning process has been proposed. This framework consists of design and production planning phases, within which there are several other activities: the redesign of the part, topological optimization, the creation of alternative build orientations (ABOs), and, as a final step, the selection of the optimal build orientation (OBO) using the multi-criteria decision method (MCDM). The results obtained after the MCDM hybrid method application clearly indicated that simultaneous topology optimization and part orientation has significant influence on the cost and time of the additive manufacturing process. The paper also proposed a further research direction that should take into consideration the mechanical as well as geometric, dimensioning and tolerances (GDT) characteristics of the part during the process of ABOs and OBO, as well as the uses of symmetry in these fields.

Keywords: topology optimization; build orientation; time and cost optimization; additive manufacturing process planning; symmetry operation; MCDM

1. Introduction

The modern market imposes new requirements for products. In order to meet these requirements, it has been important to overcome certain limitations that exist in the design and production of these products. In addition to that, the modern market also requires companies to launch innovative, high-quality products to the market quickly and cost-effectively.

In connection with the design, it is necessary to improve existing or develop new design capabilities that will enable the design of parts with increased performance, complex design, and simplified structure in a short time and in a cost-effective way.

To design parts with the mentioned characteristics, it is necessary to use production technologies that can ensure the rapid production of parts (requires a quick release to the market) and to enable production in small quantities as well as to respond to requests for personalized products. Also, it would be of great benefit if the production technology could produce complex functional and hierarchical structures, a faster distribution of products to the end user, and the optimization of the production process through the elimination of redundant tools, as well as digital data storage. It seems that additive manufacturing technologies could provide most of these requirements.

In situations characterized by increasing product complexity, tighter development budgets, and a competitive business environment, manufacturers are required to better understand product behavior during the design phase. The usual approach meant that after the end of the design phase, the initial design was moved to a dedicated group of simulation experts for further design iteration and optimization. It turned out that this approach was not good because it creates bottlenecks and slows down process efficiency. One of the requirements is that it is necessary to solve as many challenges as possible, in connection with the validation and constraints for performance and manufacturability, even in the design phase.

These conditions impose the need for companies to look for solutions to overcome these issues. A key strategy to implement simulation into the broader workflow is to put simulation-driven design early in the development cycle. This helps in reducing operating costs by preventing time and money spent fixing design flaws in later stages. Benefits of simulation design applications early in the development process are as follows [1]:

- Better achievement of the quality targets (prior to verification and testing it is possible to simulate new design under different conditions (vibration and pressure) and based on the preliminary results some structural issues could be fixed early in the design process);
- Meeting customers' expectations (time-to-market, zero defects, performance, cost expectations, etc.);
- The creation of cost-effective products (for example simulation in a virtual environment can decrease costs of creating physical prototypes, etc.).

Also, it should be noted that there are case studies in which the prototypes need to be made. After the optimization process, the prototype could be made using one of the methods of additive technology, which is becoming economically more profitable compared to the traditional approach.

The advantages and some disadvantages of PBF technology were explained in [2,3]. Several positive aspects were highlighted, including the possibility of creating functional metal prototypes, capability of building complex shapes and structures, production of end products with high parts accuracy (including high material mechanical properties and integrating functional design), production of different components in one build job, increased design freedom, fabrication of the lightweight parts as a result of topological optimization, consolidation of the parts into one assembly, etc.

Among the shortcomings, the following stand out: part size limits and slow deposition rates; costs (of machines and powder material) make this technology still expensive, but there are signs that this trend is decreasing; the reliability of the processes is still in question (due to material defects, part distortion, and residual stress); etc. In addition to the above mentioned [4,5] add the following: poor surface integrity and marks from removed support structures, a staircase effect on inclined features, and the requirement for post processing and further finishing of all functional surfaces. The advantages of additive technology in relation to conventional production from the aspect of design and production are considered by [6]. Traditional production methods are still represented in the production of various products, of greater or lesser complexity. However, if a comparative analysis between traditional and additive technology were to be made, it comes to the conclusion that additive manufacturing has certain advantages.

In order to clarify and understand the terminology, terms such as 3D printing, rapid prototyping, direct digital manufacturing, rapid manufacturing, and solid freeform fabrication are often used to describe AM processes [7]. AM is the potentially disruptive manufacturing technology in which a structural component is fabricated layer by layer via digital information [3]. The AM processes are divided into the following seven categories according to [8]:

1. Vat photopolymerization including stereolithography (SLA) and direct light processing (DLP);
2. Material jetting;
3. Binder jetting;
4. Material extrusion including fused deposition modeling (FDM) and FFF (fused filament fabrication);
5. Powder bed fusion (PBF) including selective laser sintering (SLS), selective laser melting (SLM), and direct metal laser sintering (DMLS);
6. Sheet lamination including laminated object manufacturing (LOM);
7. Direct energy deposition (DED) including 3D laser cladding and wire arc additive manufacturing (WAAM).

Among the additive technologies developed so far, technologies for the production of metal parts known as MAM (metal additive manufacturing) stand out. According to [9], there are three primary technologies relevant for metal-based AM: directed energy deposition (DED), PBF, and binder jetting. All of these technologies have their relative advantages to certain applications based on material compatibility and manufacturing limitations. MAM technologies enable the production of complex structures with near-net shape capabilities (processes that aim to produce products that are close to the final shape) from different types of metal powders.

Depending on the energy source, the PBF technology is classified into two groups: laser powder bed fusion (L-PBF) and electron beam powder bed fusion (EB-PBF). The subject of the further investigation and explanation is L-PBF techniques. The L-PBF techniques are known as selective laser melting (SLM), direct metal laser melting (DMLM), or direct metal laser sintering (DMLS), according to [10]. The L-PBF techniques are an additive manufacturing technology intended for the production of metal parts (using metal or alloy powder). L-PBF is the process where a laser beam is used to fuse the metal powder particles on the powder bed [11]. The system of tree chambers (supply chamber, powder bad chamber, and collector chamber) and recoater provides manipulation with powder. Powder material is deposited on the powder bed (with recoater), the laser beam selectively fuses the deposited powder particles based on the layer profile, then the platform is lowered by a predefined layer thickness, and the same process is repeated until the whole part is finalized [12].

The L-PBF technology has reached its mature stage, and now it can produce functional end use parts, not only prototypes [9]. Also, there are several constraints that need to be addressed during the part design phase (minimum thickness, overhangs, holes, builds orientations, etc.). If these constraints exceed their limits, it would cause some failures during the manufacturing stage [13].

Additive manufacturing has gone through a certain development path from the initial focus on the production of prototypes to the production of parts in small series with a tendency towards occupying a larger market share in the segment of large-scale production. Certain obstacles have been overcome on that development path, but there are still segments in this process that could be optimized and improved, and the planning process is certainly one of them.

Additive technologies are characterized by the fact that there is a reduction in process steps, which indicates that the total number of processes and resources required could be significantly reduced, which ultimately leads to the simplification of processes [14]. All of these facts lead to the conclusion that it is necessary to carry out detailed planning of the process, from the design phase to the production of the final part.

Challenges in AM Process Planning and Research Gaps

Companies that have acquired additive technology for their business are facing some challenges in the planning of the design and production process for AM. Regarding the additive manufacturing planning process, it is still questionable how to establish a relationship between various process parameters and final part quality (GDT properties and mechanical properties). This is still a popular research goal. The reason is that the 3D printing process is characterized with several process deficiencies, like poor geometry, dimensional accuracy, deteriorated surface finish, part shrinkage, pores and micro-cracks, and residual stress-induced defects, which affect the design of the requirements for the finished product.

In addition to the production process, the key factor is also the mechanical part itself. A mechanical part is usually a multi-feature mechanical part (MFMP) which carries on the production and design knowledge. In order to solve the mentioned problems [15] considered additional improvements in the planning phase with the aim of reducing costs, through the part orientation process that affects the quality of the part or individual functional surfaces, i.e., through supports that have a significant effect on production costs. The author also mentioned the problem of the available space of the working chamber, and in that sense, the presented work considers the procedure for separating the parts and their orientation (PBF additive technology was applied), all with the aim of obtaining a cost-effective process. The developed procedure for the automatic separation of parts, taking into account the aspect of costs, reduced production costs by 54% [15].

The tendencies in the development of additive technologies go towards more efficient planning of the additive manufacturing process and the optimization of production parameters in order to obtain a final product of high performance, with optimized characteristics and produced in an optimized way. The key elements that provide additional value are topological optimization, parts consolidation, and the simultaneous optimization of several process parameters and the integration of topology optimization with additive technologies.

Simultaneous optimization involves considering the impact of topological optimization on production costs, together with the process optimization of additive manufacturing parameters to reduce total costs [16]. In [16] the simultaneous optimization of topology and process parameters (laser power and speed), which have a certain influence on the microstructure of the material, are demonstrated. This considers the production of metal parts using one of the PBF techniques. It is estimated that certain savings in the costs of additive manufacturing could be achieved. The benefits provided by the optimization of the topology were considered through the reduction in the volume of material used, which indirectly reduces the material costs. The final results indicated that by applying this approach, the total production costs were reduced by 15% and the production time was improved by 21% [16].

In [17] the simultaneous optimization of build orientation and topology for self-supported enclosed voids in additive manufacturing based on the heat-flux approach was proposed. With the implementation of the "surface slope dependent heat flux through a domain integral of a Heaviside projected density gradient" to the density-based topology optimization algorithm, the problem of designing self-supported enclosed voids in additive manufacturing was solved.

The simultaneous optimization of the geometric orientation and support structure were applied in [18]. The authors concluded that building direction has an important role in production cost determination. Innovation in this study was the introduction of an efficient thermal model for TO in AM and the integration of the support structures into the design and optimization process.

Topological optimization and its integration with additive manufacturing were also analyzed by [3]. The author states that additive manufacturing and topological optimization were carried out separately for several years, but the latest integration of topology optimization and additive technologies arises for the following reasons:

- Topology optimization parts have very complex shapes and cannot be manufactured with traditional technological processes. Instead they can only be produced by additive manufacturing technologies.
- The other reason is the fabrication cost, which is proportional to the material and weight, which benefits additional technologies.
- Topology optimization produces parts with enhanced performance and mechanical properties, without compromising the strength of the part.

There are a plethora of papers focusing their research on optimization problems in additive manufacturing. The best results were obtained by simultaneously optimizing at least two parameters. One of them is topology optimizations, and the others are either process parameters or part orientations at the build plate. However, when it comes to the part orientation, none of the authors explicitly described the choice of orientation in a situation where you have the option to choose between the solution offered by applying software (through, for example, an optimization orientation module) and an alternative solution based on the operator's experience.

This paper presents the simultaneous topological optimization and the part orientation on the working plate (the selection of the orientation of the part is based on the feature recognition method and symmetry operations) in order to obtain more cost-effective production with PBF technology. In addition to the symmetry operation, special focus is placed on the analysis and selection of the part orientation on the work plate in a way that, in addition to the orientation solution provided by the applied software, alternative solutions based on the operator's experience were also applied.

For the conduct of the optimization process (the selection of the best part orientation), a new framework for design and process planning is proposed with the inclusion of MCDM hybrid methods. Four build orientating factors were considered, including the total build time, total build cost, support volume, and support surface.

After the introductory discussion, the next section analyzes the planning process of designing and manufacturing parts by additive technologies, and presents a new framework for the AM planning process, as well as different parameters affected by L-PBF additive technology. In the following section, the theoretical assumptions and the importance of applying finite element (FE) analysis and topological optimization in the design of parts is explained. Also, the feature recognition method, which is used when choosing ABOs, is specially explained. The next section is dedicated to the symmetry elements and application of the symmetry principle in additive technology. The following section is devoted to the application of the selected MCDM process (hybrid approach) in determining the OBOs.

The subsequent section presents the proposed framework for the AM planning process together with a case study where the planning process and optimization techniques were applied on a real example from practice. Finally, at the end of the paper, there is a section where results from the case study are summarized and a section committed to the conclusions, where advantages and disadvantages of the presented approach and guidelines for further development of this topic are given.

2. The New Framework for the AM Planning Process

For the purpose of the explanation of the planning process for additive manufacturing, several papers dealing with the topic are analyzed. Also, a new framework for the AM planning process is presented.

In [4], the focus is on the importance of creating effective process planning for the designed component/part. The SLM process is considered; however, the proposed approach is general and can be applied to any additive manufacturing dealing with the production of metal parts. The author states that the application of additive technology methods requires a close integration of the design process and production planning.

The presented model for planning design and production consists of the following three processes:

1. 3D model preparation for printing;

2. Quality assessment and inspection activities;
3. The planning of necessary finishing processes.

One of the conclusions is that a proper, detailed, and thorough planning process, with the inclusion of all necessary factors in the 3D model, contributes to the increase in costs and production time. Based on this conclusion, key parameters (costs and production time) have been used as build orientation factors in the MCDM process performed in this paper.

Process planning from the aspect of part orientation is also discussed in [6]. It is pointed out that in comparison with conventional manufacturing processes, the process planning of AM processes is totally different, and that planning is a key step in order to ensure the quality of the final product. The methodology of planning and design for the additive manufacturing process presented in this work consists of the following steps:

- Design stage: the definition of the conceptual model, analyzing the function of the part, and the topology optimization of the conceptual model. The output is a geometry model with the required mechanical properties.
- The preparation of the set of process parameters (build orientation, layer thickness, build orientation, the design of the support structure, and the selection of AM methods, materials, and machines) in order to perform the manufacturing process simulation based on the predefined parameters.
- The implementation and analysis of the simulation process. In order to obtain the most optimal solutions, it is possible to carry out several iterations.
- Manufacturing stage: the author suggests using an "in-process" monitoring system with the possibility of analyzing collected data and detecting some defects. Corrective actions could be sent back via a feed-back loop all the way to the planning or even design phase.

The presented paper further specifically analyzed the planning process for build orientation due to the significance of build orientation on the quality of the end-use part. The author emphasizes that before choosing the orientation of the part on the working plate, it is necessary to perform functional analysis and topological optimization.

Another interesting deduction about the planning process is given in [19]. Based on the preliminary analysis of several scientific papers, the authors, in their technical report, conclude that the additive manufacturing planning process consists of a set of standard operations (repairing, orientation, supports, slicing, and tool path generation), whereby in the continuation of their conclusions, they state the following:

- There are some common things/problems for all of the printing technologies (mesh repair, shape orientation, slicing, tool path planning, and external supports). But how these blocks are related to each other "is still considered as an open problem".
- These blocks cannot be treated separately—3D printing would be more predictable if the mutual relationship among these blocks could be better understood.
- Shape orientation is a strategic choice "spanning form the building time to surface quality".

According to [19], the term process planning (PP) refers to the definition of a set of individual production operations required for the production of a defined part on a specific machine.

The paper [20] offers a framework for formalizing the additive manufacturing planning problem at the operational level and can be used as a reference for focusing and solving problems related to the efficient planning of this production. The idea arose from the fact that additive manufacturing introduces a set of problems specific to this technology, such as the correct orientation of parts or placing several heterogeneous parts in the same build cycle, which are not solved by traditional approaches to planning and production scheduling. The review of the literature by the author revealed that there is no uniformity in the identification and solution of the mentioned problems in the application of additive technologies.

In [21], the focus is on two phases (product design and production for L-PBF technology) with the aim of their optimization. Product design is based on the integration of topological optimization and process simulation tools in order to redesign the initial product. The production process is based on the systematic use of simulations in order to prevent errors in production due to possible temperature variations in metal parts, as well as the occurrence of residual stress and deformations. The whole approach is based on the application of an integrated project-production PLM platform that enables the digital flow of information (digital process chain).

Based on the above presented analysis, as well as practical experience, a new framework for AM planning is proposed. The new framework is conceived with the idea of being cost effective, and providing as much information as possible, available in the planning phase, for decision-makers. Also, the framework should enable the use of modern optimization and decision-making tools, in order to facilitate these processes based on relevant data. The proposed framework for the AM planning process consists of two phases (Figure 1):

- The first phase (product design)—input in this phase is the CAD model, and the phase includes the application of different simulation tools for obtaining relevant data for part design exploration and validation. It contains the selection of parts and the implementation of FE analysis and topological optimization (TO). FE analysis is performed before and after topology optimization due to the fact that structural response before and after TO are not the same. The outcome of the product phase is a topology-optimized part, which is also the input element to the second phase.
- The second phase (process design)—this phase includes the activities of initial build preparation through the generation of ABOs, estimation/calculation of the optional optimization objectives (for the case study in this paper, these include build cost, support volume, and support surface), and the selection of the OBOs as well as the virtual machine setup to obtain appropriate data for the decision matrix (for example, build time, as is the case in this paper). The outcome of this phase is the optimal build (OB) orientation for the TO part.

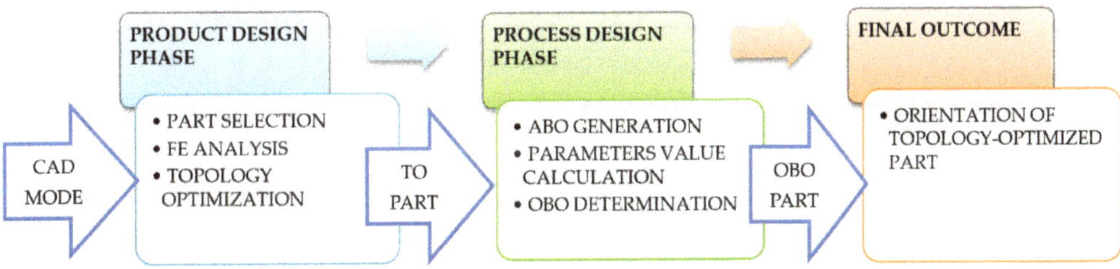

Figure 1. The overview of the new framework for the AM planning phase.

In the following sections, theoretical explanations and benefits of the proposed optimization and decision tools in the AM planning phase are given.

Part and Process Parameters Affected by Additive Technology During the Planning Process

In the process of planning additive manufacturing, it is important to know the relationships and determine how individual elements of the additive process (design, build orientation determination, etc.) affected part and process parameters.

The most important parameters, presented in [10], within the additive manufacturing process planning are shown in Table 1.

A comprehensive analysis of the set of parameters affected by the L-PBF technology was performed in [22,23]. In [22], some of the main parameters affected by build orientation were grouped as follows:

- Mechanical characteristics of the part (strength, hardness, elongation, residual stress, and material fatigue).
- Finished product accuracy (GDT and volumetric errors): Due to the possible phenomenon (shrinkage, curling, and distortion), GDT arise. Volumetric errors occur as

a consequence of the construction of the part in layers, that is, due to the phenomenon known as the "staircases effect".

Table 1. Process planning stages with main parameters.

Design for AM	Function analysis
	Topology optimization
Build orientation determination	Cost
	Mechanical properties
	Geometry properties
Support structure generation	Building process
Slicing strategy	Layer thickness
Scanning path generation	Filling pattern
	Feed rate planning

In [23], the criteria affected by the build orientation are also analyzed and divided into three categories (within which there are several subcategories): (1) technical criteria (surface properties, geometrical properties, mechanical properties, thermal and electrical properties), (2) economic criteria (cost and time), and (3) indirect criteria (resources status and logistics).

This paper analyzes topology optimization and build orientation effects on the total build cost, total build time, and support volume and surface. The reason for this is that in the planning phase it is hard to define mechanical and GDT properties of the part unless historical data about these properties is available in advance, or we have at our disposal some mathematical model or prediction algorithm that has already been developed. Also, another constraint is the fact that the OEM (original equipment manufacturer) has already proposed optimal process parameters and suggested they should not be changed during printing time. Anyway, these constraints should not in any way affect final results.

3. Optimization Elements in a New Framework for L-PBF Design and Production Process Planning

This section is dedicated to the theoretical assumptions and the importance of applying topological optimization and finite element (FE) analysis in L-PBF design and production process planning. The build orientation problem based on the feature recognition method, which is used when choosing ABOs, is explained too.

3.1. *Topology Optimization*

Topology optimization is a structural design technique that optimizes the shape and material component of a detailed part using the finite element analysis technique and various optimization techniques [16]. Bearing in mind that each final element of the structure is defined as a variable, this method enables a flexible approach and obtains a very complex final geometry.

There are several algorithms based on mass distribution optimization. The most common, and at the same time the most effective, are the solid isotropic material with penalization (SIMP) and bi-directional evolutionary structural optimization (BESO) algorithms, according to [16]. In addition to the optimization algorithm based on the mass distribution (density-based method), there are other optimization algorithms: the evolutionary structural optimization (ESO) and the level set method (LSM), as well as moving morphable components (MMC), and moving morphable voids (MMV) [24].

Topological optimization consists of the following steps, shown in Figure 2 and based on [3,25]:

- Three-dimensional modeling using appropriate CAD softwares.

- Topology optimization: Based on the results of a structural analysis of the stress distribution, the optimization algorithm removes the material from the area where the load distribution is less.
- The remodeling of the initial CAD model based on the results of the optimization results.
- Design verification using the FEM (finite element method) or in some cases prototype testing.

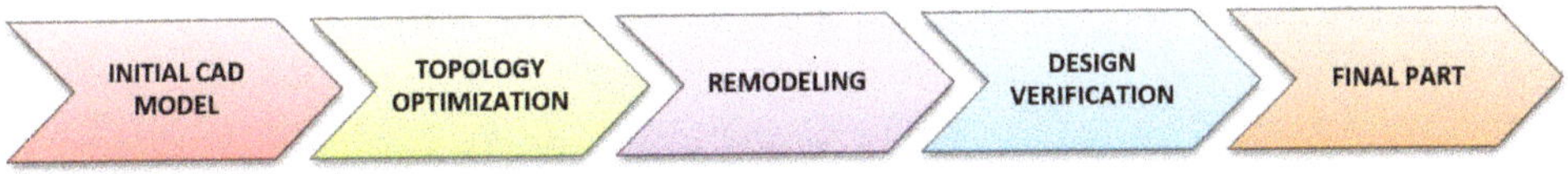

Figure 2. Steps in the topology optimization process.

There are several advantages and application areas of structural/topological optimization, according to [25], which are as follows:

- Great freedom in design because it pushes the boundaries of flexibility, and ensures improved efficiency.
- Topological optimization can generate several design variations allowing for different applications.
- Topological optimization focuses on elements of stiffness, weight, material distribution, and lightweight construction (a lighter component of equal or greater strength).
- It contributes to less wastage of materials (due to optimal material distribution).
- It shortens the time to market.

Recently, multidisciplinary optimization is also applied, meaning that the designed structure must meet multiple goals and certain limitations such as complex loads, resistance to thermal effects, limited stresses, displacements/movements, etc. [25]. The integration of materials, structures, processes, and their performance is very important and necessary in order to achieve high-performance products, multifunctional characteristics, and a light structure [26].

Topology optimization finds an increasingly intensive application in the design of parts. The latest adaptation of this method within the DfAM concept refers to the inclusion and limitations of support structures and internal structures, i.e., in the design of cellular structures, structures with internal channels, and in medicine for the production of supports for various tissues. The integration of topology optimization and additive manufacturing achieves most of their advantages and potential, and the approach as such finds more and more applications in modern production for special purposes.

3.2. Finite Element Analysis

FE analysis has an important role in the design phase of the product because it can highlight structural and strength problems and detect their location. It is used to check CAD models that have already been designed, and which could be modified in case any problems arise. Simulation analysis early in the design phase (instead of performing experiment after part is produced) could be of great help for the definition of correct orientations of the part in order to achieve the best possible mechanical and structural performances. The color coding system is applied by the FE software in order to better understand the outcomes of the analysis (the results of a von Mises stress analysis). Cold colors represent the part volume with low stress and warm colors represent the part volume with high stress, while the red color represents the maximum stress field [27].

3.3. Alternative and Optimal Build Orientation

The orientation of parts has a strong influence on many characteristics of the parts' production, and in this sense, certain rules, procedures, and design frameworks are necessary [28]. In the terminological sense, it is the process of orienting parts around the coordinate axes within the working space of the machine itself. This terminology does not refer to the translation of parts around the coordinate axes of the machine.

A key fact in considering the orientation is that the orientation of the parts is directly related to the achievement of certain quality characteristics in the final product. Some of them are dimensional accuracy, surface quality, shape accuracy, manufacturing costs, manufacturing time, the bending of components, stability, the volume of the supporting structure, the utilization of working space, the reduction in post processing, and the possibility of removing the supporting structure.

All of these quality characteristics depend on the geometry of the parts. The orientation of the parts of certain geometry in the working space allows for reaching the optimal values of these characteristics, and it is basically a process of multi-criteria optimization in order to achieve a compromise.

According to [29], there are two methods for choosing alternative orientations of parts on the machine working plate:

- Computation-based methods or direct search method: based on the direct application of nonlinear optimization-based methods and population-based optimization algorithms.
- Evaluation methods: first, a set of ABOs is defined and then an OBO is generated from this set. The generation of ABOs is realized by the following techniques: feature recognition [30], convex hull generation [31], quaternion rotation [32], and facet clustering [33].

For supporting the decision-makers and solving planning problems which include multiple (usually conflicting) criteria, one of the most appropriate solutions is the MCDM model. There are two types of MCDM models: multi attribute decision-making (MADM) models for ranking alternatives and multi objective decision-making (MODM) models [34]. According to [32], there are several differences between the decision-making methods and optimization methods:

- In decision-making methods, the alternatives are pre-selected, meaning that the space for decision-making is limited. On the contrary, for optimization methods, the decision space is not limited but is actually infinite.
- Optimization methods provide better quality output results because the objective function reaches the maximum value, but it is not suggested to use too many evaluation criteria due to the convergence problem.
- The decision-making methods do not have the convergence problem, and can take into account as many criteria as needed. This means that decision-making methods can treat part orientation more systematically.

3.4. Feature Recognition Method

In this section, the feature recognition method for choosing alternative orientations has been explained in more detail, based on the analysis of several key works.

The geometry of the part is a key carrier of information. In additive manufacturing, the "key" geometries are influenced by the whole set of parameters (the orientation of the part, overhangs that require an additional support structure, process parameters, scanning strategy, etc.) and thus form the desired mechanical and geometrical and dimensional tolerances (GDT) characteristics in the final product. This clearly indicates the importance of the selection of "key" surfaces and alternative/optimal orientations in additive manufacturing. Key explanations and a case study related to the generation of alternatives and selection of optimal orientations is provided in [35].

The selection of key geometries based on the method of feature-based recognition (the recognition of "key" shapes) is used in this paper. In this sense, for the generation of the final number of alternative orientations, a concept based on the recognition of the geometry of the part and the available knowledge base (lessons learned) regarding the orientation of the part on the working plate is applied, and the choice of the optimal orientation is completed by the application of the MADM method.

One of the first authors who defined the orientation of critical surfaces was [30]. In [33], it is suggested that it is important to define the coordinate system towards which parts are oriented, and that the z-axis points in the building direction. Also, in [30], the orientation for some specific surfaces/features like cuts, protrusions, and shells is proposed. In addition to the above mentioned, the defined rules for orientation are given in [36], along with other critical features (overhangs orientation, features with two planes, features with holes, and features with an inclined plane).

Based on the foregoing it can be concluded that the best GDT values of the parts can be obtained through the maximization and minimization of the following characteristics (in the phase of choosing alternative orientations):

- Maximize the horizontal and perpendicular faces in the z-axis (build direction).
- Maximize the cylindrical feature (hole, cone, etc.) axis in line with the z-axis.
- Maximize the total number of curved surfaces in the horizontal plane.
- Maximize the base surface area.
- Minimize angular/inclined surfaces.
- Minimize the overhanging area.
- Minimize the trapped volume.

The influence of the orientation of the parts on the working plate on the production costs (for the L-BPF process) was discussed in [37] and the following three important facts were stated:

- The orientation influences the amount of supporting structures;
- The orientation influences the height of the component in the building space;
- The orientation of the component influences the number of parts that can be manufactured simultaneously.

Based on the conducted experiment, which includes two different orientations of the same components on the working plate, it is concluded that it is necessary to first calculate the production costs of the relevant parts (based on the selected orientations) and then choose the most favorable solution. Based on this conclusion, the cost parameter has been chosen for further analysis in this paper.

4. Symmetry Operations and Symmetry Elements

Symmetry is often used to describe the balance in proportion and objects, to better understand the geometry, or to create balance. The symmetry operation is related to symmetrical transformation, and as a consequence, creates one object at the end of that movement [38]. The geometrical representation of one or more symmetry operations involves the symmetry elements. Symmetry operations and symmetry elements are presented in Table 2. The combination of these elements produces complex symmetry elements like roto-inversion axes, screw axes, and glide planes.

Table 2. Symmetry operations and their corresponding symmetry elements.

Symmetry Operation	Symmetry Element	Geometrical Entity
Rotation	Rotation axis	Axis
Inversion	Center of inversion	Center or point
Reflection	Mirror plane	Plane
Translation	Translation vector	Vector

Symmetry elements can be spotted in other objects too. Further implications and the connection of the symmetry principle to additive technology are given below.

4.1. Symmetry in ADDITIVE Technology

The subject of the research in [39] is the application of symmetry elements in other additive technologies like wire arc additive manufacturing, WAAM (sub-categories of the directed energy deposition, DED, technology). The basis for the research is the fact that material deposition techniques, combined with different process parameters, have a negative impact on the mechanical properties and dimensional and structural accuracy of the part. A comparison of the shape and physical characteristics of the weld bead for two techniques (overlapping and oscillating) is performed through the symmetry coefficient including the calculation of a symmetry coefficient for both techniques. The ultimate goal is to understand the impact of symmetry on the quality and performance of DED fabricated parts. The conclusion is that the industrial application of this approach can contribute to the improvement of quality in DED technology, as well as the acquisition of data (part geometry, symmetry, and process parameters) in real time and their implementation in the control loop will significantly improve process adjustment and its optimization.

The work in [40] proposes the simultaneous or parallel application of multiple printers (the focus is on FFM 3D technology) with the objective of reducing printing time. The proposed algorithm enables the uniform division of a large part (exploits reflective symmetry to partition models) as well as optimum balanced use of multiple printers in parallel so that there is no idle work. Although the parallel printing of divided parts is insisted on, considering the price of the printer, as well as the effort that should be invested in the preparation and monitoring of parallel printing, the presented application of symmetry for parallelization remains at the laboratory level for now.

The study in [41] is based on the fact that mechanical performance of 3D printed ceramic materials depends on both the part orientation and printing angle with respect to the loading direction. The influence of symmetry in the structure of the material (under tensile loading) is considered at the filament scale. On the basis of the tests conducted (SEM micrographs of fractured patterns), it is concluded that orientation and loading direction have a positive influence on the structure of the material.

The work in [42] presented a practical application of the generative method in creating complex and materially heterogeneous geometry, which can be manufactured as such by additive techniques. The generative method implied that, on the basis of the initially generated user-guided input mesh and the defined set of planes (as a framework for all subsequent operations), a symmetrical mesh is formed, which is then recursively re-applied for a certain number of iterations until obtaining the final product. Complex geometries are driven by the symmetry principle. The additive technology that was considered is photo polymerization.

In [43], the relationships between symmetry and additive manufacturing workflow (design/redesign process, manufacturing stage, and post processing—final part geometry and microstructure) were analyzed in detail and a connection was established. The use of symmetry in additive technologies is recognized with the aim of optimization. As for the additive technologies focus was on the analysis of properties and process control.

4.2. Interaction of Symmetry Elements as a Potential Solution for Part Orientation

In order to explain the application of symmetry elements as a potential solution to the part orientation at the working plate, the model from [39] will be used to explain how objects can be oriented in different directions.

Since symmetry elements and operations interacting with each other (simultaneously or consecutively) produce new symmetry elements and symmetry operations, this phenomena can be used for part orientation.

The application of a twofold rotation axis and an inversion (a center of inversion located on the axis) on the selected object is presented in Figure 3.

An explanation and conclusion of the presented interaction is as follows:

- Starting object (A) is performing twofold rotation (180 degrees Celsius) around axis (1) to obtain object (B), then object (B) performs inversion and is converted to object (C). If we applied the inversion operation to object (A) we would obtain object (D).

- It can be noticed that objects (C and D) are reflected images of objects (A and B), respectively. This means that, as a result of two symmetry elements, a new one (mirror plane perpendicular to the axis) emerges.

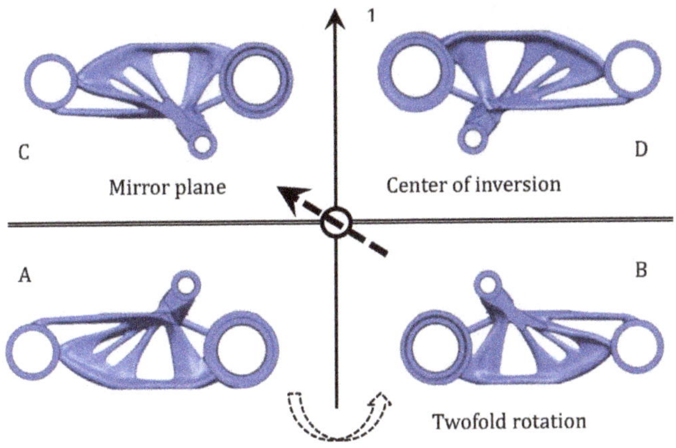

Figure 3. Scheme of twofold orientation and an inversion: position **A**—original position, position **B**—rotation of object A for 180 degrees of Celsius (mark twofold rotation in the direction of the curved dotted arrow), position **C** inversion of object B (in the direction of straight dotted arrow), position **D**—reflection of object B as well as inversion operation of object A.

If the order of symmetry elements is replaced (inversion of object A to obtain object D, and then a twofold operation: from abject A to get object B and from object D to get object C), at the end, the same results will emerge.

This brings us to the conclusions mentioned in [39], "any two symmetry operations applied in sequence to the same object create a third symmetry operation, which applies to all symmetrically equivalent objects".

5. Application of Multi-Criteria Decision-Making Process in Selecting the OBO

Based on the research available in [44], it was concluded that orientation problems (including the set of criteria) can be solved by quantitative methods and techniques, but these methods and techniques still do not have full application in advanced production technologies such as additive manufacturing. The authors suggest the improvement of quantitative and qualitative methods in such a way as to include the perspective of the decision-maker, which has been done in this paper.

Based on the research conducted in [45], the author concluded that the identification of the right MCDM techniques from the list of potential candidates is a difficult task. They conducted some research and assessment on different MCDM approaches in the selection of the manufacturing process. In the final conclusions, for the selection of the manufacturing process, they pointed to the VIKOR and TOPSIS methods as adequate methods because of the number of alternatives and parameters to be processed, adequacy in supporting a group decision, and agility during the process of decision-making.

In [46], it is emphasized that single MCDM techniques cannot yield the best solution for a designated problem, so they proposed a hybrid model which can improve "the weakness and amplify the effect and reliability of solutions acquired through single models". For their problem (prioritize risks in self-driving vehicles), the author proposes the application of hybrid multi-criteria decision-making methods employing the AHP, TOPSIS, and VIKOR.

A methodical review of the application of MCDM methods in material selection is presented in [47]. It was concluded that the combination of two or more MCDM methods is the best possible approach in the material selection process.

The MCDM helps a decision-maker to select or rank alternatives, but the first step is to quantitatively or qualitatively evaluate a group of selected criteria. The MCDM framework features four elements: alternatives (choices), criteria (attributes), weights of criteria (comparative significance), and ranking of alternative's against criteria [48]. MCDM methods were classified according to the following three criteria:

- Methods of ranking by the closeness score.
- Methods of ranking by the original score.
- Methods of ranking by the positive score.

The distinctive characteristic of methods from the first group (VIKOR and TOPSIS belong to this group) is the calculation of negative and positive ideal solutions, and then the calculation of the distances between alternatives and calculated solutions. The ranking is achieved based on the proximity to the ideal solution [48].

In [49], it is confirmed that, for situations characterized by multiple alternatives and conflicting criteria, the best solution is to use multi-attribute decision-making (MADM) techniques instead of MCDM. The authors especially mentioned the use of the AHP method for determining objective weights.

In [50] it is suggested possibility to use other available MCDM techniques, instead of TOPSIS and VIKOR, since ideal or anti-ideal solution may not exist in real case scenario.

In [51], it is emphasized the importance of the process of generating attribute weights directly from the decision-makers through interview, discussion, or questionnaire. They also classified weight assignment methods into three categories: subjective, objective, and hybrid.

Based on the above analyzed literature, it was concluded that the optimal solution to be applied for problem resolution in this paper is a hybrid MCDM approach in which the following three methods are used:

- The analytic hierarchy process (AHP) for defining the weight of attributes, and for the ranking of the ABO.
- The technique for order of preference by similarity to ideal solution (TOPSIS).
- VIKOR (multi-criteria compromise ranking).

The complete flow of the MCDM process for choosing the OBO that will be applied in this paper is shown in Figure 4.

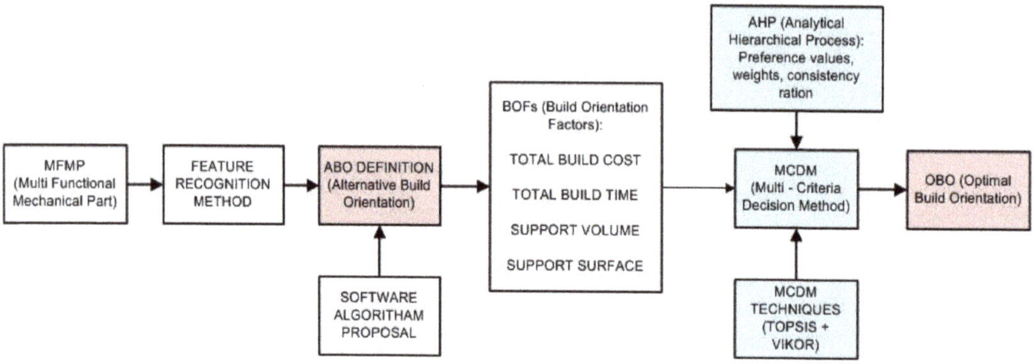

Figure 4. Scheme of the proposed MCDM process.

5.1. Analytical Hierarchy Process (AHP) Method

When it comes to the analytical hierarchy process (AHP) method, [51] explains that the majority of analyzed authors chose this method because of its ability to take into consideration, in a simple way, both quantitative and qualitative data in the decision-making process, as well as the consistency measurement for the pairwise comparison of the alternatives/parameters, which helps to minimize the inconsistency of decision-makers.

With the ability to use a multi-level hierarchical structure of objectives, criteria, and alternatives, the AHP is a structured technique and decision support tool which can be used to solve complex decision problems. In the calculation process, AHP considers the priorities of each criterion [52]. In a hybrid approach, this method is predominantly used for defining the weight of attributes (parameters or build orientation factors in additive manufacturing).

For the mutual comparison of criteria, and the construction of a pairwise comparison matrix, the Saati scale is used, defined on the interval (9, 1/9). In order to check the consistency of weights and priorities, the AHP method calculates the consistency rate, which should be less than 0.1 if consistency exists; otherwise, the preference value needs an additional check [53].

5.2. Technique for Order of Preference by Similarity to Ideal Solution—TOPSIS

This method is based on the concept that the optimal alternative has the least Euclidean distance from the positive ideal solution and the greatest distance from the negative ideal solution. Both solutions (positive and negative) are hypothetical solutions for which attribute values have the most desirable or least desirable values in relation to other criteria. The best ranked solution maximizes the benefit criteria and minimizes the cost criteria, according to [54–56].

The simplicity of the method as well as the ability to solve problems regardless of the number of criteria and alternatives is a main benefit of the TOPSIS [52].

The TOPSIS method tends towards universality in the selection of attributes for all AM methods, and it connects the evaluation of attributes with their characteristics and benefits [57].

5.3. Multi-Criteria Compromise Ranking—VIKOR

The name of the method multi-criteria compromised ranking is a Serbian name, but in English this method can be called criteria optimization and compromised solutions. VIKOR ranks alternatives and determines the optimal solution by comparing alternatives with respect to the measure of closeness to the ideal alternative. The VIKOR method is suitable for decision-making problems where attributes of a quantitative nature prevail, according to [50–52]. Further, in [52], it is said that what makes VIKOR one of the popular methods in the MCDM concept is the simplicity of the algorithm and ability to give almost accurate results.

In [58], it is emphasized that this method is suitable for use because it is a less complex method for application than others, the method is stable to changes in certain parameters, and similar results are obtained by applying more complex methods (in their case, the ELECTRE method).

6. Case Study

The case study is performed based on the proposed framework for the AM planning process (Figure 1) and an explanation is given in [21]. Each proposed step is executed in detail, including the use of adequate software with an explanation of the results.

6.1. Case Study—Phase One: Part Selection

Regarding the selection of the part for production, the selection rule related to the metal AM defined by [59] is applied. The basis for selecting a part for optimization (and subsequent production) can be an existing CAD model or a new part is designed. In the first case, the focus is on its redesign for additive manufacturing and the possibility of applying topological optimization, Figure 5.

In addition to the above, it can also be noted that the generally accepted rule among manufacturers is that if a part can be economically produced using a conventional production process, that part should probably not be produced using AM technology.

A necessary condition regarding the selected part is that it is required to have certain information related to function, loading conditions, constraints, frequency requirements, etc. The above information is necessary in order to carry out the following steps: FE analysis and topological optimization.

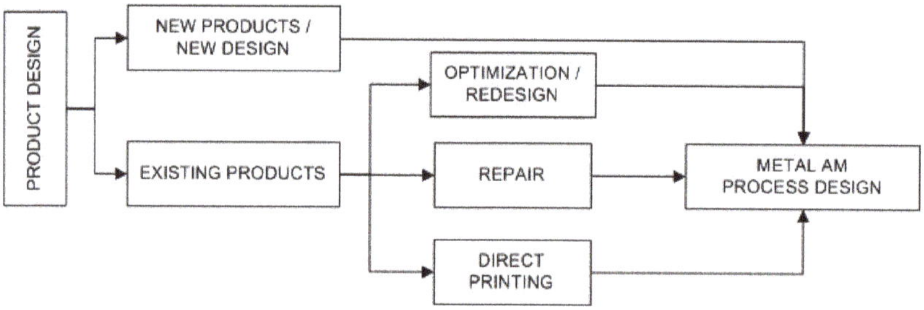

Figure 5. Procedure for the selection of the AM part for optimization/production.

In this case study, a part that is an element of the suspension system of an unmanned vehicle is considered, which serves to connect the fixed and moving parts of the suspension system and carries certain loads shown in Figure 6.

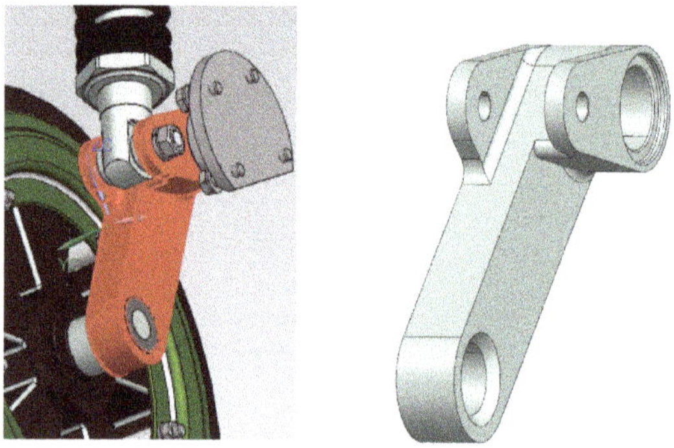

(**a**) (**b**)

Figure 6. MFMP display: (**a**) as part of suspension system and (**b**) individually.

It is a multi-functional mechanical part (MFMP), and in that sense, it consists of a certain number of planes as well as cylindrical surfaces whose axes are parallel to each other. The part is originally designed for fabrication using traditional production technologies and now it is planned to be produced using additive technology (L-PBF).

6.2. Case Study—Phase One: Perform Finite Element Analysis

The FE analysis is necessary to define the actual loads and possible displacements of the considered part, caused by the defined loads. To carry out FE analysis, it is important to define several initial parameters and then perform the simulation. The following parameters are defined in the FE analysis module (the solver is the Siemens NX NASTRAN add-on module):

- The type of load (the analysis type is structural, and the solution type is static 101 and single constraint).
- Network parameters (3D Tetrahedral Mesh).
- The definition of load characteristics (fixed and variable load was selected) as well as the magnitude and direction of action (constraint type: fixed constraint and rotation, and load type: Force 1250 N).

After defining the actual loads and forces and executing the simulation, the obtained solution was analyzed through the analysis of the load distribution and displacement of the structure. The FE analysis was performed for metal alloy steel with the following characteristics: ultimate tensile strength: 276 MPa, yield strength: 138 MPa, density: 7.829 g/c^3, and Poisson's ratio: 0.288.

Von Mises criteria are among the most commonly used criteria for checking yield conditions in different engineering fields. Figures 7 and 8 below show the results from the FE analysis for the following:

- A minimum and maximum displacement of 0.059 mm.
- Stress analysis (calculated stress is 79.15 MPa), which indicates that the part has an FOS (factor of safety) higher than 1.5.

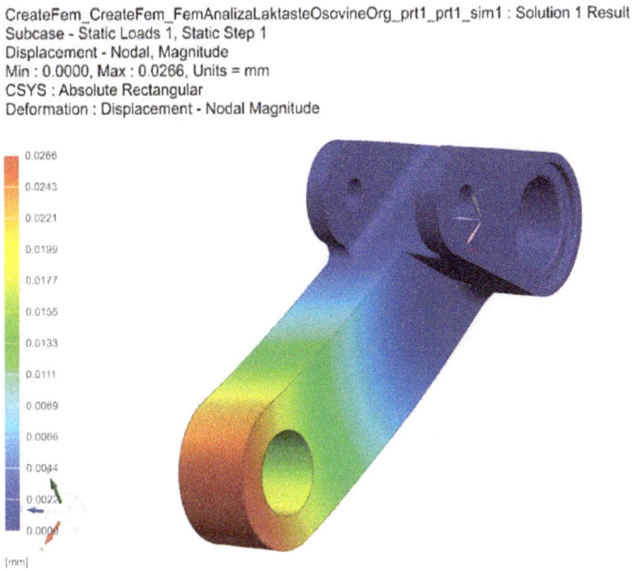

Figure 7. Color distribution of the displacement on the model.

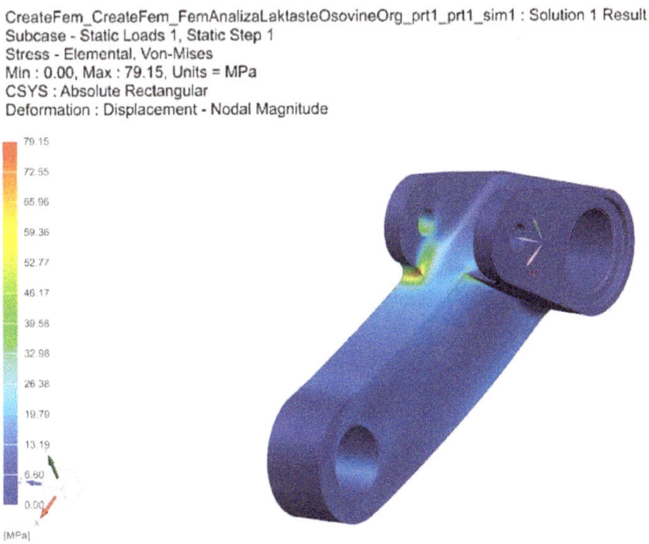

Figure 8. Von Mises equivalent stress field before optimization.

Regarding the values of yield stress (138 MPa) and maximal calculated yield stress (79.15 MPa) it can be concluded that the initial CAD design satisfies all stress constraints. This is the starting point for our optimization procedure. The current results of displacements (0.0266 mm) show that this part movement is not of great significance to the selected part and can be accepted.

6.3. Case Study—Phase One: Performing the Topology Optimization

Topology optimization is a powerful tool for obtaining the optimal design based on a finite element model of the design space and loading conditions. Topological optimization is carried out in several iterations until the optimal result is obtained. For performing the topology optimization, the NX Topology Optimizer (Siemens, Minhen, Germany) add-on module is used.

The first step is to define the design space. We started with the part body (main body in Figure 9) that will be used to define the functional requirements and our design space. Then the construction bodies are defined (shafts in Figure 9). These bodies represent areas where we want to keep a certain material around them while at the other areas of the part material are removed or optimized.

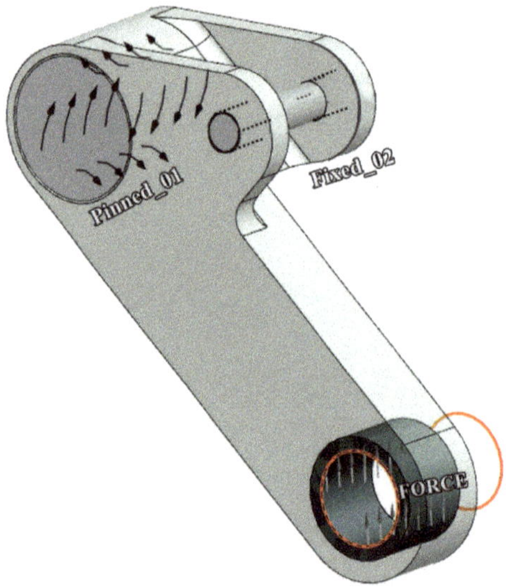

Figure 9. Initial design (main and construction bodies) for topology optimization.

The next step in performing topology optimization is to define displacement constraints and load cases (Figure 10). In this situation, the real case scenario is transferred to the software for further analysis and simulation. There are two pinning constraints (places where the part is fixed to the other suspension components—in this case, the shock absorber) and one load force positioned on the lower hole of the part where the shaft from the wheel is connected. During the movement force from the ground is pointed upward onto the shock absorber.

After all parameters are set, we can start topology optimization, and see final results (Figure 11). Topology-optimized parts are 70% lighter in weight then the initial parts (0.21 g compared to 0.698 g). This is almost max mass reduction. Since the topological optimization software could affect the geometry, the weight, and the strength of the final designs, this needs to be taken into account.

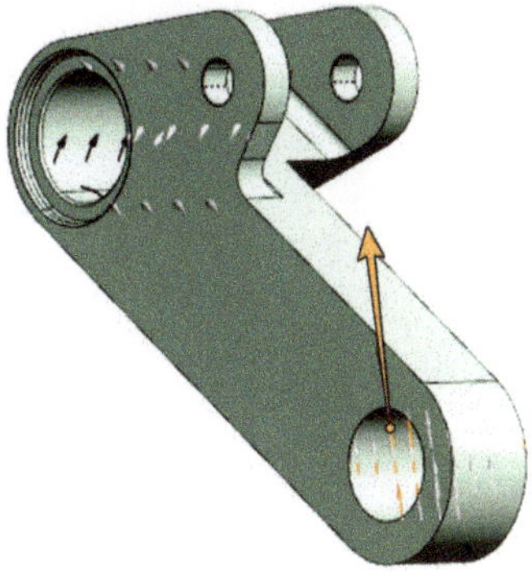

Figure 10. Fixed constraints and load force (arrow): load force is pointed upward transferring ground movement up to the next support were shock absorber is attached.

Figure 11. Final optimized part.

After performing FE analysis on the optimized geometry, Figures 12 and 13 show the displacements and stress results, as well as how the optimized part fits into the assembly (Figure 14). The results from Figures 8 and 13 are compared with initial data for the metal alloy (the optimized part form Figure 13 has a max stress of 61.16 MPa and the original part from Figure 8 has a max stress of 79.15 MPa).

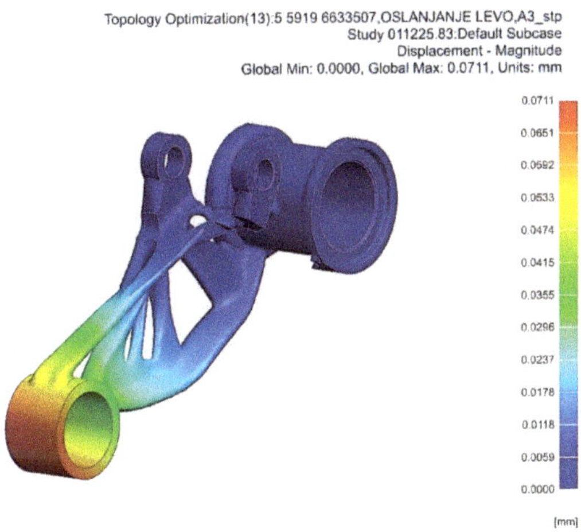

Figure 12. Displacement on the optimized part.

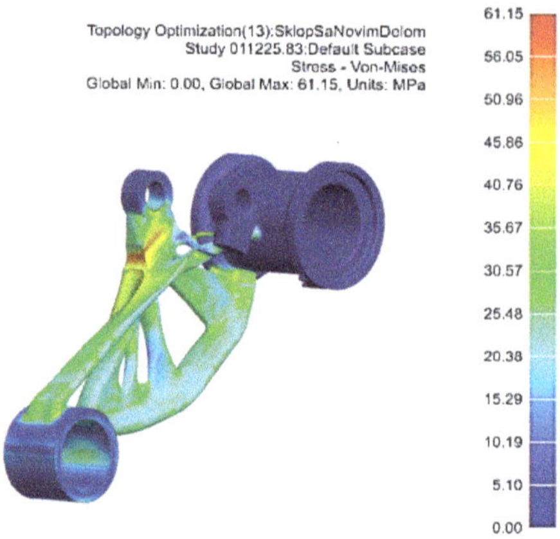

Figure 13. Von Mises equivalent stress after optimization.

Figure 14. Optimized part mounted into the assembly.

After optimization, the stress level should be at the same level or higher than in the initial design, due to the material removal in some areas of the part. In the presented case, the stress level is smaller and this requires an additional analysis of the following elements: the shape of the mesh (for example, use of hexagonal instead of tetrahedron mesh), the direction and the size of the load force, the nature of internal deformation, etc. The resulting stress after topological optimization is lower than the yield strength of the chosen metal alloy (61.16 MPa compared to 138 MPa).

6.4. Case Study—Phase Two: Process Design

The first step is the generation of ABOs. The following approach was used to select an adequate orientation on the working plate:

- Accepting the proposal generated by the software program (Materialize Magic) and selecting two options (orientations 1 and 2 in Figures 15a and 15b, respectively).
- Other orientations were proposed by the experienced operator by applying the concept of feature recognition (Figure 16) and symmetry operation to the selected part (orientations from 3 to 7 in Figure 17 from (a) to (e), respectively).

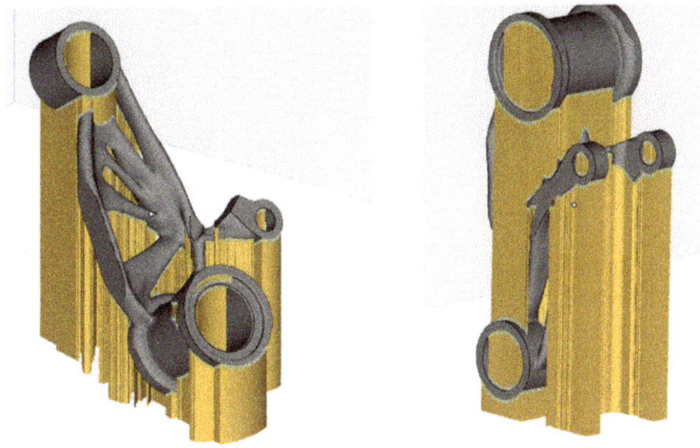

(**a**) (**b**)

Figure 15. Part orientation on the working plate chosen from the software solution: (**a**) orientation that provide minimum support surface (**b**) orientation that minimize XY projection.

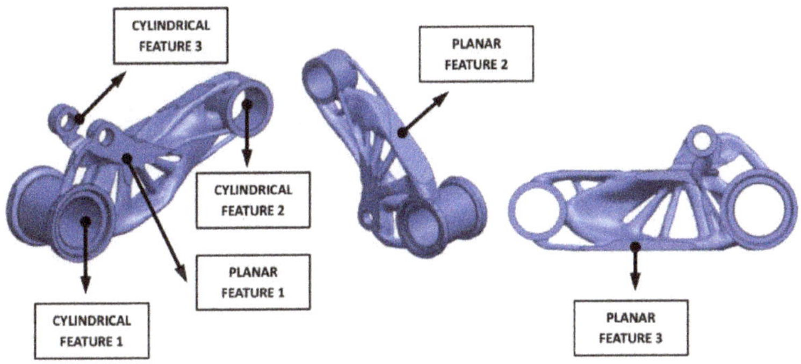

Figure 16. Feature recognition on the optimized part.

6.4.1. Generation of ABOs: Selection of Software-Defined Orientations

Together with the possibility of fine-tuning part orientation using the adequate rotation tool, software Materialize Magics also provides some advanced options (through the use of the orientation comparator) where three orientations can be calculated (the shortest Z height, the smallest support surface, and the smallest maximum XY section orientation from the original CAD file). Two software solutions have been chosen for further comparison: (1) minimum support surface (orientation 1 in Figure 15a) and (2) minimize XY projection (orientation 2 in Figure 15b), and data related to these orientations were inserted into the decision matrices. Associated data and positions of these two chosen orientations on the working plate are shown in Figure 15. The other two parameters (total build cost and time) were extracted from printing machine software (virtual print preparation) and mathematical calculation, respectively.

6.4.2. Generation of ABOs: Selection of Orientations Defined on the Basis of Feature Recognition

In the feature recognition method, the features of the input model for the topology-optimized model are recognized (Figure 16).

Based on the recognition process, the following five possible positions were considered (Figure 17 from (a) to (e)):

- Planar feature 3 parallel with the working plate (orientation 3 in Figure 17a).

- Planar feature 3 rotated 180 degrees (orientation 4 in Figure 17b).
- Cylindrical features 1 and 2 have parallel axes with the build direction (orientation 5 in Figure 17c).
- Planar planes and the working plate are under some degree (orientation 6 in Figure 17d).
- Parallel axes of the main cylindrical feature with the build direction (this orientation corresponds to the minimum Z-height orientation from the software) (orientation 7 in Figure 17e).

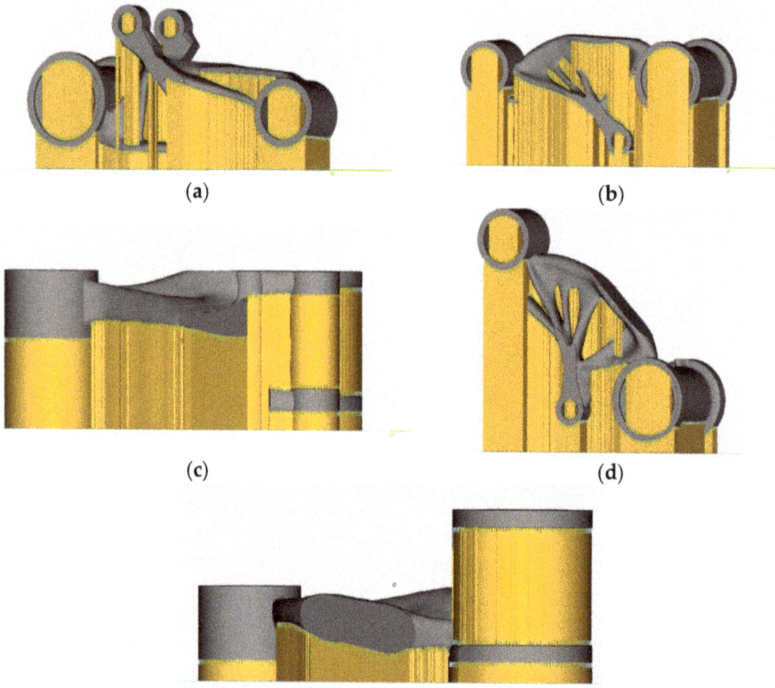

(**a**) (**b**) (**c**) (**d**) (**e**)

Figure 17. Part orientation on the working plate defined by the operator: (**a**) planar feature 3 parallel with working plate (orientation 3), (**b**) planar feature 3 rotated 180 degrees (orientation 4), (**c**) cylindrical features 1 and 2 have parallel axes with build direction (orientation 5), (**d**) planar planes and working plate are under some degree (orientation 6), (**e**) parallel axes of main cylindrical feature with build direction (this orientation corresponds to the minimum Z-height orientation from the software) (orientation 7).

6.5. Case Study—Phase Two: Application of Symmetry Operations and Elements

The analytical approach, presented in [39], will serve as the basis for the analysis of the application of symmetry in this paper.

When selecting ABOs using the feature recognition method, symmetry elements are found in the position (a, c) shown in Figure 18. These positions are defined as an asymmetric unit—meaning that the next positions (b, e) will be established from these asymmetric units and symmetrical operations to be performed, as follows:

- The original object (asymmetric unit—a) is immediately inverted from its original position through the center of inversion. These operations result in a symmetrical new object (b) which is positioned 180 degrees opposite to the original one, Figure 18a.

- The same symmetry operation (inversion) is applied to the asymmetric unit (c) in order to obtain symmetry part (e), Figure 18b.
- Other positions on the working plate do not have elements of symmetry.

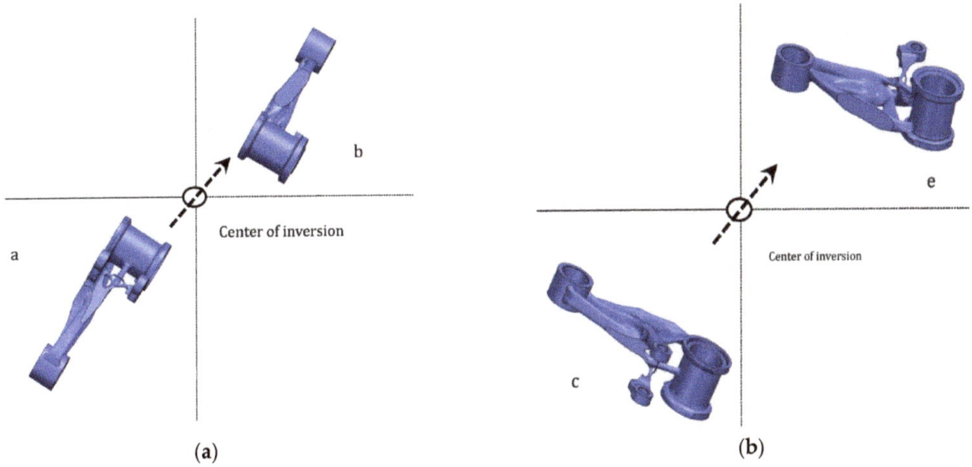

Figure 18. Use of symmetry operation in part orientation for the presented case study: (**a**) Object a inversion to obtain symmetrical new object b which is positioned 180 degrees opposite to the original one (in the direction of the dotted arrow). (**b**) The same symmetry operation (inversion) is applied to the asymmetric unit c in order to obtain symmetry part e (in the direction of the dotted arrow).

Furthermore, it is also important to cover the application of symmetry in post processing since decisions made in the previous planning stage have big influences on several aspects of the final part. So the application of symmetry can be viewed as a control activity for the following:

- Performing an analysis of GDT parameters of the final part through a comparison with the initial CAD model in order to obtain information about the occurrence of defective parts.
- Checking the existence of symmetrical formation (symmetry pattern) in the crystalline structure changes.

6.6. Case Study—Phase Two: Estimation of the Build Orientation Factors

In defining the OBOs, the first step is to determine parameters (BOFs—build orientation factors) influenced by the orientation of the part, and calculate them through mathematical calculation or extracting data from applied software.

In connection with the selection of adequate parameters, the most common parameters that are characteristic for additive manufacturing have been analyzed and refer to the state of the parts and some process parameters.

For the purposes of the case study, four parameters were chosen (print time, print cost, support volume, and support surface) on which the orientation has the greatest influence. Unlike mechanical parameters, the selected parameters are available in the planning phase, which makes the decision-making process easier. Other parameters listed above, which are not analyzed for the purposes of this paper, and which relate to GDT and mechanical characteristics, can be obtained in the planning phase through mathematical estimations or at the end of the printing process by measuring their values in the final product.

The amount of material for the supports is obtained from the Materialize Magics (Materialise, Leuven, Belgium) software for build preparation. Total build time was extracted directly from software that supports the printing machine, therefore, directly representing manufacturing/printing time. Materialize Magics provides automatic support generation and provide option for support to be later upgraded due to the design changes. Also, this software provides flexibility to adjust support geometry. For this case study, in order to provide part stability and to obtain better part quality, the support structure is generated by the combination of three support types: cones, contours, and blocks.

6.7. Case Study—Phase Two: Cost Calculation

Based on the analysis of the cost model given in [60–63] as well as data obtained from experienced operators on the machine, values were obtained for calculating the criteria of printing costs. Total printing costs are the sum of pre-processing costs, process (build) costs and post-processing costs. More explanations can be found in [63] and reference literature. For the purposes of this paper, only the costs in the process/build phase of the selected part were calculated. The total build costs of an individual part (consisting of machine, material, inert gas, and energy costs) are calculated according to the following formula:

$$C_{build}(P_i) = T_{build}(P_i) \times (C_{machine} + C_{inertgas}) + \rho \times V(P_i) \times C_{material} \times 1.1 + C_e \quad (1)$$

where

C_{build}—the cost of the building part with ith geometry (€/part);
P_i—ith geometry;
T_{build}—total build time (hour);
$C_{machine}$—machine cost per hour (€/hour);
$C_{inertgas}$—the cost of inert gas (euro/m^3);
V—part volume + support volume (mm^3);
ρ—the density of metal powder;
$C_{material}$—material cost (€/kg);
C_e—the cost of the energy consumed by the machine (euro).
Value 1.1—increase in material consumption by 10% of the non-recyclable powder.

The formula for printing costs also includes energy and machine operating costs. These costs are calculated as follows. Energy consumption costs are as follows:

$$C_e = E \times T_b \times E_R \quad (2)$$

where

C_e—the cost of the energy consumed by the machine (euro);
E—energy consumed by the machine (Kw);
T_b—total build time (hour);
E_R—energy cost rate (euro/Kw).

Total machine cost per hour $C_{machine}$ (€/part):

$$C_{machine} = \frac{\text{Machine purchase cost}}{h \times upt} + \frac{\text{Maintenance cost per year}}{upt} \quad (3)$$

where

Machine purchase cost (euro/part);
Maintenance cost per year (euro);
h—machine depreciation period (years);
upt—machine uptime (hours/year).

The data required for the calculation are partly obtained from publicly available data and part of the data was obtained by competent persons (operators and process engineers) from the laboratory where the simulation was carried out. The obtained data are entered into the decision matrices (Table 3—total build cost column).

Table 3. Decision matrices with measured values of defined BOFs.

Weights of Parameters	0.39	0.44	0.1	0.07
BOFs	**Total Build Time (Hour)**	**Total Build Cost (Euro)**	**Support Volume (mm^3)**	**Support Surface (mm^2)**
Orientation 1	12.18	488.10	55,773.19	2478.39
Orientation 2	13.42	539.77	68,668.50	2996.63
Orientation 3	7.48	305.26	36,808.62	4349.03
Orientation 4	8.47	314.10	57,164.96	4359.99
Orientation 5	6.57	273.10	40,606.09	2906.05
Orientation 6	10.43	419.50	47,515.68	3527.98
Orientation 7	5.49	224.37	20,799.81	2986.16

6.8. Case Study—Phase Two: Application of the MCDM Process in the Selection of the Optimal Build Orientation

The OBO is selected from the set of ABOs that are generated by the orientation of the part in the machine's working space (seven orientations are defined). For each selected orientation, the values for the four selected criteria (total build time, total build cost, support volume, and support surface) were either calculated or extracted from the adequate software applied in the planning phase, and hence, the decision matrices presented in Table 3 were obtained.

Each criterion has its own weighting factor that represents the aggregated values of the decision-makers. In the process of defining the weights of the selected criteria, six experts dealing with additive manufacturing (decision-makers—managers, engineers, and operators) were included in the survey. The AHP method was used for the mutual comparison of parameters and the results are shown in Table 3 (weights of parameters).

For the selection of the optimal orientation, a hybrid approach was applied using well-known multi-criteria optimization methods: TOPSIS and VIKOR, as described in [47,48].

With the TOPSIS method, the ranking of alternatives is performed based on the relative proximity of the alternative to the ideal solution, the best alternative having the biggest value. With the VIKOR method, the compromise solution is the one that is closest to the ideal solution, and in this regard, the alternative with the smallest value (distance) is also the best alternative.

All selected criteria (four in total) are of the cost type, bearing in mind that they all generate certain costs that affect the total cost of printing with the L-PBF method. This is significant due to the execution of the normalization process in both selected methods.

The obtained ranks of alternatives (Table 4 columns Rank) using two methods (TOPSIS and VIKOR) indicate that there is a maximum matching of results, which indicates consistency. On the other hand, the results obtained with the VIKOR method, for the first and last alternative (Table 4, values 0 and 1 in the Value VIKOR column), match with the negative ideal and positively ideal solution, respectively.

Table 4. Final results and ranking of alternatives.

ABO	Value TOPSIS	Rank TOPSIS	Value VIKOR	Rank VIKOR
Orientation 1	0.194636443	6	0.815373669	6
Orientation 2	0.078339882	7	1	7
Orientation 3	0.72514405	3	0.281743461	3
Orientation 4	0.64579099	4	0.38159598	4
Orientation 5	0.83972765	2	0.150856111	2
Orientation 6	0.382107763	5	0.622690496	5
Orientation 7	0.969407647	1	0	1

6.9. Sensitivity Analysis

The MCDM methods are tools for reducing subjectivity in the decision-making process. Each MDCM method characterizes a different mathematical approach, and in some cases, the application of different methods to the same problem can give different solutions, meaning that alternative choices do not depend solely on the chosen criteria but also on the chosen MCDM method. Although the results largely depend on the applied methods and analyzed problems, it is also necessary to conduct a sensitivity analysis (an analysis of the final results on the change in the value of certain parameters).

The sensitivity test can be carried out in the following ways: changing the weight value of the criterion and by the analysis of the final results obtained from the two MCDM methods. Given that the VIKOR method gives compromise solutions, the result obtained in Table 4 was checked against two conditions: (1) the condition of sufficient advantage and (2) the condition of sufficient stability.

The optimal alternative does not fulfill the condition of sufficient advantage in relation to the second alternative (the value difference 0.151 is less than the condition 0.33 = 1/(number of alternatives − 1)), but it fulfills the additional conditions from point 2.

Namely, the best alternative should meet the following conditions:

- That it is the best according to two metrics (S—overall benefit and R—individual deviation). Table 5 indicates that the optimal solution has the best scores for S and R values, hence this condition is fulfilled.
- That it ranks as first for values (υ = 0.25, υ = 0.25, and υ = 0.75, where "υ" represents the balancing factor between the overall benefit—S and maximum individual deviation—R). Table 6 shows that the optimal solution maintains the first place for different "υ" values.

Table 5. Ranking of alternatives according to S, R, and Q metrics.

	S Rank		R Rank	υ = 0.625	Q Rank
0.7700	6	0.3679	6	0.815373669	6
0.9493	7	0.4400	7	1	7
0.3138	3	0.1128	3	0.281743461	3
0.4177	4	0.1466	4	0.38159598	4
0.1784	2	0.0680	2	0.150856111	2
0.6100	5	0.2722	5	0.622690496	5
0.0189	1	0.0189	1	0	1

Table 6. Ranking of alternatives according different balancing factor (υ) values.

	υ = 0.25	υ = 0.50	υ = 0.75	Rank
OR-1	0.823445935	0.818064424	0.812682913	6
OR-2	1	1	1	7
OR-3	0.246566062	0.270017661	0.293469261	3
OR-4	0.334539392	0.365910451	0.397281509	4
OR-5	0.130287266	0.143999829	0.157712392	2
OR-6	0.610017676	0.618466222	0.626914769	5
OR-7	0	0	0	1

Since there are zero changes in the ranking of alternatives, with different values for the balancing factor—"υ", the results are stable and without sensitivity to the changes in the balancing factor "υ".

7. Discussion of the Results

The selection of adequate parameters and implementation of hybrid MCDM approaches in the AM decision process poses significant challenges.

The analysis of the weighting coefficients indicates the importance of the first two parameters (costs and time), while the remaining two parameters have no significant importance, according to experts. Regardless of the obtained results of the expert assessment, these two parameters still significantly contribute to the increase in costs (through the increased consumption of materials for the construction of the supporting structure).

All of the selected parameters are of the cost type and their value should be as low as possible, which is certainly a matter of compromise, and this is indicated by the best alternative, which has the lowest values for each parameter.

The values of the selected parameters can be obtained (either through software or calculations), even in the production planning phase, so it is not necessary to carry out the experimental phase, which shortens the preparation time and costs and provides enough information for quality decision-making.

The choice of parameters does not have to be limited to the proposed four parameters, and depends on several factors: the choice of additive technology, the choice of software for production preparation, the needs of the decision-maker, the operator's experience, etc.

The results showed that the best chosen alternative (orientation 7) is the choice of an experienced operator who based his attitude on the basis of the feature recognition approach and symmetry operations. From a more detailed analysis of the proposed software solution, that was not selected as an option in the case study (orientation solution that require minimum Z height); it can be concluded that it also matches the operator's proposal (as an orientation option). However, it is important to point out that the ranking positions from 2 to 5 (Table 3) are related to the orientations chosen by the operator, which points to the conclusion that we cannot fully rely on the software's suggestions, i.e., that it is necessary to know the basic settings of additive manufacturing planning as well as the geometry of complex parts in order to choose an adequate orientation.

The results show that there are no deviations in the rankings of the alternatives using both chosen methods, so there is a maximum correlation.

The analysis from the aspect of the printing cost parameter indicates that in the selected formula there are no costs of supporting equipment (for example, a gas generator), but only the cost of the machine is included. On the other hand, the costs as well as the operating parameters of the machine can vary, which affects the final price, so the obtained production price does not always have to be a correct reference.

8. Conclusions

This paper is focused on the planning process of the design and production of metal parts by additive manufacturing (PBF-L technology). Despite certain disputable facts (about cost and time), it was determined that this technology offers certain advantages compared to traditional production technologies, which were also explained in the introductory part of the paper.

It is proposed that the planning process be carried out in two phases (product and process design), within which the sub-phases must be carried out in the manner and in the order as specified. The limitation of the proposed framework is that its complete application requires knowledge of several areas (topology optimization and FE analysis, mathematical solutions for build parameters calculation, etc.) and that requires teamwork. The simulation of process planning and production is time consuming, requiring the implementation of very expensive software tools as well as expert knowledge in L-PBF additive technology. Speaking about L-PBF technology operators, users or experts in this field need to be familiar with machine technology, feedstock powder materials, post-processing activities, etc. In practice, this process is still labor intensive. The proposed framework is targeted towards application in L-PBF technology, but with minor changes (mainly depending on the chosen additive technology) it is applicable for the product and process planning of other available additive technologies.

Also, the paper emphasizes the importance of simultaneous topological optimization and the optimization of the orientation of the part on the working plate, with the aim of achieving an optimal solution (obtaining the final product of reduced mass that satisfies the initially set structural loads, in a cost-acceptable range).

The benefits of using simulation tools in the earliest stage of conceptual design are in providing a set of data which can help in the systematic exploration and analysis of product design (can reduce redesign in later stages and reveal systematic flaws) as well as in the analysis of process parameters in order to avoid any build cycle failures.

Based on the analysis of the literature in the field of planning, design, and production with additive technologies, it has been concluded that there is a lack of work in which the orientation of the parts on the working plate (proposed by an implemented software solution) is compared to that of an experienced operator.

Four parameters (total build time, total build cost, support volume, and support surface) were chosen as parameters for comparing the proposed orientations (seven in total), which clearly and explicitly represent the characteristics of PBF-L additive technology. The list of parameters is not final and can be arranged according to expectations and the final goal.

Although not considered in this paper, since we suppose that process parameters are constant, special attention should be paid to the concept of uncertainty, different sources of uncertainty, and uncertainty propagation in the additive manufacturing processes. Uncertainties (in process parameters, printing conditions, etc.) affect the consistency in the quality of the final product and the repeatability of the additive process. Uncertainty can be modeled by applying certain uncertainty quantification techniques in order to find optimal process parameters and increase the resilience of the whole additive process.

Related to the applied MCDM methods (TOPSIS and VIKOR), and since these methods are based on a computation of ideal or anti-ideal solutions that may not exist in a real case scenario, this should provoke researchers to look for the implementation of other MCDM methods like ANP, PROMETHEE, COPRAS, MABAC, etc. Nevertheless, the hybrid approach in the application of the MCDM method, with the inclusion of the expert opinions and the implementation of sensitivity analysis, is a suitable and valuable tool for obtaining quality decision.

In addition to the clear promotion for the acceptance of additive technology for the production of metal parts, there are some other contributions that this paper brings to wider scientific community:

- A description of efficient and economically acceptable process planning for additive manufacturing production of metal parts.
- The paper points out the importance of applying simulation tools in the process of planning and designing products based on which additional information can be obtained for decision-making processes.
- The paper also points to the fact that parts designed for production using traditional production technologies could be good candidates for production through additive manufacturing.
- The paper emphasizes the importance of including the experienced operator in the design phase and selection of production parameters for additive production. This further means that available software solutions and algorithms can provide additional but not decisive help in the decision-making process to initiate production.
- There are spaces for the application of symmetry operations and associated elements in the part orientation problem. Symmetry operations (rotation, inversion, mirror, and transition) can provide a different orientation of parts on the working plate which can further contribute to the detailed understanding of the influence of the part orientation on the mechanical and geometrical characteristics of the produced parts. This work

pointed to some of the stages in the additive manufacturing workflow (product and process design) where symmetry can contribute significantly.

Further steps in the research should be directed to the analysis of the influence of the orientation of the part on the geometric, dimensional, and mechanical characteristics. In this sense, it is necessary to carry out a specific experiment in which these characteristics would be measured, and then, based on the obtained results, alternatives would be compared and the best one selected. With this approach, a full cycle of the additive production of metal parts would be reached.

The presented phases in the preparation and planning of the additive manufacturing process together with the hybrid MCDM approach as a decision-making tool present a good framework for implementation in other similar processes.

Author Contributions: Conceptualization, S.M., Methodology, S.M. and S.Ž.; software, S.M. and S.Ž.; formal analysis, A.Đ., D.D. and V.S.; data curation, S.M., A.Đ., S.Ž., D.D. and V.S.; investigation, S.M. and S.Ž.; resources, S.M. and S.Ž.; writing—original draft preparation, S.M.; writing—review and editing, A.Đ., S.Ž., D.D. and V.S.; visualization, S.M., S.Ž. and D.D.; supervision, A.Đ., D.D. and V.S. All authors have read and agreed to the published version of the manuscript.

Funding: This research received no external funding.

Data Availability Statement: The data are available upon reasonable request from the authors.

Conflicts of Interest: The authors declare no conflicts of interest.

References

1. Sarah Gaffney. The Benefits of Simulation-Driven Design. 2022. Available online: https://resources.sw.siemens.com/en-US/white-paper-benefits-of-simulation-driven-design (accessed on 24 April 2024).
2. Sheng, H.; Xu, J.; Zhang, S.; Tan, J.; Wang, K. Build Orientation Determination of Multi-Feature Mechanical Parts in Selective Laser Melting via Multi-Objective Decision Making. *Front. Mech. Eng.* **2023**, *18*, 21. [CrossRef]
3. Prathyusha, A.; Babu, G.R. A Review on Additive Manufacturing and Topology Optimization Process for Weight Reduction Studies in Various Industrial Applications. *Mater. Today Proc.* **2022**, *62*, 109–117. [CrossRef]
4. Dotcheva, M.; Favrot, J.; Dotchev, K.; Zekonyte, J. Planning for Metal Additive Manufacturing. *Procedia Manuf.* **2020**, *51*, 710–716. [CrossRef]
5. Liu, Z. Economic Comparison of Selective Laser Melting and Conventional Subtractive Manufacturing Processes. Master's Thesis, Northeastern University Boston, Boston, MA, USA, 2017.
6. Luo, Z.; Yang, F.; Dong, G.; Tang, Y.; Zhao, Y.F. Orientation Optimization in Layer-Based Additive Manufacturing Process. In Proceedings of the ASME 2016 International Design Engineering Technical Conferences and Computers and Information in Engineering Conference, Charlotte, NC, USA, 21–24 August 2016.
7. Al-Ahmari, A.M.; Abdulhameed, O.; Khan, A.A. An Automatic and Optimal Selection of Parts Orientation in Additive Manufacturing. *Rapid Prototyp. J.* **2018**, *24*, 698–708. [CrossRef]
8. *ISO/ASTM 52900:2021*; Additive Manufacturing—General Principles—Fundamentals and Vocabulary. ISO (International Organization for Standardization): Geneva, Switzerland, 2021.
9. Dietrich, D.M.; Cudney, E.A.; Kenworthy, M. *Additive Manufacturing Change Management—Best Practices*; CRC Press, Taylor & Francis Group: Boca Raton, FL, USA, 2019.
10. Taghian, M.; Mosallanejad, M.H.; Lannunziata, E.; Del Greco, G.; Iuliano, L.; Saboori, A. Laser Powder Bed Fusion of Metallic Components: Latest Progress in Productivity, Quality, and Cost Perspectives. *J. Mater. Res. Technol.* **2023**, *27*, 6484–6500. [CrossRef]
11. Wang, H.; Fuh, J.Y.H. Metal Additive Manufacturing and Its Post-Processing Techniques. *J. Manuf. Mater. Process.* **2023**, *7*, 47. [CrossRef]
12. Özel, T.; Altay, A.; Kaftanoğlu, B.; Leach, R.; Senin, N.; Donmez, A. Focus Variation Measurement and Prediction of Surface Texture Parameters Using Machine Learning in Laser Powder Bed Fusion. *J. Manuf. Sci. Eng.* **2019**, *142*, 011008. [CrossRef]
13. Zhang, Y.; Yang, S.; Zhao, Y.F. Manufacturability Analysis of Metal Laser-Based Powder Bed Fusion Additive Manufacturing—A Survey. *Int. J. Adv. Manuf. Technol.* **2020**, *110*, 57–78. [CrossRef]
14. Gibson, I.; Rosen, D.; Stucker, B.; Khorasani, M. *Additive Manufacturing Technologies*, 3rd ed.; Springer Nature: Cham, Switzerland, 2021.
15. Reichwein, J.; Kirchner, E. Part orientation and separation to reduce process costs in additive manufacturing. *Proc. Des. Soc.* **2021**, *1*, 2399–2408. [CrossRef]
16. Ulu, E.; Huang, R.; Kara, L.B.; Whitefoot, K.S. Concurrent Structure and Process Optimization for Minimum Cost Metal Additive Manufacturing. *J. Mech. Des.* **2019**, *141*, 061701. [CrossRef]

17. Wang, C. Simultaneous Optimization of Build Orientation and Topology for Self-Supported Enclosed Voids in Additive Manufacturing. *Comput. Methods Appl. Mech. Eng.* **2021**, *388*, 114227. [CrossRef]
18. Haveroth, G.A.; Thore, C.-J.; Ausas, R.F.; Jakobsson, S.; Cuminato, J.A.; Correa, M.R. A Thermal Model for Topology Optimization in Additive Manufacturing: Design of Support Structures and Geometry Orientation. *Comput. Struct.* **2024**, *301*, 107453. [CrossRef]
19. Livesu, M.; Attene, M.; Spagnuolo, M.; Falcidieno, B. A Study of the State of the Art of Process Planning for Additive Manufacturing. 2016. Available online: https://irs.imati.cnr.it/reports/irs16-04 (accessed on 28 May 2024).
20. De Antón, J.; Villafáñez, F.; Poza, D.; López-Paredes, A. A Framework for Production Planning in Additive Manufacturing. *Int. J. Prod. Res.* **2022**, *61*, 8674–8691. [CrossRef]
21. Dalpadulo, E.; Pini, F.; Leali, F. Powder Bed Fusion Integrated Product and Process Design for Additive Manufacturing: A Systematic Approach Driven by Simulation. *Int. J. Adv. Manuf. Technol.* **2024**, *130*, 5425–5440. [CrossRef]
22. Di Angelo, L.; Di Stefano, P.; Guardiani, E. Search for the Optimal Build Direction in Additive Manufacturing Technologies: A Review. *J. Manuf. Mater. Process.* **2020**, *4*, 71. [CrossRef]
23. Wang, Y.; Zhong, R.Y.; Xu, X.; Wang, Y.; Zhong, R.Y.; Xu, X.; Wang, Y.; Zhong, R.Y.; Xu, X.; Wang, Y.; et al. A Decision Support System for Additive Manufacturing Process Selection Using a Hybrid Multiple Criteria Decision-Making Method. *Rapid Prototyp. J.* **2018**, *24*, 1544–1553. [CrossRef]
24. Tian, X.; Wu, L.; Gu, D.; Yuan, S.; Zhao, Y.; Li, X.; Ouyang, L.; Song, B.; Gao, T.; He, J.; et al. Roadmap for Additive Manufacturing: Toward Intellectualization and Industrialization. *Chin. J. Mech. Eng. Addit. Manuf. Front.* **2022**, *1*, 100014. [CrossRef]
25. Deepak; Sahini, K.; Ghose, J.; Jha, S.K.; Behera, A.; Mandal, A. Optimization and simulation of additive manufacturing processes: Challenges and opportunities—A review. In *Advances in Civil and Industrial Engineering*; Balasubramanian, K.R., Senthilkumar, V., Eds.; IGI Global: Hershey, PA, USA, 2020; pp. 187–209. [CrossRef]
26. Zhu, J.; Zhou, H.; Wang, C.; Zhou, L.; Yuan, S.; Zhang, W. A Review of Topology Optimization for Additive Manufacturing: Status and Challenges. *Chin. J. Aeronaut.* **2020**, *34*, 91–110. [CrossRef]
27. Matúš, M.; Križan, P.; Kijovský, J.; Strigáč, S.; Beniak, J.; Šooš, L. Implementation of Finite Element Method Simulation in Control of Additive Manufacturing to Increase Component Strength and Productivity. *Symmetry* **2023**, *15*, 2036. [CrossRef]
28. Leutenecker-Twelsiek, B.; Klahn, C.; Meboldt, M. Considering Part Orientation in Design for Additive Manufacturing. *Procedia CIRP* **2016**, *50*, 408–413. [CrossRef]
29. Qin, Y.; Qi, Q.; Shi, P.; Scott, P.J.; Jiang, X. Status, Issues, and Future of Computer-Aided Part Orientation for Additive Manufacturing. *Int. J. Adv. Manuf. Technol.* **2021**, *115*, 1295–1328. [CrossRef]
30. Pham, D.T.; Dimov, S.S.; Gault, R.S. Part Orientation in Stereolithography. *Int. J. Adv. Manuf. Technol.* **1999**, *15*, 674–682. [CrossRef]
31. Byun, H.-S.; Lee, K.H. Determination of the Optimal Build Direction for Different Rapid Prototyping Processes Using Multicriterion Decision Making. *Robot. Comput. Manuf.* **2005**, *22*, 69–80. [CrossRef]
32. Yu, C.; Qie, L.; Jing, S.; Yan, Y. Personalized Design of Part Orientation in Additive Manufacturing. *Rapid Prototyp. J.* **2019**, *25*, 1647–1660. [CrossRef]
33. Zhang, Y.; Harik, R.; Fadel, G.; Bernard, A. A Statistical Method for Build Orientation Determination in Additive Manufacturing. *Rapid Prototyp. J.* **2019**, *25*, 187–207. [CrossRef]
34. Gade, P.K.; Osuri, M. Evaluation of Multi Criteria Decision Making Methods for Potential Use in Application Security. Master's Thesis, School of Computing, Blekinge Institute of Technology, Blekinge, Sweden, 2014.
35. Zhang, Y.; Bernard, A.; Gupta, R.K.; Harik, R. Feature Based Building Orientation Optimization for Additive Manufacturing. *Rapid Prototyp. J.* **2016**, *22*, 358–376. [CrossRef]
36. Frank, D.; Fadel, G. Expert system-based selection of the preferred direction of build for rapid prototyping processes. *J. Intell. Manuf.* **1995**, *6*, 339–345. [CrossRef]
37. Reiher, T.; Lindemann, C.; Jahnke, U.; Deppe, G.; Koch, R. Holistic Approach for Industrializing AM Technology: From Part Selection to Test and Verification. *Prog. Addit. Manuf.* **2017**, *2*, 43–55. [CrossRef]
38. Pecharsky, V.K.; Zavalij, P.V. Finite Symmetry Elements and Crystallographic Point Groups. In *Fundamentals of Powder Diffraction and Structural Characterization of Materials*; Springer: Boston, MA, USA, 2009. [CrossRef]
39. Uralde, V.; Veiga, F.; Suarez, A.; Aldalur, E.; Ballesteros, T. Symmetry Analysis in Wire Arc Direct Energy Deposition for Overlapping and Oscillatory Strategies in Mild Steel. *Symmetry* **2023**, *15*, 1231. [CrossRef]
40. Hatton, H.; Khalid, M.; Manzoor, U.; Murray, J. Symmetry-Based Decomposition for Optimised Parallelisation in 3D Printing Processes. *Int. J. Adv. Manuf. Technol.* **2023**, *127*, 2935–2954. [CrossRef]
41. Hedjazi, L.; Belhabib, S.; D'orlando, A.; Guessasma, S. Breaking Material Symmetry to Control Mechanical Performance in 3D Printed Objects. *Symmetry* **2022**, *15*, 28. [CrossRef]
42. Bader, C.; Oxman, N. Recursive Symmetries for Geometrically Complex and Materially Heterogeneous Additive Manufacturing. *Comput. Des.* **2016**, *81*, 39–47. [CrossRef]
43. Uralde, V.; Veiga, F.; Aldalur, E.; Suarez, A.; Ballesteros, T. Symmetry and its application in metal additive manufacturing (MAM). *Symmetry* **2022**, *14*, 1810. [CrossRef]
44. Ransikarbum, K.; Pitakaso, R.; Kim, N.; Ma, J. Multicriteria Decision Analysis Framework for Part Orientation Analysis in Additive Manufacturing. *J. Comput. Des. Eng.* **2021**, *8*, 1141–1157. [CrossRef]
45. Ghaleb, A.M.; Kaid, H.; Alsamhan, A.; Mian, S.H.; Hidri, L. Assessment and Comparison of Various MCDM Approaches in the Selection of Manufacturing Process. *Adv. Mater. Sci. Eng.* **2020**, *2020*, 4039253. [CrossRef]

46. Bakioglu, G.; Atahan, A.O. AHP Integrated TOPSIS and VIKOR Methods with Pythagorean Fuzzy Sets to Prioritize Risks in Self-Driving Vehicles. *Appl. Soft Comput.* **2020**, *99*, 106948. [CrossRef]
47. Emovon, I.; Oghenenyerovwho, O.S. Application of MCDM Method in Material Selection for Optimal Design: A Review. *Results Mater.* **2020**, *7*, 100115. [CrossRef]
48. Li, Y.; He, X.; Martínez, L.; Zhang, J.; Wang, D.; Liu, X.A. Comparative Analysis of Three Categories of Multi-Criteria Decision-Making Methods. *Expert Syst. Appl.* **2023**, *238*, 121824. [CrossRef]
49. Bachchhav, B.; Bharne, S.; Choudhari, A.; Pattanshetti, S. Selection of Spot Welding Electrode Material by AHP, TOPSIS, and SAW. *Mater. Today Proc.* **2023**, S2214785323007976. [CrossRef]
50. Chakraborty, S.; Raut, R.D.; Rofin, T.; Chakraborty, S. A Comprehensive and Systematic Review of Multi-Criteria Decision-Making Methods and Applications in Healthcare. *Health Anal.* **2023**, *4*, 100232. [CrossRef]
51. Zhou, M.; Chen, Y.-W.; Liu, X.-B.; Cheng, B.-Y.; Yang, J.-B. Weight Assignment Method for Multiple Attribute Decision Making with Dissimilarity and Conflict of Belief Distributions. *Comput. Ind. Eng.* **2020**, *147*, 106648. [CrossRef]
52. Sarı, F. Forest Fire Susceptibility Mapping via Multi-Criteria Decision Analysis Techniques for Mugla, Turkey: A Comparative Analysis of VIKOR and TOPSIS. *For. Ecol. Manag.* **2020**, *480*, 118644. [CrossRef]
53. Safian, E.E.M.; Nawawi, A.H. The Evolution of Analytical Hierarchy Process (AHP) as a Decision Making Tool in Property Sectors. 2011. Available online: https://www.researchgate.net/publication/254445031 (accessed on 10 May 2024).
54. Mukhametzyanov, I.; Pamučar, D. A Sensitivity Analysis in MCDM Problems: A Statistical Approach. *Decis. Making Appl. Manag. Eng.* **2018**, *1*, 51–80. [CrossRef]
55. Miloš, M.; Bogdan, N.; Miroslav, R. *Business and Engineering Decision-Making Using Multi-Criteria Optimization Methods*; Faculty of Engineering Sciences, University of Kragujevac: Kragujevac, Serbia, 2015.
56. Dragan, P. *Operational Research—Deterministic Methods and Models*; RABEK: Beograd, Serbia, 2017.
57. Sartini, M.; Luca, M.; Claudio, F.; Marco, M. a multi-criteria decision-making approach to optimize the part build orientation in additive manufacturing. *Proc. Des. Soc.* **2023**, *3*, 293–302. [CrossRef]
58. Vladimir, M.; Aleksic, A.; Sokolovic, V.; Milenkov, M. Ranking of key performance indicators of the overhaul process of technical systems. *Int. J. Ind. Eng. Theory Appl. Pract.* **2024**, *31*, 31–65.
59. Chen, Z.; Han, C.; Gao, M.; Kandukuri, S.Y.; Zhou, K. A Review on Qualification and Certification for Metal Additive Manufacturing. *Virtual Phys. Prototyp.* **2021**, *17*, 382–405. [CrossRef]
60. Lamei, Z. A Comprehensive Cost Estimation for Additive Manufacturing. Master's Thesis, Faculty of the Graduate School of Wichita State University, Wichita, KS, USA, 2021.
61. Rickenbacher, L.; Spierings, A.; Wegener, K. An Integrated Cost-Model for Selective Laser Melting (SLM). *Rapid Prototyp. J.* **2013**, *19*, 208–214. [CrossRef]
62. Fera, M.; Fruggiero, F.; Costabile, G.; Lambiase, A.; Pham, D.T. A New Mixed Production Cost Allocation Model for Additive Manufacturing (MiProCAMAM). *Int. J. Adv. Manuf. Technol.* **2017**, *92*, 4275–4291. [CrossRef]
63. Malbašić, S.; Nedić, B.; Đorđević, A.; Živković, S. The role of the cost and quality in additive manufacturing. *J. Eng. Manag. Inf. Technol.* **2023**, *1*, 11–18. [CrossRef]

symmetry

MDPI

Article

Application of a Fractional Order PI Controller for a Speed Servo Drive Control

Pavol Bistak [1,*], Igor Bélai [1], Igor Bélai, Jr. [1], Damir Vrancic [2,3] and Mikulas Huba [1]

1 Institute of Automotive Mechatronics, Faculty of Electrical Engineering and Information Technology, Slovak University of Technology in Bratislava, Ilkovičova 3, 841 04 Bratislava, Slovakia; igor.belai@stuba.sk (I.B.); igor_belai@stuba.sk (I.B.J.); mikulas.huba@stuba.sk (M.H.)
2 Department of Systems and Control, Jozef Stefan Institute, Jamova cesta 39, 1000 Ljubljana, Slovenia; damir.vrancic@ijs.si
3 Faculty of Industrial Engineering Novo mesto, Šegova ulica 112, 8000 Novo mesto, Slovenia
* Correspondence: pavol.bistak@stuba.sk

Abstract: This paper deals with the tuning of the parameters of a fractional-order PI controller for the speed control of an electric servo drive in which the torque is set by a torque generator. The controller parameters are tuned using the multiple dominant pole method (MDPM), while the fractional order integrator is approximated by the Oustaloup method. The input parameters required for tuning the controller using MDPM are calculated using the optimization algorithm presented in this paper. This algorithm selects the optimal parameters from a set of points in three-dimensional space, based on the symmetry around a central point. The controller tuning is performed for the normalized control loop model. The obtained optimized normalized fractional order PI controller can then be applied to a real servo drive with specific parameters. The proposed tuning was also verified experimentally, comparing the obtained closed-loop responses with those of the integer-order PI controller. Both simulation and experimental results showed a significant reduction in the integral of the absolute error at the disturbance step compared to a control loop using an integer-order PI controller. This results in a faster output response to load torque steps and a smaller control error in a real servo drive.

Keywords: control loop; fractional order controller; Oustaloup's approximation; servo drive; speed control

1. Introduction

Fractional order control is based on fractional calculus, a generalization of standard calculus that uses integral and derivative of fractional order. Fractional calculus defines an operator for the derivative and integral. This operator can be called the integrodifferentiator [1] and is given by the Formula (1), where a and t are the limits of the operation and μ is the order of the derivative or integration.

$$ {}_aD_t^{\mu} f(t) = \begin{cases} \dfrac{d^{\mu}}{dt^{\mu}} f(t) & \Re(\mu) > 0, \\ 1 & \Re(\mu) = 0, \\ \displaystyle\int_a^t f(\tau)(d\tau)^{-\mu} & \Re(\mu) < 0 \end{cases} \tag{1} $$

The Laplace transform $\mathcal{L}$ of the derivative/integral of a function $f(t)$ of fractional order μ is [2]:

$$ \mathcal{L}\left\{ {}_aD_t^{\mu} f(t) \right\} = s^{\mu} F(s) \tag{2} $$

where s is a Laplace operator and

$$ F(s) = \mathcal{L}\{f(t)\} \tag{3} $$

There are various approaches to the definition of the fractional order integrodifferentiation operator, such as the definitions by Grünwald-Letnikov, Riemann-Liouville, or Caputo [3]. Based on these definitions, numerical algorithms have been derived to compute the fractional order derivative/integral from a given number of input samples, e.g., as in [4].

Another way to implement a fractional order operator is to approximate it by integer and finite transfer functions, which are summarized in [2]. These approximations lead to transfer functions of integer order, where $N \in \mathbb{N}^{+}$ is the order of the approximation:

$$s^{\mu} \approx \frac{b_N s^N + b_{N-1} s^{N-1} + \cdots + b_0 s^0}{a_N s^N + a_{N-1} s^{N-1} + \cdots + a_0 s^0} = \frac{M_A(s)}{N_A(s)} \\ a_i \in \mathbb{R}, b_i \in \mathbb{R}, a_i \geq 0, b_i \geq 0 \quad \forall \quad i \in \langle 0, N \rangle \tag{4}$$

where b_0 to b_N are the coefficients of the numerator and a_0 to a_N are the coefficients of the denominator of the transfer function. The numerator and denominator polynomials are denoted as $M_A(s)$ and $N_A(s)$.

Linear proportional-integral (PI) controllers are often used to control the torque and speed of electrical machines. These controllers are popular because of their simplicity and ease of implementation. Several tuning methods have been published that have proven themselves in practice.

In electric servo drives, control structures with a fractional-order PID controller (FOPID) [5] were tested, which has more degrees of freedom in terms of the number of adjustable parameters compared to the standard integer order PI or PID controllers. The generalized transfer function of the FOPID controller $G_c(s)$ is given in (5), where $U(s)$ is the controller output, $E(s)$ is the control error, k_p, k_i, and k_d are the gains of the proportional, integral, and derivative components, λ is the order of the integrator, and μ is the order of the derivative. Note that the parameters λ and μ can be real numbers.

$$G_c(s) = \frac{U(s)}{E(s)} = k_p + k_i \frac{1}{s^{\lambda}} + k_d s^{\mu}, \quad \lambda > 0, \mu > 0 \tag{5}$$

The following is a list of works in which a fractional order PI (FOPI) or PID (FOPID) controller is used to control an electric servo drive with different tuning procedures.

The speed control of a DC motor using a FOPID controller whose output is the reference rotor voltage is described in [6]. The tuning of the controller parameters is based on the specification of the phase margin of the open loop. The performance of the control loop was verified by simulation and without investigating the effect of the load torque on the motor speed.

A method for calculating the parameters of an FOPI speed controller for a servo drive with a torque generator is described in [7]. The phase margin method was used to tune the controller parameters, whereby the controlled system was replaced by a first-order system and an integrator. The characteristics of the speed control loop were tested experimentally on two servo drives. The first was a DC servo drive with rotor current control. The experimental servo drive with a vector-controlled permanent magnet synchronous motor (PMSM) was the second. The experiments showed a faster response to setpoint tracking compared to the servo drive with an integer order PI controller.

The FOPI controller was also used in [8] to control the speed of a PMSM with a torque generator, where integer-order PI controllers were used to control the flux and torque components of the stator current vector and the FOPI controller was used only for speed control (as in the experimental part of this paper). The order of the controller presented in [8] was time-dependent. This resulted in less overshoot during the setpoint change and a lower error in disturbance rejection than with the constant-order FOPI controller. The performance of the control loop was verified experimentally.

Fractional-order PID controllers were also used in motor speed and current vector torque cascade control loops in servo drive with PMSM [9]. The parameters of the controllers were calculated using particle swarm optimization. The simulation results of the speed control loop were compared with FOPID and PID controllers. A significantly smaller error was achieved with the FOPID controllers.

The use of FOPI controllers to control the speed and the stator current vector of the PMSM was presented in [10]. The control structure was supplemented by a disturbance observer. The parameters of the controllers were adjusted depending on the magnitude of the observed load torque. The performance of the closed-loop was verified by simulations. The results showed a faster response of the closed-loop and a reduction in oscillations due to the disturbance observer.

In [11], a fractional order PD position controller is used in a PMSM servo drive. The output of the controller is the setpoint for the torque component of the stator current vector. The steady state error caused by the disturbance is suppressed by a linear extended disturbance observer (LESO) of integer order. The parameters of the position controller were tuned using the phase margin method. In the paper, experimental results are compared with a servo drive using either an integer order PD controller or a fractional-order PD controller. The servo drive with an integer order position controller was characterized by overshoot of the tracking responses, while there was no overshoot with the fractional-order controller.

The application of the FOPI speed controller to a servo drive with a vector-controlled induction motor is described in [12]. The parameters of the FOPI controller were set to achieve a shorter settling time and less overshoot compared to a conventional PI speed controller, which was verified by simulation and on a test rig.

The application of the FOPID controller in a model for tracking control of a robot manipulator with two degrees of freedom was used in [13]. The controllers were tuned using the phase margin method. The authors compared fractional and integer order PID controllers. The system with the FOPID controller was found to be more robust to external disturbances, load variations, and noise in the feedback channel.

As can be seen from the above review, the use of a fractional order controller can improve the quality of control by reducing settling time and/or improving disturbance rejection (changes in load torque).

The aim of this work was to develop and verify experimentally a FOPI speed controller tuning method in a servo drive with a torque generator implemented. The method should be based on knowledge of the parameters of the torque generator and the mechanical subsystem of the servo drive, and its application should minimize the integral of the absolute error at a disturbance (load torque) step.

The novelty is that the FOPI speed controller is tuned to a specific implementation of a fractional order integrator. This means that the properties of a fractional order integrator, which is approximated by the Oustaloup method, are taken into account when tuning the controller. Besides the controller gains and the integrator order, the parameters of the controller tuning are also the lower and upper limits of the frequency band of the approximated fractional-order integrator. This approach was chosen because existing FOPI controller tuning methods only allow the controller gains and order of the integral component to be computed by assuming the implementation of an ideal fractional-order integrator. When the fractional-order integrator is approximated by a rational transfer function using the Oustaloup method, its frequency response matches that of the ideal integrator only in a certain frequency band. The lower limit of this band is usually close to zero. However, increasing the lower frequency of an approximated fractional-order integrator can improve the output response at the disturbance step. Our approach outperforms existing FOPID methods, especially in disturbance step responses. In addition, the tuning of the controller parameters is performed for a normalized process (gain and a time delay equal to one). The gain and other parameters of the FOPI controller, including the frequency band of the fractional-order approximated integrator, can then be recalculated during implementation based on the actual gain and time delay of the controlled process, which is a servo drive with an implemented torque generator. The actual parameters of the FOPI controller are calculated by a combination of analytical and optimization methods developed by the authors of the paper.

In this paper, it is assumed that an electric servo drive with an implemented torque generator is the controlled system. It can be represented by the integrator plus dead time (IPDT) transfer function. This way of representing an electromechanical system of a drive is given, for example, in [14]. The transfer functions of the process (system) are then

$$\begin{aligned} S_c(s) &= \frac{\omega(s)}{M_m^*(s)} = e^{-T_d s}\frac{K_s}{s} \\ S_d(s) &= \frac{\omega(s)}{M_L(s)} = \frac{K_s}{s} \end{aligned} \tag{6}$$

where the rotor angular velocity $\omega(s)$ is the output of the system, T_d is the transport delay (dead time), and K_s is the gain of the system. The reference motor torque $M_m^*(s)$ is the control variable and the load torque $M_L(s)$ is the disturbance variable. The transport delay T_d is determined by the transport delay of the torque generator T_{GM} and the length of the sampling period of the speed controller T_s in the discrete controller implementation as follows:

$$T_d = T_{GM} + T_s/2 \tag{7}$$

The torque generator is implemented in the electrical inverter with a special motor control algorithm. The actual control system, which is presented in Section 3.2, uses vector control [15] to control the motor torque.

The system gain K_s is the inverse value of the moment of inertia J, but for generalization, the variable K_s is used to denote the gain of the system:

$$K_s = J^{-1} \tag{8}$$

The structure of the speed control loop with a fractional-order PI controller is shown in Figure 1, where ω^* is the reference speed, K_p is the gain of the proportional term of the controller, K_i is the inverse of the integration time constant, and $F_I(s)$ is the reference speed filter. The filter is used to suppress the overshoot of the actual motor speed to the setpoint change ω^*. The overshoot is caused by zeros in the closed loop transfer function.

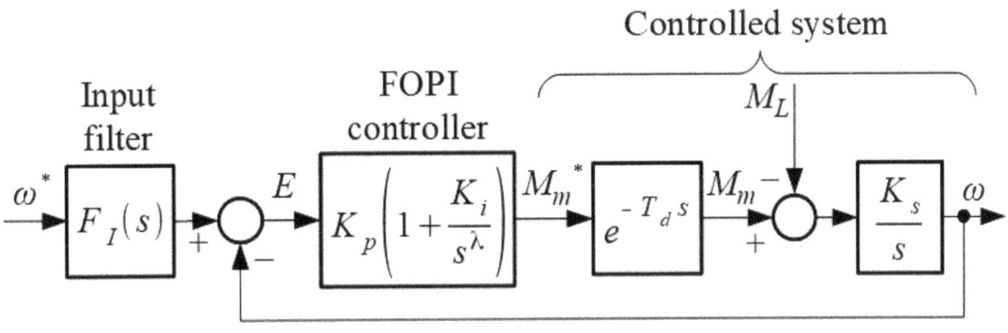

Figure 1. Speed control loop structure with fractional order PI (FOPI) controller.

If the fractional order integrator $1/s^\lambda$ is approximated by a transfer function of integer order (4), where $\mu = -\lambda \wedge F_I(s) = 1$, then the error transfer functions are:

$$\begin{aligned} G_{e,A}(s) &= \frac{E(s)}{\omega^*(s)} = \frac{s e^{T_d s} N_A(s)}{s e^{T_d s} N_A(s) + K_p K_i (N_A(s) + K_i M_A(s))} \\ G_{eL,A}(s) &= \frac{E(s)}{M_L(s)} = \frac{K_s e^{T_d s} N_A(s)}{s e^{T_d s} N_A(s) + K_p K_s (N_A(s) + K_i M_A(s))} \end{aligned} \tag{9}$$

The IE for the disturbance step is as follows:

$$IE_d = \frac{\omega_b^{\lambda-1}}{K_p K_i} \quad (20)$$

2.2. Normalizing the Control Loop

By normalizing the control loop, the transport delay T_d can be replaced by a unit delay and the system gain K_s by a unit gain. By applying the following substitution:

$$\xi = T_d s \quad (21)$$

the control loop can be represented by Figure 2, with the overlines indicating the normalized parameters.

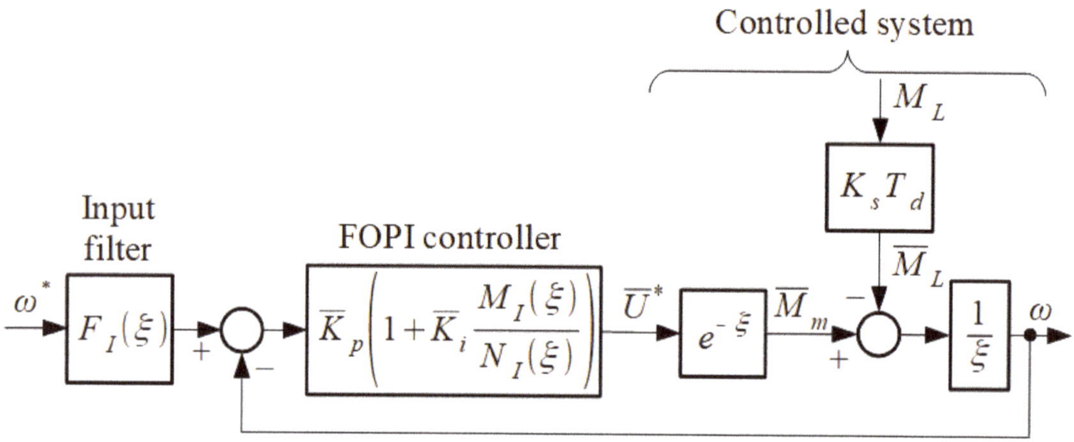

Figure 2. Structure of a normalized control loop with a fractional order PI controller with an integral component approximated by Oustaloup's method.

The formulas for calculating the normalized parameters of the controller and the integrator, which are approximated by Oustaloup's method (14), are as follows

$$\begin{gathered}
\overline{K}_p = K_p K_s T_d\,, \quad \overline{K}_i = K_i T_d^{\lambda}\,, \quad \overline{\omega}_b = \omega_b T_d\,, \quad \overline{\omega}_h = \omega_h T_d \\
\overline{\omega}_j = \overline{\omega}_b \left(\frac{\overline{\omega}_h}{\overline{\omega}_b}\right)^{\frac{2j-\lambda}{2N}} = \omega_j T_d\,, \quad \overline{\omega}_j' = \overline{\omega}_b \left(\frac{\overline{\omega}_h}{\overline{\omega}_b}\right)^{\frac{2j-2+\lambda}{2N}} = \omega_j' T_d \\
\overline{K}_o = \overline{\omega}_h^{1-\lambda} = K_o T_d^{1-\lambda}\,, \quad M_I(\xi) = \overline{K}_o \prod_{j=1}^{N} \xi + \overline{\omega}_j'\,, \quad N_I(\xi) = \xi \prod_{j=1}^{N} \xi + \overline{\omega}_j
\end{gathered} \quad (22)$$

The transfer functions of the normalized control loop without filtering the reference speed are:

$$G_r(\xi) = \frac{\omega(\xi)}{\omega^*(\xi)} = \frac{\overline{K}_p N_I(\xi) + \overline{K}_p \overline{K}_i M_I(\xi)}{\xi e^{\xi} N_I(\xi) + \overline{K}_p N_I(\xi) + \overline{K}_p \overline{K}_i M_I(\xi)} = \frac{M_{Or}(\xi)}{N_O(\xi)} \quad (23)$$

$$G_d(\xi) = \frac{\omega(\xi)}{\overline{M}_L(\xi)} = -\frac{e^{\xi} N_I(\xi)}{\xi e^{\xi} N_I(\xi) + \overline{K}_p N_I(\xi) + \overline{K}_p \overline{K}_i M_I(\xi)} = -\frac{M_{Od}(\xi)}{N_O(\xi)} \quad (24)$$

where

$$\begin{aligned} M_{Or}(\xi) &= \overline{K}_p N_I(\xi) + \overline{K}_p \overline{K}_i M_I(\xi) \\ M_{Od}(\xi) &= e^{\xi} N_I(\xi) \\ N_O(\xi) &= \xi e^{\xi} N_I(\xi) + \overline{K}_p N_I(\xi) + \overline{K}_p \overline{K}_i M_I(\xi) \end{aligned} \tag{25}$$

Similar to the structure shown in Figure 1, it is possible to filter the reference speed signal using a filter $F_I(\xi)$ that compensates the zeros of the transfer function $G_r(\xi)$ and one of its real poles $-\xi_0 = -T_d s_0$:

$$F_I(\xi) = \frac{\xi_0^{-1}\xi + 1}{N_I(\xi) + \overline{K}_i M_I(\xi)} \overline{K}_i \overline{K}_o \prod_{j=1}^{N} \overline{\omega}_j' \tag{26}$$

If the speed reference signal is filtered by $F_I(\xi)$, then the normalized integral of the error $\overline{IE}_r$ for the step setpoint signal is

$$\overline{IE}_r = \frac{\prod_{j=1}^{N} \overline{\omega}_j + \overline{K}_i \overline{K}_o \sum_{i=1}^{N} \left(\frac{1}{\overline{\omega}_i'} \prod_{j=1}^{N} \overline{\omega}_j' \right)}{\overline{K}_i \overline{K}_o \prod_{j=1}^{N} \overline{\omega}_j'} - \frac{1}{\xi_0} = \frac{IE_r}{T_d} \tag{27}$$

The normalized integral of the error $\overline{IE}_d$ for the disturbance step is as follows:

$$\overline{IE}_d = \frac{\overline{\omega}_b^{\lambda-1}}{\overline{K}_p \overline{K}_i} = \frac{IE_d}{K_s T_d^2} \tag{28}$$

2.3. *Tuning the FOPI Controller Parameters*

The methods for calculating the parameters of a fractional order controller can be divided into two groups: analytical and optimization methods. In some works, the analytical calculation of the parameters of the fractional-order PI/PID controller is performed by first calculating the gains and time constants of the integer order controller. These values are then used in the fractional-order controller, whereby the orders of the integrator or the derivative terms are additionally tuned [12,18]. Such a tuning approach can provide some improvement in control performance compared to an integer order PI/PID controller, but cannot be considered optimal.

For the analytical calculation of the parameters of fractional-order PI/PID controller, methods based on the frequency responses of the open or closed loop are used instead. With such methods, the gains and time constants of a fractional-order PI/PID controller can be calculated for specific orders of the integral and derivative components [7,19]. In most cases, however, the orders of the integral and derivative components are calculated analytically [6,11,13,20–22].

Optimization methods tune the controller parameters, including the order of the integral and derivative components, to minimize the value of the optimization function. The optimization function is based on integral criteria to evaluate the quality of control [23], or on phase and gain margin requirements [24]. The approaches use different types of optimization algorithms to tune the parameters of a fractional-order PI/PID controller, including the gray wolf algorithm [25], particle swarm optimization [26], or Ant-Lion optimization [23].

The above-mentioned works, in which the FOPID controller is tuned by analytical or optimization methods, are based on control loop transfer functions that include a fractional-order integrodifferentiation operator s^{μ}. In a real control loop, this operator is replaced by a component whose properties are more or less similar to an ideal fractional order integrodifferentiator.

When an integrodifferentiator is approximated using Oustaloup's method, the lower and upper bounds of the frequency band are specified, which define the region of close similarity between the frequency characteristics of the approximated and ideal integrodifferentiators. As shown in [27], the lower limit of the frequency band of the Oustaloup integrator (ω_b) influences the disturbance rejection of the system. Increasing ω_b increases the disturbance rejection. In other words, when the parameters of the controller are calculated analytically for an ideal integrodifferentiator, its characteristics are changed by changing ω_b. Such a change causes the change in the control loop response compared to the original specifications.

Therefore, this paper presents a method to tune the FOPI controller for a normalized control loop in Figure 2, where the fractional order integrator is approximated by a rational transfer function (14). The method for calculating the controller parameters is a combination of analytical and optimization methods. The normalized controller gains $\overline{K}_p$ and $\overline{K}_i$ are calculated analytically for the given values of $\overline{\omega}_b$, $\overline{\omega}_h$ and N. The last four parameters are calculated by the optimization algorithm in such a way that the value of the integral of the absolute error is minimized at the disturbance step, whereby the control signal must not exhibit excessive deviations.

2.3.1. Calculation of the Normalized Gains of the FOPI Controller

The multiple dominant pole method (MDPM) presented in [28], which is based on the closed loop transfer function, was used to derive the formulas to calculate the normalized gains of the FOPI controller. The characteristic polynomial of the transfer function can also contain exponential terms, so that the method can also be applied to systems with transport delays. With this method, the controller parameters $\overline{K}_p$ and $\overline{K}_i$ are calculated in such a way that the transfer function of the closed control loop has a double dominant real pole $-\xi_0$. The normalized controller parameters can be calculated using the following equations:

$$\begin{aligned} 0 &= N_O(\xi)\big|_{\xi=-\xi_0} \\ 0 &= \left.\frac{dN_O(\xi)}{d\xi}\right|_{\xi=-\xi_0} \end{aligned} \tag{29}$$

After substituting for $N_O(\xi)$ in (25), the system of Equation (29) has the form

$$\begin{aligned} 0 &= -\xi_0 e^{-\xi_0} N_I(\xi_0) + \overline{K}_p N_I(\xi_0) + \overline{K}_p \overline{K}_i M_I(\xi_0) \\ 0 &= A(\xi_0) + \overline{K}_p B(\xi_0) + \overline{K}_p \overline{K}_i C(\xi_0) \end{aligned} \tag{30}$$

where the following values apply for $A(\xi_0)$, $B(\xi_0)$, $C(\xi_0)$, $M_I(\xi_0)$ and $N_I(\xi_0)$:

$$\begin{aligned} A(\xi_0) &= \left.\frac{d(\xi e^{\xi} N_I(\xi))}{d\xi}\right|_{\xi=-\xi_0} \\ B(\xi_0) &= \left.\frac{dN_I(\xi)}{d\xi}\right|_{\xi=-\xi_0} \\ C(\xi_0) &= \left.\frac{dM_I(\xi)}{d\xi}\right|_{\xi=-\xi_0} \\ M_I(\xi_0) &= M_I(\xi)\big|_{\xi=-\xi_0} \\ N_I(\xi_0) &= N_I(\xi)\big|_{\xi=-\xi_0} \end{aligned} \tag{31}$$

The solution of (30) is as follows:

$$\begin{aligned} \overline{K}_p &= \frac{M_I(\xi_0)A(\xi_0) + \xi_0 e^{-\xi_0} N_I(\xi_0) C(\xi_0)}{N_I(\xi_0)C(\xi_0) - M_I(\xi_0)B(\xi_0)} \\ \overline{K}_i &= -\frac{N_I(\xi_0)\left(A(\xi_0) + \xi_0 e^{-\xi_0} B(\xi_0)\right)}{M_I(\xi_0)A(\xi_0) + \xi_0 e^{-\xi_0} N_I(\xi_0) C(\xi_0)} \end{aligned} \tag{32}$$

Expression (32) is used to calculate the values of $\overline{K}_p$ and $\overline{K}_i$ for the specified dominant pole $-\xi_0$. The values of ξ_0 are determined together with the order of the fractional order integrator λ and the lower limit of the frequency band of the approximated integrator $\overline{\omega}_b$ using an algorithm described in Section 2.3.2.

2.3.2. The Optimum Values for ξ_0, λ, and $\overline{\omega}_b$

The transfer function of the closed control loop $G_r(\xi)$ is of order $N+2$, where $N \geq 1$. Therefore, in addition to the $-\xi_0$ pole, it has other poles, the number and position of which depend on the order and other parameters of the approximated integrator. The additional poles can have a considerable influence on the closed control loop. An unsuitable setting of the parameters of the approximated integrator can lead to oscillations or even instability of the control loop. Therefore, the algorithm proposed here searches for the values of ξ_0, λ, and $\overline{\omega}_b$ for the specified N and $\overline{\omega}_h$ in order to minimize the value of the integral of absolute error (IAE) at the disturbance step:

$$IAE = \int_0^\infty |\omega^*(t) - \omega(t)| dt \tag{33}$$

In addition, the deviations of the control signal from the one-pulse function (1P) are evaluated at the setpoint and disturbance steps, where the 1P function is defined in [29]. The deviations can be calculated using the following expression [30]:

$$TV_1(\overline{U}^*) = \sum_c \left|\overline{U}^*_{c+1} - \overline{U}^*_c\right| - \left|2\overline{U}^*_{max} - \overline{U}^*_\infty - \overline{U}^*_0\right| \tag{34}$$

where c is the number of samples. $\overline{U}^*_0$, $\overline{U}^*_\infty$, $\overline{U}^*_{\max}$ are the initial, the final steady state, and the maximum value of the control signal for the setpoint ω^* and the disturbance $\overline{M}_L$ steps, respectively.

The optimization objective is expressed by the function Γ_d in (35), where IAE_d is the integral of the absolute error at the disturbance step, ε_r is the maximum allowable shape deviation at the setpoint or disturbance step, $TV_{1r}(\overline{U}^*)$ and $TV_{1d}(\overline{U}^*)$ are the shape deviations of the control signal from the 1P function at the setpoint and disturbance step, respectively, and $k \in \mathbb{N}$ is the cycle number of the optimization algorithm given below. The values of IAE_d, $TV_{1r}(\overline{U}^*)$, and $TV_{1d}(\overline{U}^*)$ are determined by a simulation in which the setpoint step is executed first and then the disturbance step.

$$\begin{gathered}
\Gamma_d = \min\left(IAE_d(\overline{\omega}_b, \xi_0, \lambda)\right) \cap \left(TV_{1r}(\overline{U}^*) \leq \varepsilon_r\right) \cap \left(TV_{1d}(\overline{U}^*) \leq \varepsilon_r\right) \\
\overline{\omega}_b \in \langle \overline{\omega}^k_{b,\min}, \overline{\omega}^k_{b,\max} \rangle = \overline{\Omega}^k_b, \quad \xi_0 \in \langle \xi^k_{0,\min}, \xi^k_{0,\max} \rangle = \Xi^k_0 \\
\lambda \in \langle \lambda^k_{\min}, \lambda^k_{\max} \rangle = \Lambda^k
\end{gathered} \tag{35}$$

The authors of the article have proposed an algorithm that searches the three-dimensional space $\mathbf{H}^k = \overline{\Omega}^k_b \times \Xi^k_0 \times \Lambda^k$ in several cycles. When searching the space $\mathbf{H}^k$, the values of the variables $\overline{\omega}_b$, ξ_0 and λ are changed with the step ΔP^k_n according to (36), where the index n is one of the variables in Table 1. N_{oP} is the number of all tested values of a particular variable (i.e., the values of ω_b, ξ_0, or λ) applied in one cycle of the algorithm.

$$\begin{gathered}
\Delta P^k_n = \begin{cases} \dfrac{P^1_{n,\max} - P^1_{n,\min}}{N_{oP} - 1} & k = 1 \\[2ex] \dfrac{P^{k-1}_{n,\max} - P^{k-1}_{n,\min}}{2^{1/3} \times (N_{oP} - 1)} & k > 1 \end{cases} \\
n \in \{1,2,3\}, N_{oP} \in \mathbb{N}, N_{oP} \geq 5
\end{gathered} \tag{36}$$

Table 1. Relations between the variables of the optimization function Γ_d and the variables of (36).

Variable in (36)	Corresponding Variable $n = 1$	$n = 2$	$n = 3$
P_n	$\overline{\omega}_b$	ξ_0	λ
ΔP_n^k	$\Delta\overline{\omega}_b^k$	$\Delta\xi_0^k$	$\Delta\lambda^k$
$P_{n,\min}^k$	$\overline{\omega}_{b,\min}^k$	$\xi_{0,\min}^k$	$\lambda_{\min}^k$
$P_{n,\max}^k$	$\overline{\omega}_{b,\max}^k$	$\xi_{0,\max}^k$	$\lambda_{\max}^k$

The size ("volume") of the searched space is halved with each cycle k, as shown in Figure 3, but the number of tested values of the variables (for which IAE_d, TV_{1r}, and TV_{1d} are calculated) remains unchanged. The limits of the searched interval in the k-th cycle are

$$\begin{aligned} P_{n,\min}^k &= P_{n,opt}^{k-1} - \tfrac{N_{oP}}{2}\Delta P_n^k \;\cap\; P_{n,\min}^k \geq P_{n,\min}^1 \\ P_{n,\max}^k &= P_{n,opt}^{k-1} + \tfrac{N_{oP}}{2}\Delta P_n^k \;\cap\; P_{n,\max}^k \leq P_{n,\max}^1 \end{aligned} \tag{37}$$

where $P_{n,opt}^{k-1}$ is the value of the parameter P_n that satisfies (35) in the $k-1$ cycle. The Formula (37) is valid for $k > 1$. The values of the parameter P_n applied in cycle k are symmetrically distributed around a central value $P_{n,opt}^{k-1}$. The user specifies the range of parameter changes P_n in the first cycle of the algorithm ($k = 1$).

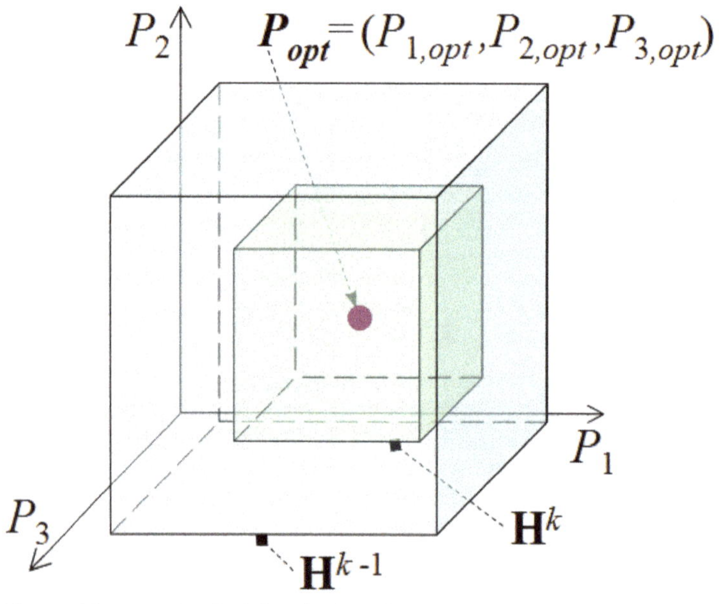

Figure 3. The space **H** in the k-th cycle of the algorithm.

Figure 4 shows the flowchart of the algorithm for selecting the values of $\overline{\omega}_b$, ξ_0, and λ so that expression (35) applies. The algorithm is executed in k_{max} cycles. The innermost loop of the algorithm is the loop in which the value of the parameter $P_3 = \lambda$ is calculated. This loop is run through N_{oP}^3 times in one cycle. For $N_{oP} = 19$ and $k_{max} = 20$, the innermost loop of the algorithm, in which the parameters of the controller and the fractional order integrator are calculated, is run through 137,180 times. The output variables of the algorithm are: $\overline{\omega}_{b,opt}$, $\xi_{0,opt}$, λ_{opt}, $\overline{K}_{p,opt}$, $\overline{K}_{i,opt}$, $\overline{IAE}_{r,opt}$, $\overline{IAE}_{d,opt}$.

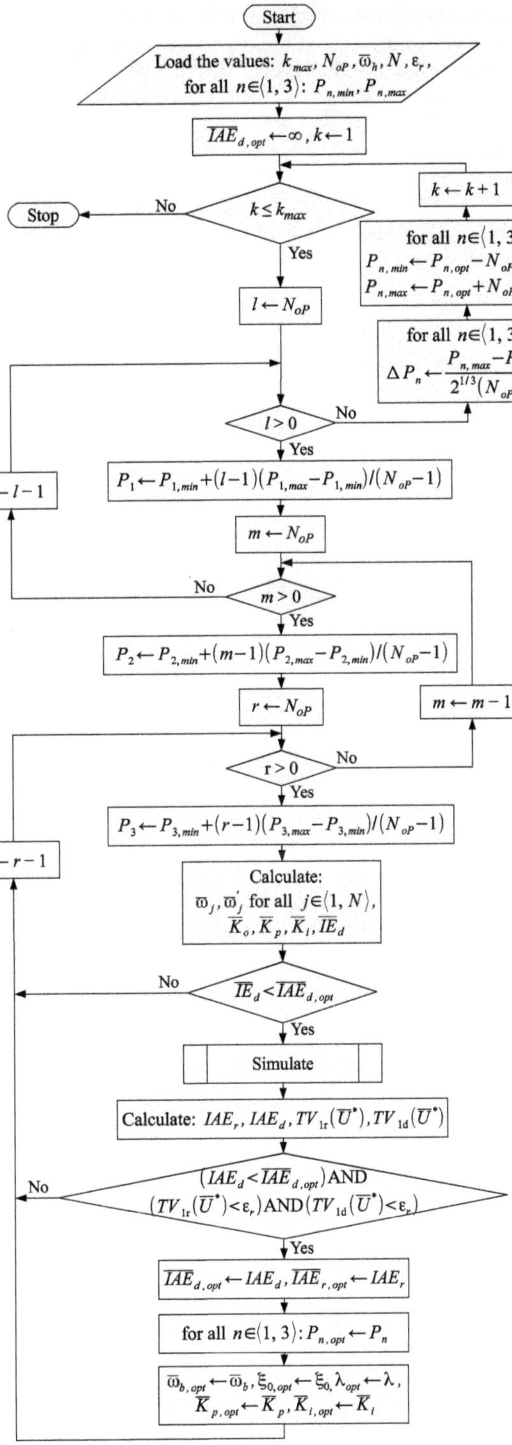

Figure 4. Flowchart of algorithm using symmetrically distributed points in 3D space to select $\overline{\omega}_b$, ξ_0, and λ values.

Matlab R 2018b with Symbolic Math Toolbox was used to compute the parameters of the normalized FOPI controller using the proposed optimization algorithm. Simulink V 9.2 and FOMCON Toolbox V 1.50.3 were used to simulate the FOPI controller.

2.4. PI Controller Tuning

To compare the performance of the FOPI controller with that of the PI controller, the tuning of the integer order PI controller that minimizes the IAE at the disturbance step is presented below.

The structure of the control loop is the same as in Figure 2. The polynomials in the numerator and denominator of the integrator are as follows

$$M_I(\xi)|_{\lambda=1} = 1, \quad N_I(\xi)|_{\lambda=1} = \xi \tag{38}$$

and the transfer functions $G_r(\xi)$ and $G_d(\xi)$ (23) become:

$$G_{1r}(\xi) = \frac{\overline{K}_p\xi + \overline{K}_p\overline{K}_i}{e^{\xi} + \overline{K}_p\xi + \overline{K}_p\overline{K}_i} \tag{39}$$

$$G_{1d}(\xi) = \frac{-e^{\xi}\xi}{e^{\xi} + \overline{K}_p\xi + \overline{K}_p\overline{K}_i} \tag{40}$$

The expression for calculating the gains of a PI controller ($\lambda = 1$) is now as follows:

$$\overline{K}_p|_{\lambda=1} = \xi_0 e^{-\xi_0}(2-\xi_0), \quad \overline{K}_i|_{\lambda=1} = \xi_0\frac{1-\xi_0}{2-\xi_0} \tag{41}$$

where $-\xi_0$ is the double dominant real pole of the transfer functions $G_{1r}(\xi)$ and $G_{1d}(\xi)$.

The reference speed filter $F_I(\xi)$

$$F_I(\xi)|_{\lambda=1} = \frac{\xi_0^{-1}\xi + 1}{\overline{K}_i^{-1}\xi + 1} \tag{42}$$

compensates for the zero in the numerator of the transfer function $G_{1r}(\xi)$ and a real pole $-\xi_0$.

The $\overline{IE}$ values at the setpoint and disturbance steps when applying the $F_I(\xi)$ filter are (42):

$$\overline{IE}_r|_{\lambda=1} = \frac{1}{\overline{K}_i} - \frac{1}{\xi_0} = \frac{1}{\xi_0(1-\xi_0)} \tag{43}$$

$$\overline{IE}_d|_{\lambda=1} = \frac{1}{\overline{K}_p\overline{K}_i} = \frac{e^{\xi_0}}{\xi_0^2(1-\xi_0)} \tag{44}$$

The minimum values of the $\overline{IE}$ and the corresponding values of $\xi_0, \overline{K}_p, \overline{K}_i$ are

$$\begin{array}{llll} \overline{IE}_{r,min} = 4, & \xi_0 = 0.5, & \overline{K}_p = 0.4549, \overline{K}_i = 0.1667, & \lambda = 1 \\ \overline{IE}_{d,min} = 12.6387, & \xi_0 = 0.5858, & \overline{K}_p = 0.4612, \overline{K}_i = 0.1716, & \lambda = 1 \end{array} \tag{45}$$

and since there are no overshoots in the setpoint and disturbance steps, the $\overline{IAE}$ values are identical to the $\overline{IE}$ values:

$$\overline{IAE}_{r,min}|_{\lambda=1} = \overline{IE}_{r,min}|_{\lambda=1}, \quad \overline{IAE}_{d,min}|_{\lambda=1} = \overline{IE}_{d,min}|_{\lambda=1} \tag{46}$$

A comparison of the achieved results with the fully analytical PI controller design using the triple real dominant pole method in [31] shows that the new methodology gives two optimal controller parameter sets instead of a single set of parameters—one optimal for setpoint steps, the other for disturbance steps. However, this only confirms other results of [31] obtained by the experimental performance portrait method (PPM). PPM showed that for different weighting of setpoint and disturbance steps, there will also be different optimal settings of the controller (see Table 1 in [31]).

2.5. Experimental Workstation

The performance of the speed control loop with the FOPI controller tuned by the proposed method described in Section 2.3 was verified on a workstation whose block diagram is shown in Figure 5. The workstation consists of two servo drives, a motion controller, and a personal computer running Matlab R 2023a software (Mathworks, Natick, MA, USA) and Automation Studio V 4.6 (Bernecker & Reiner, Eggelsberg, Austria).

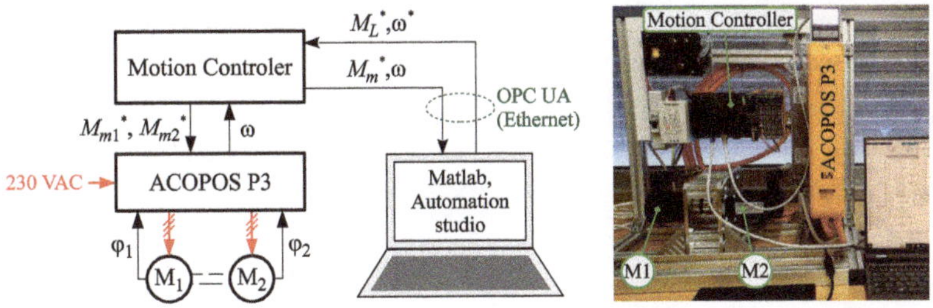

Figure 5. Block diagram and a photography of the workstation.

The servo drives contain two permanent magnet synchronous motors (M_1, M_2) of type 8LVA23 with a rated power $P_N = 400$ W and a rated speed $n_N = 3000$ rpm. The shafts of the motors are connected via a rigid coupling. One of the motors is speed-controlled, while the second motor generates the load torque M_L. Absolute position sensors with the current rotor positions φ_1 and φ_2 are integrated in the motors. The information about the current rotor position is processed by an ACOPOS P3 frequency inverter (Bernecker & Reiner) to control the torque of the motors and calculate the actual speed ω. The speed controller is implemented in a motion control unit of type X20CP1586 (Bernecker & Reiner), where the control algorithm is executed with a sampling period T_s.

The reference speed ω^* and the load torque M_L^* are sent from Matlab to the motion controller via OPC UA. Matlab receives the values for the target motor torque M_m^* and the actual speed ω from the motion controller. The motion controller sends the target motor torque values M_{m1}^* and M_{m2}^* to the frequency inverter and receives the actual speed ω from it.

The speed controller was implemented in the motion controller using Matlab and the Automation Studio Target for Simulink Toolbox. Using the toolbox, Matlab compiles the program for the control algorithm in C language and saves it in the Automation Studio project. This loads the program into the memory of the motion controller and executes it.

The basic form of the fractional order PI controller was created in Simulink. The integrator of the controller had the structure of a sequentially connected first-order system with the first-order integrator according to (14), which was then transformed into a discrete form using Tustin's method [32].

The controlled system parameters used to calculate the process and controller parameters are listed in Table 2.

Table 2. Parameters of the controlled system.

Symbol	Value	Unit	Description
J	6.5×10^{-6}	kgm^2	Moment of inertia
K_s	15,385	kg^{-1}m^{-2}	System gain
T_{GM}	5	ms	Torque generator transport delay
T_s	0.4	ms	Sampling period

The value of the moment of inertia J was obtained during the autotuning of the torque generators in Automation Studio software. The system gain K_s was calculated from the moment of inertia according to (8). The torque generator transport delay T_{GM} has been identified from the speed responses to step changes in the reference torque M_m^*. The sampling period $T_s = 0.4$ ms corresponds to the minimum possible program cycle length for the X20CP1586 motion controller.

3. Results

The results fall into two groups.

The first group is represented by tables with calculated optimal values of the normalized FOPI controller parameters. The calculations of the parameter values in these tables were performed using the method presented in Section 2.3. The controller parameters have been calculated for the specified values of the upper limit of the frequency band of the approximated integrator $\overline{\omega}_h$ and for the selected orders of the integrator transfer function N. These results are presented below in Section 3.1.

Experimental results on a speed actuator with FOPI and PI controller represent the second group of achieved results. The parameters of the FOPI controller were calculated using the results in Section 3.1. The description of the experiments and their results are in Section 3.2.

3.1. Optimization Results

A simulation model was created in Simulink based on Figure 2 and the methods presented in Sections 2.3.1 and 2.3.2. The parameters of the normalized FOPI controller and the normalized fractional-order integrator, approximated by Oustaloup's method, were calculated for the chosen values of $\overline{\omega}_h$ and N. During the simulations, unit steps of the reference speed ω^* and the normalized disturbance $\overline{M}_L$ were applied. The allowable shape deviation of the control signal from the 1P signal for the reference and disturbance steps, the number of algorithm cycles, and the number of different values of the variables in an algorithm cycle were as follows: $\varepsilon_r = 1 \times 10^{-6}$, $k_{max} = 20$, $N_{oP} = 19$, respectively. The normalized parameters, including the normalized $\overline{IAE}$ values, are shown in Tables 3–13. The calculation time for the values of one row of the table took between two and eight hours, depending on the values of $\overline{\omega}_h$ and N.

Table 3. Optimized controller parameters and achieved $\overline{IAE}$ values, $\overline{\omega}_h = 0.2$.

N	$\overline{\omega}_b$	ξ_0	λ	$\overline{\mathbf{K}}_\mathbf{p}$	$\overline{\mathbf{K}}_\mathbf{i}$	$\overline{\mathbf{IAE}}_\mathbf{r}$	$\overline{\mathbf{IAE}}_\mathbf{d}$
1	0.19904	0.58542	1.0430	0.46118	0.16015	9.1293	12.6327
2	0.19954	0.58517	1.0903	0.46118	0.14840	14.1279	12.6328
3	0.19931	0.58510	1.0619	0.46118	0.15533	19.1416	12.6331
5	0.19935	0.58496	1.1298	0.46120	0.13930	29.1419	12.6382

$\overline{\omega}^1_{b,min} = 0.1$, $\overline{\omega}^1_{b,max} = 0.2$, $\xi^1_{0,min} = 0.2$, $\xi^1_{0,max} = 0.8$, $\lambda^1_{min} = 0.3$, $\lambda^1_{max} = 2$.

Table 4. Optimized controller parameters and achieved $\overline{IAE}$ values, $\overline{\omega}_h = 0.25$.

N	$\overline{\omega}_b$	ξ_0	λ	$\overline{\mathbf{K}}_\mathbf{p}$	$\overline{\mathbf{K}}_\mathbf{i}$	$\overline{\mathbf{IAE}}_\mathbf{r}$	$\overline{\mathbf{IAE}}_\mathbf{d}$
1	0.24075	0.27282	1.1908	0.62507	0.14912	5.5068	8.1764
2	0.23876	0.27227	1.1578	0.62593	0.15600	9.6124	8.1700
3	0.24390	0.27314	1.2597	0.62616	0.13527	13.5996	8.1836
5	0.23122	0.26760	1.0828	0.62736	0.17065	22.2419	8.2751

$\overline{\omega}^1_{b,min} = 0.15$, $\overline{\omega}^1_{b,max} = 0.25$, $\xi^1_{0,min} = 0.1$, $\xi^1_{0,max} = 0.9$, $\lambda^1_{min} = 0.3$, $\lambda^1_{max} = 2$.

Table 5. Optimized controller parameters and achieved $\overline{IAE}$ values, $\overline{\omega}_h = 0.3$.

N	$\overline{\omega}_b$	ξ_0	λ	$\overline{\mathbf{K}}_\mathbf{p}$	$\overline{\mathbf{K}}_\mathbf{i}$	$\overline{\mathbf{IAE}}_\mathbf{r}$	$\overline{\mathbf{IAE}}_\mathbf{d}$
1	0.27968	0.32034	1.0834	0.60629	0.18876	5.0844	7.8575
2	0.28473	0.32234	1.1002	0.60617	0.18499	8.4988	7.8632
3	0.27806	0.31896	1.0658	0.60819	0.19173	12.0398	7.8838
5	0.28868	0.32531	1.1438	0.60412	0.17630	18.6460	7.8586

$\overline{\omega}^1_{b,min} = 1 \times 10^{-4}$, $\overline{\omega}^1_{b,max} = 0.3$, $\xi^1_{0,min} = 0.1$, $\xi^1_{0,max} = 0.9$, $\lambda^1_{min} = 0.1$, $\lambda^1_{max} = 2$.

Table 6. Optimized controller parameters and achieved $\overline{IAE}$ values, $\overline{\omega}_h = 0.5$.

N	$\overline{\omega}_b$	ξ_0	λ	$\overline{\mathbf{K}}_\mathbf{p}$	$\overline{\mathbf{K}}_\mathbf{i}$	$\overline{\mathbf{IAE}}_\mathbf{r}$	$\overline{\mathbf{IAE}}_\mathbf{d}$
1	0.49136	0.42308	1.7353	0.60432	0.12606	4.3456	7.7850
2	0.48887	0.42156	1.5779	0.60506	0.14037	6.3713	7.7865
3	0.48093	0.42119	1.3	0.60365	0.17067	8.4360	7.7925
5	0.48363	0.41924	1.3892	0.60469	0.15948	12.4959	7.8157

$\overline{\omega}^1_{b,min} = 1 \times 10^{-4}$, $\overline{\omega}^1_{b,max} = 0.5$, $\xi^1_{0,min} = 0.1$, $\xi^1_{0,max} = 0.9$, $\lambda^1_{min} = 0.1$, $\lambda^1_{max} = 2$.

Table 7. Optimized controller parameters and achieved $\overline{IAE}$ values, $\overline{\omega}_h = 1$.

N	$\overline{\omega}_b$	ξ_0	λ	$\overline{\mathbf{K}}_\mathbf{p}$	$\overline{\mathbf{K}}_\mathbf{i}$	$\overline{\mathbf{IAE}}_\mathbf{r}$	$\overline{\mathbf{IAE}}_\mathbf{d}$
1	0.40311	0.44050	1.0811	0.63654	0.19193	4.0884	7.6043
2	0.83559	0.52196	1.9890	0.65084	0.18033	4.8221	7.1337
3	0.83715	0.52363	1.9896	0.64986	0.18092	5.9138	7.1334
5	0.83348	0.51830	2.0	0.65323	0.17888	8.1150	7.1329

$\overline{\omega}^1_{b,min} = 1 \times 10^{-4}$, $\overline{\omega}^1_{b,max} = 1$, $\xi^1_{0,min} = 0.1$, $\xi^1_{0,max} = 0.9$, $\lambda^1_{min} = 0.1$, $\lambda^1_{max} = 2$.

Table 8. Optimized controller parameters and achieved $\overline{IAE}$ values, $\overline{\omega}_h = 2$.

N	$\overline{\omega}_b$	ξ_0	λ	$\overline{\mathbf{K}}_\mathbf{p}$	$\overline{\mathbf{K}}_\mathbf{i}$	$\overline{\mathbf{IAE}}_\mathbf{r}$	$\overline{\mathbf{IAE}}_\mathbf{d}$
1	1.0712	0.52406	1.9963	0.67959	0.21140	3.6584	7.4545
2	0.96845	0.49373	1.9124	0.73147	0.19081	4.3024	6.9584
3	1.1133	0.56681	2.0	0.71028	0.23658	4.7885	6.6255
5	1.1377	0.58334	2.0	0.70271	0.24507	6.1010	6.6065

$\overline{\omega}^1_{b,min} = 1 \times 10^{-4}$, $\overline{\omega}^1_{b,max} = 2$, $\xi^1_{0,min} = 0.1$, $\xi^1_{0,max} = 0.9$, $\lambda^1_{min} = 0.1$, $\lambda^1_{max} = 2$.

Table 9. Optimized controller parameters and achieved $\overline{IAE}$ values, $\overline{\omega}_h = 3$.

N	$\overline{\omega}_b$	ξ_0	λ	$\overline{\mathbf{K}}_\mathbf{p}$	$\overline{\mathbf{K}}_\mathbf{i}$	$\overline{\mathbf{IAE}}_\mathbf{r}$	$\overline{\mathbf{IAE}}_\mathbf{d}$
1	1.2077	0.55501	1.9913	0.68786	0.23922	3.5730	7.3271
2	1.1599	0.53677	1.9913	0.71464	0.22907	4.0651	7.0761
3	1.0413	0.52033	1.8448	0.74531	0.20657	4.6112	6.7212
5	1.2261	0.58440	2.0	0.73461	0.25918	5.4803	6.4695

$\overline{\omega}^1_{b,min} = 1 \times 10^{-4}$, $\overline{\omega}^1_{b,max} = 2$, $\xi^1_{0,min} = 0.1$, $\xi^1_{0,max} = 0.9$, $\lambda^1_{min} = 0.1$, $\lambda^1_{max} = 2$.

Table 10. Optimized controller parameters and achieved $\overline{IAE}$ values, $\overline{\omega}_h = 5$.

N	$\overline{\omega}_b$	ξ_0	λ	$\overline{\mathbf{K}}_\mathbf{p}$	$\overline{\mathbf{K}}_\mathbf{i}$	$\overline{\mathbf{IAE}}_\mathbf{r}$	$\overline{\mathbf{IAE}}_\mathbf{d}$
1	1.3231	0.57339	2.0	0.70114	0.26177	3.5106	7.2091
2	1.3004	0.56600	2.0	0.71213	0.25719	3.8814	7.0998
3	1.2405	0.54600	1.9913	0.73529	0.24315	4.2876	6.9254
5	1.1330	0.55400	1.8168	0.75484	0.22603	5.1232	6.4903

$\overline{\omega}^1_{b,min} = 1 \times 10^{-4}$, $\overline{\omega}^1_{b,max} = 2$, $\xi^1_{0,min} = 0.1$, $\xi^1_{0,max} = 0.9$, $\lambda^1_{min} = 0.1$, $\lambda^1_{max} = 2$.

Table 11. Optimized controller parameters and achieved $\overline{IAE}$ values, $\overline{\omega}_h = 10$.

N	$\overline{\omega}_b$	ξ_0	λ	$\overline{\mathbf{K}}_\mathbf{p}$	$\overline{\mathbf{K}}_\mathbf{i}$	$\overline{\mathbf{IAE}}_\mathbf{r}$	$\overline{\mathbf{IAE}}_\mathbf{d}$
1	1.4152	0.58932	2.0	0.71148	0.27957	3.4653	7.1150
2	1.4104	0.58849	2.0	0.71473	0.27899	3.7222	7.0728
3	1.3693	0.57426	1.9963	0.72664	0.26902	4.0140	6.9968
5	0.9369	0.51061	1.6065	0.75571	0.18844	4.8956	6.7499

$\overline{\omega}^1_{b,min} = 1 \times 10^{-4}, \overline{\omega}^1_{b,max} = 2, \xi^1_{0,min} = 0.1, \xi^1_{0,max} = 0.9, \lambda^1_{min} = 0.1, \lambda^1_{max} = 2.$

Table 12. Optimized controller parameters and achieved $\overline{IAE}$ values, $\overline{\omega}_h = 20$.

N	$\overline{\omega}_b$	ξ_0	λ	$\overline{\mathbf{K}}_\mathbf{p}$	$\overline{\mathbf{K}}_\mathbf{i}$	$\overline{\mathbf{IAE}}_\mathbf{r}$	$\overline{\mathbf{IAE}}_\mathbf{d}$
1	1.4573	0.59854	1.9956	0.71654	0.28731	3.4434	7.0670
2	1.4381	0.58726	2.0	0.72267	0.28225	3.6287	7.0504
3	1.4666	0.60071	2.0	0.71949	0.29073	3.8349	7.0115
5	1.4094	0.58031	2.0	0.73801	0.27741	4.2996	6.8839

$\overline{\omega}^1_{b,min} = 1 \times 10^{-4}, \overline{\omega}^1_{b,max} = 2, \xi^1_{0,min} = 0.1, \xi^1_{0,max} = 0.9, \lambda^1_{min} = 0.1, \lambda^1_{max} = 2.$

Table 13. Optimized controller parameters and achieved $\overline{IAE}$ values, $\overline{\omega}_h = 50$.

N	$\overline{\omega}_b$	ξ_0	λ	$\overline{\mathbf{K}}_\mathbf{p}$	$\overline{\mathbf{K}}_\mathbf{i}$	$\overline{\mathbf{IAE}}_\mathbf{r}$	$\overline{\mathbf{IAE}}_\mathbf{d}$
1	1.2936	0.59928	1.9250	0.72134	0.24988	3.4322	7.0396
2	1.4773	0.60060	1.9927	0.72146	0.29036	3.5456	7.0321
3	1.4601	0.58954	2.0	0.72784	0.28607	3.7038	7.0127
5	1.4399	0.58346	2.0	0.73578	0.28190	4.0470	6.9422

$\overline{\omega}^1_{b,min} = 1 \times 10^{-4}, \overline{\omega}^1_{b,max} = 2, \xi^1_{0,min} = 0.1, \xi^1_{0,max} = 0.9, \lambda^1_{min} = 0.1, \lambda^1_{max} = 2.$

3.2. *Laboratory Experiments*

Experiments were performed with the servo system described in Section 2.5. The servo system consists of a controlled drive with a torque generator and a load drive that generates load torque steps.

3.2.1. Description of the Experiments

One experiment with an integer order PI controller and a series of experiments with a FOPI speed controller were performed on the workstation. Each experiment evaluated the response of the actual speed ω to a step change in:

- the reference speed from the value ω_1^* to the value ω_2^* at a constant load torque $M_L = M_{L,1}$ at time $t = t_1$,
- the load torque from the value $M_{L,1}$ to the value $M_{L,2}$ at a constant actual speed $\omega = \omega_2^*$ at time $t = t_2$.

The specific values for the reference speed and the load torque can be found in Table 14. The time t refers to the start of the experiment.

Table 14. Reference values and timing of the experiment.

Symbol	Value	Unit
$M_{L,1}$	0.05	Nm
$M_{L,2}$	0.2	Nm
t_1	1	s
t_2	2	s
ω_1^*	40	rad/s
ω_2^*	80	rad/s

3.2.2. Actual Speed Controller Parameters

The parameters of the speed controller and the fractional order integrator were determined from the normalized parameters given in Tables 3–13 on the basis of the parameters listed in Table 2. The formulas for converting the normalized parameters to the actual parameters are as follows

$$\omega_b = \frac{\overline{\omega}_b}{T_d}, \quad \omega_h = \frac{\overline{\omega}_h}{T_d}, \quad K_o = \left(\frac{\overline{\omega}_h}{T_d}\right)^{1-\lambda}, \quad K_p = \frac{\overline{K}_p}{K_s T_d}, \quad K_i = \frac{\overline{K}_i}{T_d^{\lambda}}, \quad s_0 = \frac{\xi_0}{T_d}$$
$$\omega_j = \frac{\overline{\omega}_b}{T_d}\left(\frac{\overline{\omega}_h}{\overline{\omega}_b}\right)^{\frac{2j-\lambda}{2N}}, \quad \omega_j' = \frac{\overline{\omega}_b}{T_d}\left(\frac{\overline{\omega}_h}{\overline{\omega}_b}\right)^{\frac{2j-2+\lambda}{2N}}, \quad j \in \mathbb{N},\ 1 \le j \le N \tag{47}$$

Experiments with the FOPI controller were carried out with parameters calculated for:

- $N = 3$ and $\overline{\omega}_h \in \{0.3, 0.5, 1, 2, 3, 5, 10\}$.
- $\overline{\omega}_h = 5$ and $N \in \{1, 2, 3, 5\}$,

The value $N = 3$ in the first set of experiments was chosen as the average of the interval 1 to 5. The values $\overline{\omega}_h \ge 0.3$ were chosen because there is a significant decrease in the value of $\overline{IAE}_d$. For $\overline{\omega}_h = 5$ in the second set of experiments, no time constant less than twice the sampling period $T_s = 0.4$ ms appears in the transfer function of the approximated fractional-order integrator (this is not the case for $\overline{\omega}_h \ge 10$). This $\overline{\omega}_h$ setting guarantees the fastest output response for this tuning method and for this system.

The calculated controller parameters are listed in Table 15.

Table 15. PI and FOPI controller parameters used in the experiments.

$\overline{\omega}_h$	N	ω_b [rad/s]	ω_h [rad/s]	$K_o \times 10^3$	λ	$K_p \times 10^3$ [Nms/rad]	K_i [s^{-1}]	s_0 [rad/s]
–	–	–	–	–	1	5.7643	32.99479	112.654
0.3	3	53.473	57.692	765.81	1.0658	7.6022	52.11632	61.338
0.5	3	92.487	96.154	254.16	1.3000	7.5454	158.9838	80.998
1	3	160.990	192.308	5.4923	1.9896	8.1230	6334.704	100.698
2	3	214.096	384.615	2.6000	2.0	8.8783	8749.260	109.002
3	3	200.250	576.923	4.6495	1.8448	9.3161	3377.414	100.063
5	3	238.558	961.538	1.1040	1.9913	9.1909	8590.072	105.000
10	3	263.327	1923.08	5.3475	1.9963	9.0828	9757.242	110.435
5	1	254.442	961.538	1.0400	2.0	8.7640	9680.843	110.267
5	2	250.077	961.538	1.0400	2.0	8.9014	9511.465	108.846
5	5	217.885	961.538	3.6603	1.8168	9.4353	3189.564	106.538

In a speed control loop with an FOPI controller, the reference speed ω^* is filtered by a filter $F_I(s)$ (18), where the polynomials $M_I(s)$ and $N_I(s)$ are given in (14). For an integer order PI controller, the transfer function of the speed setpoint filter is given by (48).

$$F_I(s)|_{\lambda=1} = \frac{s_0^{-1}s + 1}{K_i^{-1}s + 1} \tag{48}$$

3.2.3. Experimental Results

Figures 6 and 7 show the experimentally determined responses of the motor speed and the reference torque to step changes in the reference speed and the load torque. The noise of the constant motor speed is caused by the torque pulsations of the motor, which are caused by the permanent magnets in the magnetic circuit of the motor. The amplitude of this pulsating torque component is less than 0.05 Nm, but due to the low moment of inertia J, it manifests itself as a visible noise in the motor speed. The frequency of the pulsating component of the motor torque depends on the motor speed.

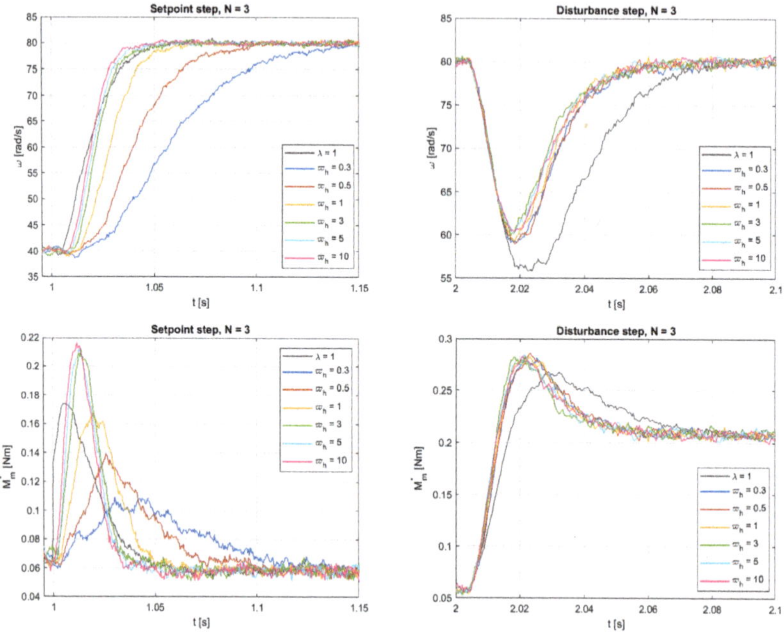

Figure 6. The responses of actual speed ω and reference torque M_m^* to reference speed and load torque steps with integer PI ($\lambda = 1$) and FOPI speed controller, for $N = 3$ and $\overline{\omega}_h = \text{var}$.

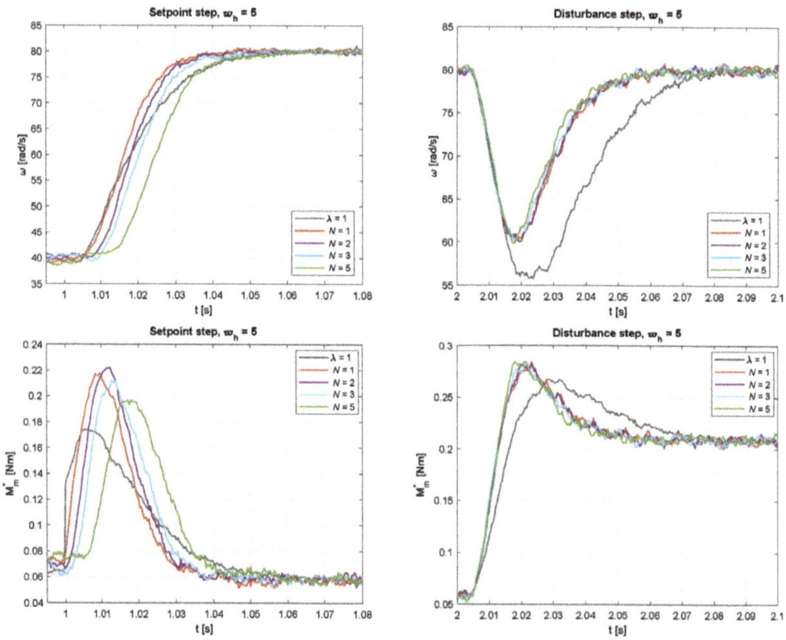

Figure 7. The responses of actual speed ω and reference torque M_m^* to reference speed and load torque steps with integer PI ($\lambda = 1$) and FOPI speed controller, for $\overline{\omega}_h = 5$ and $N = \text{var}$.

In the experiments, the results of which are shown in Figure 6, the fractional order integrator was approximated by the third order transfer function ($N = 3$) for different values of the upper limit of the normalized frequency band of the integrator $\overline{\omega}_h$. The reference tracking performance improves with increasing $\overline{\omega}_h$. In contrast, the disturbance rejection performance does not visibly depend on $\overline{\omega}_h$.

The results of experiments with the same upper limit of the normalized frequency band of the integrator ($\overline{\omega}_h = 5$), but with different order N ($N \in \{1, 2, 3, 5\}$), are shown in Figure 7. The fastest tracking response is obtained with $N = 1$, i.e., with the simplest integrator approximation. Similar to the previous experiment, the disturbance rejection performance does not seem to depend on N.

4. Discussion

This section compares the expected IAE values of the normalized control loop with PI and FOPI controllers. It also evaluates the extent to which the experimental IAE values match the predicted values.

4.1. Comparison of Loop Dynamics with FOPI and PI Controllers for Normalized Control Loop

As already mentioned, Tables 3–13 show the normalized FOPI parameters that achieve optimum disturbance rejection with the permissible shape deviation of the control signal. In the mentioned tables, the calculated values of $\overline{\omega}_{b,opt}$, $\xi_{0,opt}$, λ_{opt}, $\overline{K}_{p,opt}$, and $\overline{K}_{i,opt}$ for the specified upper limit of the integrator frequency band $\overline{\omega}_h$ and the specified order of the approximated integrator N are listed.

The values of $\overline{IAE}_r$ and $\overline{IAE}_d$ from Tables 3–13 versus $\overline{\omega}_h$ for $N = 1, 2, 3$ and 5 are shown in Figure 8. The horizontal gray lines represent the optimal value of $\overline{IAE}_r = 4.1214$ and $\overline{IAE}_d = 12.6387$ with an integer order PI controller ($\lambda = 1$).

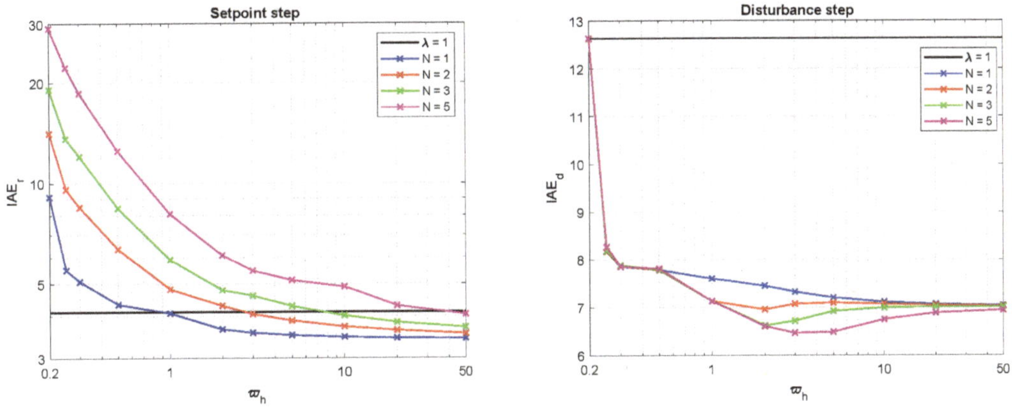

Figure 8. Plots of $\overline{IAE}_r$ and $\overline{IAE}_d$ versus $\overline{\omega}_h$ for N = 1, 2, 3, 5 ($IAE_r = \overline{IAE}_r$, $IAE_d = \overline{IAE}_d$).

The comparison of the $\overline{IAE}_r$ and $\overline{IAE}_d$ waveforms for integer-order and fractional-order PI controllers in Figure 8 shows the following:

$$\begin{array}{ll} \overline{IAE}_r\big|_{\lambda=1} < \overline{IAE}_r\big|_{\lambda\neq1} & \text{for} \quad \overline{\omega}_h < 1 \\ \overline{IAE}_d\big|_{\lambda=1} > \overline{IAE}_d\big|_{\lambda\neq1} & \text{for} \quad \overline{\omega}_h \geq 0.2 \end{array} \tag{49}$$

The higher the order of the approximated integrator, the higher the $\overline{IAE}_r$. The lowest value of $\overline{IAE}_r$ is reached for $N = 1$.

The $\overline{IAE}_d$ values are always lower for $\overline{\omega}_h \in \langle 0.2, 50\rangle$ than when using an integer order PI controller. The lowest value $\overline{IAE}_d = 6.4903$ is obtained for $N = 5, \overline{\omega}_h = 5$. This value of $\overline{IAE}_d$ is 46.1% less than the value of $\overline{IAE}_d = 12.0387$ obtained with the integer order PI controller. The order of the integrator approximation N has no significant influence on the value of $\overline{IAE}_d$. The values of $\overline{IAE}_d$ for $N = 1$ and $N = 5$ differ from each other in a range of 0.014 to 13.26 percent. The smallest difference is at $\overline{\omega}_h = 0.3$ and the largest difference at $\overline{\omega}_h = 3$. It is to be expected that the $\overline{IAE}_d$ value would be even lower at around $\overline{\omega}_h = 3$ for $N > 5$.

4.2. Comparison of Expected and Actual Control Loop Characteristics

To check the correctness of the conversion of the normalized controller parameters given in Tables 3–13 to parameters for the real system, the predicted values of IAE_r and IAE_d were calculated for each experiment. These were compared with the actual values from the experiments in Table 16.

In Table 16, the IAE values for the setpoint and disturbance steps are denoted as $IAE_{r,exp}$ and $IAE_{d,exp}$, respectively. The values of $IAE_{r,exp}$ were calculated from the actual speed samples within the time interval from 1 s to 1.15 s. The values of $IAE_{d,exp}$ were calculated from the actual speed samples within the time interval from 2.005 s to 2.115 s. For comparison, the theoretical IAE values were calculated from

$$IAE_{r,opt} = \overline{IAE}_r T_d(\omega_2^* - \omega_1^*), \quad IAE_{d,opt} = \overline{IAE}_d K_s T_d^2 (M_{L,2} - M_{L,1}) \tag{50}$$

and are also listed in Table 16. The variables δIAE_r and δIAE_d were calculated using the following formula

$$\delta IAE_r = 100 \times \frac{IAE_{r,exp} - IAE_{r,opt}}{IAE_{r,opt}}, \quad \delta IAE_d = 100 \times \frac{IAE_{d,exp} - IAE_{d,opt}}{IAE_{d,opt}} \tag{51}$$

and represent the relative error between the IAE values in the experiment and the IAE calculated from (50). The values in Table 16 show that the relative error between the calculated values of IAE and IAE from the experiment is less than four percent, indicating a high level of agreement between the model and the real system.

Table 16. Integrals of absolute error for setpoint and disturbance steps.

$\overline{\omega}_h$	N	$IAE_{r,exp}$	$IAE_{r,opt}$	δIAE_r [%]	$IAE_{d,exp}$	$IAE_{d,opt}$	δIAE_d [%]
–	–	0.84349	0.85725	−1.61	0.79857	0.78866	1.26
0.3	3	2.46165	2.50428	−1.70	0.49976	0.49196	1.59
0.5	3	1.73665	1.75469	−1.03	0.49411	0.48625	1.62
1	3	1.21870	1.23007	−0.92	0.45999	0.47451	−3.06
2	3	0.99412	0.99601	−0.19	0.42606	0.41344	3.05
3	3	0.94369	0.95129	−0.80	0.42277	0.41941	2.87
5	3	0.88048	0.89182	−1.27	0.44311	0.43215	2.54
10	3	0.82341	0.83491	−1.38	0.45167	0.43661	3.45
5	1	0.72675	0.73021	−0.47	0.46402	0.44985	3.15
5	2	0.79895	0.80733	−1.04	0.45325	0.44303	2.31
5	5	1.06061	1.06562	−0.47	0.41472	0.40500	2.40

As expected, the minimum value of $IAE_{d,exp} = 0.41472$ is at $\overline{\omega}_h = 5, N = 5$. This value is 48.1% less than the value of $IAE_{d,exp} = 0.79857$ obtained with the integer order PI controller.

4.3. Comparison with Results from Other Papers

The speed control loop of a servo drive with a torque generator and an FOPI speed controller is presented in [7,8,10,12]. The speed of a DC motor [7], a PMSM [7,8,10] and an induction motor [12] was controlled in these papers. In both the experimental servo drives [7,8,12] and the simulations [10], the dynamics of the torque generator response was conditioned by the tuning of the torque generator.

In our case, the torque generator channel exhibits a rather significant transport delay $T_{GM} = 5$ ms, which is due to the internal parameter settings of the ACOPOS P3 frequency inverter. We were not able to reduce this delay. It is clear that this transport delay affects the dynamics of the speed control loop, which is reflected in a slower response to the setpoint step and a higher control error at the load torque step than in a servo drive with a faster torque generator (or with a lower transport delay T_{GM}). The control error at the disturbance step is also influenced by the gain K_s, which in our case was several times higher than in the reported papers.

The presented speed controller tuning method was designed to achieve the fastest possible speed response. However, a first look at the simulation and experimental results presented in [7,8,10,12] shows a faster response and smaller control inaccuracy for the load torque step than in our paper. This is due to the high transport delay of our torque generator T_{GM} and the high value of K_s.

In order to roughly compare the characteristics of the speed control loop of the servo drive with FOPI controller tuned by the method presented in this paper with the results presented in cited papers [7,8,10,12], simulations were performed and the magnitude of the speed error $\Delta\omega = \omega^* - \omega$ and the settling time T_{set} were evaluated. The values of K_s and the value of the load torque step M_L were set in the simulations based on the data presented in the respective paper. The torque generator transport delay T_{GM} was not specified in any of the papers and was therefore set to the same value in all simulations, $T_{GM} = 0.5$ ms, which approximately corresponds to the real transport delays of the current control loops in the torque generators of the DC motors and the PMSMs. The FOPI controller parameters in the simulations were calculated for $\overline{\omega}_h = 3$, $N = 3$. The results of the simulations are listed in Table 17. The index "No" indicates results from the cited papers.

Table 17. Speed error and speed settling time in servo drives [7,8,10,12] compared to a servo drive tuned by the presented method.

No	K_s [$kg^{-1}m^{-2}$]	M_L [Nm]	$\Delta\omega_{No}$ [rad/s]	$T_{set,No}$ [ms]	$\Delta\omega$ [rad/s]	T_{set} [ms]
[7]	167	2.2	2	147	0.42	10
[8]	500	5	1	20	0.22	10
[10]	167	2	1	15	0.42	10
[12]	120	6	1.4	40	0.85	10

$T_{GM} = 0.5$ ms, $\overline{\omega}_h = 3$, $N = 3$.

The results in Table 17 show that the tuning of the FOPI controller parameters by the presented method achieves lower speed error and shorter settling time for the load torque step than those obtained in the cited papers.

5. Conclusions

This article describes a method for tuning the parameters of a fractional-order PI (FOPI) speed controller. The tuning of the controller parameters is based on minimizing the value of IAE at a disturbance step, while limiting the deviation of the control signal from an ideal 1P pulse. These two requirements make it possible to minimize the settling time with an overshoot of zero or almost zero.

The tuning of the controller parameters is performed for a normalized process (delay and gain equal to 1) and a controller where the fractional order integrator is approximated by a rational transfer function. The approximation of the fractional order integrator is based on the Oustaloup method and guarantees a zero error in the steady state under disturbance. Tables with normalized parameters of the FOPI controller were calculated for eleven values of the upper limit of the frequency band and for four orders ($N = 1, 2, 3, 5$) of the integrator approximated by the Oustaloup method. The tables also contain the values of the integral of the absolute error (IAE) at the setpoint and disturbance steps for the normalized process.

The characteristics of the control loop with the FOPI controller were compared with those of the integer order PI controller. The aim was to compare the values of the IAE at the setpoint and disturbance steps. The parameters of the integer order PI controller were set to minimize the IAE at the disturbance step. The comparison of the IAE values for an integer order PI controller and a FOPI controller confirms that the FOPI controller can significantly increase the tracking and disturbance rejection performance. In the best case, the IAE value in the disturbance step of the FOPI controller is almost half of the IAE value with an ordinary PI controller (integer order).

When using a fractional-order PI controller in a real servo drive, the actual controller parameters are recalculated from the normalized parameters based on the actual characteristics of the servo drive. Similarly, the actual IAE values can be calculated from the tabulated values.

The characteristics of the control loop were tested on a servo system with a pair of industrial servo drives. The responses of the motor speed to setpoint speed and load torque steps were evaluated. The IAE values at the setpoint and disturbance steps were calculated from the actual rotor speed samples. Comparison of the IAE values calculated from the experimental results and the tabulated values for the normalized system confirmed the accuracy of the controller design and the correctness of the calculated IAE values for the normalized control loop.

Finally, the limitations of this study can be briefly summarized as follows. First, the optimized parameters of the normalized FOPI controller presented in Section 3.1 are only applicable when controlling an IPDT system. An electric servo drive with a torque generator can be considered as such a system. Second, the fractional-order integrator in the FOPI controller must be approximated by the Oustaloup method, which results in a continuous transfer function of the chosen order. A proper conversion method to discrete form must be applied in the digital implementation. Third, the optimized FOPI controller parameters were computed for the first to fifth order Oustaloup approximation of the fractional order integrator. The computations were not performed for higher orders due to the increased computational requirements on the computer executing the FOPI controller parameter optimization algorithm. Fourth, the optimized FOPI controller parameters were not calculated even for $\overline{\omega}_h > 50$. However, from the plots of $\overline{IAE}_r$ and $\overline{IAE}_d$ versus $\overline{\omega}_h$, it can be inferred that higher values of $\overline{\omega}_h$ would not result in a significant reduction in the values of $\overline{IAE}_r$ and $\overline{IAE}_d$. Fifth, the application and applicability of the calculated parameters of the normalized FOPI controller were experimentally validated on the servo drive, which allowed to correctly verify the behavior of the speed control loop only for $\overline{\omega}_h \leq 5$.

Author Contributions: Writing—original draft preparation, I.B., I.B.J., P.B., M.H. and D.V.; writing—review and editing, I.B., P.B., M.H. and D.V.; simulations, I.B.; experiments, I.B.J.; project administration, P.B. All authors have read and agreed to the published version of the manuscript.

Funding: This research was supported in part by the following grants: Grant No. 1/0637/23 financed by the Scientific Grant Agency of the Ministry of Education, Research, Development and Youth of the Slovak Republic (VEGA); Grant No. APVV-21-0125 financed by the Slovak Research and Development Agency; Research Program P2-0001 (Systems and Control) and research project L2-3166 (Supervisory control system for plant-wide optimization of wastewater treatment plant operation) financed by the Slovenian Research and Innovation Agency.

Institutional Review Board Statement: Not applicable.

Informed Consent Statement: Not applicable.

Data Availability Statement: Data are contained within the article.

Acknowledgments: Supported by E-Academia Slovaca, a non-profit organisation, Sadmelijská 1, 831 06 Bratislava, Slovakia.

Conflicts of Interest: The authors declare no conflicts of interest.

Abbreviations

The following abbreviations are used in this manuscript:

DC	Direct Current
FOPI	Fractional-Order Proportional-Integral
FOPID	Fractional-Order Proportional-Integral-Derivative
IAE	Integral of Absolute Error
IE	Integral of Error
IPDT	Integrator Plus Dead-Time
LESO	Linear Extended State Observer
MDPM	Multiple Dominant Pole Method
OPC UA	Open Platform Communications Unified Architecture
PI	Proportional-Integral
PID	Proportional-Integral-Derivative
PMSM	Permanent Magnet Synchronous Motor
PPM	Performance Portrait Method
TV	Total Variance

Nomenclature

The following symbols are used in this manuscript:

k	Cycle number of the FOPI controller parameter optimization algorithm
k_d	Gain of the derivative component of the FOPID controller
k_i	Gain of the integral component of the FOPID controller
k_{max}	The total number of cycles of the FOPI controller parameter optimization algorithm
k_p	Gain of the proportional component of the FOPID controller
n_N	Rated speed of the motor
s	Laplace operator
s_0	Absolute value of the double real pole in the speed control loop transfer function
t	Time
t_1	Time of the reference speed step in the experiment
t_2	Time of the load torque step in the experiment
E	Control error
$E_{\infty,A}$	Steady-state error at the setpoint step
$E_{\infty L,A}$	Steady-state error at the disturbance step
$F_I(s)$	Transfer function of the reference speed filter
$F_I(\xi)$	Transfer function of the normalized reference speed filter
$G_{1,d}(\xi)$	Closed loop transfer function for a disturbance step with the normalized PI controller
$G_{1,r}(\xi)$	Closed loop transfer function with the normalized PI controller
$G_{e,A}(s)$	Error transfer function for a setpoint step
$G_{eL,A}(s)$	Error transfer function for a disturbance step
$G_d(s)$	Closed loop transfer function for a disturbance step with the FOPI controller
$G_d(\xi)$	Normalized $G_d(s)$
$\widehat{G}_o^{\kappa}(s)$	Transfer function of the fractional-order derivative approximated by the Oustaloup method
$G_r(s)$	Closed loop transfer function with the FOPI controller
$G_r(\xi)$	Normalized $G_r(s)$
$\mathbf{H}^k$	Three-dimensional space of parameters $\overline{\omega}_b$, ξ_0, and λ in the k-th cycle of the optimization algorithm
$IAE_{d,exp}$	The value of the integral of absolute error at the disturbance step retrieved from the experiment
$IAE_{d,opt}$	Calculated value of the integral of absolute error at the disturbance step when using the optimized parameters of the normalized FOPI controller
$IAE_{r,exp}$	The value of the integral of absolute error at the setpoint step retrieved from the experiment
$IAE_{r,opt}$	Calculated value of the integral of the absolute error at the setpoint step when using the optimized parameters of the normalized FOPI controller
$\overline{IAE_d}$	Normalized integral of absolute error at the disturbance step

$\overline{IAE}_{d,min}$	Minimum $\overline{IAE}_d$ value
$\overline{IAE}_{d,opt}$	Integral of absolute error at the disturbance step when the optimized parameters of the normalized FOPI controller are used
$\overline{IAE}_{r,min}$	Minimum $\overline{IAE}_r$ value
$\overline{IAE}_{r,opt}$	Integral of absolute error at the setpoint step when the optimized parameters of the normalized FOPI controller are used
IE_d	Integral of error at the disturbance step
$\overline{IE}_d$	Normalized integral of error at the disturbance step
$\overline{IE}_{d,min}$	Minimum $\overline{IE}_d$ value
IE_r	Integral of error at the setpoint step
$\overline{IE}_r$	Normalized integral of absolute error at the setpoint step
$\overline{IE}_{r,min}$	Minimum $\overline{IE}_r$ value
J	Moment of inertia
K_i	Gain of the integral component of the FOPI controller
$\overline{K}_i$	Normalized K_i
$\overline{K}_{i,opt}$	The value of $\overline{K}_i$ after the optimization algorithm has been completed
K_o	Coefficient in the modified form of the Oustaloup approximation
$\overline{K}_o$	Normalized K_o
K_p	Gain of the proportional component of the FOPI controller
$\overline{K}_p$	Normalized K_p
$\overline{K}_{p,opt}$	The value of $\overline{K}_p$ after the optimization algorithm has been completed
K_s	Gain of the system
$M_A(s)$	Numerator polynomial of a transfer function approximating a fractional-order derivative or integral
$M_I(s)$	Numerator polynomial in the modified form of the Oustaloup approximation
$M_I(\xi)$	Numerator polynomial in the normalized Oustaloup approximation
M_L	Load torque
$\overline{M}_L$	Normalized load torque
M_L^*	Reference load torque
M_m	Motor torque
$\overline{M}_m$	Normalized motor torque
M_m^*	Reference motor torque
M_{m1}^*	Reference torque of the motor No. 1
M_{m2}^*	Reference torque of the motor No. 2
$M_{Od}(s)$	Numerator polynomial of the transfer function $G_d(s)$
$M_{Od}(\xi)$	Numerator polynomial of the transfer function $G_d(\xi)$
$M_{Or}(s)$	Numerator polynomial of the transfer function $G_r(s)$
$M_{Or}(\xi)$	Numerator polynomial of the transfer function $G_r(\xi)$
N	Order of the transfer function of a fractional-order integrator approximated by the Oustaloup method
$N_A(s)$	Denominator polynomial of a transfer function approximating a fractional-order derivative or integral
$N_I(s)$	Denominator polynomial in the modified form of the Oustaloup approximation
$N_I(\xi)$	Denominator polynomial in the normalized Oustaloup approximation
$N_O(s)$	Denominator polynomial of the transfer functions $G_d(s)$ and $G_r(s)$
$N_O(\xi)$	Denominator polynomial of the transfer functions $G_d(\xi)$ and $G_r(\xi)$
N_{oP}	The number of all tested values of a particular variable (i.e., the values of $\overline{\omega}_b$, ξ_0, or λ) applied in one cycle of the optimization algorithm
P_n	Designates one of the parameters: $\overline{\omega}_b$, ξ_0, or λ
$P_{n,max}^k$	Maximum value of parameter P_n in k-th cycle of optimizing algorithm
$P_{n,min}^k$	Minimum value of parameter P_n in k-th cycle of optimizing algorithm
$P_{n,opt}^{k-1}$	Optimum value of parameter P_n in the optimizing algorithm cycle $k-1$
P_N	Rated power of the motor
T_d	Transport delay in the control channel of the system
T_{GM}	Transport delay of the torque generator
T_s	Sampling period of the discrete speed controller
T_{set}	Settling time
$TV_1(\overline{U}^*)$	Total variation in the normalized control signal from the one-pulse function

$TV_{1d}(\overline{u}^*)$	Total variation in the normalized control signal from the one-pulse function at the disturbance step
$TV_{1r}(\overline{u}^*)$	Total variation in the normalized control signal from the one-pulse function at the setpoint step
u	The output of the FOPI controller
$\overline{u}^*$	Normalized control signal
$\overline{u}_0^*$	Initial value of the normalized control signal
$\overline{u}_c^*$	Sample No. c of the normalized control signal
$\overline{u}_{max}^*$	Maximum value of the normalized control signal
$\overline{u}_\infty^*$	Steady state value of the normalized control signal
${}_aD_t^\mu$	Integrodifferentiator operator, where a, t are the limits of the operation
γ_j	Angular frequency representing a pole in the Oustaloup approximation
$\gamma_j^{'}$	Angular frequency representing a zero in the Oustaloup approximation
δIAE_d	Relative deviation between experimental and calculated IAE_d value
δIAE_r	Relative deviation between experimental and calculated IAE_r value
ε_r	maximum allowable shape deviation at the setpoint or disturbance step
λ	Fractional order of the integral
λ_{max}^1	Maximum value of λ in the first cycle of the optimization algorithm
λ_{min}^1	Minimum value of λ in the first cycle of the optimization algorithm
λ_{opt}	The value of λ after the optimization algorithm has been completed
ξ	Normalized Laplace operator
ξ_0	Absolute value of the double dominant real pole in the normalized closed-loop transfer function
$\xi_{0,max}^1$	Maximum value of ξ_0 in the first cycle of the optimization algorithm
$\xi_{0,min}^1$	Minimum value of ξ_0 in the first cycle of the optimization algorithm
$\xi_{0,opt}$	The value of ξ_0 after the optimization algorithm has been completed
μ	Fractional order of the derivative
κ	Fractional order of the derivative
φ_1	Actual angular position of motor M_1
φ_2	Actual angular position of motor M_2
ω	Actual angular speed
ω^*	Reference angular speed
ω_1^*, ω_2^*	The reference values of the motor speed in the experiment
ω_b	The lower limit of the frequency band in which the fractional-order derivative/integrator approximation is valid when the Oustaloup method is used
$\overline{\omega}_b$	Normalized ω_b
$\overline{\omega}_{b,max}^1$	Maximum value of $\overline{\omega}_b$ in the first cycle of the optimization algorithm
$\overline{\omega}_{b,min}^1$	Minimum value of $\overline{\omega}_b$ in the first cycle of the optimization algorithm
$\overline{\omega}_{b,opt}$	The value of $\overline{\omega}_b$ after the optimization algorithm has been completed
ω_h	Upper limit of the frequency band in which the fractional-order derivative/integrator approximation is valid when the Oustaloup method is used
$\overline{\omega}_h$	Normalized ω_h
ω_j	Angular frequency representing a pole in the modified form of the Oustaloup approximation
$\overline{\omega}_j$	Normalized ω_j
$\omega_j^{'}$	Angular frequency representing a zero in the modified form of the Oustaloup approximation
$\overline{\omega}_j^{'}$	Normalized $\omega_j^{'}$
Γ_d	Optimizing function used to tune $\overline{\omega}_b$, ξ_0, and λ values
ΔP_n^k	Step to change the value of one of the parameters $\overline{\omega}_b$, ξ_0, or λ in the k-th cycle of the optimization algorithm
$\Delta\omega$	Speed error at load torque step
Λ^k	Interval of λ values to be applied in the k-th cycle of the optimization algorithm
Ξ_0^k	Interval of ξ_0 values to be applied in the k-th cycle of the optimization algorithm
Ω_b^k	Interval of ω_b values to be applied in the k-th cycle of the optimization algorithm
$\mathcal{L}$	Laplace transform

References

1. Wiora, J.; Wiora, A. Influence of Methods Approximating Fractional-Order Differentiation on the Output Signal Illustrated by Three Variants of Oustaloup Filter. *Symmetry* **2020**, *12*, 1898. [CrossRef]
2. Vinagre, B.; Podlubný, I.; Hernández, A.; Feliu, V. Some approximations of fractional order operators used in control theory and applications. *J. Fract. Calc. Appl. Anal.* **2000**, *4*, 47–66.
3. Shah, P.; Agashe, S. Review of fractional PID controller. *Mechatronics* **2016**, *38*, 29–41. [CrossRef]
4. Diethelm, K.; Ford, N.; Luchko, Y. Algorithms for the fractional calculus: A selection of numerical methods. *Comput. Methods Appl. Mech. Eng.* **2005**, *194*, 743–773. [CrossRef]
5. Podlubný, I. Fractional-Order Systems and $PI^{\lambda}D^{\mu}$-Controllers. *IEEE Trans. Autom. Control.* **1999**, *44*, 208–214. [CrossRef]
6. Petráš, I. Fractional-Order feedback control of a DC motor. *J. Electr. Eng.* **2009**, *60*, 117–128.
7. Lino, P.; Maione, G.; Stasi, S.; Padula, F.; Visioli, A. Synthesis of Fractional-order PI Controllers and Fractional-order Filters for Industrial Electrical Drives. *IIEEE/CAA J. Autom. Sin.* **2017**, *4*, 58–69. [CrossRef]
8. Chen, L.; Chen, G.; Li, P.; Lopes, A.; Tenreiro Machado, J.; Xu, S. A variable-order fractional proportional-integral controller and its application to a permanent magnet synchronous motor. *Alex. Eng. J.* **2020**, *59*, 3247–3254. [CrossRef]
9. Jakovljević, B.; Lino, P.; Maione, G. Optimized Current and Speed Fractional-Order PID Control in Electrical Drives. In *Proceedings of the International Conference on Fractional Differentiation and Its Applications (ICFDA'21)*; Dzielinski, A., Sierociuk, D., Ostalczyk, P., Eds.; Springer: Cham, Switzerland, 2022; pp. 141–152. [CrossRef]
10. Apte, A.; Thakar, U.; Joshi, V. Disturbance observer based speed control of PMSM using fractional order PI controller. *IEEE/CAA J. Autom. Sin.* **2019**, *6*, 316–326. [CrossRef]
11. Wang, S.; Li, B.; Chen, P.; Yu, W.; Peng, Y.; Luo, Y. A fractional-order active disturbance rejection control for permanent magnet synchronous motor position servo system. *Asian J. Control* **2024**, *26*, 3137–3147. [CrossRef]
12. Kumar, D.M.; Mudaliar, H.K.; Cirrincione, M.; Mehta, U.; Pucci, M. Design of a Fractional Order PI (FOPI) for the Speed Control of a High-Performance Electrical Drive with an Induction Motor. In Proceedings of the 21st International Conference on Electrical Machines and Systems (ICEMS), Jeju, Republic of Korea, 7–10 October 2018; pp. 1198–1202. [CrossRef]
13. Angel, L.; Viola, J. Control Performance Assessment of Fractional-Order PID Controllers Applied to Tracking Trajectory Control of Robotic Systems. *Wseas Trans. Syst. Control* **2022**, *17*, 62–73. [CrossRef]
14. Bélai, I.; Huba, M.; Burn, K.; Cox, C. PID and filtered PID control design with application to a positional servo drive. *Kybernetika* **2019**, *55*, 540–560. [CrossRef]
15. Phung Quang, N.; Dittrich, J.A. *Vector Control of Three-Phase AC Machines—System Development in the Practice*, 2nd ed.; Springer: Berlin/Heidelberg, Germany, 2015. [CrossRef]
16. Oustaloup, A.; Levron, F.; Mathieu, B.; Nanot, F. Frequency-band complex noninteger differentiator: Characterization and synthesis. *IEEE Trans. Circuits Syst. I Fundam. Theory Appl.* **2000**, *47*, 25–39. [CrossRef]
17. Deniz, F.; Alagoz, B.; Tan, N.; Koseoglu, M. Revisiting four approximation methods for fractional order transfer function implementations: Stability preservation, time and frequency response matching analyses. *Annu. Rev. Control* **2020**, *49*, 239–257. [CrossRef]
18. Singhal, R.; Padhee, S.; Kaur, G. Design of Fractional Order PID Controller for Speed Control of DC Motor. *Int. J. Sci. Res. Res. Publ.* **2012**, *2*, 1–8.
19. Leuzzi, R.; Lino, P.; Maione, G.; Stasi, S.; Padula, F.; Visioli, A. Combined Fractional Feedback-Feedforward Controller Design for Electrical Drives. In Proceedings of the ICFDA'14 International Conference on Fractional Differentiation and Its Applications 2014, Catania, Italy, 23–25 June 2014; pp. 1–6. [CrossRef]
20. Dulf, É.H.; Şuşcă, M.; Kovács, L. Novel Optimum Magnitude Based Fractional Order Controller Design Method. *IFAC-PapersOnLine* **2018**, *51*, 912–917. [CrossRef]
21. Wang, R.; Pi, Y. Fractional-order PI Speed Control for Permanent Magnet Synchronous Motor. In Proceedings of the 2012 IEEE International Conference on Mechatronics and Automation, Chengdu, China, 5–8 August 2012; pp. 2303–2308. [CrossRef]
22. Li, X.; Gao, L. A Simple Frequency-domain Tuning Method of Fractional-order PID Controllers for Fractional-order Delay Systems. *Int. J. Control Autom. Syst.* **2022**, *20*, 2159–2168. [CrossRef]
23. Pradhan, R.; Majhi, S.K.; Pradhan, J.K.; Pati, B.B. Optimal fractional order PID controller design using Ant lion Optimizer. *Ain Shams Eng. J.* **2020**, *11*, 281–291. [CrossRef]
24. Dastjerdi, A.A.; Vinagre, B.M.; Chen, Y.; HosseinNia, S.H. Linear fractional order controllers; A survey in the frequency domain. *Annu. Rev. Control* **2019**, *47*, 51–70. [CrossRef]
25. Verma, S.K.; Yadav, S.; Nagar, S.K. Optimization of Fractional Order PID Controller Using Grey Wolf Optimizer. *J. Control Autom. Electr. Syst.* **2017**, *28*, 314–322. [CrossRef]
26. Paducel, I.; Safirescu, C.O.; Dulf, E.H. Fractional Order Controller for Wind Turbines. *Appl. Sci.* **2022**, *12*, 8400. [CrossRef]
27. Bélai, I.; Bélai, I. Electric Servo Drive with Fractional-Order PI Speed Controller. In Proceedings of the 2023 24th International Conference on Process Control (PC), Strbske Pleso, Slovakia, 6–9 June 2023; pp. 6–11. [CrossRef]
28. Viteckova, M.; Vitecek, A. Use of multiple dominant pole method for controller tuning. In Proceedings of the 13th International Carpathian Control Conference (ICCC), High Tatras, Slovakia, 28–31 May 2012; pp. 757–762. [CrossRef]
29. Huba, M.; Skogestad, S.; Fikar, M.; Hovd, M.; Johansen, T.; Rohal'-Ilkiv, B. *Selected Topics on Constrained and Nonlinear Control*; STU Bratislava—NTNU Trondheim: Bratislava, Slovakia, 2011; p. 104.

30. Huba, M.; Bistak, P.; Vrancic, D. Parametrization and Optimal Tuning of Constrained Series PIDA Controller for IPDT Models. *Mathematics* **2023**, *11*, 4229. [CrossRef]
31. Huba, M. Performance measures, performance limits and optimal PI control for the IPDT plant. *J. Process. Control* **2013**, *23*, 500–515. [CrossRef]
32. Franklin, G.F.; Powell, J.D.; Workman, M. *Digital Control of Dynamic Systems*, 3rd ed.; Ellis-Kagle Press: Half Moon Bay, CA, USA, 2022.

symmetry

MDPI

Article

Symmetry-Optimized Dynamical Analysis of Optical Soliton Patterns in the Flexibly Supported Euler–Bernoulli Beam Equation: A Semi-Analytical Solution Approach

Muhammad Umer and Paweł Olejnik *

Department of Automation, Biomechanics and Mechatronics, Lodz University of Technology, 1/15 Stefanowski St., 90-537 Lodz, Poland; muhammad.umer@dokt.p.lodz.pl
* Correspondence: pawel.olejnik@p.lodz.pl

Abstract: This study employs spatial optimization principles to investigate the nonlinear vibration of a flexibly supported Euler–Bernoulli beam, a (1 + 1)-dimensional system subjected to axial loads. The modified Khater method, a crucial tool in mechanical engineering, is utilized to analyze analytical solutions, which include a symmetric spatial representation of the waveform as an integral part of each solution. Notably, periodic soliton solutions for the nonlinear model closely align with numerical and approximate analytical solutions, demonstrating the accuracy of our modeling approach. Density diagrams, contour diagrams, and Poincaré maps depicting the obtained analytical solutions are presented to elucidate their accuracy and provide visual confirmation of the optimized engineering model's physical significance. The planar dynamical system is derived through the Galilean transformation by employing mathematical models and appropriate parameter values, thereby further refining problem understanding. Sensitivity analysis is conducted, and phase portraits with equilibrium points are illustrated by analyzing a special case of the investigated dynamical system, emphasizing its symmetrical properties. Lastly, we perform a global analysis to identify periodic, quasi-periodic, and chaotic behaviors, with an extra weak forcing term confirmed by Poincaré maps and a two-dimensional symmetric basin of the largest Lyapunov exponent.

Keywords: Euler–Bernoulli beam; analytical solution; approximate methods; equilibrium points; dynamical analysis; chaos; Lyapunov exponents

MSC: 05E05; 34C25; 35A24; 35C08; 37M05; 37N30; 65P20; 70S10; 74K10

1. Introduction

The demand for engineered construction is continually increasing. In structural engineering, the investigation of vibrations in beams is of great importance, especially in the context of tall structures, aerospace vehicles, large bridges, and various industrial applications. As the oscillation's amplitude increases, these structures experience nonlinear vibrations, which can result in material fatigue and structural damage. The repercussions become more pronounced as the system approaches its inherent frequency. Consequently, precise mathematical and numerical analysis is imperative to comprehend the nonlinear vibration characteristics of these structures.

The design of such buildings necessitates careful consideration of multiple factors to optimize performance and extend their lifespan. Dynamic reactions of structures play a significant role in the design process. Distributed parameters and continuous systems, exemplified by the nonlinear vibration of beams, are addressed using linear and nonlinear partial differential equations (PDEs) in both spatial and temporal dimensions. Attaining precise or closed-form solutions for nonlinear issues has proven challenging.

Researchers have employed two primary categories of approximation solutions for initial boundary-value problems: numerical approaches [1,2] as well as approximate analytical approaches [3,4]. Perturbation methods have not been directly applied to solve nonlinear PDEs and their appropriate boundary conditions, especially in severely nonlinear systems. Consequently, the Galerkin method is employed to transform the initial partial differential equations into a set of nonlinear ordinary differential equations. Subsequently, these governing equations are analytically resolved in the time domain.

Numerous researchers have addressed the issue of vibrating beams by formulating partial differential equations of motion with diverse boundary conditions [5–13]. Bayat et al. [14] conducted an extensive investigation into the analytical evaluation of vibrating tapered beams, achieving notable progress in developing analytical solutions for nonlinear equations devoid of very small parameters. These advancements have been instrumental in approximating solutions for nonlinear oscillators.

Various classical methodologies, including perturbation techniques, have been employed to tackle the governing nonlinear differential equations for investigating nonlinear vibrations. Noteworthy methods include the Max-Min Approach [15], Homotopy Analysis Method [16,17], Iteration Perturbation Method [18], ADM-Padé technique [19], Homotopy Perturbation Method (HPM) [20], Adomian Decomposition [21], Energy Balance Method [22,23], Multistage Adomian Decomposition [24], Variational Iteration Method [25,26], Monotone Iteration Schemes [27], Hamiltonian Approach [28], Navier and Levy-type Solution [29,30], and Parameter Expansion Method [31].

A critical aspect of investigating nonlinear physical mechanisms involves exploring solutions in the form of traveling waves for nonlinear PDEs, which find applications in engineering sciences, mathematics, and technological fields. Nonlinear partial and ordinary differential equations (PDEs and ODEs) are crucial for simulating various significant phenomena in sciences such as mechanical engineering, biology, chemistry, and finance, as demonstrated in the literature [32–35].

Although numerous works exist on approximate analytical solutions in mechanical engineering, a gap persists in the literature regarding semi-analytical solutions. Therefore, this study aims to uncover soliton solutions with the aid of semi-analytical methods. The chosen methodologies encompass the G'/G-expansion method [36], the Sardar sub-equation method [37], the modified simple equation method [38], the generalized Jacobi elliptic function method [39], the modified extended *tanh* scheme [40], the Kudryashov method [41], the improved Fan sub-equation method [42], the extended rational sine-cosine method [43], the unified method [44,45], the extended algebraic method [46], the new auxiliary equation technique [47], bifurcation analysis methods [48,49], and others.

According to Jhangeer et al. [50,51], the perturbed Fokas–Lenells equation has been demonstrated to have bifurcations, soliton structures, and chaotic dynamics. Solitons play a significant role in various physical phenomena and manifest in diverse forms, including kinks, light breathers, periodic structures, darkness, envelopes, and more. Imran et al. [52] show saddle-node bifurcation while studying the fractional space-time nonlinear Chen–Lee–Liu equation's shift from periodic to quasi-periodic behavior. The work analyzes solitonic structures using direct algebraic methods and Galilean transformations to examine multi-dimensional bifurcations of dynamical solutions. A chaotic structure and multi-stability indicate a higher degree of complexity in the equation's behavior.

In this investigation, we apply the Modified Khater Method (MKM)—a methodology not previously applied in the field of mechanical engineering of beams. Application of this effective technique to our experimental equation yields a visualization of novel wave patterns. Utilizing MKM, periodic soliton solutions, bright solutions, soliton-like solutions, mixed soliton solutions, and solitary bright solutions are attained. These results are expressed in terms of trigonometric and hyperbolic functions. The findings presented in this research have not been previously documented in the existing literature. The solutions developed in this study are new and hold significant utility across other scientific disciplines.

The Winkler model, introduced in 1867, incorporates the typical displacement of a structure. This model establishes a linear algebraic relationship between the normal displacement of the structure and the contact pressure [53]. Utilizing a set of mutually parallel and independent spring components to represent the soil medium, the Winkler model allows for a more straightforward comparison of the system's nonlinear behavior compared to other approaches [54,55]. Wu and Liu [56] employed the technique of differential quadrature to address the buckling equation of a single-span Bernoulli-Euler beam. In 2006, they proposed the Parameterized-Perturbation method as a solution for highly nonlinear equations.

Osman and Omer [57] elucidated the relationship between curvature and bending moment in large-deformation Euler–Bernoulli beams, emphasizing distinctions between linear and nonlinear theories. Their work cautions against the indiscriminate use of nonlinear mathematical curvature, providing a numerical example for practical clarity. Pirbodaghi et al. [58] explored the nonlinear vibration characteristics of Euler–Bernoulli beams with geometric nonlinearity under axial loads using the homotopy analysis approach. They also examined the influence of vibration amplitude on nonlinear frequency and buckling load. In a study by Burgreen [59], the natural vibrations of a buckling beam supported at both ends were explored using a discretization method that considered a single mode of vibration. According to Burgreen, the buckling beam's natural frequencies are vibration amplitude-dependent.

Abinash and Sundararajan [60] extend the Fragile Points Method (FPM) to analyze the behavior of isotropic and functionally graded Euler–Bernoulli beams under static bending, free vibration, and mechanical buckling. This is achieved through a meshless approach that utilizes discontinuous polynomial test and trial functions, along with numerical flux corrections, to enhance consistency. Pratiwi et al. [61] presents a Python-based tool that is validated against analytical solutions and commercial finite element solvers to efficiently and accurately analyze the structural response of wind turbine blades under aerodynamic loading using complex Euler–Bernoulli Beam theory and the polygon algorithm. Ataman and Szcześniak [62] analyze the dynamic response of a Bernoulli–Euler beam on a three-parameter inertial basis to moving forces. Deformable foundation properties, velocities, and foundation models all have an impact on beam dynamic deflection. The findings are a baseline for studying more complicated engineering structures under moving loads like road or railroad vehicles.

Upon examining the aforementioned achievements, the primary objective of this work is to derive the mathematical equation that describes the vibration behavior of clamped-clamped Euler–Bernoulli beams, considering their geometric nonlinearity. These beams are fixed at one end, and their geometric nonlinearity arises from the nonlinear interactions between strain and displacement, a topic frequently addressed in existing literature. This type of nonlinearity stems from various factors, including stretching in the middle of the structure, high curvatures in structural parts, and significant rotation of elements.

Initially, the governing nonlinear PDE was simplified to a solitary nonlinear ODE using the Galerkin technique under the assumption that only the basic mode was stimulated. Subsequently, this problem was analytically solved in the time domain using the MKM approach employed in this work. Finally, the results obtained from the proposed approach are compared with numerical solutions.

Finally, in relation to practical applications within the domain of engineering design and optimization, the precise semi-analytical solutions offered by the model can be utilized for the design and optimization of structures that involve Euler–Bernoulli beams. This application ensures enhanced reliability and performance, as demonstrated in studies such as [4,9,53].

Similarly, regarding vibration control and mitigation, gaining insight into the diverse, dynamic behaviors of beams can assist in formulating efficient vibration control and mitigation solutions. These solutions are essential for enhancing the durability and safety of engineering structures, as evidenced in [5,8,63–66].

The subsequent sections follow this sequence: Section 2 outlines the formulation of the problem. In Section 3, we illustrate the traveling wave solutions of the model under consideration. Section 4 presents the visualization and discussion of the dynamics of wave patterns, while Section 5.1 showcases phase portraits of the given planar dynamical system, incorporating bifurcation analysis. Moreover, Section 5.2 demonstrates the sensitivity of the system corresponding to initial conditions, and Section 5.3 depicts the chaotic behavior of the system with extra small harmonic forcing (perturbation) term, i.e., later verified with the help of Poincaré section and Lyapunov exponents spectra. Final conclusions drawn from these patterns are presented in Section 6.

2. Formulation of the Problem

A linear beam is supported by a flexible base and possesses properties such as length $\hat{L}$, cross-sectional area $\hat{A}$, mass per unit length $\hat{\mu}$, moment of inertia $\hat{I}$, and modulus of elasticity $\hat{E}$. Additionally, the beam is subjected to an axial force of magnitude $\hat{F}$ as shown in Figure 1. Assumptions include a uniform cross-sectional area and homogeneous material, in accordance with the Euler–Bernoulli beam theory. According to this theory, post-deformation, cross-sectional planes maintain their planar shape, while lines perpendicular to the central plane retain their perpendicularity. However, lines running across the cross-section do not change in length.

Three fundamental assumptions underpin the theory:

- Neglect of deformation within the same plane.
- Dismissal of transverse shear forces (resulting in cross-section rotation solely caused by bending).
- The incompressibility condition, which suggests the absence of transverse typical strains.

References supporting these assumptions include [65,67].

The equation of motion, considering the impact of mid-plane stretching, is expressed as follows:

$$\hat{E}\hat{I}\frac{\partial^4\hat{W}}{\partial\hat{X}^4}+\hat{\mu}\frac{\partial^2\hat{W}}{\partial\hat{t}^2}+\hat{F}\frac{\partial^2\hat{W}}{\partial\hat{X}^2}+\hat{C}\frac{\partial\hat{W}}{\partial\hat{X}}+\hat{K}\hat{W}-\frac{\hat{E}\hat{A}}{2\hat{L}}\frac{\partial^2\hat{W}}{\partial\hat{X}^2}\int_0^L\left(\frac{\partial\hat{W}}{\partial\hat{X}}\right)^2 d\hat{X}=V(\hat{X},\hat{t}). \quad (1)$$

The viscous damping coefficient is represented by $\hat{C}$, the foundation modulus is denoted by $\hat{K}$, and $\hat{W}(\hat{X},\hat{t})$ is an unknown function, and V represents the distributed load in the transverse direction.

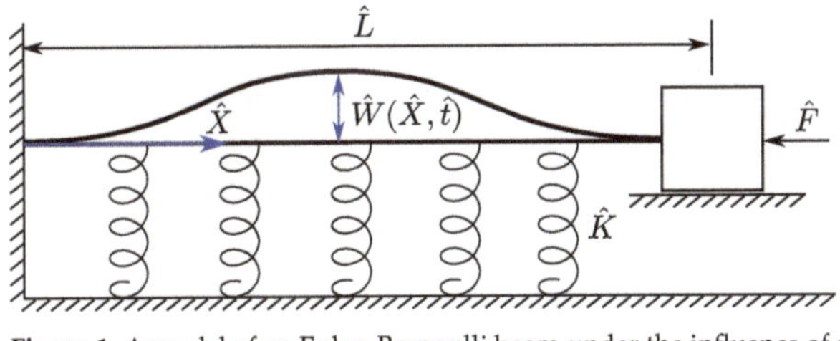

Figure 1. A model of an Euler–Bernoulli beam under the influence of an axial load.

Let us assume that the non-conservative forces are negligible, meaning that the terms at $\hat{C}$ and V are equal to zero. Therefore, Equation (1) can be expressed in the following manner:

$$\hat{E}\hat{I}\frac{\partial^4\hat{W}}{\partial\hat{X}^4}+\hat{\mu}\frac{\partial^2\hat{W}}{\partial\hat{t}^2}+\hat{F}\frac{\partial^2\hat{W}}{\partial\hat{X}^2}+\hat{K}\hat{W}-\frac{\hat{E}\hat{A}}{2\hat{L}}\frac{\partial^2\hat{W}}{\partial\hat{X}^2}\int_0^L\left(\frac{\partial\hat{W}}{\partial\hat{X}}\right)^2 d\hat{X}=0. \quad (2)$$

For enhanced convenience, we employ the following non-dimensional variables:

$$\bar{X}=\frac{\hat{X}}{\hat{L}},\quad \bar{W}=\frac{\hat{W}}{\hat{R}},\quad \bar{t}=\hat{t}\sqrt{\frac{\hat{E}\hat{I}}{\hat{\mu}\hat{L}^4}},\quad \bar{F}=\frac{\hat{F}\hat{L}^2}{\hat{E}\hat{I}},\quad \bar{K}=\frac{\hat{K}\hat{L}^4}{\hat{E}\hat{I}}. \quad (3)$$

Here, the symbol $\hat{R}$ represents the radius of gyration of the cross-section, which is calculated as $\hat{R} = \sqrt{\hat{I}/\hat{A}}$. Therefore, Equation (2) yields:

$$\frac{\partial^4 \bar{W}}{\partial \bar{X}^4} + \frac{\partial^2 \bar{W}}{\partial \bar{t}^2} + \bar{F}\frac{\partial^2 \bar{W}}{\partial \bar{X}^2} + \bar{K}\bar{W} - \frac{1}{2}\frac{\partial^2 \bar{W}}{\partial \bar{X}^2}\int_0^L \left(\frac{\partial \bar{W}}{\partial \bar{X}}\right)^2 d\bar{X} = 0. \tag{4}$$

By assuming that $\bar{W}(\bar{X}, \bar{t})$ can be expressed as the product of $\delta(\bar{X})$ and $\omega(\bar{t})$, where $\delta(\bar{X})$ represents the first eigenmode of the beam [66], and applying the Galerkin technique, we can derive the equation of motion as follows:

$$\ddot{\omega}_{(\bar{t})} + \alpha\omega_{(\bar{t})} + \beta\omega^3_{(\bar{t})} = 0\,, \tag{5}$$

where α controls the linear stiffness, β controls the amount of nonlinearity in the restoring force, $\alpha = \alpha_1 + \alpha_2\bar{F} + \bar{K}$ and the values of α_1, α_2, and β are as follows:

$$\alpha_1 = \frac{\int_0^1 \delta^{iv}\delta dx}{\int_0^1 \delta^2 dx}, \qquad \alpha_2 = \frac{\int_0^1 \delta''\delta dx}{\int_0^1 \delta^2 dx}, \qquad \beta = \frac{-0.5\int_0^1 (\delta'' \int_0^1 \delta'^2 dx)\delta dx}{\int_0^1 \delta^2 dx}. \tag{6}$$

Equation (5) describes the governing nonlinear vibration behavior of Euler–Bernoulli beams. The equation is governed by the initial conditions specified at the center of the beam:

$$\omega_{(0)} = A, \quad \dot{\omega}_{(0)} = 0\,, \tag{7}$$

where A stands for the dimensionless maximum amplitude of oscillation, the focus is on analyzing the natural response of the beam. This analysis starts with a specific displacement with no initial velocity, emphasizing the natural vibrational properties without any external or damping effects.

In this study, our initial attempt involved applying the Sardar sub-equation method to derive solutions for the equation. However, this approach proved unsuccessful, primarily due to square roots in the solution, hindering the separation of variables. Consequently, we turned to the modified Khater method, which proved to be a more suitable approach for addressing our problem.

3. The Traveling Wave Solutions

In this section, our focus is on finding the traveling wave solutions to Equation (1).

We generate wave patterns for the Euler–Bernoulli beam using the MKM based on Equation (5).

By employing the balancing strategy outlined in Appendix A, wherein we compare the highest-order linear and nonlinear terms, we determine the value of n. Specifically, we select the linear term $\ddot{\omega}_{(\bar{t})}$, denoted as $n+2$, and the nonlinear term $\omega^3_{(\bar{t})}$, denoted as $3n$, from Equation (5). Hence, we have $n+1 = 3n$. Solving this equation yields $n = 1$, see [68] which we then substitute into Equation (A4). Thus, the resulting equation becomes:

$$V(\tau) = \lambda_0 + \lambda_1\Re(\tau)\,, \tag{8}$$

where $\Re(\tau)$ is a solution of the ODE:

$$\dot{\Re}(\tau) = \ln(v)(\sigma_1 + \sigma_2\Re(\tau) + \sigma_3\Re^2(\tau))\,. \tag{9}$$

By substituting Equations (8) and (9) into Equation (5) and performing simplifications, we derive a system of equations that provides the following set of solutions:

$$\lambda_0 = \lambda_0, \quad \lambda_1 = \frac{2\lambda_0\sigma_3}{\sigma_2}\,. \tag{10}$$

The set of solutions for Equation (1) is obtained by using Equation (10):

1: If $\delta < 0$ and $\sigma_3 \neq 0$, then:

$$\begin{aligned}
&\bar{W}_1(\bar{X},\bar{t}) = \frac{\lambda_0\sqrt{-\delta}}{\sigma_2}\tan\left(\frac{\sqrt{-\delta}}{2}\tau\right), \quad \bar{W}_2(\bar{X},\bar{t}) = -\frac{\lambda_0\sqrt{-\delta}}{\sigma_2}\cot\left(\frac{\sqrt{-\delta}}{2}\tau\right),\\
&\bar{W}_3(\bar{X},\bar{t}) = \frac{\lambda_0\sqrt{-\delta}}{\sigma_2}\left(\tan\left(\sqrt{-\delta}\tau\right) \pm \sqrt{mc}\sec\left(\sqrt{-\delta}\tau\right)\right),\\
&\bar{W}_4(\bar{X},\bar{t}) = -\frac{\lambda_0\sqrt{-\delta}}{\sigma_2}\left(\cot\left(\sqrt{-\delta}\tau\right) \pm \sqrt{mc}\csc\left(\sqrt{-\delta}\tau\right)\right),\\
&\bar{W}_5(\bar{X},\bar{t}) = \frac{\lambda_0\sqrt{-\delta}}{2\sigma_2}\left(\tan\left(\frac{\sqrt{-\delta}}{4}\tau\right) - \cot\left(\frac{\sqrt{-\delta}}{4}\tau\right)\right).
\end{aligned} \tag{11}$$

2: If $\delta > 0$ and $\sigma_3 \neq 0$, then:

$$\begin{aligned}
&\bar{W}_6(\bar{X},\bar{t}) = -\frac{\lambda_0\sqrt{\delta}}{\sigma_2}\tanh\left(\frac{\sqrt{\delta}}{2}\tau\right), \quad \bar{W}_7(\bar{X},\bar{t}) = -\frac{\lambda_0\sqrt{\delta}}{\sigma_2}\coth\left(\frac{\sqrt{\delta}}{2}\tau\right),\\
&\bar{W}_8(\bar{X},\bar{t}) = -\frac{\lambda_0\sqrt{\delta}}{\sigma_2}\left(\tanh\left(\sqrt{\delta}\tau\right) \pm \iota\sqrt{mc}\,\mathrm{sech}\left(\sqrt{\delta}\tau\right)\right),\\
&\bar{W}_9(\bar{X},\bar{t}) = -\frac{\lambda_0\sqrt{\delta}}{\sigma_2}\left(\coth\left(\sqrt{\delta}\tau\right) \pm \sqrt{mc}\,\mathrm{csch}\left(\sqrt{\delta}\tau\right)\right),\\
&\bar{W}_{10}(\bar{X},\bar{t}) = -\frac{\lambda_0\sqrt{\delta}}{2\sigma_2}\left(\tanh\left(\frac{\sqrt{\delta}}{4}\tau\right) + \coth\left(\frac{\sqrt{\delta}}{4}\tau\right)\right).
\end{aligned} \tag{12}$$

3: If $\sigma_1\sigma_3 > 0$ and $\sigma_2 = 0$, then:

$$\begin{aligned}
&\bar{W}_{11}(\bar{X},\bar{t}) = \frac{\left(\sigma_2 + 2\sigma_3\left(\sqrt{\frac{\sigma_1}{\sigma_3}}\tan(\sqrt{\sigma_1\sigma_3}\tau)\right)\right)\lambda_0}{\sigma_2},\\
&\bar{W}_{12}(\bar{X},\bar{t}) = \frac{\left(\sigma_2 - 2\sigma_3\left(\sqrt{\frac{\sigma_1}{\sigma_3}}\cot(\sqrt{\sigma_1\sigma_3}\tau)\right)\right)\lambda_0}{\sigma_2},\\
&\bar{W}_{13}(\bar{X},\bar{t}) = \frac{\left(\sigma_2 + 2\sigma_3\left(\sqrt{\frac{\sigma_1}{\sigma_3}}(\tan(2\sqrt{\sigma_1\sigma_3}\tau) \pm \sqrt{mc}\sec(2\sqrt{\sigma_1\sigma_3}\tau))\right)\right)\lambda_0}{\sigma_2},\\
&\bar{W}_{14}(\bar{X},\bar{t}) = \frac{\left(\sigma_2 + 2\sigma_3\left(\sqrt{\frac{\sigma_1}{\sigma_3}}(-\cot(2\sqrt{\sigma_1\sigma_3}\tau) \pm \sqrt{mc}\csc(2\sqrt{\sigma_1\sigma_3}\tau))\right)\right)\lambda_0}{\sigma_2},\\
&\bar{W}_{15}(\bar{X},\bar{t}) = \frac{\left(\sigma_2 + \sigma_3\left(\sqrt{\frac{\sigma_1}{\sigma_3}}\left(\tan\left(\frac{\sqrt{\sigma_1\sigma_3}}{2}\tau\right) - \cot\left(\frac{\sqrt{\sigma_1\sigma_3}}{2}\tau\right)\right)\right)\right)\lambda_0}{\sigma_2}.
\end{aligned} \tag{13}$$

4: If $\sigma_1\sigma_3 < 0$ and $\sigma_2 = 0$, then:

$$\begin{aligned}
&\bar{W}_{16}(\bar{X},\bar{t}) = \frac{\left(\sigma_2 - 2\sigma_3\left(\sqrt{-\frac{\sigma_1}{\sigma_3}}\tanh(\sqrt{-\sigma_1\sigma_3}\tau)\right)\right)\lambda_0}{\sigma_2},\\
&\bar{W}_{17}(\bar{X},\bar{t}) = \frac{\left(\sigma_2 - 2\sigma_3\left(\sqrt{-\frac{\sigma_1}{\sigma_3}}\coth(\sqrt{-\sigma_1\sigma_3}\tau)\right)\right)\lambda_0}{\sigma_2},\\
&\bar{W}_{18}(\bar{X},\bar{t}) = \frac{\left(\sigma_2 - 2\sigma_3\left(\sqrt{-\frac{\sigma_1}{\sigma_3}}(\tanh(2\sqrt{-\sigma_1\sigma_3}\tau) \pm \iota\sqrt{mc}\,\mathrm{sech}(2\sqrt{-\sigma_1\sigma_3}\tau))\right)\right)\lambda_0}{\sigma_2},\\
&\bar{W}_{19}(\bar{X},\bar{t}) = \frac{\left(\sigma_2 - 2\sigma_3\left(\sqrt{-\frac{\sigma_1}{\sigma_3}}(\coth(2\sqrt{-\sigma_1\sigma_3}\tau) \pm \sqrt{mc}\,\mathrm{csch}(2\sqrt{-\sigma_1\sigma_3}\tau))\right)\right)\lambda_0}{\sigma_2},\\
&\bar{W}_{20}(\bar{X},\bar{t}) = \frac{\left(\sigma_2 - \sigma_3\left(\sqrt{-\frac{\sigma_1}{\sigma_3}}\left(\tanh\left(\frac{\sqrt{-\sigma_1\sigma_3}}{2}\tau\right) + \coth\left(\frac{\sqrt{-\sigma_1\sigma_3}}{2}\tau\right)\right)\right)\right)\lambda_0}{\sigma_2}.
\end{aligned} \tag{14}$$

5: If $\sigma_1 = \sigma_3$ and $\sigma_2 = 0$, then:

$$\begin{aligned}
&\bar{W}_{21}(\bar{X},\bar{t}) = \frac{(\sigma_2 + 2\sigma_3(\tan(\sigma_1\tau)))\lambda_0}{\sigma_2}, \quad \bar{W}_{22}(\bar{X},\bar{t}) = \frac{(\sigma_2 - 2\sigma_3(\cot(\sigma_1\tau)))\lambda_0}{\sigma_2}, \\
&\bar{W}_{23}(\bar{X},\bar{t}) = \frac{(\sigma_2 + 2\sigma_3(\tan(2\sigma_1\tau) \pm \sqrt{mc}\sec(2\sigma_1\tau)))\lambda_0}{\sigma_2}, \\
&\bar{W}_{24}(\bar{X},\bar{t}) = \frac{(\sigma_2 + 2\sigma_3(-\cot(2\sigma_1\tau) \pm \sqrt{mc}\csc(2\sigma_1\tau)))\lambda_0}{\sigma_2}, \\
&\bar{W}_{25}(\bar{X},\bar{t}) = \frac{(\sigma_2 + \sigma_3(\tan(\frac{\sigma_1}{2}\tau) - \cot(\frac{\sigma_1}{2}\tau)))\lambda_0}{\sigma_2}.
\end{aligned} \tag{15}$$

6: If $\sigma_1 = -\sigma_3$ and $\sigma_2 = 0$, then:

$$\begin{aligned}
&\bar{W}_{26}(\bar{X},\bar{t}) = \frac{(\sigma_2 - 2\sigma_3(\tanh(\sigma_1\tau)))\lambda_0}{\sigma_2}, \quad \hat{W}_{27}(\hat{X},\hat{t}) = \frac{(\sigma_2 - 2\sigma_3(\coth(\sigma_1\tau)))\lambda_0}{\sigma_2}, \\
&\bar{W}_{28}(\bar{X},\bar{t}) = \frac{(\sigma_2 + 2\sigma_3(-\tanh(2\sigma_1\tau) \pm \iota\sqrt{mc}\,\mathrm{sech}(2\sigma_1\tau)))\lambda_0}{\sigma_2}, \\
&\bar{W}_{29}(\bar{X},\bar{t}) = \frac{(\sigma_2 + 2\sigma_3(-\coth(2\sigma_1\tau) \pm \sqrt{mc}\,\mathrm{csch}(2\sigma_1\tau)))\lambda_0}{\sigma_2}, \\
&\bar{W}_{30}(\bar{X},\bar{t}) = \frac{(\sigma_2 - \sigma_3(\tanh(\frac{\sigma_1}{2}\tau) + \coth(\frac{\sigma_1}{2}\tau)))\lambda_0}{\sigma_2}.
\end{aligned} \tag{16}$$

7: If $\sigma_2^2 = 4\sigma_1\sigma_3$, then $\bar{W}_{31}(\bar{X},\bar{t}) = \left(1 - \frac{4\sigma_1\sigma_3(\sigma_2\tau\ln(v) + 2)}{\sigma_2^3\tau\ln(v)}\right)\lambda_0.$

8: If $\sigma_2 = \mu, \sigma_1 = q\mu\ (q \neq 0), \sigma_3 = 0$, then $\bar{W}_{32}(\bar{X},\bar{t}) = \frac{(\sigma_2 + 2\sigma_3(v^{\mu\tau} - q))\lambda_0}{\sigma_2}.$

9: If $\sigma_2 = \sigma_3 = 0$, then $\bar{W}_{33}(\bar{X},\bar{t}) = \frac{(\sigma_2 + 2\sigma_3\sigma_1\tau\ln(v))\lambda_0}{\sigma_2}.$

10: If $\sigma_2 = \sigma_1 = 0$, then $\bar{W}_{34}(\bar{X},\bar{t}) = \left(1 - \frac{2}{\sigma_2\tau\ln(v)}\right)\lambda_0.$

11: If $\sigma_1 = 0$ and $\sigma_2 \neq 0$, then

$$\begin{aligned}
\bar{W}_{35}(\bar{X},\bar{t}) &= \left(1 - \frac{2m}{\cosh(\sigma_2\tau) - \sinh(\sigma_2\tau) + m}\right)\lambda_0, \\
\bar{W}_{36}(\bar{X},\bar{t}) &= \left(1 - \frac{2(\cosh(\sigma_2\tau) + \sinh(\sigma_2\tau))}{\cosh(\sigma_2\tau) - \sinh(\sigma_2\tau) + c}\right)\lambda_0.
\end{aligned} \tag{17}$$

12: If $\sigma_2 = \mu, \sigma_3 = q\mu\ (q \neq 0), \sigma_1 = 0$, then

$$\bar{W}_{37}(\bar{X},\bar{t}) = \left(1 + \frac{2\sigma_3 m v^{\mu\tau}}{(c - qmv^{\mu\tau})\sigma_2}\right)\lambda_0. \tag{18}$$

The presented approach marks the first application of solving the Euler–Bernoulli beam problem using a symmetric spatial representation of the waveform as part of each solution, which includes the τ function in $\bar{W}_i(\bar{X},\bar{t})\ \forall\, i \in 1\ldots37$. Following the derivation of solutions, as detailed in Equation (10), their accuracy was validated by reintegrating them into the original Equation (5). Upon substitution, all solutions satisfied the equation, thus affirming their accuracy.

3.1. *Strengths and Weaknesses*

3.1.1. Strengths

- **Direct method**: Possibly producing quicker and more effective results, the modified Khater method looks for solutions directly rather than using iterative methods.

- **Multiple exact solutions**: It can often compute more than 1 exact solution to the same PDE. This gives you flexibility in how to analyze the behavior of your system and explore different scenarios.

3.1.2. Weaknesses

- **Limited applicability**: Not all nonlinear PDEs can be solved by the modified Khater approach. Especially complicated equations or ones with certain nonlinearities might not work well with it.
- **Limited theoretical framework**: The modified Khater approach may have a less developed theoretical framework than some well-known analytical techniques with a solid theoretical basis.

4. Visualization and Discussion of the Symmetric Wave Patterns

This study showcases the physical significance of the model through a representation of three- and two-dimensional density and contour diagrams, which illustrate the results obtained from numerical computations. These diagrams depict periodic soliton patterns, with each figure accompanied by a detailed list of model parameter values chosen carefully for accuracy.

In Figures 2 and 3, we present a series of plots depicting the functions of selected solutions, $\bar{W}_6(\bar{x}, \bar{t})$ and $\bar{W}_{37}(\bar{x}, \bar{t})$, as described in Equations (12) and (18). Utilizing various types of plots allows us to illustrate the expected and correctly derived analytical solutions presented in the previous chapters. To assess the analytical solutions for the vibrations of the examined beam, density diagrams, and contour plots were employed to visualize and comprehend the behavior of this structure in time and space. The horizontal axis represents time $\bar{t}$, the vertical axis represents position $\bar{X}$, and density or contour levels represent the values of the deflection function $\bar{W}(\bar{x}, \bar{t})$. These visual tools provide insights into several different aspects of the vibrations of the examined beam.

In Figures 2 and 3e,f, the distribution of amplitude over time and space is illustrated. The values of the function $\bar{W}(\bar{x}, \bar{t})$ are depicted using shades, revealing how the amplitude changes along the beam and over time as well. In Figure 3, we observe blurred and less distinct cyclically appearing regions compared to Figure 2. Additionally, under certain assumed boundary conditions and vibration frequencies, density diagrams revealed standing and traveling wave phenomena, where the deflection exhibits a characteristic pattern resembling a standing wave. Contour plots depict the dominant modes of vibration in the beam, with different contours corresponding to different vibration modes. As a result of this modal analysis, Figure 3 indicates a greater unevenness in the distribution of modes for the solution $\bar{W}_{37}(\bar{x}, \bar{t})$.

Figure 4a,b illustrate the influence of the β parameter on the dynamical response of $\bar{W}_6(\bar{X}, \bar{t})$ at a specific time and position $\bar{X}$. In Figure 4a, it is evident that when time is held constant, the β parameter affects the amplitude of the wave without inducing any phase difference. Conversely, in Figure 4b, the β parameter does not impact the amplitude but causes a slight forward shift in the wave, resulting in a phase difference.

The fourth-order Runge–Kutta (RK4) numerical integration algorithm has been employed to numerically solve Equation (5). The obtained numerical solution serves as a means of comparison to validate our semi-analytical results and to demonstrate their closeness to the solutions derived from Equation (12), particularly $\bar{W}_6(\bar{X}, \bar{t})$ as depicted in Figure 5. The approach involves discretizing the differential equation into small steps and iteratively calculating the approximate solution at each step.

Utilizing this precise and stable numerical method, we successfully captured the behavior of the system described by Equation (5). The numerical solutions exhibit satisfactory agreement with the semi-analytical solutions of the system $\bar{W}_6(\bar{X}, \bar{t})$, confirming the reliability of our novel methodology in accurately depicting the dynamics of the system. This alignment between numerical and semi-analytical results highlights the strength of the numerical algorithm in approximating the mathematical model (5).

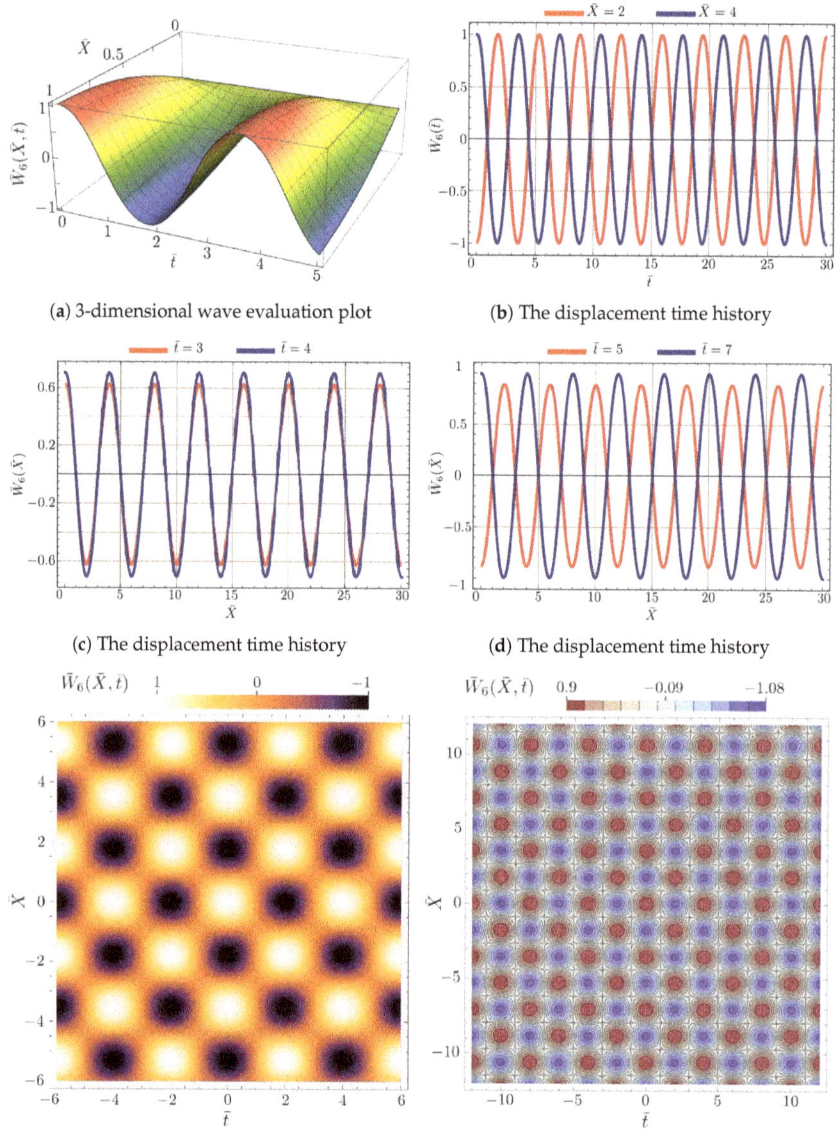

(**a**) 3-dimensional wave evaluation plot (**b**) The displacement time history

(**c**) The displacement time history (**d**) The displacement time history

(**e**) Density plot (**f**) Contour diagram

Figure 2. Dynamical behavior of the investigated beam on the solution $\bar{W}_6(\bar{X},\bar{t})$ in the three-dimensional wave evaluation plot, time-dependent two-dimensional displacement plots, density, and contour diagrams for the model parameters: $\alpha = \pi$, $\beta = 0.15$, $\sigma_1 = -0.1$, $\sigma_2 = 2$, $\sigma_3 = 3$, $a_0 = -1.7$, $\delta = 5.2$.

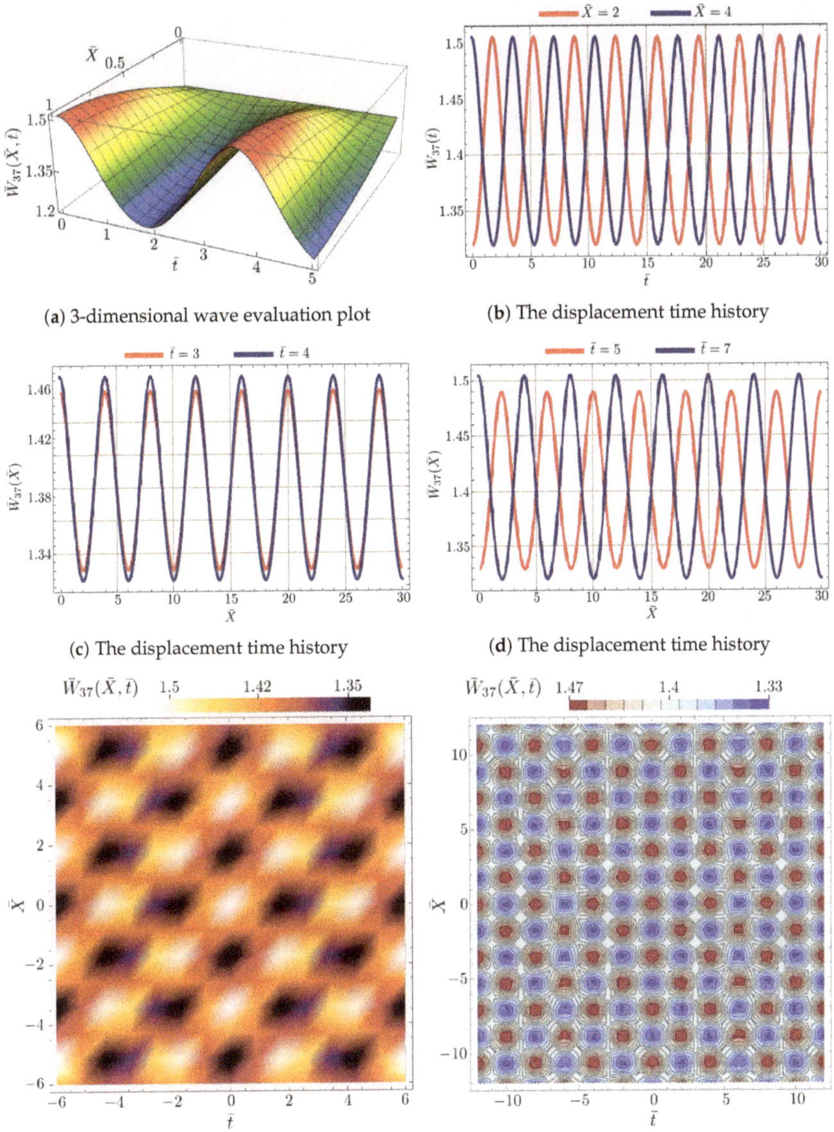

(**a**) 3-dimensional wave evaluation plot (**b**) The displacement time history

(**c**) The displacement time history (**d**) The displacement time history

(**e**) Density plot (**f**) Contour diagram

Figure 3. Dynamical behavior of the investigated beam on the solution $\bar{W}_{37}(\bar{X},\bar{t})$ in the three-dimensional wave evaluation plot, time-dependent two-dimensional displacement plots, density, and contour diagrams for the model parameters: $\alpha = \pi$, $\beta = 0.15$, $\sigma_1 = 0$, $\sigma_2 = 4$, $\sigma_3 = 2$, $a_0 = 1$, $m = 1, c = 3, v = 1.1, q = 0.5, \mu = 4$.

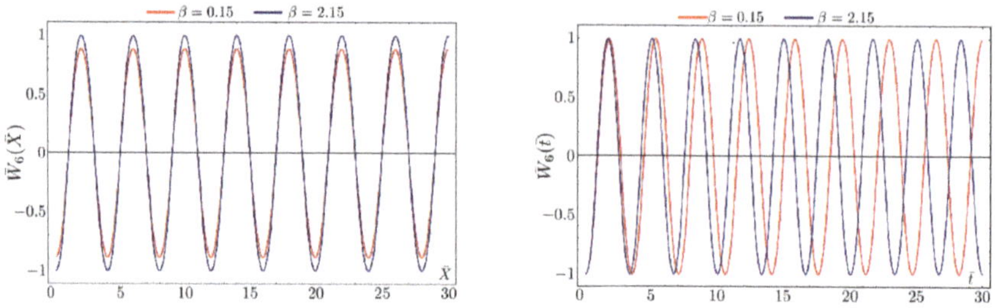

(a) (b)

Figure 4. Influence of β parameter on the response $\bar{W}_6(\bar{X},\bar{t})$ in the t-dependent 2-dimensional displacement plots for the model parameters: $\alpha = \pi, \sigma_1 = -0.1, \sigma_2 = 2, \sigma_3 = 3, a_0 = -1.7, \delta = 5.2$. (**a**) The time history when $\bar{t}$ is fixed; (**b**) The time history when $\bar{X}$ is fixed.

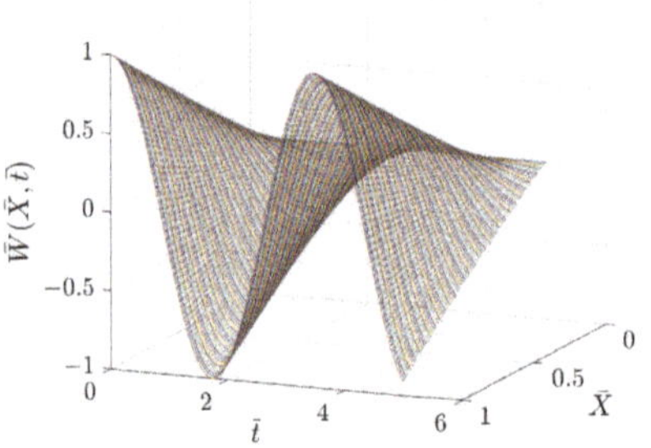

Figure 5. Numerical solution of the ODE (5) with model parameters $\alpha = \pi$ and $\beta = 0.15$.

5. Dynamical Analysis

This section of the work explores the examined equation to unveil unexplored yet intriguing dynamics. The theories of sensitivity analysis, bifurcation, and chaos will be employed for this purpose. Given its applicability to a broad spectrum of independent variables, all subsequent calculations will be based on Equation (5).

5.1. Computation and Analysis of Equilibrium Points

After substituting $\dot{\omega} = y$ into Equation (5) and replacing $\hat{t}$ with t, the resulting planar dynamical system is obtained:

$$\begin{cases} \dfrac{d\omega}{dt} &= y(t), \\ \dfrac{dy}{dt} &= -\beta\omega^3(t) - \alpha\omega(t)\,. \end{cases} \tag{19}$$

In relation to System (19), the first integral takes the form of a Hamiltonian

$$G(\omega, y) = \frac{y^2}{2} + \frac{\beta}{4}y^4 + \frac{\alpha}{2}y^2 = H, \tag{20}$$

where H represents the Hamiltonian constant. The vector field of System (19) governs the phase orbits of this planar dynamical system.

Hence, it is important to examine various phase profiles of the System (19) using different parameters. The System (19) exhibits three equilibrium points for non-zero parameters α and β:

$$V_1 = (0,0), \quad V_2 = \left(\sqrt{\frac{-\alpha}{\beta}}, 0\right), \quad V_3 = \left(-\sqrt{\frac{-\alpha}{\beta}}, 0\right). \tag{21}$$

The expression for the Jacobian of the linearized System (19) is given by

$$J(\omega, y) = \begin{vmatrix} 0 & 1 \\ -3\beta\omega^2 - \alpha & 0 \end{vmatrix} = 3\beta\omega^2 + \alpha. \tag{22}$$

The equilibrium points $(V_i, 0), i = 1, 2, 3$ exhibit distinct characteristics determined by the value of $J(\omega, y)$, as shown in Figure 6.

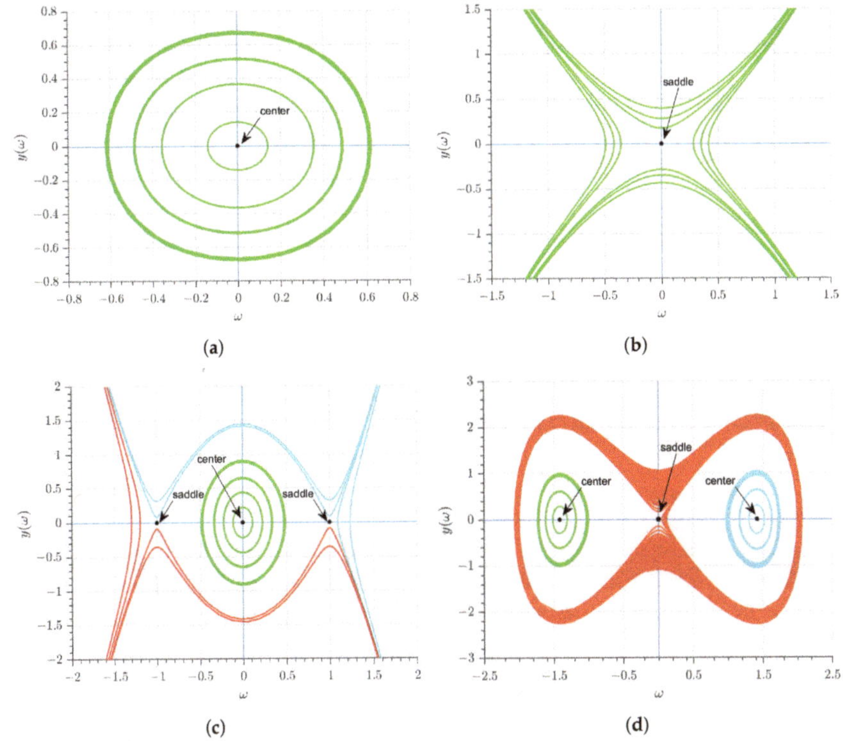

Figure 6. Phase portrait analysis of equilibrium points. (**a**) Case 1: $\alpha > 0$ and $\beta > 0$; (**b**) Case 2: $\alpha < 0$ and $\beta < 0$; (**c**) Case 3: $\alpha > 0$ and $\beta < 0$; (**d**) Case 4: $\alpha < 0$ and $\beta > 0$.

They act as saddle points when $J(\omega, y) < 0$, as centers when $J(\omega, y) > 0$, and as cuspidal points when $J(\omega, y) = 0$. To illustrate the phase portrait analysis of System (19), we explored various combinations of the parameters. The phase portraits illustrating the dynamical behavior of the system in Figure 6 depend on the following configurations of parameters:

- **Case 1:** $\alpha > 0$ and $\beta > 0$ Three equilibrium points are obtained from the System (19) by assigning specific values to the free parameters, such as α, $\beta = 1$: $V_1 = (0, 0)$, $V_2 = (\iota, 0)$, and $V_3 = (-\iota, 0)$. The only actual point, denoted as V_1, is illustrated in Figure 6a, as V_2 and V_3 are imaginary.
- **Case 2:** $\alpha < 0$ and $\beta < 0$ Three equilibria are obtained from the System (19) with specific values assigned to α, $\beta = -1$: $V_1 = (0, 0)$, $V_2 = (-\iota, 0)$, and $V_3 = (\iota, 0)$. The only actual point V_1, is shown in Figure 6b, as V_2 and V_3 are imaginary.
- **Case 3:** $\alpha > 0$ and $\beta < 0$ Three equilibria are obtained from the System (19) by assigning $\alpha = 1$ and $\beta = -1$: $V_1 = (0, 0)$, $V_2 = (1, 0)$, and $V_3 = (-1, 0)$. In this case, V_2 and V_3 indicate saddle points, while V_1 represents a center; see Figure 6c.

- **Case 4:** $\alpha < 0$ and $\beta > 0$ Three equilibria are obtained from the System (19) with specific values $\alpha = -2$ and $\beta = 1$: $V_1 = (0,0)$, $V_2 = (1.4142, 0)$, and $V_3 = (-1.4142, 0)$. In this case, V_2 and V_3 represent centers, while V_1 is a saddle point; see Figure 6d.

5.2. The Sensitivity Analysis

This section addresses the sensitivity analysis of the complex structure described by Equation (19) from an optimization perspective.

Figure 7a–d depicts three distinct configurations of initial conditions alongside several cases. Specifically, in Figure 7e, the red curve corresponds to $(U, V) = (0.3, 0)$, the blue curve to $(U, V) = (0.4, 0)$, and the black curve to $(U, V) = (0.5, 0)$, indicating transient time. During this transient period, as illustrated in Figure 7e, the system demonstrates insensitivity. However, upon transitioning beyond the transient state, as evidenced in Figure 7a–c, System (19) exhibits a notably high level of sensitivity.

At the end, the comparison was conducted using various initial values, specifically $(0.3, 0)$, $(0.4, 0)$, and $(0.5, 0)$, as illustrated in Figure 7d. The results clearly indicate that even minor variations in the initial values of System (19) significantly impact the final output. Consequently, it can be inferred that the investigated model is highly sensitive to initial conditions, lacking a transitional state.

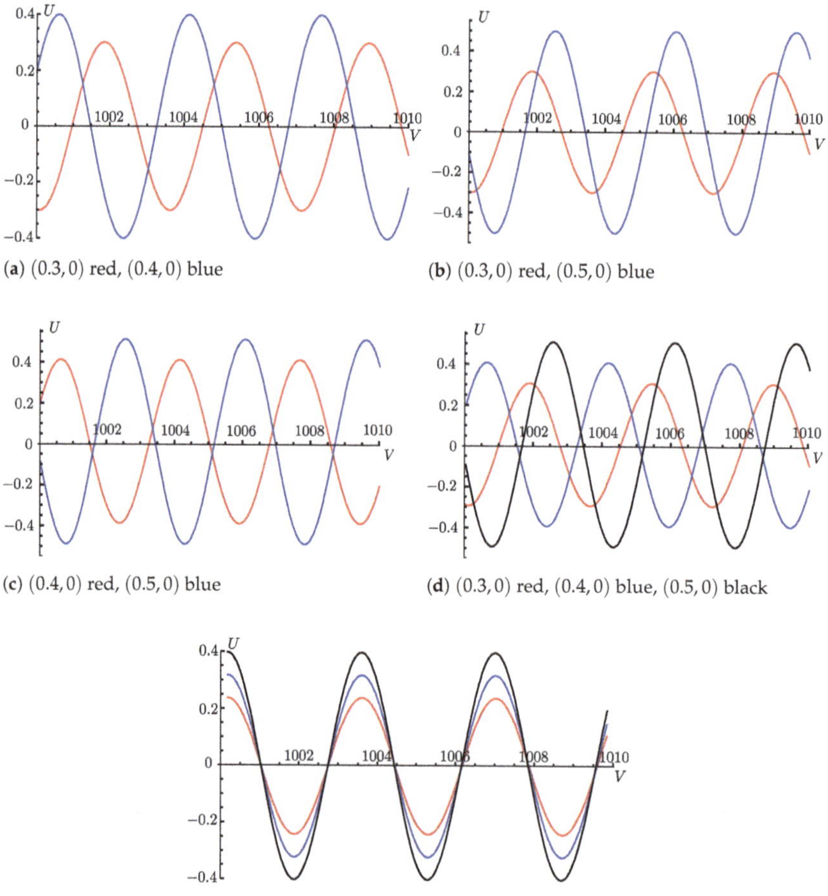

(**a**) $(0.3, 0)$ red, $(0.4, 0)$ blue

(**b**) $(0.3, 0)$ red, $(0.5, 0)$ blue

(**c**) $(0.4, 0)$ red, $(0.5, 0)$ blue

(**d**) $(0.3, 0)$ red, $(0.4, 0)$ blue, $(0.5, 0)$ black

(**e**) $(0.3, 0)$ red, $(0.4, 0)$ blue, $(0.5, 0)$ black line, where time is transient

Figure 7. Sensitivity plots of the nonlinear dynamical behavior of the examined beam for different initial conditions (U_0, V_0) superposed on the states (U, V). The system parameters: $\alpha = \pi$, $\beta = 0.15$.

5.3. *Quasi-Periodic and Chaotic Dynamics*

The primary focus of this section is on describing the quasi-periodic, chaotic, and periodic dynamics governed by the 2-DOF ODE under investigation. Equation (19) is now supplemented with the weak forcing term $\varepsilon\cos(\vartheta t)$. Therefore, the following system may be expressed using Equation (19), including an extra forcing term (a form of perturbation):

$$\begin{cases} \dfrac{d\omega}{dt} = y, \\ \dfrac{dy}{dt} = -\beta\omega^3 - \alpha\omega + \varepsilon\cos(\vartheta t), \end{cases} \tag{23}$$

where ϑ denotes the angular frequency and ε describes the small amplitude of the harmonic force. The introduction of the external periodic force, absent in System (19), is now incorporated into System (23). To explore the various dynamic effects covered by the description in Equation (1), a weak forcing term with parameters ε and $\vartheta = \pi$ is introduced while still considering the sustained influence of an external force with a certain excitation frequency, acting vertically at one end, and simultaneously taking into account specific physical properties of the model.

Figures 8–10 depict quasi-periodic, chaotic, and periodic two-dimensional phase plane orbits versus time $t \in [100, 200]$ s, respectively.

The dynamical responses shown in Figures 8 and 9 are observed in the appropriate phase space and are obtained for the same set of model parameters, differing only in the signs of α and β. For instance, a time history spanning 20,000 s demonstrated in Figure 9 confirms a very weak dissipation of energy, resulting in a prolonged convergence time to the steady, albeit chaotic, dynamical state. In Figure 8, the periodic system response is found to be somewhat faster, as confirmed by the closed red Poincaré map, albeit with a quasi-periodic behavioral shift.

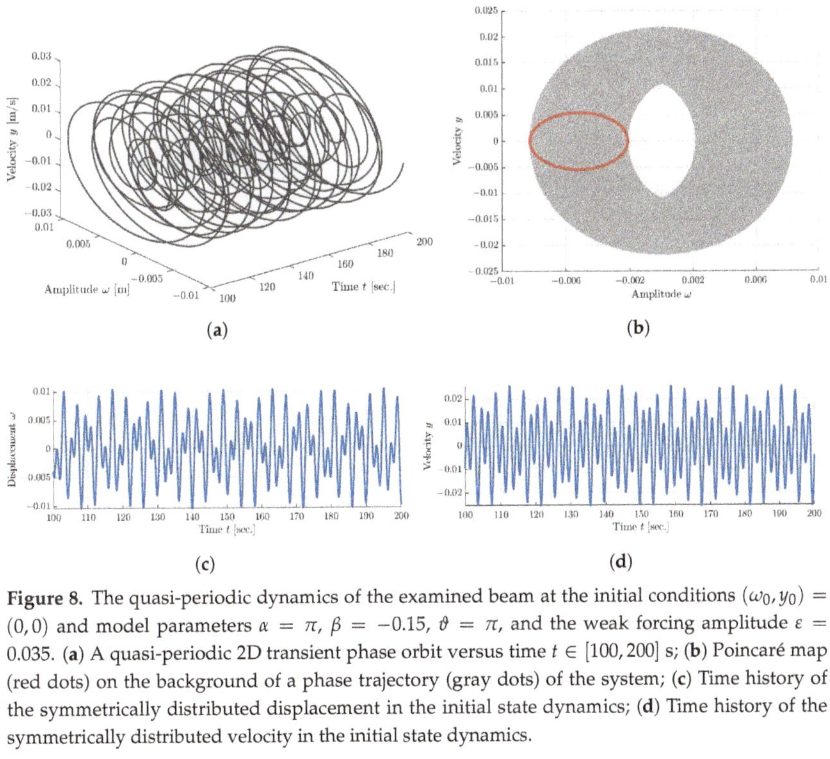

Figure 8. The quasi-periodic dynamics of the examined beam at the initial conditions $(\omega_0, y_0) = (0, 0)$ and model parameters $\alpha = \pi$, $\beta = -0.15$, $\vartheta = \pi$, and the weak forcing amplitude $\varepsilon = 0.035$. (**a**) A quasi-periodic 2D transient phase orbit versus time $t \in [100, 200]$ s; (**b**) Poincaré map (red dots) on the background of a phase trajectory (gray dots) of the system; (**c**) Time history of the symmetrically distributed displacement in the initial state dynamics; (**d**) Time history of the symmetrically distributed velocity in the initial state dynamics.

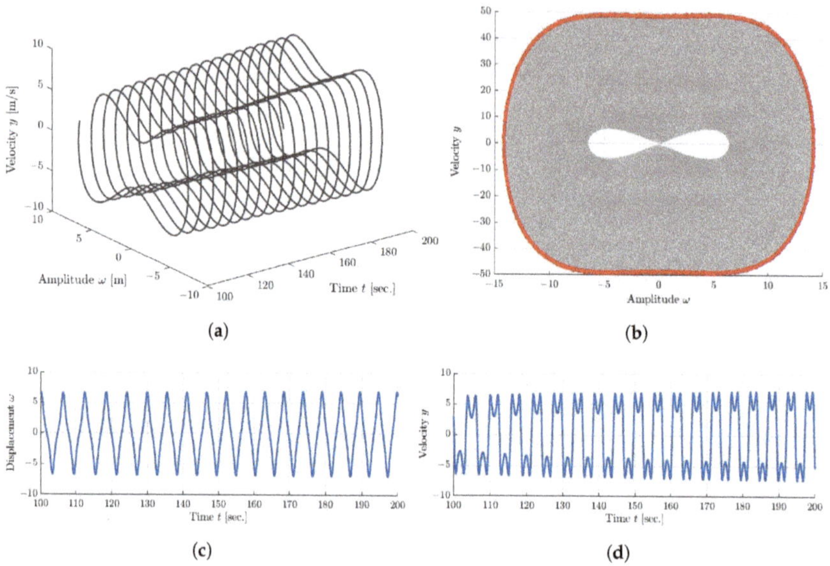

Figure 9. The chaotic dynamics of the examined beam proved by an irregular Poincaré map extended over a narrow symmetric region of the phase plane at the initial conditions $(\omega_0, y_0) = (0,0)$, model parameters $\alpha = -\pi$, $\beta = 0.15$, $\vartheta = \pi$, and the small harmonic forcing amplitude $\varepsilon = 0.035$. (**a**) A chaotic 2D transient phase orbit versus time $t \in [100, 200]$ s; (**b**) A steady-state Poincaré map (red dots) on the background of the full phase trajectory; (**c**) Time history of the symmetrically distributed displacement in the initial state dynamics; (**d**) Time history of the symmetrically distributed velocity in the initial state dynamics.

The dynamic responses, as illustrated in Figure 10, are observed in the corresponding phase plane for different sets of model parameters: $\alpha = 3.41$, $\beta = 2.15$, $\vartheta = \pi/2$, and a small amplitude of $\varepsilon = 0.035$. For example, the 60000-s time history depicted in Figure 10 confirms a prolonged convergence time to steady and periodic dynamics.

The dynamical system described by Equation (23) exhibits chaotic behavior under weak forcing, as depicted in Figure 9 for a steady-state irregular solution.

In addition to the Poincaré maps, the presence of quasi-periodic, chaotic, and periodic behavior is confirmed by the Lyapunov exponent spectra, presented in Table 1.

Table 1. Lyapunov exponents spectra.

Figure	t_{end}	λ_1	λ_2
Figure 8	2000	0.000010	−0.000010
Figure 9	2000	0.170928	−0.170928
Figure 10	2000	0.000686	−0.000686

From the physics point of view, the influence of parameter α variation is illustrated in Figure 11a and the initial conditions imposed on the position and initial velocity on the dynamics of vibrations of the considered beam in Figure 11b. It is evident that both dependencies exhibit a symmetric nature of the physical system with respect to the zero velocity value, indicating a boundary of direction change. Within the range $\alpha = (-0.7; 0.7)$, the motion may exhibit chaotic behavior, while outside of this range, it remains periodic, assuming that the remaining parameters of the model remain constant, with values of $\beta = 2.15$, $\varepsilon = 0.035$, and $\theta = \pi/2$ (as depicted in the particular dynamic response in Figure 10). In this case, periodic motion was observed, confirming the significance of the special value of parameter $\alpha = 3.41$, located outside the window $(-0.7; 0.7)$ in which the dynamical response is mostly expected to be unstable.

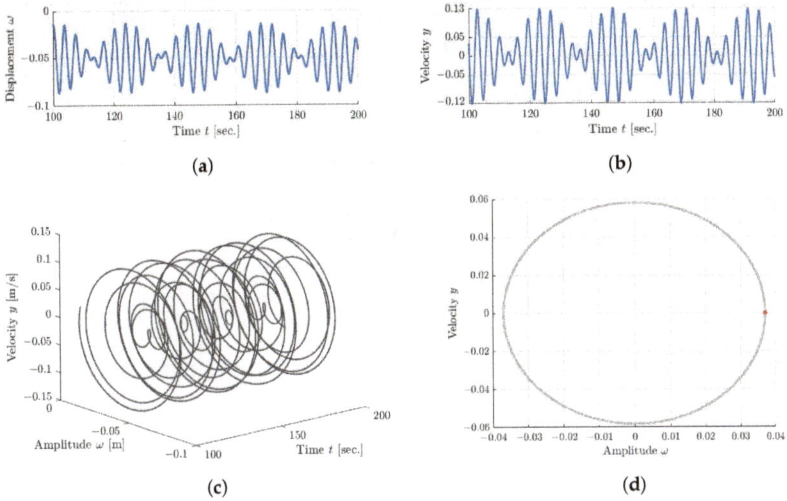

Figure 10. The periodic dynamical behavior of the examined beam proved by an irregular Poincaré map extended over a narrow symmetric region of the phase plane at the initial conditions $(\omega_0, y_0) = (0, 0)$ and model parameters $\alpha = 3.41$, $\beta = 2.15$, $\vartheta = \pi/2$, and the small forcing amplitude $\varepsilon = 0.035$. (**a**) Time history of the symmetrically distributed displacement in the initial state dynamics; (**b**) Time history of the symmetrically distributed velocity in the initial state dynamics; (**c**) A periodic 2D transient phase orbit versus time $t \in [100, 200]$ s; (**d**) Poincaré map (red dots) on the background of a phase trajectory (grey dots) of the system.

Subsequently, we chose one of the values of parameter α and examined the sensitivity of the investigated dynamical system to changes in initial conditions, as visible in Figure 11b. A series of dark points symmetrically distributed on a yellow background can be observed. In these areas, the system will be more sensitive to changes in the pair of initial conditions (ω, y), and in places of almost black color, where the largest Lyapunov exponent exceeds 0.01, chaotic or quasi-periodic motion will occur. It is interesting to note that these areas consist of scattered points, yet the map maintains its symmetry.

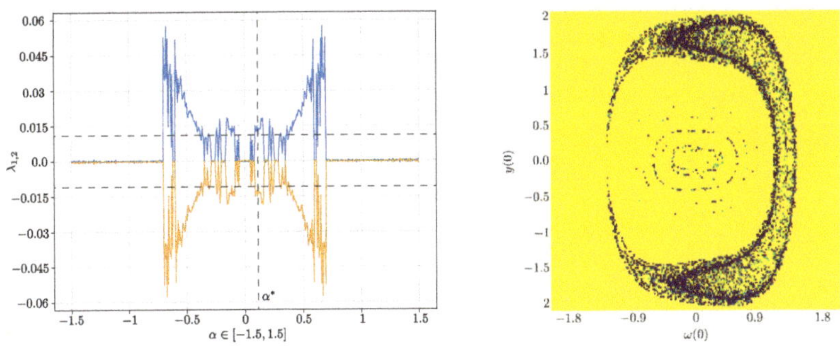

(**a**) Symmetric distribution of the Lyapunov spectrum $\lambda_{1,2}$ versus parameter α of the beam model

(**b**) Two-dimensional symmetric basin of the largest Lyapunov exponent for $\alpha^* = 0.1$

Figure 11. Global illustration showing the influence of varying the parameter α of the model beam on the distribution of Lyapunov exponents (**a**) and their dependence on the initial conditions $\omega(0)$ and $y(0)$ (**b**), depicted across a 200×200 rectangular grid basin ($\alpha = \alpha^*$, $\beta = 2.15$, $\varepsilon = 0.035$, $\theta = \pi/2$).

6. Conclusions

In this study, the symmetry-optimized method of solution for a boundary- and initial-value problem, coupled with its dynamical analysis, enabled us to tackle two primary tasks. Firstly, we aimed to derive precise, explicit semi-analytical solutions. Secondly, we sought to analyze the dynamical behavior of the integrable Euler–Bernoulli beam model, representing a two-dimensional dynamical system subjected to axial load from one end and vertical forcing from the other. Employing the modified Khater approach allowed us to obtain precise, explicit solutions, including periodic soliton solutions presented in polynomials as well as rational function forms. The existence of these solutions was found to depend on the fulfillment of stable and favorable conditions, as illustrated through various graphical representations.

Furthermore, the phase portraits of the extracted two-degree-of-freedom dynamical system governing the nonlinear vibration behavior of the analyzed Euler–Bernoulli beams reveal planar orbits with equilibrium points of two types: center and saddle points. These results, showcasing bifurcations of solutions in the investigated system, hold promise for applications in exploring the dynamics and observational aspects of models used in engineering, bio-mathematics, mathematical physics, optics, and fluid dynamics.

Additionally, alongside the axial load, we introduced a small harmonic horizontal force acting in a perturbed manner on the second end of the investigated dynamical system. Subsequently, several techniques of dynamical analysis were employed to detect various kinds of periodic or even chaotic behavior. Utilizing phase plots, Poincaré maps, time history plots, Lyapunov exponent spectra, and their basins facilitated the demonstration of the existence of quasi-periodic, chaotic, and periodic dynamics within the harmonically and weakly forced system. The results illustrate specific cases of the model equation's dynamics on symmetry-optimized global maps, depicting the system's behavioral dependency on initial conditions and model parameters.

Furthermore, our analysis has shown symmetry in the system's sensitivity to initial conditions. Remarkably, even minor changes in the initial values lead to significant differences in the system's behavior. In summary, the findings of the current study reveal the effectiveness of the proposed approaches, which will be useful in assessing symmetric soliton dynamics as well as phase patterns of nonlinear phenomena.

Author Contributions: Conceptualization, M.U.; methodology, M.U.; software, M.U. and P.O.; validation, P.O.; formal analysis, M.U.; investigation, M.U. and P.O.; resources, M.U. and P.O.; data curation, M.U. and P.O.; writing—original draft preparation, M.U. and P.O.; writing—review and editing, M.U. and P.O.; visualization, M.U. and P.O.; supervision, P.O.; project administration, M.U. All authors have read and agreed to the published version of the manuscript.

Funding: This research received no external funding.

Data Availability Statement: The data are available upon reasonable request from the authors.

Conflicts of Interest: The authors declare no conflicts of interest.

Nomenclature

$\hat{X}$	Spatial coordinate along the length of the beam
$\hat{t}$	Time variable
$\hat{L}$	Length of the beam
$\hat{A}$	Cross-sectional area of the beam
$\hat{\mu}$	Mass per unit length of the beam
$\hat{F}$	Axial force
$\hat{C}$	Viscous Damping coefficient (set to zero in this context)
$\hat{K}$	Foundation modulus
$\hat{E}$	Young's modulus (modulus of elasticity) of the beam material
$\hat{I}$	Moment of inertia of the beam's cross-section
$\hat{W}(\hat{X},\hat{t})$	An unknown function, often used to denote the deflection of a beam
$\hat{V}(\hat{X},\hat{t})$	Distributed load in the transverse direction (set to zero in this context)

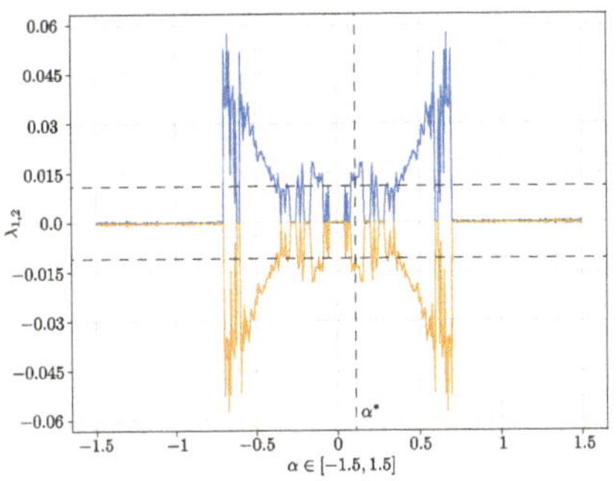

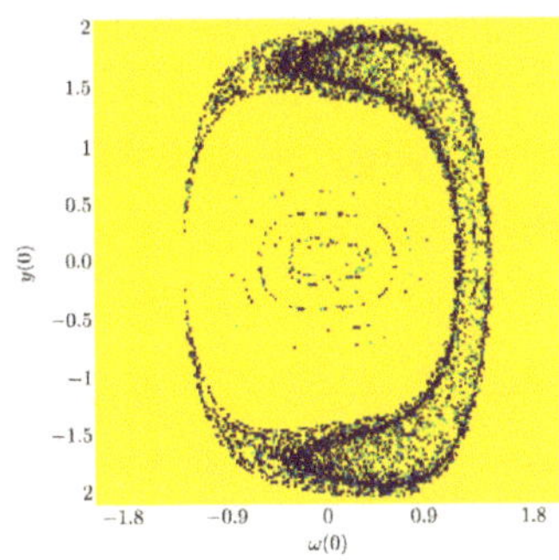

Appendix A. Analytical Solution Using the Modified Khater Method

We present the modified technique, see [68–70], for generating a new wave pattern within the analyzed model. Here are the key steps of this approach:

Step 1: Consider a generic n-th order PDE:

$$K(Y, Y_x, Y_{xx}, \dots, Y, Y_t, Y_{tt}, \dots) = 0. \tag{A1}$$

The function $Y = Y(x,t)$ is unknown, while K is a polynomial function with respect to the provided variables.

Step 2: Introduce the symmetric wave transformation:

$$\tau = \delta(x)\omega(t), \quad Y(x,t) = V(\tau), \tag{A2}$$

where $\delta(x)$ represents the first eigenmode of the beam [66]. Apply the transformation (A2) to transform the PDE (A1) into an ODE:

$$E(V, V_\tau, V_{\tau\tau}, \dots) = 0. \tag{A3}$$

Step 3: The general solution of the nonlinear ODE (A3) can be demonstrated as below:

$$V(\tau) = \sum_{i=o}^{n} \lambda_i \Re^i(\tau), \tag{A4}$$

where λ_i are arbitrary constants with values ranging from $1 \le i \le n$ and $\Re(\tau)$ is the solution of the equation:

$$\dot{\Re}(\tau) = \ln(v)\Big(\sigma_1 + \sigma_2 \Re(\tau) + \sigma_3 \Re^2(\tau)\Big), \tag{A5}$$

where, for convenience $v \in \mathbb{R} \setminus \{0,1\}$ replaces V, and σ_1, σ_2 and σ_3 are constants.

After assuming $\delta = \sigma_2^2 - 4\sigma_1\sigma_3$, 12 cases of the solutions of Equation (A5) appear:

1: If $\delta < 0$ and $\sigma_3 \neq 0$, then:

$$\begin{aligned}
&\Re_1(\tau) = -\frac{\sigma_2}{2\sigma_3} + \frac{\sqrt{-\delta}}{2\sigma_3}\tan\left(\frac{\sqrt{-\delta}}{2}\tau\right), \quad \Re_2(\tau) = -\frac{\sigma_2}{2\sigma_3} - \frac{\sqrt{-\delta}}{2\sigma_3}\cot\left(\frac{\sqrt{-\delta}}{2}\tau\right), \\
&\Re_3(\tau) = -\frac{\sigma_2}{2\sigma_3} + \frac{\sqrt{-\delta}}{2\sigma_3}\Big(\tan\big(\sqrt{-\delta}\tau\big) \pm \sqrt{mc}\sec\big(\sqrt{-\delta}\tau\big)\Big), \\
&\Re_4(\tau) = -\frac{\sigma_2}{2\sigma_3} - \frac{\sqrt{-\delta}}{2\sigma_3}\Big(\cot\big(\sqrt{-\delta}\tau\big) \pm \sqrt{mc}\csc\big(\sqrt{-\delta}\tau\big)\Big), \\
&\Re_5(\tau) = -\frac{\sigma_2}{2\sigma_3} + \frac{\sqrt{-\delta}}{4\sigma_3}\left(\tan\left(\frac{\sqrt{-\delta}}{4}\tau\right) - \cot\left(\frac{\sqrt{-\delta}}{4}\tau\right)\right).
\end{aligned} \tag{A6}$$

2: If $\delta > 0$ and $\sigma_3 \neq 0$, then:

$$\begin{aligned}
&\Re_6(\tau) = -\frac{\sigma_2}{2\sigma_3} - \frac{\sqrt{\delta}}{2\sigma_3}\tanh\left(\frac{\sqrt{\delta}}{2}\tau\right), \quad \Re_7(\tau) = -\frac{\sigma_2}{2\sigma_3} - \frac{\sqrt{\delta}}{2\sigma_3}\coth\left(\frac{\sqrt{\delta}}{2}\tau\right), \\
&\Re_8(\tau) = -\frac{\sigma_2}{2\sigma_3} - \frac{\sqrt{\delta}}{2\sigma_3}\Big(\tanh\big(\sqrt{\delta}\tau\big) \pm \iota\sqrt{mc}\,\mathrm{sech}\big(\sqrt{\delta}\tau\big)\Big), \\
&\Re_9(\tau) = -\frac{\sigma_2}{2\sigma_3} - \frac{\sqrt{\delta}}{2\sigma_3}\Big(\coth\big(\sqrt{\delta}\tau\big) \pm \sqrt{mc}\,\mathrm{csch}\big(\sqrt{\delta}\tau\big)\Big), \\
&\Re_{10}(\tau) = -\frac{\sigma_2}{2\sigma_3} - \frac{\sqrt{\delta}}{4\sigma_3}\left(\tanh\left(\frac{\sqrt{\delta}}{4}\tau\right) + \coth\left(\frac{\sqrt{\delta}}{4}\tau\right)\right).
\end{aligned} \tag{A7}$$

3: If $\sigma_1\sigma_3 > 0$ and $\sigma_2 = 0$, then:

$$\begin{aligned}
&\Re_{11}(\tau) = \sqrt{\frac{\sigma_1}{\sigma_3}}\tan(\sqrt{\sigma_1\sigma_3}\tau), \quad \Re_{12}(\tau) = -\sqrt{\frac{\sigma_1}{\sigma_3}}\cot(\sqrt{\sigma_1\sigma_3}\tau),\\
&\Re_{13}(\tau) = \sqrt{\frac{\sigma_1}{\sigma_3}}(\tan(2\sqrt{\sigma_1\sigma_3}\tau) \pm \sqrt{mc}\sec(2\sqrt{\sigma_1\sigma_3}\tau)),\\
&\Re_{14}(\tau) = \sqrt{\frac{\sigma_1}{\sigma_3}}(-\cot(2\sqrt{\sigma_1\sigma_3}\tau) \pm \sqrt{mc}\csc(2\sqrt{\sigma_1\sigma_3}\tau)),\\
&\Re_{15}(\tau) = \frac{1}{2}\sqrt{\frac{\sigma_1}{\sigma_3}}\left(\tan\left(\frac{\sqrt{\sigma_1\sigma_3}}{2}\tau\right) - \cot\left(\frac{\sqrt{\sigma_1\sigma_3}}{2}\tau\right)\right).
\end{aligned} \tag{A8}$$

4: If $\sigma_1\sigma_3 < 0$ and $\sigma_2 = 0$, then:

$$\begin{aligned}
&\Re_{16}(\tau) = -\sqrt{-\frac{\sigma_1}{\sigma_3}}\tanh(\sqrt{-\sigma_1\sigma_3}\tau), \quad \Re_{17}(\tau) = -\sqrt{-\frac{\sigma_1}{\sigma_3}}\coth(\sqrt{-\sigma_1\sigma_3}\tau),\\
&\Re_{18}(\tau) = -\sqrt{-\frac{\sigma_1}{\sigma_3}}(\tanh(2\sqrt{-\sigma_1\sigma_3}\tau) \pm \iota\sqrt{mc}\,\mathrm{sech}(2\sqrt{-\sigma_1\sigma_3}\tau)),\\
&\Re_{19}(\tau) = -\sqrt{-\frac{\sigma_1}{\sigma_3}}(\coth(2\sqrt{-\sigma_1\sigma_3}\tau) \pm \sqrt{mc}\,\mathrm{csch}(2\sqrt{-\sigma_1\sigma_3}\tau)),\\
&\Re_{20}(\tau) = -\frac{1}{2}\sqrt{-\frac{\sigma_1}{\sigma_3}}\left(\tanh\left(\frac{\sqrt{-\sigma_1\sigma_3}}{2}\tau\right) + \coth\left(\frac{\sqrt{-\sigma_1\sigma_3}}{2}\tau\right)\right).
\end{aligned} \tag{A9}$$

5: If $\sigma_1 = \sigma_3$ and $\sigma_2 = 0$, then:

$$\begin{aligned}
&\Re_{21}(\tau) = \tan(\sigma_1\tau), \quad \Re_{22}(\tau) = -\cot(\sigma_1\tau),\\
&\Re_{23}(\tau) = \tan(2\sigma_1\tau) \pm \sqrt{mc}\sec(2\sigma_1\tau),\\
&\Re_{24}(\tau) = -\cot(2\sigma_1\tau) \pm \sqrt{mc}\csc(2\sigma_1\tau),\\
&\Re_{25}(\tau) = \frac{1}{2}\left(\tan\left(\frac{\sigma_1}{2}\tau\right) - \cot\left(\frac{\sigma_1}{2}\tau\right)\right).
\end{aligned} \tag{A10}$$

6: If $\sigma_1 = -\sigma_3$ and $\sigma_2 = 0$, then:

$$\begin{aligned}
&\Re_{26}(\tau) = -\tanh(\sigma_1\tau), \quad \Re_{27}(\tau) = -\coth(\sigma_1\tau),\\
&\Re_{28}(\tau) = -\tanh(2\sigma_1\tau) \pm \iota\sqrt{mc}\,\mathrm{sech}(2\sigma_1\tau),\\
&\Re_{29}(\tau) = -\coth(2\sigma_1\tau) \pm \sqrt{mc}\,\mathrm{csch}(2\sigma_1\tau),\\
&\Re_{30}(\tau) = -\frac{1}{2}\left(\tanh\left(\frac{\sigma_1}{2}\tau\right) + \coth\left(\frac{\sigma_1}{2}\tau\right)\right).
\end{aligned} \tag{A11}$$

7: If $\sigma_2^2 = 4\sigma_1\sigma_3$, then $\Re_{31}(\tau) = \dfrac{-2\sigma_1(\sigma_2\tau\ln(v) + 2)}{\sigma_2^2\tau\ln(v)}$.

8: If $\sigma_2 = \mu, \sigma_1 = q\mu\ (q \neq 0), \sigma_3 = 0$, then $\Re_{32}(\tau) = v^{\mu\tau} - q$.

9: If $\sigma_2 = \sigma_3 = 0$, then $\Re_{33}(\tau) = \sigma_1\tau\ln(v)$.

10: If $\sigma_2 = \sigma_1 = 0$, then $\Re_{34}(\tau) = \dfrac{-1}{\sigma_3\tau\ln(v)}$.

11: If $\sigma_1 = 0$ and $\sigma_2 \neq 0$, then

$$\begin{aligned}
&\Re_{35}(\tau) = -\frac{m\sigma_2}{\sigma_3(\cosh(\sigma_2\tau) - \sinh(\sigma_2\tau) + m)},\\
&\Re_{36}(\tau) = -\frac{\sigma_2(\sinh(\sigma_2\tau) + \cosh(\sigma_2\tau))}{\sigma_3(\sinh(\sigma_2\tau) + \cosh(\sigma_2\tau) + c)}.
\end{aligned} \tag{A12}$$

12: If $\sigma_2 = \mu, \sigma_3 = q\mu \ (q \neq 0), \sigma_1 = 0$, then

$$\Re_{37}(\tau) = \frac{mv^{\mu\tau}}{c - qmv^{\mu\tau}}. \tag{A13}$$

In this context, we establish the definitions of hyperbolic and trigonometric functions in the following manner:

$$\begin{aligned}
\sinh(\tau) &= \frac{mv^{\tau} - cv^{-\tau}}{2}, & \cosh(\tau) &= \frac{mv^{\tau} + cv^{-\tau}}{2}, & \tanh(\tau) &= \frac{mv^{\tau} - cv^{-\tau}}{mv^{\tau} + cv^{-\tau}}, \\
\coth(\tau) &= \frac{mv^{\tau} + cv^{-\tau}}{mv^{\tau} - cv^{-\tau}}, & \operatorname{csch}(\tau) &= \frac{2}{mv^{\tau} - cv^{-\tau}}, & \operatorname{sech}(\tau) &= \frac{2}{mv^{\tau} + cv^{-\tau}}, \\
\sin(\tau) &= \frac{mv^{\iota\tau} - cv^{-\iota\tau}}{2\iota}, & \cos(\tau) &= \frac{mv^{\iota\tau} + cv^{-\iota\tau}}{2}, & \tan(\tau) &= -\iota\frac{mv^{\iota\tau} - cv^{-\iota\tau}}{mv^{\iota\tau} + cv^{-\iota\tau}}, \\
\cot(\tau) &= \iota\frac{mv^{\iota\tau} + cv^{-\iota\tau}}{mv^{\iota\tau} - cv^{-\iota\tau}}, & \csc(\tau) &= \frac{2\iota}{mv^{\iota\tau} - cv^{-\iota\tau}}, & \sec(\tau) &= \frac{2}{mv^{\iota\tau} + cv^{-\iota\tau}},
\end{aligned} \tag{A14}$$

where constants m and c are both arbitrary.

Step 4: The value of i remains consistently positive when employing the balancing approach to determine n in ODE (A3) through a comparison of the highest-order linear and nonlinear terms.

Step 5: We establish a system of algebraic equations by substituting Equations (A4) and (A5) into Equation (A3) and setting the coefficients of powers of $\Re(\tau)$ to zero. Subsequently, in Section 4, we visualize the results through graph plotting.

References

1. Shi, Y.; Mei, C. A finite element time domain modal formulation for large amplitude free vibrations of beams and plates. *J. Sound Vib.* **1996**, *193*, 453–464. [CrossRef]
2. Sarma, B.S.; Varadan, T.K. Lagrange-type formulation for finite element analysis of non-linear beam vibrations. *J. Sound Vib.* **1983**, *86*, 61–70. [CrossRef]
3. Qaisi, M.I. Application of the harmonic balance principle to the nonlinear free vibration of beams. *Appl. Acoust.* **1993**, *40*, 141–151. [CrossRef]
4. Azrar, L.; Benamar, R.; White, R.G. Semi-analytical approach to the non-linear dynamic response problem of S-S and C-C beams at large vibration amplitudes part I: General theory and application to the single mode approach to free and forced vibration analysis. *J. Sound Vib.* **1999**, *224*, 183–207. [CrossRef]
5. Arvin, H.; Bakhtiari-Nejad, F. Non-linear modal analysis of a rotating beam. *Int. J. Non-Linear Mech.* **2011**, *46*, 877–897. [CrossRef]
6. Bahrami, M.N.; Arani, M.K.; Saleh, N.R. Modified wave approach for calculation of natural frequencies and mode shapes in arbitrary non-uniform beams. *Sci. Iran.* **2011**, *18*, 1088–1094. [CrossRef]
7. Freno, B.A.; Cizmas, P.G.A. A computationally efficient non-linear beam model. *Int. J. Non-Linear Mech.* **2011**, *46*, 854–869. [CrossRef]
8. Zohoor, H.; Kakavand, F. Vibration of Euler-Bernoulli and Timoshenko beams in large overall motion on flying support using finite element method. *Sci. Iran.* **2012**, *19*, 1105–1116. [CrossRef]
9. Chen, J.S.; Chen, Y.K. Steady state and stability of a beam on a damped tensionless foundation under a moving load. *Int. J. Non-Linear Mech.* **2011**, *46*, 180–185. [CrossRef]
10. Andreaus, U.; Placidi, L.; Rega, G. Soft impact dynamics of a cantilever beam: Equivalent SDOF model versus infinite-dimensional system. *Proc. Inst. Mech. Eng. Part C J. Mech. Eng. Sci.* **2011**, *225*, 2444–2456. [CrossRef]
11. Jang, T.S.; Baek, H.S.; Paik, J.K. A new method for the non-linear deflection analysis of an infinite beam resting on a non-linear elastic foundation. *Int. J. Non-Linear Mech.* **2011**, *46*, 339–346. [CrossRef]
12. Sapountzakis, E.J.; Dikaros, I.C. Non-linear flexural-torsional dynamic analysis of beams of arbitrary cross section by BEM. *Int. J. Non-Linear Mech.* **2011**, *46*, 782–794. [CrossRef]
13. Campanile, L.F.; Jahne, R.; Hasse, A. Exact analysis of the bending of wide beams by a modified elastic approach. *Proc. Inst. Mech. Eng. Part C J. Mech. Eng. Sci.* **2011**, *225*, 2759–2764. [CrossRef]
14. Bayat, M.; Pakar, I.; Bayat, M. Analytical study on the vibration frequencies of tapered beams. *Lat. Am. J. Solids Struct.* **2011**, *8*, 149–162. [CrossRef]
15. He, J.H. Max-min approach to nonlinear oscillators. *Int. J. Nonlinear Sci. Numer. Simul.* **2008**, *9*, 207–210. [CrossRef]
16. Sedighi, H.M.; Shirazi, K.H.; Zare, J. An analytic solution of transversal oscillation of quintic non-linear beam with homotopy analysis method. *Int. J. Non-Linear Mech.* **2012**, *47*, 777–784. [CrossRef]

17. Liao, S.J. An analytic approximate approach for free oscillations of self-excited systems. *Int. J. Non-Linear Mech.* **2004**, *39*, 271–280. [CrossRef]
18. Eigoli, A.K.; Vossoughi, G.R. A periodic solution for friction drive microrobots based on the iteration perturbation method. *Sci. Iran.* **2011**, *18*, 368–374. [CrossRef]
19. Noghrehabadi, A.; Ghalambaz, M.; Ghanbarzadeh, A. A new approach to the electrostatic pull-in instability of nanocantilever actuators using the ADM-Pade technique. *Comput. Math. Appl.* **2012**, *64*, 2806–2815. [CrossRef]
20. Shadloo, M.S.; Kimiaeifar, A. Application of homotopy perturbation method to find an analytical solution for magnetohydrodynamic flows of viscoelastic fluids in converging/diverging channels. *Proc. Inst. Mech. Eng. Part C J. Mech. Eng. Sci.* **2011**, *225*, 347–353. [CrossRef]
21. Soroush, R.; Koochi, A.; Kazemi, A.S.; Noghrehabadi, A.; Haddadpour, H.; Abadyan, M. Investigating the effect of Casimir and van der Waals attractions on the electrostatic pull-in instability of nano-actuators. *Phys. Scr.* **2010**, *82*, 045801. [CrossRef]
22. He, J.H. Preliminary report on the energy balance for nonlinear oscillations. *Mech. Res. Commun.* **2002**, *29*, 107–111. [CrossRef]
23. Bayat, M.; Shahidi, M.; Barari, A.; Domairry, G. Analytical evaluation of the nonlinear vibration of coupled oscillator systems. *Z. Naturforschung A* **2011**, *66*, 67–74. [CrossRef]
24. Evirgen, F.; Ozdemir, N. Multistage adomian decomposition method for solving NLP problems over a nonlinear fractional dynamical system. *J. Comput. Nonlinear Dyn.* **2011**, *6*, 021003. [CrossRef]
25. Khosrozadeh, A.; Hajabasi, M.A.; Fahham, H.R. Analytical approximations to conservative oscillators with odd nonlinearity using the variational iteration method. *J. Comput. Nonlinear Dyn.* **2013**, *8*, 014502. [CrossRef]
26. He, J.H. A short remark on fractional variational iteration method. *Phys. Lett. A* **2011**, *375*, 3362–3364. [CrossRef]
27. Hasanov, A. Some new classes of inverse coefficient problems in non-linear mechanics and computational material science. *Int. J. Non-Linear Mech.* **2011**, *46*, 667–684. [CrossRef]
28. He, J.H. Hamiltonian approach to nonlinear oscillators. *Phys. Lett. A* **2010**, *374*, 2312–2314. [CrossRef]
29. Naderi, A.; Saidi, A.R. Buckling analysis of functionally graded annular sector plates resting on elastic foundations. *Proc. Inst. Mech. Eng. Part C J. Mech. Eng. Sci.* **2011**, *225*, 312–325. [CrossRef]
30. Baferani, A.H.; Saidi, A.R.; Jomehzadeh, E. An exact solution for free vibration of thin functionally graded rectangular plates. *Proc. Inst. Mech. Eng. Part C J. Mech. Eng. Sci.* **2011**, *225*, 526–536. [CrossRef]
31. He, J.H. Modified Lindstedt-Poincare methods for some strongly non-linear oscillations: Part I: Expansion of a constant. *Int. J. Non-Linear Mech.* **2002**, *37*, 309–314. [CrossRef]
32. Rezazadeh, H.; Inc, M.; Baleanu, D. New solitary wave solutions for variants of (3 + 1)-dimensional Wazwaz-Benjamin-Bona-Mahony equations. *Front. Phys.* **2020**, *8*, 332. [CrossRef]
33. Jin, S.; Liu, N.; Yu, Y. Time complexity analysis of quantum algorithms via linear representations for nonlinear ordinary and partial differential equations. *J. Comput. Phys.* **2023**, *487*, 112149. [CrossRef]
34. Ullah, N.; Rehman, H.U.; Imran, M.A.; Abdeljawad, T. Highly dispersive optical solitons with cubic law and cubic-quintic-septic law nonlinearities. *Results Phys.* **2020**, *17*, 103021. [CrossRef]
35. Zhao, D.; Lu, D.; Salama, S.A.; Khater, M.M. Stable novel and accurate solitary wave solutions of an integrable equation: Qiao model. *Open Phys.* **2021**, *19*, 742–752. [CrossRef]
36. Baishya, C.; Rangarajan, R. A new application of G'/G-expansion method for travelling wave solutions of fractional PDEs. *Int. J. Appl. Eng. Res.* **2018**, *13*, 9936–9942.
37. Younas, U.; Baber, M.Z.; Yasin, M.W.; Sulaiman, T.A.; Ren, J. The generalized higher-order nonlinear Schrodinger equation: Optical solitons and other solutions in fiber optics. *Int. J. Mod. Phys. B* **2023**, *37*, 2350174. [CrossRef]
38. Biswas, A.; Yildirim, Y.; Yasar, E.; Zhou, Q.; Moshokoa, S.P.; Belic, M. Optical solitons for Lakshmanan-Porsezian-Daniel model by modified simple equation method. *Optik* **2018**, *160*, 24–32. [CrossRef]
39. Zayed, E.M.; Alngar, M.E. Optical solitons in birefringent fibers with Biswas-Arshed model by generalized Jacobi elliptic function expansion method. *Optik* **2020**, *203*, 163922. [CrossRef]
40. Raslan, K.R.; Ali, K.K.; Shallal, M.A. The modified extended tanh method with the Riccati equation for solving the space-time fractional EW and MEW equations. *Chaos Solitons Fractals* **2017**, *103*, 404–409. [CrossRef]
41. Akbari, M. Application of Kudryashov method for the Ito equations. *Appl. Appl. Math. Int. J. AAM* **2017**, *12*, 9.
42. Feng, D.; Luo, G. The improved Fan sub-equation method and its application to the SK equation. *Appl. Math. Comput.* **2009**, *215*, 1949–1967. [CrossRef]
43. Mahak, N.; Akram, G. Exact solitary wave solutions by extended rational sine-cosine and extended rational sinh-cosh techniques. *Phys. Scr.* **2019**, *94*, 115212. [CrossRef]
44. Raza, N.; Rafiq, M.H. Abundant fractional solitons to the coupled nonlinear Schrodinger equations arising in shallow water waves. *Int. J. Mod. Phys. B* **2020**, *34*, 2050162. [CrossRef]
45. Qin, M.; Wang, Y.; Yuen, M. Optimal System, Symmetry Reductions and Exact Solutions of the (2+ 1)-Dimensional Seventh-Order Caudrey-Dodd-Gibbon-KP Equation. *Symmetry* **2024**, *16*, 403. [CrossRef]
46. Younas, U.; Sulaiman, T.A.; Ren, J. Dynamics of optical pulses in fiber optics with stimulated Raman scattering effect. *Int. J. Mod. Phys. B* **2023**, *37*, 2350080. [CrossRef]
47. Riaz, M.B.; Jhangeer, A.; Martinovic, J.; Kazmi, S.S. Dynamics and Soliton Propagation in a Modified Oskolkov Equation: Phase Plot Insights. *Symmetry* **2023**, *15*, 2171. [CrossRef]

48. Rafiq, M.H.; Jhangeer, A.; Raza, N. The analysis of solitonic, supernonlinear, periodic, quasiperiodic, bifurcation and chaotic patterns of perturbed Gerdjikov-Ivanov model with full nonlinearity. *Commun. Nonlinear Sci. Numer. Simul.* **2023**, *116*, 106818. [CrossRef]
49. Jhangeer, A.; Raza, N.; Rezazadeh, H.; Seadawy, A. Nonlinear self-adjointness, conserved quantities, bifurcation analysis and travelling wave solutions of a family of long-wave unstable lubrication model. *Pramana* **2020**, *94*, 1–9. [CrossRef]
50. Jhangeer, A.; Rezazadeh, H.; Seadawy, A. A study of travelling, periodic, quasiperiodic and chaotic structures of perturbed Fokas-Lenells model. *Pramana* **2021**, *95*, 1–11. [CrossRef]
51. Jhangeer, A.; Hussain, A.; Junaid-U-Rehman, M.; Baleanu, D.; Riaz, M.B. Quasi-periodic, chaotic and travelling wave structures of modified Gardner equation. *Chaos Solitons Fractals* **2021**, *143*, 110578. [CrossRef]
52. Imran, M.; Jhangeer, A.; Ansari, A.R.; Riaz, M.B.; Ghazwani, H.A. Investigation of space-time dynamics of perturbed and unperturbed Chen-Lee-Liu equation: Unveiling bifurcations and chaotic structures. *Alex. Eng. J.* **2024**, *97*, 283–293. [CrossRef]
53. Gorbunov-Posadov, M.I. Design of structure upon elastic foundations. *Proc. VICSMFE* **1961**, *1*, 643–648.
54. Soldatos, K.P.; Selvadurai, A.P.S. Flexure of beams resting on hyperbolic elastic foundations. *Int. J. Solids Struct.* **1985**, *21*, 373–388. [CrossRef]
55. Al-Hosani, K.; Fadhil, S.; El-Zafrany, A. Fundamental solution and boundary element analysis of thick plates on Winkler foundation. *Comput. Struct.* **1999**, *70*, 325–336. [CrossRef]
56. Wu, T.Y.; Liu, G. A differential quadrature as a numerical method to solve differential equations. *Comput. Mech.* **1999**, *24*, 197–205. [CrossRef]
57. Kopmaz, O.; Gundogdu, O. On the curvature of an Euler-Bernoulli beam. *Int. J. Mech. Eng. Educ.* **2003**, *31*, 132–142. [CrossRef]
58. Pirbodaghi, T.; Ahmadian, M.T.; Fesanghary, M. On the homotopy analysis method for non-linear vibration of beams. *Mech. Res. Commun.* **2009**, *36*, 143–148. [CrossRef]
59. Burgreen, D. Free vibrations of a pin-ended column with constant distance between pin ends. *J. Appl. Mech.* **2021**, *18*, 135–139. [CrossRef]
60. Malla, A.; Natarajan, S. Fragile points method for Euler–Bernoulli beams. *Eur. J. Mech.-A/Solids* **2024**, *106*, 105319. [CrossRef]
61. Fudlailah, P.; Allen, D.H.; Cordes, R. Verification of Euler–Bernoulli beam theory model for wind blade structure analysis. *Thin-Walled Struct.* **2024**, *202*, 111989. [CrossRef]
62. Ataman, M.; Szcześniak, W. Influence of Inertial Vlasov Foundation Parameters on the Dynamic Response of the Bernoulli-Euler Beam Subjected to A Group of Moving Forces-Analytical Approach. *Materials* **2022**, *15*, 3249. [CrossRef] [PubMed]
63. He, X.; Song, Y.; Han, Z.; Zhang, S.; Jing, P.; Qi, S. Adaptive inverse backlash boundary vibration control design for an Euler-Bernoulli beam system. *J. Frankl. Inst.* **2020**, *357*, 3434–3450. [CrossRef]
64. Wang, Z.; Wu, W.; Görges, D.; Lou, X. Sliding mode vibration control of an Euler-Bernoulli beam with unknown external disturbances. *Nonlinear Dyn.* **2022**, *110*, 1393–1404. [CrossRef]
65. Rao, S.S. *Vibration of Continuous Systems*, 2nd ed.; John Wiley & Sons: Hoboken, NJ, USA, 2019.
66. Tse, F.S.; Morse, I.E.; Hinkle, R.T. *Mechanical Vibrations*; Allyn and Bacon: Boston, MA, USA, 1963.
67. Barari, A.; Kaliji, H.D.; Ghadimi, M.; Domairry, G. Non-linear vibration of Euler-Bernoulli beams. *Lat. Am. J. Solids Struct.* **2011**, *8*, 139–148. [CrossRef]
68. Khater, M.M.; Seadawy, A.R.; Lu, D. Elliptic and solitary wave solutions for Bogoyavlenskii equations system, couple Boiti-Leon-Pempinelli equations system and Time-fractional Cahn-Allen equation. *Results Phys.* **2017**, *7*, 2325–2333. [CrossRef]
69. Hussain, A.; Jhangeer, A.; Abbas, N.; Khan, I.; Sherif, E.S.M. Optical solitons of fractional complex Ginzburg-Landau equation with conformable, beta, and M-truncated derivatives: A comparative study. *Adv. Differ. Equ.* **2020**, *2020*, 612. [CrossRef]
70. Riaz, M.B.; Awrejcewicz, J.; Jhangeer, A.; Junaid-U-Rehman, M. A Variety of New Traveling Wave Packets and Conservation Laws to the Nonlinear Low-Pass Electrical Transmission Lines via Lie Analysis. *Fractal Fract.* **2021**, *5*, 170. [CrossRef]

symmetry

MDPI

Article

A Symmetric Multiprocessor System-on-a-Chip-Based Solution for Real-Time Image Dehazing

Dat Ngo [1] and Bongsoon Kang [2,*]

[1] Department of Computer Engineering, Korea National University of Transportation, Chungju 27469, Republic of Korea; datngo@ut.ac.kr
[2] Department of Electronic Engineering, Dong-A University, Busan 49315, Republic of Korea
* Correspondence: bongsoon@dau.ac.kr; Tel.: +82-51-200-7703

Abstract: The acquisition of digital images is susceptible to haze, and images captured under such adverse conditions may impact high-level applications designed for clean input data. Image dehazing emerges as a practical solution to this problem, as it can be employed to pre-process images immediately after acquisition. This paper presents a concise review of impactful algorithms, including those based on deep learning models, to identify the existing gap in real-time processing capabilities. Subsequently, a real-time dehazing system on a multiprocessor system-on-a-chip (MPSoC) platform is introduced to bridge this gap. The proposed system balances the trade-off between dehazing performance and computational complexity; hence, the name "Symmetric" is coined. Additionally, the entire system is implemented in programmable logic and wrapped by an interface circuit supporting double-buffering, rendering it highly suitable for seamless integration into existing camera systems. Implementation results on a Zynq UltraScale+ MPSoC ZCU106 Evaluation Kit demonstrate a maximum operating frequency of 356.51 MHz, equivalent to a maximum processing speed of 40.27 frames per second for DCI 4K resolution.

Keywords: image dehazing; deep learning; real-time processing; MPSoC

1. Introduction

Image dehazing (also known as image defogging or visibility restoration) is a long-standing problem in computer vision due to its ill-posed nature. One of the earliest attempts at addressing this challenging problem dates back to the work of Vincent [1] in 1972. Over the years, a myriad of relevant studies have emerged, ranging from heuristic approaches (such as enhancement-based [2,3] and prior-based [4,5] methods) to data-driven techniques (such as deep learning methods [6–9]). As a result, the research field has now matured, with a strong focus on practical and application-oriented solutions, where dehazing algorithms are required to be computationally efficient for broad deployment. An illustrative example of this trend can be found in Adobe's integration of image dehazing capabilities within the Camera Raw plugin of its renowned image editing application, Photoshop [10].

Recent years have witnessed rapid developments in self-driving vehicles and smart surveillance systems, where computer vision algorithms play crucial roles. Integrating image dehazing into these systems presents a key requirement, that is, processing speed. For instance, Bosch's multi-purpose camera [11] is a system-on-a-chip (SoC) device designed for video-based driver assistance systems, and it can generate up to 45 frames per second (fps) at 2048 × 1280 resolution. If a dehazing algorithm with a processing speed of 10 fps were to be implemented, a bottleneck would arise, leading to significant performance loss. To maintain the high performance and smooth functioning of Bosch's camera, the dehazing algorithm must handle images at a minimum speed of 25 or 30 fps, depending on whether the video encoding system is PAL or NTSC. This example highlights the critical importance of processing speed in real-time computer vision systems.

The following section summarizes the five-decade development of image dehazing, with a primary focus on daytime single-image approaches. It also highlights a trade-off between performance and algorithmic complexity. Sections 3 and 4 then detail the proposed solution based on multiprocessor system-on-a-chip (MPSoC) to balance this trade-off. Our contributions can be summarized as follows:

- We incorporate a self-calibrating feature, enabling the proposed algorithm to handle various haze conditions effectively.
- We present a real-time high-quality hardware implementation, facilitating the practical deployment of the proposed algorithm.

Experimental results are also presented to validate the real-time processing capability and performance, comparing the proposed solution with the base algorithm and state-of-the-art methods. Section 5 discusses future development directions and concludes the paper.

2. Image Dehazing Chronicle

Generally, image dehazing algorithms can be broadly categorized into two groups: heuristic and data-driven methods. These two categories differ in the origin of the utilized image features. Specifically, heuristic methods are grounded on handcrafted features discovered through engineering efforts. Conversely, data-driven methods focus on architecture design to learn the most representative features from the abundant data. This paper further classifies heuristic methods into enhancement-based and prior-based and data-driven methods into restoration-based and generation-based approaches. The following subsections chronicle major milestones in the development of single-image dehazing, along with high-impact studies exemplifying each individual category.

2.1. Heuristic Methods

2.1.1. Enhancement-Based Approach

The presence of haze causes atmospheric scattering and absorption, wherein part of the incoming light scatters directly into the camera's aperture, leading to increased brightness. The remaining light attenuates in the transmission medium before reaching the aperture, resulting in faintness. Consequently, hazy images exhibit poor visibility. To address this, enhancement-based methods aim to improve low-level features such as contrast and brightness. For example, Kim et al. [2] introduced the block-overlapped histogram equalization method, which spreads out highly populated intensities to enhance global contrast. This computationally inexpensive method is suitable for mobile phones and security cameras. However, for images with imperceptible background noise, this method may increase noise contrast, reducing the signal-to-noise ratio (SNR).

In line with this, Oakley and Satherley [3] proposed a physical-model-based contrast enhancement method to compensate for the adverse effects of a turbid atmosphere on digital images. They also noticed the SNR reduction problem and devised a temporal filter, but the problem persisted. Ancuti and Ancuti [12] adopted multiscale image fusion to alleviate the visibility reduction problem. They transformed a single input image using white balance and contrast enhancement to generate multiple variants of the input for image fusion. After that, they constructed Laplacian pyramids and conducted fusion using guidance weights derived from saliency, luminance, and chrominance. While multiscale image fusion guarantees dehazing results with fine details, it can hinder real-time hardware implementation due to up-sampling and down-sampling processes that require many frame buffers.

Similarly, Galdran [13] attempted to reverse the effects of atmospheric scattering and absorption through multiscale image fusion. A single input image undergoes artificial under-exposure and contrast enhancement to mitigate the haze-induced problems of brightness increase and contrast degradation. The resulting variants, expressed as Laplacian pyramids, are then input into the fusion process, where the weighting function is derived from the pixel-wise contrast and saturation maps, and while artificial under-exposure renders this method robust to noise amplification, it can also darken the dehazing results.

2.1.2. Prior-Based Approach

Enhancement-based methods focus on visibility restoration by manipulating low-level features, but they often overlook haze's impact on image degradation. To address this, researchers have modeled image formation in a turbid atmosphere using optical physics, with the most widely used model being the Koschmieder model.

$$\mathbf{I}(x) = \mathbf{J}(x)t(x) + \mathbf{A}[1 - t(x)], \tag{1}$$

where $\mathbf{I} \in \mathbb{R}^{\mathrm{H}\times\mathrm{W}\times 3}$ denotes the hazy image, $\mathbf{J} \in \mathbb{R}^{\mathrm{H}\times\mathrm{W}\times 3}$ the clean image, $t \in \mathbb{R}^{\mathrm{H}\times\mathrm{W}}$ the transmission map, and $\mathbf{A} \in \mathbb{R}^{1\times 1\times 3}$ the global atmospheric light. H and W represent the height and width of images, and x denotes the spatial coordinates of pixels. The terms $\mathbf{J}(x)t(x)$ and $\mathbf{A}[1 - t(x)]$ correspond to the multiplicative and additive attenuation of the incoming light due to absorption and scattering. This model assumes a constant transmission map across color channels, whereas in reality, it is wavelength-dependent.

Another approach, prior-based methods, leverages prior knowledge to estimate the transmission map and global atmospheric light, then reverses Equation (1) to restore visibility. He et al. [4] proposed that in local image patches (excluding white and bright regions), pixels have extremely low intensities in at least one color channel, a concept known as the dark channel prior. For a local patch $\Omega(x)$ centered at x, this prior is represented by Equation (2). By substituting $\mathbf{I}$, $\mathbf{A}$, and t for $\mathbf{J}$, a direct relation between $\mathbf{A}$ and t is established. He et al. [4] also suggested that the global atmospheric light corresponds to the brightest pixel in the top 0.1% of highest intensities in the dark channel.

$$\min_{y\in\Omega(x)} \left[\min_{c\in\{\mathrm{R,G,B}\}} \mathbf{J}^c(y) \right] \approx 0. \tag{2}$$

Despite its simplicity, the method devised by He et al. [4] is highly effective, though it may cause color distortion in the sky region where the dark channel prior does not hold. Combining multiple priors can help address these limitations. For instance, Tang et al. [14] adopted random forest regression to estimate the transmission map from four image features: dark channel, contrast, saturation, and hue disparity, extracted at four different scales. They adapted the method of He et al. [4] by using the median (instead of the largest) of the top 0.1% of dark channel values for atmospheric light, improving robustness at the cost of a prolonged execution time.

The prior knowledge presented in the aforementioned dehazing solutions is verifiable with local image patches but not with global image context. Accordingly, Berman et al. [15] introduced a non-local prior, noting that colors in clean images form tight clusters in RGB space, spread throughout the image. They employed k-means clustering to identify these clusters and infer transmission values from their distance to the camera. The global atmospheric light estimation was similar to the method of He et al. [4]. This non-local prior is effective and versatile, as demonstrated in [16–18]. However, it shares common problems with other prior-based methods, such as a tendency to produce over-saturated dehazing results.

2.2. *Data-Driven Methods*

2.2.1. Restoration-Based Approach

To enhance the generalizability of dehazing algorithms, researchers have incorporated deep learning techniques, notably convolutional neural networks (CNNs). Cai et al. [6] proposed DehazeNet, which infers the transmission map from a single image. The approach employs a CNN to extract low-level features like contrast, saturation, and edge details. Maxout layers enhance feature robustness, and convolutional layers with different kernel sizes induce scale-invariant characteristics. Multiscale features undergo a max-pooling layer to enhance resilience against minor displacements in the input image. Finally, a bilateral ReLU performs nonlinear regression to estimate the transmission map. Cai et al. [6] utilized the method of He et al. [4] to obtain the global atmospheric light, necessary for recovering clean images based on the Koschmieder model.

Haze-induced image degradation affects all red, green, and blue channels. However, Wang et al. [19] observed that it predominantly impacts the luminance channel. They developed a lightweight variant of DehazeNet to estimate the transmission map from the image's luminance, reducing computational costs while maintaining performance. Dudhane and Murala [20] extended the research of Cai et al. [6] and Wang et al. [19] by employing two DehazeNet-like networks to estimate two transmission maps in RGB and YCbCr color spaces, combining them with a fusion network to obtain the final transmission map. This method improved performance but increased computational costs. Recently, Sahu et al. [21] presented a dual-channel DehazeNet to improve the accuracy of transmission map estimation. To attain computational efficiency, they implemented their proposed model on an FPGA board, where the input images were downsampled to 32×32 pixels for real-time processing.

Ren et al. [22] proposed an alternative approach, which has also been widely referenced in subsequent studies. They devised a deep CNN that estimates the transmission map in a coarse-to-fine manner. They employed convolutional layers with large receptive fields to learn the coarse structure and layers with small receptive fields to refine the transmission map, ensuring smoothness while preserving discontinuities.

Despite their potential for learning complex and abstract patterns from images, the aforementioned methods solely utilized CNNs for estimating the transmission map. Additionally, the lack of real ground-truth data for training CNNs limits these methods, rendering them susceptible to the domain-shift problem.

2.2.2. Generation-Based Approach

The seminal work of Goodfellow et al. [23] on generative adversarial networks, coupled with the increasing adoption of the autoencoder architecture [24], has given rise to generation-based dehazing. Pan et al. [25] proposed a physics-based network involving hazy–clean generation followed by clean–hazy regeneration, using a separate discriminator to ensure consistency with the real input. The authors also incorporated the Koschmieder model to facilitate the regeneration. However, the network's capability is constrained by this physical model and may fail with complex phenomena.

In contrast to the method of Pan et al. [25], Liu et al. [26] improved upon previous work [27] with GridDehazeNet+, an enhanced multiscale network that dehazes images and is purely data-driven without relying on the Koschmieder model. GridDehazeNet+ processes images through pre-processing, multiscale image fusion, and post-processing stages. The multiscale processing employs a grid-like data flow with self-attention to combine data at different scales. Liu et al. [26] also addressed the domain-shift problem by utilizing intra-task knowledge transfer, training a teacher network with synthetic images and initializing a student network with its weights, then training with translated images via CycleGAN [28]. Anecdotally, using these translated images for model training is a provisional solution to the domain-shift problem, as they are still artificially generated.

Inspired by the concept of layer disentanglement [29], Li et al. [30] introduced an unsupervised network, which was trained to generate the transmission map and global atmospheric light in addition to the clean image. By reconstructing the hazy image using the Koschmieder model, the network can supervise itself during parameter optimization. This self-supervision capability significantly aids data preparation, though lacking clean image domain knowledge may hinder an optimal parameter search.

Recently, Xu et al. [8] introduced a U-Net-like network for video dehazing with a multiscale encoder and a prior-scene decoder. The multiscale encoder extracts feature maps at various scales, while the prior-scene decoder layers learn features related to the prior and scene. Recurrent features from adjacent video frames are aligned and aggregated to generate the clean image. The network, trained on synthesized hazy videos, remains susceptible to the domain-shift problem and fails to meet real-time processing requirements.

Wu et al. [9] sought to mitigate the domain-shift problem by incorporating diverse degradation types in hazy image synthesis, modifying the Koschmieder model to adjust light conditions, atmospheric light color bias, and JPEG compression effects. However, given that the distribution of the synthesized hazy images does not align with that of real hazy images, their proposed method remains a provisional solution. Sahu et al. [31] proposed Oval-Net, an encoder–decoder network with spatial and channel attention mechanisms, for end-to-end image dehazing. Oval-Net was trained using synthetic datasets, and the authors acknowledged that this could reduce the network's reliability in real-world circumstances.

The primary concern with deep-learning-based methods is their high computational complexity. Even a simple network for image classification can contain millions of parameters, necessitating significant effort for hyper-parameter tuning and hindering fast and efficient implementation for widespread deployment. Chen et al. [32] addressed these challenges with a lightweight dehazing network using an autoencoder architecture, incorporating difference convolution to integrate low-level prior information and a content-guided attention mechanism for handling haze heterogeneity; while this network exhibited relative speed and efficiency, it still falls short of real-time high-quality image processing.

Most data-driven methods are trained on a mix of synthetic and real-world images. With the increasing prevalence of text-to-image models like StableDiffusion [33] and DALL-E 2 [34], this trend is expected to continue. Nonetheless, the inclusion of synthetic images may exacerbate the domain-shift problem, as discussed by Shumailov et al. [35]. Artificially generated images do not share a similar distribution with real-world images, potentially reducing network generalizability.

In summary, data-driven methods have demonstrated superior performance over heuristic approaches in various computer vision tasks. Nevertheless, their limitations, such as high computational cost and limited generalizability, may render them less favorable for practical applications.

2.3. Summary

Table 1 presents a summary of the daytime single-image dehazing methods discussed above. Generally, heuristic methods are computationally efficient but susceptible to noise, and their results tend to align with human perception. However, they may face challenges when applied to diverse circumstances. On the other hand, data-driven methods offer improved generalizability but come with a higher computational cost, and their results often align better with quantitative assessment metrics. Notably, nearly all data-driven methods are susceptible to the domain-shift problem due to the lack of real-world training images.

Table 1. Summary of daytime single-image dehazing chronicle.

Category		Representative Studies	Pros and Cons
Heuristic	Enhancement-based	[2,3,12,13]	Pros Low computational cost Subjectively favoring results
	Prior-based	[4,14,15]	Cons Noise amplification Lack of generalizability
Data-driven	Restoration-based	[6,19,20,22]	Pros Improved generalizability Quantitatively favoring results
	Generation-based	[8,25,26,30,32]	Cons High computational cost Domain-shift problem

More importantly, data-driven methods often require graphics processing units (GPUs) for model inference. Since this computing platform is power-consuming and expensive, it is unsuitable for implementation on edge devices, such as CCTVs or cameras mounted on autonomous driving vehicles. In sharp contrast, the proposed MPSoC-based solution presented in the following section is fast and compact, occupying less than one-fifth of the hardware resources available on a mid-size FPGA device (XCZU7EV-2FFVC1156), as demonstrated in Section 4.2. This makes the proposed MPSoC-based solution a preferable option over data-driven methods for real-time high-quality image dehazing.

3. Proposed Algorithm

As data-driven methods are not yet ready for widespread deployment, this paper presents an alternative for real-time high-quality single-image dehazing: a symmetric MPSoC-based solution that balances the trade-off between dehazing performance and computational complexity. Building upon our previous work of linear-time single-image dehazing [36], the proposed algorithm incorporates the following features (as illustrated in Figure 1):

- A self-calibrating feature that enables the algorithm to handle different haze conditions effectively.
- A real-time high-quality hardware implementation that facilitates the practical deployment of the proposed algorithm.

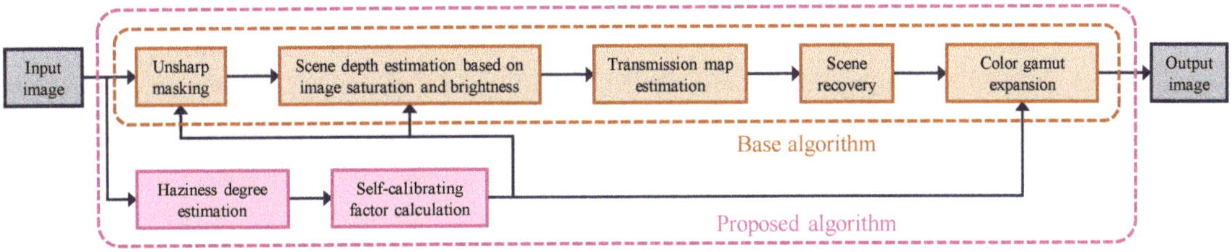

Figure 1. Block diagram of the proposed algorithm.

3.1. Base Algorithm

In [36], we presented an $\mathcal{O}(N)$ dehazing method, where N denotes the number of image pixels. This method enhances the visibility of hazy images through several steps. Initially, a pre-processing step involving unsharp masking is applied to the input image to enhance edge details based on local image statistics. Next, image visibility is restored using a dehazing step grounded on the improved color attenuation prior. However, this dehazing step may introduce artifacts like dynamic range reduction. To address this, a post-processing step, namely color gamut expansion, is employed to ensure an artifact-free output. Interested readers are referred to [36] for a more comprehensive description.

Let $\mathcal{P}$, $\mathcal{D}$, and $\mathcal{H}$ denote the pre-processing, dehazing, and post-processing stages of the base algorithm. The clean image $\mathbf{J}$ is derived from the hazy image $\mathbf{I}$ as follows:

$$\mathbf{J} = \mathcal{H}\{\mathcal{D}[\mathcal{P}(\mathbf{I})]\}, \tag{3}$$

where spatial coordinates are omitted for clarity. The responses of these three stages to input images are fixed, irrespective of whether images are affected by haze. Hence, the following subsection outlines our contribution in adopting a haziness degree estimator [37] to make $\mathcal{P}$, $\mathcal{D}$, and $\mathcal{H}$ aware of haze conditions. More precisely, we introduce a self-calibrating weight ω into $\mathcal{P}$, $\mathcal{D}$, and $\mathcal{H}$ to restore the clean image as $\mathbf{J} = \mathcal{H}\{\omega, \mathcal{D}[\omega, \mathcal{P}(\omega, \mathbf{I})]\}$. Depending on the haze condition of the input image, the value of ω varies, thus enabling the fine-tuning of all three processing stages for appropriate enhancement.

In [36], we demonstrated that the base algorithm achieves performance comparable to data-driven methods, such as those proposed by Cai et al. [6] and Ren et al. [22], while exhibiting significantly lower computational costs. However, real-time processing requirements through software implementation remain challenging. The fastest implementation, representing the base algorithm, processes only ten 640 × 480 frames per second (fps), falling short of the desired 25 fps.

The subsequent subsections focus on two main aspects. Firstly, efforts are made to incorporate a self-calibrating feature into the base algorithm to enhance performance further. Secondly, a comparative evaluation is conducted to assess the effectiveness of the proposed improvements. Additionally, Section 4 presents an MPSoC-based solution to address the real-time processing constraint.

3.2. Self-Calibration on Haze Conditions

The Koschmieder model describes the transmission map $t(x)$ as an exponential function of the scene depth $d(x)$, denoted as $t(x) = \exp[-\beta \cdot d(x)]$, where β represents the atmospheric scattering coefficient. This implies that the haze distribution depends on scene depth, allowing the dehazing algorithm to handle various types of haze, from mild to dense. In a prior study [38], we introduced a framework for generating a piece-wise linear weight using the haziness degree estimator [37]. This weight is combined with the scene depth in a multiplicative manner to address different scenarios:

- **Haze-free images**. The weight is set to zero, zeroing the scene depth. Consequently, $t(x) = 1$ is achieved throughout the image, meaning that no image dehazing is performed.
- **Mildly-to-moderately hazy images**. The weight assumes a value ω_e, where $0 < \omega_e < 1$, based on the haziness degree estimate, reducing the dehazing power to prevent artifacts.
- **Densely hazy images**. The weight is set to one, imposing no constraints on the scene depth, allowing maximum dehazing power.

By incorporating this adaptive weight, the base algorithm can effectively adapt to various haze conditions, improving results for different types of hazy images. Figure 2a illustrates this weighting scheme, where ω and ρ represent the weight and haziness degree estimate, respectively. The haziness degree range is divided into three regions using two predefined parameters, ρ_1 and ρ_2. The weighting scheme is expressed as follows:

$$\omega = \begin{cases} 0 & \rho < \rho_1 \\ \dfrac{\rho - \rho_1}{\rho_2 - \rho_1} & \rho_1 \le \rho \le \rho_2 \\ 1 & \rho > \rho_2 \end{cases}. \tag{4}$$

In [38], evaluation results indicated that dehazing performance for densely hazy images was unimpressive, suggesting that greater dehazing power might improve results. Consequently, in this study, we have modified the original weighting scheme by allowing the weight (ω) to extend beyond the range $[0, 1]$, up to a predefined value of $\mathcal{W}$, as illustrated in Figure 2b. This modification enables the algorithm to effectively "see" through a thicker haze, surpassing the capabilities of prior-based dehazing methods. The proposed weighting scheme is expressed as follows:

$$\omega = \begin{cases} 0 & \rho < \rho_1 \\ \dfrac{\rho - \rho_1}{\rho_2 - \rho_1} & \rho_1 \le \rho \le \rho_2 \\ \left(\dfrac{\mathcal{W} - 1}{1 - \rho_2}\right)\rho + \dfrac{1 - \mathcal{W}\rho_2}{1 - \rho_2} & \rho > \rho_2 \end{cases}. \tag{5}$$

Figure 2 illustrates a comparison between the original weight presented in [38] and our proposed weight to highlight their differences. It features a densely hazy image from the IVC dataset [39] and showcases two dehazing results obtained using the two weights, respectively. Parameters ρ_1 and ρ_2 are set to 0.8811 and 0.9344, as described in [40], and $\mathcal{W}$ is fixed at 1.2. Subjective evaluation shows that the dehazing result in Figure 2d is less favorable compared to the result with our proposed weight in Figure 2e.

Our contribution extends beyond the weighting scheme, including how the self-calibrating weight is incorporated into the algorithm. In [38], the self-calibrating weight was applied to both the dehazing and post-processing stages, while the pre-processing stage remained unchanged. The pre-processing stage focused on white-balancing the input image to skip the estimation of the global atmospheric light $\mathbf{A}$ (in [38], the global atmospheric light was set to a fixed value of $\{1, 1, 1\}$, under the assumption that image intensities were normalized within the range $[0, 1]$). In contrast, the proposed algorithm uses unsharp masking in the pre-processing stage to enhance distant edge details obscured by haze. Consequently, we have also equipped this pre-processing stage with the self-calibrating weight to prevent overshooting in haze-free images.

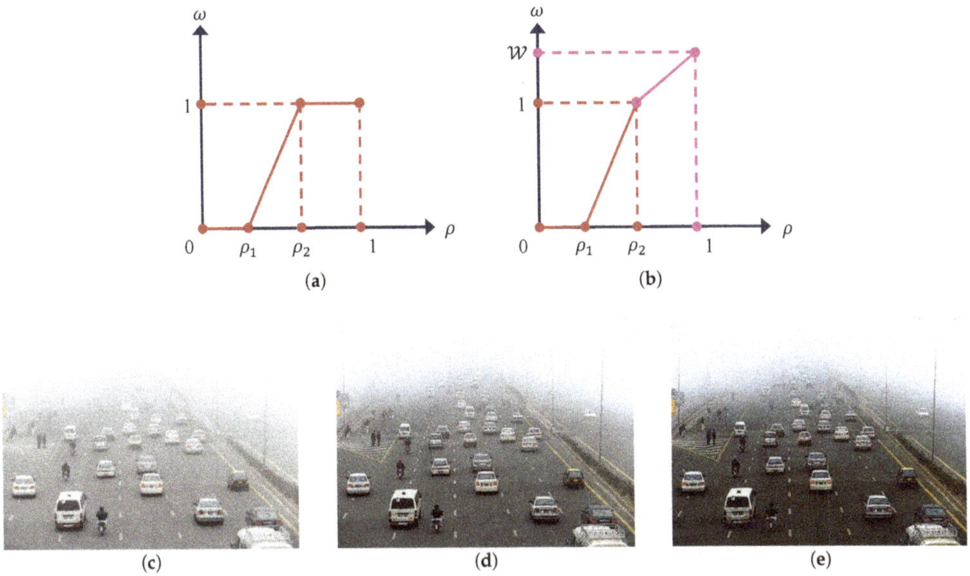

Figure 2. Illustration of piece-wise linear weights for incorporating the self-calibrating feature. (**a**) The original weight presented in [38]. (**b**) Our proposed weight. (**c**) A densely hazy image. (**d**) Dehazing result with the original weight. (**e**) Dehazing result with the proposed weight.

3.3. Objective Evaluation

To validate the performance of the proposed algorithm, we conducted a comparative analysis against four methods, including the base algorithm and those proposed by Cai et al. [6], Liu et al. [27], and Li et al. [30]. We used five public datasets for evaluation: FRIDA2 [41], D-HAZY [42], O-HAZE [43], I-HAZE [44], and Dense-Haze [45]. The benchmark methods have been introduced in Section 2.

The FRIDA2 dataset consists of 320 computer-rendered images of road scenes, with 66 haze-free and 264 hazy images representing four distinct haze conditions. D-HAZY is another synthetic dataset containing 1472 pairs of indoor hazy/clean images, where haze was synthesized using scene depth information from a Microsoft Kinect camera. In contrast, O-HAZE, I-HAZE, and Dense-Haze are real-world datasets consisting of 45, 30, and 55 image pairs, respectively, depicting outdoor, indoor, and both outdoor and indoor scenes.

To assess the experimental results, we employed two metrics: feature similarity extended to color images (FSIMc) [46] and tone-mapped image quality index (TMQI) [47]. Both metrics provide scores ranging from zero to one, where higher scores indicate better results. The obtained FSIMc and TMQI scores for each dataset, along with their average scores, are presented in Table 2.

The results demonstrate that the proposed algorithm, enhanced with the new self-calibrating weighting scheme, consistently outperforms the base algorithm in all test scenarios. Additionally, it is also ranked higher than the other three data-driven benchmark methods. This result suggests that even though the proposed method is a heuristic approach, it effectively addresses the limitation of limited generalizability, thanks to the new weighting scheme. With its efficacy confirmed, the next section will introduce a corresponding hardware accelerator to enhance its practical usability.

Table 2. Objective evaluation using feature similarity extended to color images (FSIMc) and tone-mapped image quality index (TMQI). The best results are highlighted in bold.

	Method \ Dataset	FRIDA2 [41]	D-HAZY [42]	O-HAZE [43]	I-HAZE [44]	Dense-Haze [45]	Overall
FSIMc	Cai et al. [6]	0.7963	**0.8874**	0.7865	0.8482	0.5573	0.7725
	Liu et al. [27]	0.8003	0.8747	0.8030	0.7416	0.5564	0.7552
	Li et al. [30]	0.7849	0.7383	0.6997	0.7564	0.5763	0.7111
	Base algorithm [36]	0.8016	0.8763	0.8112	0.8586	0.5728	0.7807
	Proposed algorithm	**0.8029**	0.8733	**0.8265**	**0.8677**	**0.5799**	**0.7846**
TMQI	Cai et al. [6]	**0.7366**	**0.7966**	0.8413	0.7598	0.5723	0.7312
	Liu et al. [27]	0.6970	0.7938	0.8267	0.6107	0.5196	0.6896
	Li et al. [30]	0.7176	0.6817	0.6566	0.6936	0.5107	0.6520
	Base algorithm [36]	0.7242	0.7841	**0.8951**	**0.8204**	0.5921	0.7354
	Proposed algorithm	0.7244	0.7790	0.8913	0.8101	**0.6040**	**0.7357**

4. MPSoC-Based Solution

4.1. Real-Time Hardware Implementation

Previous studies [32,36] have reported that software implementations of dehazing algorithms are unable to achieve a processing speed of at least 25 fps, failing to meet real-time processing requirements. This observation underscores the critical need for hardware implementation. In this study, we develop a hardware accelerator for the proposed algorithm using Verilog HDL [48] (IEEE Standard 1364-2005) and validate its performance on a Zynq UltraScale+ MPSoC ZCU106 Evaluation Kit [49].

Before implementing the hardware accelerator, let us revisit the block diagram in Figure 1. It is important to note that all operations in the base algorithm, including unsharp masking, image dehazing, and color gamut expansion, are pixel-wise. In contrast, our additions to the base algorithm, involving haziness degree estimation and self-calibrating factor calculation, are performed on a per-frame basis. This difference poses a challenging problem in synchronizing data flows within the proposed algorithm. Delaying unsharp masking, image dehazing, and color gamut expansion until the haziness degree estimate becomes available is impractical, as it leads to flickering issues.

To address this problem, we leveraged the high similarity between consecutive video frames, a common characteristic in various video types resulting from the natural continuity of motion and scenes in real-world scenarios. Numerous video processing and analysis techniques, such as motion estimation, video stabilization, object tracking, and video compression, have effectively exploited this characteristic.

Figure 3 shows a plot of structural similarity values [50] for the initial 300 frames of a video. The plot demonstrates that each frame exhibits a strong resemblance to its preceding and following frames, as indicated by the red-dotted oval, except during abrupt video changes highlighted by the blue-dotted and pink-dotted ovals. Given the infrequency of these scene changes, it is feasible to compute the haziness degree estimate for a specific frame and apply the computed value to the subsequent frame. This approach not only addresses the synchronization problem but also significantly reduces the required hardware resources for implementation.

After addressing the synchronization problem, the proposed algorithm can be readily implemented at the register-transfer level using standard design techniques. It is partitioned into blocks similar to the block diagram in Figure 1. By exploiting the pipeline parallelism, each block corresponds to a processing stage in the pipeline, allowing simultaneous processing of pixels from the previous stage, thus increasing the throughput. The resulting hardware accelerator is then encapsulated by an interface circuit to adhere to the AXI bus communication protocol [51]. Our interface circuit supports a double-buffering scheme, enabling the accelerator to seamlessly process the input video stream. Xilinx Vivado v2019.1 [52] was employed to develop a hardware intellectual property (IP) and program the Zynq UltraScale+ MPSoC ZCU106 Evaluation Kit.

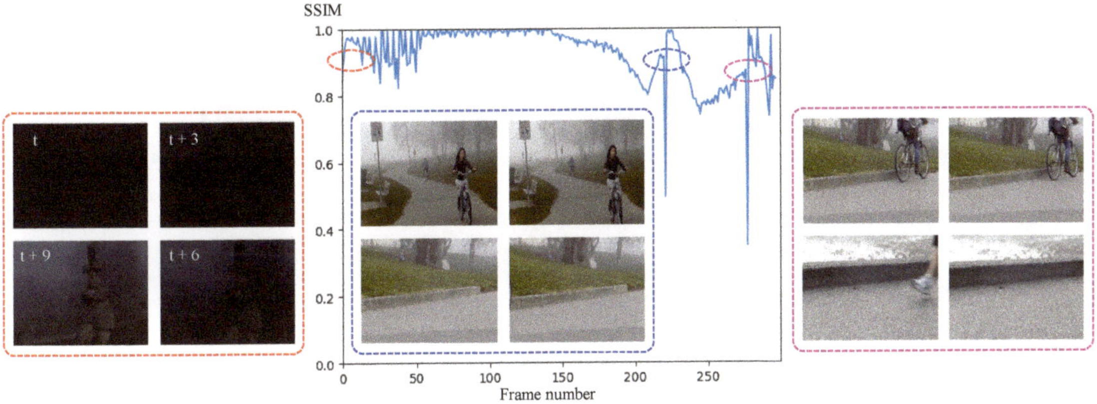

Figure 3. Plot of structural similarity (SSIM) values of the first 300 frames in a video. Red-dotted oval indicates frames of similar SSIM values, while blue-dotted and pink-dotted ovals indicate frames of abrupt changes in SSIM values.

Figure 4 provides an overview of our MPSoC-based solution. The input video stream is processed by a verification platform running on a host computer. This platform acts as an intermediary between our MPSoC-based solution and users. It receives, packages, and sends commands received from users, as well as video data, to our hardware IP within the evaluation kit. The kit features a Zynq UltraScale+ MPSoC device, comprising a quad-core ARM processor, a dual-core real-time processor, a graphics-processing unit, and a mid-size FPGA device (XCZU7EV-2FFVC1156) [49]. The ARM processor is referred to as the processing system (PS), and the FPGA device is referred to as the programmable logic (PL). We have developed an application called the hardware controller, which runs on the PS and is responsible for interfacing our hardware IP (located in the PL) with the outside world.

In this setup, the verification platform acquires the video stream from a camera and gathers user-inputted data through its graphical user interface. Following a handshaking process, the platform forwards the collected data to the hardware controller in the PS, which in turn relays the received data to the hardware IP in the PL. Subsequently, the hardware IP processes the data and generates an interrupt signal upon completion. The hardware controller acknowledges the signal and transmits the processed data back to the verification platform, where the input–output data are displayed side-by-side to users for ease of verification.

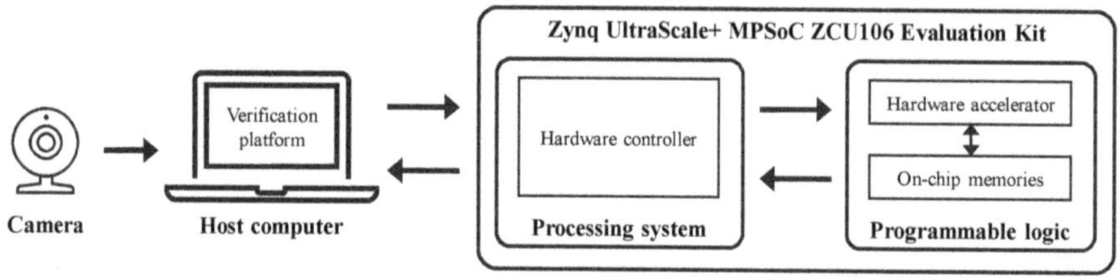

Figure 4. Overview of the proposed MPSoC-based solution.

4.2. Hardware Implementation Results

We utilized Xilinx Vivado v2019.1 [52] to synthesize the proposed hardware IP on the FPGA device. The implementation results, as summarized in Table 3, demonstrate that our hardware IP occupies only a modest portion of the available hardware resources. Specifically, it consumes 9.95% of slice registers, 19.86% of slice look-up tables (LUTs), and 17.47% of block RAMs (BRAMs). The FPGA device used in this study belongs to the Zynq UltraScale+ family, which features UltraRAMs and BRAMs. However, the proposed hardware accelerator does not contain any frame buffers, only line memories for filtering operations. Thus, BRAMs are adequate, leaving UltraRAMs available for other applications requiring frame buffers.

Table 3. Hardware implementation results for the proposed algorithm. LUT stands for look-up table, and the symbol # denotes quantities.

Xilinx Vivado v2019.1			
Device	**XCZU7EV-2FFVC1156**		
Slice Logic Utilization	**Available**	**Used**	**Utilization**
Slice registers (#)	460,800	45,832	9.95%
Slice LUTs (#)	230,400	45,761	19.86%
BRAMs	312	54.5	17.47%
Minimum period		2.81 ns	
Maximum frequency		356.51 MHz	

Furthermore, Table 3 shows that the proposed hardware accelerator can operate with a minimum clock period of 2.81 nanoseconds, allowing it to handle up to 356.51 megapixels per second. The maximum processing speed (S_{max}) in fps for a given frame's resolution of $H \times W$ can be calculated as follows:

$$S_{max} = \frac{f_{max}}{(H + VB)(W + HB)}, \quad (6)$$

where f_{max} represents the maximum frequency reported in Table 3, and VB and HB denote the vertical and horizontal blank periods, respectively. Table 4 presents the S_{max} values for various resolutions, ranging from Full HD (1920×1080) to DCI 4K (4096×2160), demonstrating that the proposed hardware IP exceeds the real-time processing requirement. For DCI 4K resolution, it achieves a maximum processing speed of 40.27 fps, making it highly suitable for real-world computer vision systems, irrespective of the color encoding scheme employed.

Moreover, we conducted a comparative assessment of the proposed accelerator with existing designs for single-image dehazing [53–55]. Park and Kim [53] and Zhang and Zhao [54] presented their own approaches to implementing the method of He et al. [4]. Specifically, they explored alternative methods to estimate the global atmospheric light more cost-effectively. For instance, Park and Kim [53] divided the image into 12 non-overlapping regions and searched for atmospheric light candidates in each region. Subsequently, they selected the brightest pixel among the candidates as the atmospheric light. Meanwhile, Zhang and Zhao [54] approximated the atmospheric light as the largest pixel in the locally filtered image (using a minimum filter).

Table 4. Maximum processing speeds in frames per second for various image resolutions. The symbol # denotes quantities.

Standard		Resolution	Required Clock Cycles (#)	Processing Speed (S_{max})
Full HD		1920 × 1080	2,076,601	171.68
Quad HD		2560 × 1440	3,690,401	96.60
	UW4K	3840 × 1600	6,149,441	57.97
4K	UHD TV	3840 × 2160	8,300,401	42.95
	DCI 4K	4096 × 2160	8,853,617	40.27

Table 5 illustrates that our hardware IP has the smallest footprint in terms of slice registers and LUTs while achieving the fastest processing speed. Notably, to the best of our knowledge, the proposed hardware IP, along with our previous design in [55], are the sole two hardware implementations equipped with the self-calibrating feature. Regarding digital signal processors (DSPs), they tend to be costly and are specifically designed for computationally intensive tasks, such as matrix multiplication in CNNs. Given that image dehazing frequently serves as a pre-processing step in high-level computer vision systems, it is preferable to reserve DSPs for more complex tasks like object recognition and localization. In this context, both of our previous and proposed designs excel by eschewing the use of DSPs. Through minimal resource utilization and objective evaluation, the proposed MPSoC-based solution achieves a balance between dehazing performance and computational complexity, hence termed "symmetric".

Nonetheless, it is essential to acknowledge that our design necessitates a considerable amount of memory, primarily utilized as line memories in filtering operations. Considering the significant impact of these operations on the base algorithm's performance, eliminating them is not a viable option. In future studies, we will explore solutions to reduce memory requirements without compromising performance.

Table 5. Comparison with contemporary hardware accelerators for single-image dehazing. NA stands for not available, and the symbol # denotes quantities.

Hardware Utilization	Park and Kim [53]	Zhang and Zhao [54]	Lee et al. [55]	Proposed Design
Registers (#)	53,400	NA	53,216	45,832
LUTs (#)	64,000	NA	49,799	45,761
DSPs (#)	42	NA	0	0
Memory (Mbits)	3.2	NA	1.4	2.0
Maximum frequency (MHz)	88.70	116.00	271.37	356.51
Maximum video resolution	SVGA	Quad HD	DCI 4K	DCI 4K
Self-calibrating feature	Unequipped	Unequipped	Equipped	Equipped

5. Conclusions

In this paper, we introduce a symmetric MPSoC-based solution to address the growing demand for real-time high-quality image dehazing. Our proposed method balances the trade-off between dehazing performance and computational complexity. It enhances the base algorithm by incorporating a self-calibrating feature, enabling efficient handling of various haze conditions. Furthermore, we have improved the piece-wise linear weighting scheme to enhance haze removal under dense-haze conditions. Subsequently, we have designed a corresponding hardware accelerator using Verilog HDL and verified its effectiveness against existing implementations.

However, we have identified three main limitations in our proposed solution. Firstly, it is inefficient in memory usage due to the extensive utilization of filtering operations. As these operations are crucial to the proposed algorithm's performance, further refinement of the design demands substantial effort. Secondly, the proposed algorithm relies on several parameters that necessitate careful fine-tuning for optimal performance, which is a laborious and time-consuming process. Finally, there is no encryption applied to the image data, posing a security risk. We defer the resolution of these three challenging problems to future research endeavors.

Author Contributions: Conceptualization, B.K.; methodology, B.K. and D.N.; software, D.N.; validation, D.N.; formal analysis, D.N.; investigation, D.N.; data curation, D.N.; writing—original draft preparation, D.N.; writing—review and editing, B.K. and D.N.; visualization, D.N.; supervision, B.K. All authors have read and agreed to the published version of the manuscript.

Funding: This work was supported by the National Research Foundation of Korea (NRF) grant funded by the Korea government (MSIT) (NRF-2023R1A2C1004592).

Data Availability Statement: Data are available in a publicly accessible repository. The data presented in this study are openly available in [41–45].

Conflicts of Interest: The authors declare no conflicts of interest.

References

1. Vincent, R. An ERTS Multispectral Scanner experiment for mapping iron compounds. In Proceedings of the Eight International Symposium on Remote Sensing of Environment, Ann Arbor, MI, USA, 2–6 October 1972; pp. 1239–1247.
2. Kim, T.K.; Paik, J.K.; Kang, B.S. Contrast enhancement system using spatially adaptive histogram equalization with temporal filtering. *IEEE Trans. Consum. Electron.* **1998**, *44*, 82–87. [CrossRef]
3. Oakley, J.P.; Satherley, B.L. Improving image quality in poor visibility conditions using a physical model for contrast degradation. *IEEE Trans. Image Process* **1998**, *7*, 167–179. [CrossRef] [PubMed]
4. He, K.; Sun, J.; Tang, X. Single Image Haze Removal Using Dark Channel Prior. *IEEE Trans. Pattern Anal. Mach. Intell.* **2011**, *33*, 2341–2353. [CrossRef] [PubMed]
5. Zhu, Q.; Mai, J.; Shao, L. A Fast Single Image Haze Removal Algorithm Using Color Attenuation Prior. *IEEE Trans. Image Process.* **2015**, *24*, 3522–3533. [CrossRef]
6. Cai, B.; Xu, X.; Jia, K.; Qing, C.; Tao, D. DehazeNet: An End-to-End System for Single Image Haze Removal. *IEEE Trans. Image Process.* **2016**, *25*, 5187–5198. [CrossRef]
7. Li, R.; Pan, J.; He, M.; Li, Z.; Tang, J. Task-Oriented Network for Image Dehazing. *IEEE Trans. Image Process.* **2020**, *29*, 6523–6534. [CrossRef]
8. Xu, J.; Hu, X.; Zhu, L.; Dou, Q.; Dai, J.; Qiao, Y.; Heng, P.A. Video Dehazing via a Multi-Range Temporal Alignment Network with Physical Prior. In Proceedings of the IEEE/CVF Conference on Computer Vision and Pattern Recognition (CVPR), Vancouver, BC, Canada, 18–22 June 2023; pp. 18053–18062. [CrossRef]
9. Wu, R.; Duan, Z.; Guo, C.; Chai, Z.; Li, C. RIDCP: Revitalizing Real Image Dehazing via High-Quality Codebook Priors. In Proceedings of the IEEE/CVF Conference on Computer Vision and Pattern Recognition (CVPR), Vancouver, BC, Canada, 18–22 June 2023; pp. 22282–22291. [CrossRef]
10. Adobe. Vignette, Grain, and Dehaze Effects in Camera Raw. Available online: https://helpx.adobe.com/camera-raw/using/vignette-grain-effects-camera-raw.html (accessed on 6 September 2023).
11. Bosch. Multi Purpose Camera: Combination of Classic Cutting Edge Computer Vision Algorithms and Artificial Intelligence Methods. Available online: https://www.bosch-mobility.com/en/solutions/camera/multi-purpose-camera/ (accessed on 12 June 2023).
12. Ancuti, C.O.; Ancuti, C. Single image dehazing by multi-scale fusion. *IEEE Trans. Image Process.* **2013**, *22*, 3271–3282. [CrossRef] [PubMed]
13. Galdran, A. Image dehazing by artificial multiple-exposure image fusion. *Signal Process.* **2018**, *149*, 135–147. [CrossRef]
14. Tang, K.; Yang, J.; Wang, J. Investigating Haze-Relevant Features in a Learning Framework for Image Dehazing. In Proceedings of the 2014 IEEE Conference on Computer Vision and Pattern Recognition, Columbus, OH, USA, 23–28 June 2014; pp. 2995–3002. [CrossRef]
15. Berman, D.; Treibitz, T.; Avidan, S. Single Image Dehazing Using Haze-Lines. *IEEE Trans. Pattern. Anal. Mach. Intell.* **2020**, *42*, 720–734. [CrossRef]
16. Hu, H.M.; Guo, Q.; Zheng, J.; Wang, H.; Li, B. Single Image Defogging Based on Illumination Decomposition for Visual Maritime Surveillance. *IEEE Trans. Image Process.* **2019**, *28*, 2882–2897. [CrossRef]
17. Afridi, I.U.; Bashir, T.; Khattak, H.A.; Khan, T.M.; Imran, M. Degraded image enhancement by image dehazing and Directional Filter Banks using Depth Image based Rendering for future free-view 3D-TV. *PLoS ONE* **2019**, *14*, e0217246. [CrossRef]
18. Berman, D.; Levy, D.; Avidan, S.; Treibitz, T. Underwater Single Image Color Restoration Using Haze-Lines and a New Quantitative Dataset. *IEEE Trans. Pattern Anal. Mach. Intell.* **2020**. [CrossRef] [PubMed]
19. Wang, A.; Wang, W.; Liu, J.; Gu, N. AIPNet: Image-to-Image Single Image Dehazing with Atmospheric Illumination Prior. *IEEE Trans. Image Process.* **2019**, *28*, 381–393. [CrossRef] [PubMed]

20. Dudhane, A.; Murala, S. RYF-Net: Deep Fusion Network for Single Image Haze Removal. *IEEE Trans. Image Process.* **2020**, *29*, 628–640. [CrossRef] [PubMed]
21. Sahu, G.; Seal, A.; Yazidi, A.; Krejcar, O. A Dual-Channel Dehaze-Net for Single Image Dehazing in Visual Internet of Things Using PYNQ-Z2 Board. *IEEE Trans. Autom. Sci. Eng.* **2024**, *21*, 305–319. [CrossRef]
22. Ren, W.; Pan, J.; Zhang, H.; Cao, X.; Yang, M.H. Single Image Dehazing via Multi-scale Convolutional Neural Networks with Holistic Edges. *Int. J. Comput. Vis.* **2020**, *128*, 240–259. [CrossRef]
23. Goodfellow, I.J.; Pouget-Abadie, J.; Mirza, M.; Xu, B.; Warde-Farley, D.; Ozair, S.; Courville, A.; Bengio, Y. Generative adversarial nets. In Proceedings of the 27th International Conference on Neural Information Processing Systems—Volume 2, Montreal, ON, Canada, 8–13 December 2014; pp. 2672–2680.
24. Kramer, M.A. Nonlinear principal component analysis using autoassociative neural networks. *AIChE J.* **1991**, *37*, 233–243. [CrossRef]
25. Pan, J.; Dong, J.; Liu, Y.; Zhang, J.; Ren, J.; Tang, J.; Tai, Y.W.; Yang, M.H. Physics-Based Generative Adversarial Models for Image Restoration and Beyond. *IEEE Trans. Pattern Anal. Mach. Intell.* **2020**. *43*, 2449–2462. [CrossRef]
26. Liu, X.; Shi, Z.; Wu, Z.; Chen, J.; Zhai, G. GridDehazeNet+: An Enhanced Multi-Scale Network With Intra-Task Knowledge Transfer for Single Image Dehazing. *IEEE Trans. Intell. Transp. Syst.* **2023**, *24*, 870–884. [CrossRef]
27. Liu, X.; Ma, Y.; Shi, Z.; Chen, J. GridDehazeNet: Attention-Based Multi-Scale Network for Image Dehazing. In Proceedings of the 2019 IEEE/CVF International Conference on Computer Vision (ICCV), Seoul, Republic of Korea, 27 October–2 November 2019; pp. 7313–7322. [CrossRef]
28. Zhu, J.; Park, T.; Isola, P.; Efros, A.A. Unpaired Image-to-Image Translation Using Cycle-Consistent Adversarial Networks. In Proceedings of the 2017 IEEE International Conference on Computer Vision (ICCV), Venice, Italy, 22–29 October 2017; pp. 2242–2251. [CrossRef]
29. Li, B.; Gou, Y.; Liu, J.Z.; Zhu, H.; Zhou, J.T.; Peng, X. Zero-Shot Image Dehazing. *IEEE Trans. Image Process.* **2020**, *29*, 8457–8466. [CrossRef]
30. Li, B.; Gou, Y.; Gu, S.; Liu, J.Z.; Zhou, J.T.; Peng, X. You Only Look Yourself: Unsupervised and Untrained Single Image Dehazing Neural Network. *Int. J. Comput. Vis.* **2021**, *129*, 1754–1767. [CrossRef]
31. Sahu, G.; Seal, A.; Jaworek-Korjakowska, J.; Krejcar, O. Single Image Dehazing via Fusion of Multilevel Attention Network for Vision-Based Measurement Applications. *IEEE Trans. Instrum. Meas.* **2023**, *72*, 4503415. [CrossRef]
32. Chen, Z.; He, Z.; Lu, Z.M. DEA-Net: Single image dehazing based on detail-enhanced convolution and content-guided attention. *arXiv* **2023**, arXiv:2301.04805. [CrossRef]
33. Rombach, R.; Blattmann, A.; Lorenz, D.; Esser, P.; Ommer, B. High-Resolution Image Synthesis with Latent Diffusion Models. *arXiv* **2022**, arXiv:2112.10752. [CrossRef]
34. Ramesh, A.; Dhariwal, P.; Nichol, A.; Chu, C.; Chen, M. Hierarchical Text-Conditional Image Generation with CLIP Latents. *arXiv* **2022**, arXiv:2204.06125. [CrossRef]
35. Shumailov, I.; Shumaylov, Z.; Zhao, Y.; Gal, Y.; Papernot, N.; Anderson, R. The Curse of Recursion: Training on Generated Data Makes Models Forget. *arXiv* **2023**, arXiv:2305.17493. [CrossRef]
36. Ngo, D.; Lee, G.D.; Kang, B. Singe Image Dehazing With Unsharp Masking and Color Gamut Expansion. *IEEE Access* **2022**, *10*, 102462–102474. [CrossRef]
37. Ngo, D.; Lee, G.D.; Kang, B. Haziness Degree Evaluator: A Knowledge-Driven Approach for Haze Density Estimation. *Sensors* **2021**, *21*, 3896. [CrossRef] [PubMed]
38. Ngo, D.; Lee, S.; Kang, U.J.; Ngo, T.M.; Lee, G.D.; Kang, B. Adapting a Dehazing System to Haze Conditions by Piece-Wisely Linearizing a Depth Estimator. *Sensors* **2022**, *22*, 1957. [CrossRef]
39. Ma, K.; Liu, W.; Wang, Z. Perceptual evaluation of single image dehazing algorithms. In Proceedings of the 2015 IEEE International Conference on Image Processing (ICIP), Quebec City, QC, Canada, 27–30 September 2015; pp. 3600–3604. [CrossRef]
40. Ngo, D.; Lee, S.; Lee, G.D.; Kang, B. Automating a Dehazing System by Self-Calibrating on Haze Conditions. *Sensors* **2021**, *21*, 6373. [CrossRef]
41. Tarel, J.; Hautiere, N.; Caraffa, L.; Cord, A.; Halmaoui, H.; Gruyer, D. Vision Enhancement in Homogeneous and Heterogeneous Fog. *IEEE Intell. Transp. Syst. Mag.* **2012**, *4*, 6–20. [CrossRef]
42. Ancuti, C.; Ancuti, C.; Vleeschouwer, C. D-HAZY: A dataset to evaluate quantitatively dehazing algorithms. In Proceedings of the 2016 IEEE International Conference on Image Processing (ICIP), Phoenix, AZ, USA, 25–28 September 2016; pp. 2226–2230. [CrossRef]
43. Ancuti, C.; Ancuti, C.; Timofte, R.; Vleeschouwer, C. O-HAZE: A Dehazing Benchmark with Real Hazy and Haze-Free Outdoor Images. In Proceedings of the 2018 IEEE/CVF Conference on Computer Vision and Pattern Recognition Workshops (CVPRW), Salt Lake City, UT, USA, 18–22 June 2018; pp. 867–8678. [CrossRef]
44. Ancuti, C.; Ancuti, C.; Timofte, R.; De Vleeschouwer, C. I-HAZE: A dehazing benchmark with real hazy and haze-free indoor images. *arXiv* **2018**, arXiv:1804.05091.
45. Ancuti, C.; Ancuti, C.; Sbert, M.; Timofte, R. Dense-Haze: A Benchmark for Image Dehazing with Dense-Haze and Haze-Free Images. In Proceedings of the 2019 IEEE International Conference on Image Processing (ICIP), Taipei, Taiwan, 22–25 September 2019; pp. 1014–1018. [CrossRef]

46. Zhang, L.; Zhang, L.; Mou, X.; Zhang, D. FSIM: A Feature Similarity Index for Image Quality Assessment. *IEEE Trans. Image Process.* **2011**, *20*, 2378–2386. [CrossRef]
47. Yeganeh, H.; Wang, Z. Objective Quality Assessment of Tone-Mapped Images. *IEEE Trans. Image Process.* **2013**, *22*, 657–667. [CrossRef] [PubMed]
48. *Std 1364-2005*; IEEE Standard for Verilog Hardware Description Language. Revision of IEEE Std 1374-2001; IEEE: New York, NY, USA, 2006; pp. 1–590. [CrossRef]
49. Xilinx. ZCU106 Evaluation Board: User Guide (UG1244). Available online: https://docs.xilinx.com/v/u/en-US/ug1244-zcu106-eval-bd (accessed on 25 July 2023).
50. Wang, Z.; Bovik, A.C.; Sheikh, H.R.; Simoncelli, E.P. Image quality assessment: From error visibility to structural similarity. *IEEE Trans. Image Process.* **2004**, *13*, 600–612. [CrossRef] [PubMed]
51. ARM. AMBA. Available online: https://developer.arm.com/Architectures/AMBA (accessed on 8 September 2023).
52. Xilinx. Vivado Design Suite User Guide: Release Notes, Installation, and Licensing (UG973). Available online: https://www.xilinx.com/support/documentation/sw_manuals/xilinx2019_1/ug973-vivado-release-notes-install-license.pdf (accessed on 31 December 2021).
53. Park, Y.; Kim, T.H. A video dehazing system based on fast airlight estimation. In Proceedings of the 2017 IEEE Global Conference on Signal and Information Processing (GlobalSIP), Montreal, ON, Canada, 14–16 November 2017; pp. 779–783. [CrossRef]
54. Zhang, B.; Zhao, J. Hardware Implementation for Real-Time Haze Removal. *IEEE Trans. Very Large Scale Integr. (VLSI) Syst.* **2017**, *25*, 1188–1192. [CrossRef]
55. Lee, S.; Ngo, D.; Kang, B. Design of an FPGA-Based High-Quality Real-Time Autonomous Dehazing System. *Remote Sens.* **2022**, *14*, 1852. [CrossRef]

symmetry

MDPI

Article

On Maximum Guaranteed Payoff in a Fuzzy Matrix Decision-Making Problem with a Fuzzy Set of States

Svajone Bekesiene [1,*] and Serhii Mashchenko [2]

1 Logistics and Defense Technology Management Science Group, General Jonas Zemaitis Military Academy of Lithuania, Silo 5a, LT-10322 Vilnius, Lithuania
2 Department of System Analysis and Decision-Making Theory, Faculty of Computer Science and Cybernetics, Taras Shevchenko National University of Kyiv, 64/13, Volodymyrska Street, 01601 Kyiv, Ukraine; mashchenko@knu.ua
* Correspondence: svajone.bekesiene@lka.lt

Abstract: The current study delves into a fuzzy matrix decision-making problem involving fuzzy sets of states. It establishes that a maximum guaranteed payoff constitutes a type-2 fuzzy set defined on the real line. Additionally, it provides the associated type-2 membership function. Moreover, the paper illustrates that the maximum guaranteed payoff type-2 fuzzy set of the decision-making problem can be broken down, based on the secondary membership grades, into a finite collection of fuzzy numbers. Each of these fuzzy numbers represents the maximum guaranteed payoff of the corresponding decision-making problem with a crisp set of states. This set corresponds to a specific cut of the original fuzzy set of states. Some properties of the maximum guaranteed payoff type-2 fuzzy set are investigated, and illustrative examples are provided. Since the problem formulation is symmetrical with respect to alternatives and states of nature, the results obtained can be used in the case of a fuzzy set of alternatives.

Keywords: decision-making problem; maximum guaranteed payoff; type-2 fuzzy set

1. Introduction

A decision problem modeling in the formal theory requires [1]:

- alternatives (choices of a DM);
- states (events);
- the payoff associated with each alternative and each state.

This is often presented as a payoff matrix (decision matrix). The rows of this matrix are associated with alternatives, and the columns are associated with states [1].

We note that, at its core, the matrix decision-making problem is symmetrical with respect to alternatives and states of nature. These elements of the problem differ only in that the alternatives characterize the actions of the DM, and the states of nature are characterized by some objective reality, which should not be taken literally. There may well be situations in which actions are dictated by nature (for example, circumstances related to weather conditions or natural forces). Therefore, the division into alternatives and states of nature is conditional and is used only as an element of system analysis that uses symmetry.

The principle of utility maximization was axiomatically substantiated in Von Neumann and Morgenstern [2] and Savage [3]. This principle consists of choosing an alternative that maximizes the so-called decision criterion (the utility function of alternatives). The type of a decision criterion depends on the availability of some additional information about:

- the type of uncertainty;
- the set of states;
- the risk features of a DM.

In conventional decision-making scenarios under uncertainty, it is typically assumed that there exists a probability distribution across the space of states, leading to what is known as decision-making under risk. In this context, DMs assess and choose among alternatives while considering the probabilities associated with various states of nature. To solve this problem, statistical criteria are used—for instance, Bayesian criteria, variance minimization, etc. In situations where information regarding the probability distribution is unavailable, this model gives rise to what is termed as a decision-making problem under ignorance. In this case, one uses various decision-making criteria like the maxmin (the Wald criterion), the maxmax (the optimistic criterion), the minimax regret (the Savage criterion), and the Hurwicz criterion. Unfortunately, the assumptions of the classical decision-making theory do not necessarily hold, for probabilities of real-world events are sometimes imprecise or non-measurable. In addition, a set of alternatives, a set of states, and payoffs may not be known precisely both in conditions of ignorance and in conditions of risk. The desire to take these factors into account led to the application of fuzzy set (FS) theory [4–12]. The corresponding works include approaches to solving decision problems with:

- a fuzzy set of alternatives [4,5];
- fuzzy states [4–6];
- a fuzzy set of states [1,7];
- fuzzy probabilities of states [8–12];
- fuzzy payoffs [1,8];
- fuzzy information [4–6].

The following contributions transform classical decision theory into fuzzy decision theory. Ignorance represents a specific instance of uncertainty within decision-making problems; thus, certain approaches rooted in fuzzy set (FS) theory designed for handling uncertainty can be utilized in cases of ignorance as well. In [6], Tanaka et al. explored a decision-making problem wherein the uncertainty surrounding the interpretation of events was captured using fuzzy sets (FSs), while the uncertainty regarding the likelihood of events occurring was quantified using probabilities. The authors introduced definitions related to worth, entropy, and quantity specifically tailored to fuzzy information within their paper. These concepts play crucial roles in analyzing decision-making processes under the combined influence of fuzzy logic and statistic uncertainty. Based on these definitions, an investment problem was analyzed. In [4], Tanaka et al. investigated properties of the fuzzy Bayes formula and the fuzzy observation system derived from FS theory. The analysis made it possible to consider the main elements of a fuzzy decision-making problem, which are states, alternatives, and other available information as fuzzy events. In [5], Tanaka et al. merged fuzzy set (FS) theory with statistical decision theory to address decision problems involving fuzzy events. They formulated fuzzy decision-making problems based on the concept of fuzzy events and introduced definitions related to entropy, the value of information, and the amount of information within this context. On the other hand, in [7], Mashchenko explored a method for resolving decision-making problems under uncertainty using a fuzzy set of states and crisp payoffs. By combining fuzzy set theory with crisp payoffs, Mashchenko proposed a method to handle decision-making scenarios where states are described imprecisely but payoffs are known crisply. In this method, a DM maximizes utilities simultaneously for all states. A type-2 fuzzy relation was constructed, which characterizes the utility of alternatives. The concept of a maximizing weak solution was introduced and its properties were explored in the referenced paper. Subsequently, this method was further developed in [13,14] for decision-making problems with objectives represented as fuzzy sets of preference relations. Additionally, in [1], Jain investigated a decision-making approach tailored for systems where either the state of the system or the utilities of alternatives, or both, were described using fuzzy sets (FSs). Through this research, Jain aimed to provide a methodology to address decision-making scenarios characterized by imprecise or uncertain information. The problem reduces to choosing, in a certain sense, the best FS from a collection of fuzzy estimates of alternatives. Each fuzzy estimate is an image of the FS of states under a mapping, which is specified by the payoff matrix. The method uses the Zadeh concept of a maximizing set to determine the FS of a solution to the problem. Next, an alternative is selected. This alternative is a compromise between the value of the utility and the degree of the membership to the solution FS. The idea of using a maximizing set to determine the solution FS does not correspond to any of the known optimality criteria of expected utility theory, which is a drawback of the method and limits its application. In [8], Whalen conducted a comparative analysis of different types of methodologies for choosing alternatives under uncertainty. These are:

- the classical statistical analysis;
- the maxmin approach;
- the analysis of fuzzy statistical solutions [9,10];
- the possibilistic decision-making algorithm [11] and its development;
- the *L*-fuzzy risk minimization algorithm [12], which uses Z-fuzzy sets [15].

These approaches vary based on their underlying assumptions regarding the quality and quantity of information available concerning the likelihood or probability of different states and the utility associated with the outcomes (alternative-state pairs). Each approach may make different assumptions about the precision of the information available, the form in which it is represented (e.g., probabilistic or fuzzy), and the degree of uncertainty accounted for in the decision-making process. These differences in assumptions can significantly influence the strategies and methodologies employed in addressing decision-making problems under uncertainty.

Advances in the development of the theory of fuzzy numbers (FNs) have made it possible to generalize the standard criteria of crisp decision-making to cases of payoffs in the form of FNs and use them directly. The following decision-making criteria under ignorance were generalized [16]:

- the maxmin (the Wald criterion);
- the maxmax (an optimistic criterion);
- the minimax regret (the Savage criterion);
- the Hurwicz criterion.

In [16], when studying a multicriteria problem with fuzzy parameters in the form of triangular FNs, Larbani examined a multi-objective two-person zero-sum game scenario, where the first player acted as the decision maker (DM), and the second player represented nature. In addressing this problem, Larbani employed the maxmin criterion, a decision-making approach under uncertainty. While our review does not encompass all the relevant literature, several conclusions can still be drawn from the existing research:

- Utilizing fuzzy sets (FSs) to represent states offers a more intrinsic and nuanced depiction of decision-making models under conditions of uncertainty compared to crisp sets.
- A FS of alternatives, a FS of states, and fuzzy payoffs describe different elements of a decision-making model under uncertainty and are of interest for research.
- Using FNs allows one to quite effectively solve decision-making problems under uncertainty by means of the fuzzy arithmetic.
- In the context of decision-making, there has been a lack of investigation into models utilizing payoffs represented as FNs alongside decision-making criteria under ignorance, specifically concerning fuzzy sets of states. This gap in research suggests an opportunity for further exploration and development in this area.

This article focuses on the exploration of decision-making processes under conditions of ignorance, specifically within the framework of fuzzy sets of states. The central place among criteria for decision-making under ignorance is occupied by the maxmin criterion (the Wald criterion). This stems from the fact that the maxmin criterion is widely used in practice in cases where it is necessary to completely eliminate a risk. In addition, the maxmin criterion is the mathematical basis of other criteria in conditions of ignorance. For instance, the minimax regret criterion is represented as the maxmin criterion for a negative relative loss function, the optimistic criterion is represented as the maxmin criterion for negative payoffs, and the Hurwicz criterion is represented as the linear convolution of the maxmin and optimistic criteria. In this article, we are going to investigate an application of the maxmin criterion for a decision-making model under ignorance with a FS of states. For the sake of simplicity, we investigate the maximum guaranteed payoff without focusing on an 'optimal' alternative. Furthermore, the significance of such a study can be elucidated by the understanding that decision-making problems under uncertainty hold interest beyond the pursuit of identifying an 'optimal' alternative. At times, the maximum guaranteed payoff holds independent interest, as decision-making theory's scope extends to encompass forecasting and analyzing uncertainties from the perspective of a decision-maker, as well as external agents. The aim of such an analysis is often directed towards informing decisions concerning alterations in the prerequisites, conditions, and outcomes of situations characterized by uncertainty. These decisions may involve adjustments in factors such as awareness levels, model formulations, and other relevant parameters. The formalization of a set of states through the utilization of a fuzzy set framework enables the incorporation of not only uncertainty stemming from the decision-maker's assessment of state admissibility but also the inherent fuzziness associated with delineating which states are feasible within the decision-making model. An example of such FSs of states could be 'possible states', 'probable states', 'expected states', etc.

The principal aims of this article are delineated as follows:

- To provide a rationale supporting the claim that a fuzzy set (FS) of states within a decision-making scenario under ignorance leads to a type-2 fuzzy set (T2FS) of maximum guaranteed payoff. This T2FS is characterized by a simplified and practical form tailored for real-world applications, in contrast to the more generalized form of T2FS.
- To thoroughly investigate the properties of this specific T2FS.
- To develop a decomposition method aimed at constructing a T2FS representing the maximum guaranteed payoff.
- To demonstrate, with the help of an example, that the approach that we develop here enables us to solve a fuzzy decision-making problem under ignorance in the situation where standard decision-making criteria fail.

The practical significance of our findings lies in their ability to effectively model the inherent vagueness in human judgment and the ambiguity surrounding the acceptability of states during the decision-making process under conditions of ignorance. By acknowledging and accounting for these factors, our research offers valuable insights and methodologies for addressing uncertainty and making informed decisions in real-world contexts.

This article is organized as follows: After this introduction, in Section 2, we recall some definitions and some basic results about MAX and MIN operations on FNs, a maximum guaranteed payoff in a fuzzy matrix decision-making problem, and T2FSs to be used later. In Section 3, we formulate the decision-making problem with a fuzzy set of states. Section 4 proposes an idea for solving this problem. At the end of Section 4, we conclude that the resulting maximum guaranteed payoff is a T2FS on the real line. Section 5.1 is devoted to the definition of a maximum guaranteed payoff T2FS and results that simplify its construction method. Section 5.2 is concerned with the calculation algorithm. Some useful properties of a maximum guaranteed payoff T2FS to a decision-making problem for a FS of states are studied in Section 5.3. In Section 5.4, we consider the example of constructing the resulting T2FS and give a simple interpretation of it. In addition, we study the ability of the developed approach to find a solution to a decision-making problem under ignorance in the case where the standard decision-making criteria fail. Section 6 is devoted to a discussion of the results. In the last section, some conclusions are pointed out.

2. Materials and Methods

2.1. MAX and MIN Operations on Fuzzy Numbers

In [17], Dubois and Prade introduced the concept of a fuzzy number, defining it as a normal and convex fuzzy set (FS) defined on the real line $\mathbb{R}$. In broader terms, a fuzzy number (FN) is conceptualized as a normal fuzzy set (FS) with bounded support, characterized by a membership function (MF) that is upper semicontinuous and quasi-concave, as described in reference [18]. This definition encapsulates fuzzy numbers as having continuous membership values across their domains, with a degree of concavity in their MF, contributing to their smooth and well-defined properties. One pivotal challenge in the theory of fuzzy numbers revolves around ordering them, a task facilitated by employing mathematical operations such as maximum (MAX) and minimum (MIN). This process is crucial for comparing and arranging fuzzy numbers, which is vital for various decision-making and analytical purposes within fuzzy systems and applications. The idea of using the MAX and MIN operations was first proposed by Ambrosio and Martini [19] for fuzzy symbols. A fuzzy symbol is an analog of a FS, according to Fung and Fu [20]. The MF of a fuzzy symbol is a mapping from one complete and linearly ordered space to another. This MF and the MF of a FN enjoy similar properties. In [21], Klir and Yuan defined the MAX and MIN operations for classical FNs and investigated some basic properties of these operations. They showed that the threesome (Φ, MIN, and MAX) is a distributive lattice, where Φ is the set of FNs on $\mathbb{R}$. In [22], Zhang and Hirota developed an algebraic theory of lattices for FNs. In [23], Tahayoria et al. extended the employment of the MAX and MIN operations to the case of convex FSs on $\mathbb{R}$ with MFs, which do not necessarily have to be continuous. In [24], Chiu and Wang suggested an approach towards simplifying the application of the MAX and MIN operations for two FNs with continuous MFs. In [25], Shirin and Saha worked out an algorithm for computing the MAX and MIN of any two 'triangular' FNs and visualizing the resulting MF. In [26], Mashchenko investigated the MIN operation in the case of a FS of operands.

According to [21], for FNs A and B with the MFs $\mu_A(r)$ and $\mu_B(r)$, $r \in \mathbb{R}$, respectively, the minimum $MIN = \min\{A, B\}$ is defined by the FN $MIN = \{(r, \mu_{MIN}(r)) : r \in \mathbb{R}\}$ with the MF

$$\mu_{MIN}(r) = \max\{\min\{\mu_A(r_A), \mu_B(r_B)\} : r = \min\{r_A, r_B\},\ r_A, r_B \in \mathbb{R}\},\ r \in \mathbb{R}. \tag{1}$$

To calculate $\mu_{MIN}(r)$, the idea of demonstrating a FN by its cuts is employed in [17]. To be more specific, one represents MFs of the FNs A, B, and MIN in the form

$$\mu_A(r) = \max_{u\in[0,1]} u1_{[A]_u}(r),\ \mu_B(r) = \max_{u\in[0,1]} u1_{[B]_u}(r),\ \mu_{MIN}(r) = \max_{u\in[0,1]} u1_{[MIN]_u}(r), \tag{2}$$

where the closed intervals $[A]_u = [(A)_u^L, (A)_u^H]$, $[B]_u = [(B)_u^L, (B)_u^H]$, and $[MIN]_u = [(MIN)_u^L, (MIN)_u^H]$ are u-cuts, $u \in [0,1]$ of the FNs A, B, and MIN, respectively. Here, we denote by $(\cdot)_u^L$ and $(\cdot)_u^H$ the lower and upper end points of the closed interval $[\cdot]_u = [(\cdot)_u^L, (\cdot)_u^H]$ of the u-cut, $u \in [0,1]$. These u-cuts are crisp sets with the MFs

$$1_{[A]_u}(r) = \begin{cases} 1, & r \in [A]_u; \\ 0, & r \notin [A]_u; \end{cases}\ 1_{[B]_u}(r) = \begin{cases} 1, & r \in [B]_u; \\ 0, & r \notin [B]_u; \end{cases}\ 1_{[MIN]_u}(r) = \begin{cases} 1, & r \in [MIN]_u; \\ 0, & r \notin [MIN]_u; \end{cases}$$

$r \in \mathbb{R}$, respectively. According to [17], Formula (1) implies that the u-cut $[MIN]_u$ of the FN $MIN = \min\{A, B\}$ is provided by

$$[MIN]_u = [(MIN)_u^L, (MIN)_u^H] = [\min\{(A)_u^L, (B)_u^L\}, \min\{(A)_u^H, (B)_u^H\}]. \tag{3}$$

Thus, Formula (2) entails the representations

$$\mu_{MIN}(r) = \max\left\{u \in [0,1] :\ (MIN)_u^L \le r \le (MIN)_u^H\right\},\ r \in \mathbb{R} \tag{4}$$

and

$$MIN = \{(r,u) : r \in [(MIN)_u^L, (MIN)_u^H],\ u \in [0,1]\} = \{([(MIN)_u^L, (MIN)_u^H], u) : u \in [0,1]\} \quad (5)$$

Similarly, we obtain formulae for calculating the maximum $MAX = \max\{A,B\}$ as the FN $MAX = \{(r, \mu_{MAX}(r)) : r \in \mathbb{R}\}$ with the MF

$$\mu_{MAX}(r) = \max\{\min\{\mu_A(r_A), \mu_B(r_B)\} : r = \max\{r_A, r_B\},\ r_A, r_B \in \mathbb{R}\},\ r \in \mathbb{R}. \quad (6)$$

The u-cut $[MAX]_u$ of the FN $MAX = \max\{A,B\}$ is provided by

$$[MAX]_u = [(MAX)_u^L, (MAX)_u^H] = [\max\{(A)_u^L, (B)_u^L\}, \max\{(A)_u^H, (B)_u^H\}]. \quad (7)$$

We represent the MF μ_{MAX} and the FN MAX as follows:

$$\mu_{MAX}(r) = \max\{u \in [0,1] :\ (MAX)_u^L \leq r \leq (MAX)_u^H\},\ r \in \mathbb{R} \quad (8)$$

and

$$MAX = \{(r,u) : r \in [(MAX)_u^L, (MAX)_u^H],\ u \in [0,1]\} = \{([(MAX)_u^L, (MAX)_u^H], u) : u \in [0,1]\}, \quad (9)$$

respectively.

The lattice (Φ, MIN, MAX) can also be expressed as the pair $(\Phi, \precsim)$, where $\precsim$ is a fuzzy partial order, which is defined by $A \precsim B \Leftrightarrow MIN\{A,B\} = A$ or otherwise $A \precsim B \Leftrightarrow MAX\{A,B\} = B$. This method of FNs ranking leads to the conclusion that, in some cases, the FNs A and B are incomparable. Therefore, the set Φ of FNs is not linearly ordered, unlike the set of real numbers. This property of fuzzy partial order limits its use for FNs ranking, since it does not guarantee the uniqueness of choice. To resolve this problem, a lot of special methods for FNs ranking have been developed, which ensure a unique choice. A review of ranking methods can be found in [27]. However, applying these FNs ranking methods for calculating the minimum (maximum) leads to a subset of the MIN (MAX). Thus, as opposed to crisp numbers, as far as FNs are concerned, it is important to understand the main problem that a DM faces. If it is more important to choose a unique minimum (maximum) FN, then it is necessary to use one of the methods for FNs ranking that is suitable under the given conditions and then take the minimum (maximum) that is equal to this FN. This FN is a subset of the MIN (MAX) only. If it is more important to obtain the correct value of the minimum (maximum), then Formula (1) (Formula (6)) should be used. In this case, the uniqueness of the choice is not guaranteed. Since, in this article, our concern is the correct values of the minimum and maximum, we shall use Formulae (1) and (6).

2.2. *Maximum Guaranteed Payoff in a Fuzzy Matrix Decision-Making Problem*

The problem of decision-making under ignorance is conveniently formalized using a matrix (we denote this by $\tilde{F} = (F_{ij})_{i \in M, j \in J}$) of the payoffs presented in Table 1. In the matrix $\tilde{F} = (F_{ij})_{i \in M, j \in J}$, to the rows $i \in M = \{1, \ldots, m\}$, $|M| = m$, we associate the alternatives feasible for the DM. The DM needs to choose one of these alternatives. To the columns $j \in J = \{1, \ldots, l\}$, $|J| = l$, we associate the states (events), one of which can occur.

Table 1. The matrix representing the payoffs.

Alternatives	States			
	1	2	...	l
1	F_{11}	F_{12}	...	F_{1l}
2	F_{21}	F_{22}	...	F_{2l}
⋮	⋮	⋮	⋱	⋮
m	F_{m1}	F_{m2}	...	F_{ml}

In the matrix $\tilde{F} = (F_{ij})_{i \in M, j \in J}$, to the rows $i \in M = \{1, \ldots, m\}$, $|M| = m$, we associate the alternatives feasible for the DM. The DM needs to choose one of these alternatives. To the columns $j \in J = \{1, \ldots, l\}$, $|J| = l$, we associate the states (events), one of which can occur. We denote by $|\cdot|$ the cardinality of a set. Each element F_{ij} of the matrix, $\tilde{F}$ represents a payoff (a utility, a win) in the form of the FN with the MF $\mu_{F_{ij}}(r)$, $r \in \mathbb{R}$, that the DM obtains if the alternative $i \in M$ has been chosen and the state $j \in J$ has occurred. For the DM, the objective is to select an alternative with a maximum payoff when the state is unknown. We represent this problem in the form $D(J) = \langle M, J, \tilde{F} \rangle$. Assume that information about the probabilities of states is not available or that a decision is made so seldom that we cannot use this information. According to the maxmin criterion (the Wald criterion), a maximum guaranteed payoff is calculated by the formula

$$G(J) = \max_{i \in M} \min_{j \in J} F_{ij}. \tag{10}$$

For the convenience of subsequent presentation, the set J of states is indicated hereinafter as the parameter in the maximum guaranteed payoff $G(J)$. According to Section 2.1, the maximum guaranteed payoff is the FN $G(J) = \left\{(r, \mu_{G(J)}(r)) : r \in \mathbb{R}\right\}$ on $\mathbb{R}$. Formulae (1) and (6) imply that the MF of the FN $G(J) = \max_{i \in M} \min_{j \in J} F_{ij}$ is given by

$$\mu_{G(J)}(r) = \max\left\{ \min_{j \in J} \mu_{F_{ij}}(r_{ij}) : \ r = \max_{i \in M} \min_{j \in J} r_{ij}, \ r_{ij} \in \mathbb{R}, \ i \in M, \ j \in J \right\}. \tag{11}$$

To calculate the MF $\mu_{G(J)}(r)$, we represent the FN $G(J)$ by its cuts. To this end, we write the MFs of the FNs F_{ij}, $i \in M, j \in J$, and $G(J)$ as follows:

$$\mu_{F_{ij}}(r) = \max_{u \in [0,1]} u 1_{[F_{ij}]_u}(r), \ i \in M, \ j \in J \text{ and } \mu_{G(J)}(r) = \max_{u \in [0,1]} u 1_{[G(J)]_u}(r), \tag{12}$$

where the closed intervals $[F_{ij}]_u = [(F_{ij})^L_u, (F_{ij})^H_u]$ and $[G(J)]_u = [(G(J))^L_u, (G(J))^H_u]$ are u-cuts, $u \in [0,1]$, of the FNs F_{ij}, $i \in M, j \in J$, and $G(J)$, respectively. These u-cuts are crisp sets with the MFs

$$1_{[F_{ij}]_u}(r) = \begin{cases} 1, & r \in [F_{ij}]_u; \\ 0, & r \notin [F_{ij}]_u; \end{cases} \quad 1_{[G(J)]_u}(r) = \begin{cases} 1, & r \in [G(J)]_u; \\ 0, & r \notin [G(J)]_u; \end{cases}$$

$r \in \mathbb{R}$, respectively. Formulae (3) and (7) imply that the u-cut $[G(J)]_u$ of the FN $G(J) = \max_{i \in M} \min_{j \in J} F_{ij}$ is given by

$$[G(J)]_u = [G(J)^L_u, G(J)^H_u] = [\max_{i \in M} \min_{j \in J} (F_{ij})^L_u, \max_{i \in M} \min_{j \in J} (F_{ij})^H_u]. \tag{13}$$

By (12), this entails the following representations of the MF $\mu_{G(J)}$ and the FN $G(J)$

$$\mu_{G(J)}(r) = \max\{u \in [0,1] : \ (G(J))^L_u \le r \le (G(J))^H_u\}, \ r \in \mathbb{R} \tag{14}$$

and

$$G(J) = \{(r,u) : r \in [(G(J))^L_u, (G(J))^H_u],\ u \in [0,1]\} = \{([(G(J))^L_u, (G(J))^H_u], u) : u \in [0,1]\}, \quad (15)$$

respectively.

2.3. Type-2 Fuzzy Sets

The concept of type-2 fuzzy sets (T2FSs) was introduced by Zadeh in reference [28] as a broader framework encompassing type-1 fuzzy sets (T1FSs). As outlined by Mizumoto and Tanaka in reference [29], a T2FS, symbolized as $\tilde{C}$, defined on a crisp set X is distinguished by its fuzzy MF $M_{\tilde{C}} : X \to [0,1]^{[0,1]}$. For fixed $x' \in X$, the value of $M_{\tilde{C}}(x')$ is the T1FS $M_{\tilde{C}}(x') = \{(u, \mu_{\tilde{M}_{\tilde{C}}(x')}(u)) : u \in U_{x'}\}$ on the set $U_{x'} \subseteq [0,1]$ of the primary membership degrees u of x' to the T2FS $\tilde{C}$ with the corresponding MF $\mu_{\tilde{M}_{\tilde{C}}(x')}(u)$, $u \in U_{x'}$, where the value $\mu_{\tilde{M}_{\tilde{C}}(x')}(u)$ is the secondary grade of the pair (x,u). The following depiction of the T2FS

$$\tilde{C} = \{(x, \tilde{M}_{\tilde{C}}(x')) : x \in X\} = \{(x, \{(u, \mu_{\tilde{M}_{\tilde{C}}(x)}(u)) : u \in U_x\}) : x \in X\}$$

is referred to as the vertical slice approach.

Building upon the concepts introduced by Karnik and Mendel [30], Mendel and John proposed an alternative definition in their work [31]. Additionally, Harding et al. [32] made several amendments to these definitions: the T2FS $\tilde{C}$ on X is given by $\tilde{C} = \{((x,u), \eta_{\tilde{C}}(x,u)) : x \in X,\ u \in [0,1]\}$, where

$$\eta_{\tilde{C}}(x,u) = \begin{cases} \mu_{M_{\tilde{C}}(x)}(u), & u \in U_x; \\ 0, & \text{otherwise} \end{cases}$$

is the type-2 membership function (T2MF).

Remark 1. *The primary degree u is related to the degree of presence of some property (defining a given fuzzy set) for $x \in X$. By secondary degree, we mean, by [33], the degree of truth of the corresponding primary u degree of this property for x.*

According to [31], we use notions of the embedded T2FSs and T1FSs for a T2FS $\tilde{C} = \{((x,u), \eta_{\tilde{C}}(x,u)) : x \in X,\ u \in [0,1]\}$. Letting $u_x = \mu_{C^{e1}}(x) \in [0,1]$ is a unique primary degree of membership for each $x \in X$, where $\mu_{C^{e1}}(x)$, $x \in X$ is the MF of the T1FS $C^{e1} = \{(x, \mu_{C^{e1}}(x)) : x \in X\}$. The T1FS C^{e1} and the T2FS $\tilde{C}^{e2} = \{((x,u_x), \eta_{\tilde{C}^{e2}}(x,u_x)) : x \in X\}$ with $\eta_{\tilde{C}^{e2}}(x,u_x)) = \eta_{\tilde{C}}(x, \mu_{C^{e1}}(x)))$, $x \in X$ are called embedded in the T2FS $\tilde{C}$.

Remark 2. *According to [31], the collection $\tilde{C} = \{((x,u), \eta_{\tilde{C}}(x,u)) : x \in X,\ u \in [0,1]\}$ is the classical union of its elements in the sense of T1FSs. In addition, each T2FS can be represented as a collection of all possible embedded T2FSs.*

We use two special cases of T2FSs in view of [13,26]. Letting $\Omega = \{\eta_{\tilde{C}}(x,u) : \eta_{\tilde{C}}(x,u) > 0, x \in X, u \in [0,1]\}$ is the finite set of all possible positive values of secondary grades for the T2FS $\tilde{C} = \{((x,u), \eta_{\tilde{C}}(x,u)) : x \in X,\ u \in [0,1]\}$.

Definition 1 [13]. *We say that an embedded T2FS $\tilde{C}^{e2}_\alpha = \{((x,u_x), \eta_{\tilde{C}^{e2}_\alpha}(x,u_x)) : x \in X\}$ in the T2FS $\tilde{C}$ has a constant secondary grade $\alpha \in \Omega$ if, for each $x \in X$, the unique primary degree $u_x = \mu_{C^{e1}_\alpha}(x) \in [0,1]$ exists for which $\eta_{\tilde{C}^{e2}_\alpha}(x, \mu_{C^{e1}(\alpha)}(x)) \equiv \alpha$.*

In this definition, $\mu_{C^{e1}_\alpha}(x)$, $x \in X$ is the MF of the embedded T1FS $C^{e1}_\alpha = \{(x, \mu_{C^{e1}_\alpha}(x)) : x \in X\}$ in the T2FS $\tilde{C}$.

Remark 3 [26]. *For the T2FS $\tilde{C}$ and each $\alpha \in \Omega$, there is the unique embedded T1FS $C^{e1}_\alpha = \{(x, \mu_{C^{e1}_\alpha}(x)) : x \in X\}$ that corresponds to the embedded T2FS $\tilde{C}^{e2}_\alpha$ with a con-*

stant secondary grade α. *Hence,* $\tilde{C}^{e2}_{\alpha} = \{(C^{e1}_{\alpha}, \alpha)\} = \{(\{(x, \mu_{C^{e1}_{\alpha}}(x)) : x \in X\}, \alpha)\} = \{((x, \mu_{C^{e1}_{\alpha}}(x)), \alpha) : x \in X\}$.

Moreover, we examine an additional specific instance of a T2FS.

Definition 2 [26]. *We say that the T2FS* $\tilde{C}$ *is decomposable by secondary grades into a collection of embedded T2FSs with constant secondary grades if there are the T2FSs* $\tilde{C}^{e2}_{\alpha} = \{((x, \mu_{C^{e1}_{\alpha}}(x)), \alpha) : x \in X\} = \{(C^{e1}_{\alpha}, \alpha)\}$ *with constant secondary grades* $\alpha \in \Omega$, *respectively, which are embedded in the T2FS* $\tilde{C}$, *satisfying* $\tilde{C} = \{\tilde{C}^{e2}_{\alpha} : \alpha \in \Omega\}$.

Remark 4. *If the T2FS* $\tilde{C}$ *is decomposable by secondary grades* $\alpha \in \Omega$ *into the collection* $\tilde{C} = \{\tilde{C}^{e2}_{\alpha} : \alpha \in \Omega\}$ *of embedded T2FSs with constant secondary grades, then the T2FS* $\tilde{C}$ *is represented in the form of a collection* $\tilde{C} = \{(C^{e1}_{\alpha}, \alpha) : \alpha \in \Omega\}$ *of embedded T1FSs* C^{e1}_{α}, $\alpha \in \Omega$, *each of which is assigned the constant secondary grade* $\alpha \in \Omega$, *respectively.*

3. Formulation of the Problem

Consider a fuzzy decision-making problem $D(N) = \langle M, N, \tilde{F} \rangle$ with a matrix of fuzzy payoffs F_{ij}, $i \in M$, $j \in N$ specified in the form of FNs with the corresponding membership functions $\mu_{F_{ij}}(r)$, $r \in \mathbb{R}$. Here, $M = \{1, 2, \ldots, m\}$ is the set of alternatives, $|M| = m$; $N = \{1, 2, \ldots, n\}$ is the set of states, $|N| = n$. According to (10) and (11), with $J = N$, the maximum guaranteed payoff is given by

$$G(N) = \max_{i \in M} \min_{j \in N} F_{ij} \tag{16}$$

with the MF

$$\mu_{G(N)}(r) = \max\{\min_{j \in N} \mu_{F_{ij}}(r_{ij}) : r = \max_{i \in M} \min_{j \in N} r_{ij},\ r_{ij} \in \mathbb{R},\ i \in M,\ j \in N\}. \tag{17}$$

Let $\tilde{N} = \{(j, \mu_{\tilde{N}}(j)) : j \in N\}$ be some FS with the MF $\mu_{\tilde{N}}(j)$, $j \in N$ on the set N of states. We shall call $\tilde{N}$ the FS of states. The following question arises: 'What is the maximum guaranteed payoff to a fuzzy decision-making problem in the case when the set of states is fuzzy?'. The corresponding value will be denoted by $\max_{i \in M} \min_{(j, \mu_{\tilde{N}}(j)) \in \tilde{N}} F_{ij}$. In addition, we represent a fuzzy decision-making problem for the FS $\tilde{N}$ of states in the form $D(\tilde{N}) = \langle M, \tilde{N}, \tilde{F} \rangle$. Another natural question is 'When is there a need for such problem formulation?' To answer this question, we consider the following examples.

Assume we know expert estimates of the state probabilities but we may make a decision only once. In this case, it is not reasonable to use statistical decision-making criteria, for example, the expectation value criterion. Completely ignoring information about probabilities is also not rational. Why do not we interpret expert estimates of probabilities as degrees of membership of a FS of states? In this example, the maximum guaranteed payoff is the result of calculating the value $\max_{i \in M} \min_{(j, \mu_{\tilde{N}}(j)) \in \tilde{N}} F_{ij}$. The idea of interpreting the probabilities of states as degrees of membership in some FS of states is only given as a hypothetical example. We shall not consider the validity of such an interpretation in this article. Also, this should not be considered as the only case in which the problem formulation under consideration may occur.

4. Main Idea

For each fixed $r \in \mathbb{R}$, we consider the mapping $G^r : 2^N \to [0, 1]$ given by

$$G^r(J) = \max\{\min_{j \in N} \mu_{F_{ij}}(r_{ij}) : r = \max_{i \in M} \min_{j \in J} r_{ij},\ r_{ij} \in \mathbb{R},\ i \in M,\ j \in J\}, J \subseteq N. \tag{18}$$

In accordance with (11), the mapping G^r links each subset $J \subseteq N$ of states with the value of the MF $\mu_{G(J)}(r)$ of the FN

$$G(J) = \{(r, \mu_{G(J)}(r)) : r \in \mathbb{R}\} \tag{19}$$

of the maximum guaranteed payoff $G(J) = \max_{i \in M} \min_{j \in J} F_{ij}$ to the decision-making problem $D(J) = \langle M, J, \tilde{F} \rangle$, which is

$$G^r(J) = \mu_{G(J)}(r),\ r \in \mathbb{R}. \tag{20}$$

With Zadeh's extension principle [34] at hand, we extend the domain 2^N of the mapping G^r to the collection of FSs $\tilde{N}$ that are defined on the set N of states and generalize Formulae (18) and (19) to this case. We denote by $\tilde{G} = \max_{i \in M} \min_{(j, \mu_{\tilde{N}}(j)) \in \tilde{N}} F_{ij}$ the maximum guaranteed payoff to the decision-making problem $D(\tilde{N}) = \langle M, \tilde{N}, \tilde{F} \rangle$ for the FS $\tilde{N}$ of states, and we denote by $M_{\tilde{G}}(r)$ the relevant MF. In this case, for each fixed $r = r^*$, the value of the MF $M_{\tilde{G}}(r)$ coincides with the image $G^{r^*}(\tilde{N})$ of the FS $\tilde{N}$ of states under the mapping G^{r^*}, which is

$$M_{\tilde{G}}(r^*) = G^{r^*}(\tilde{N}). \tag{21}$$

Following Zadeh's extension principle [34], it can be shown that the image of the FS $\tilde{N}$ of states under the mapping G^{r^*} is the FS:

$$G^{r^*}(\tilde{N}) = \{(u, \mu_{G^{r^*}(\tilde{N})}(u)) : u \in [0,1]\} \tag{22}$$

with the MF

$$\mu_{G^{r^*}(\tilde{N})}(u) = \max\{\alpha :\ \alpha \in [0,1],\ u = G^{r^*}(N_\alpha)\}, \tag{23}$$

$u \in \operatorname{supp}(G^{r^*}(\tilde{N}))$, where the set

$$\operatorname{supp}(G^{r^*}(\tilde{N})) = \{u \in [0,1] :\ u = G^{r^*}(N_\alpha);\ \alpha \in [0,1]\} \tag{24}$$

is the support of the FS $G^{r^*}(\tilde{N})$;

$N_\alpha = \{j \in N : \mu_{\tilde{N}}(j) \geq \alpha\}$ is the α-cut, $\alpha \in [0,1]$ of the FS $\tilde{N} = \{(j, \mu_{\tilde{N}}(j)) : j \in N\}$ of states; $G^{r^*}(N_\alpha)$ is the image of the α-cut N_α, $\alpha \in [0,1]$ of the FS $\tilde{N}$ of states under the mapping G^{r^*} (see (18)); the equality

$$G^{r^*}(N_\alpha) = \mu_{G(N_\alpha)}(r^*) \tag{25}$$

holds, where $\mu_{G(N_\alpha)}(r^*)$ is the MF value of the FN $G(N_\alpha)$ by (20) with $J = N_\alpha$.

Remark 5. *Let $\Omega = \{\mu_{\tilde{N}}(j) : j \in N\}$ be the set of membership degrees values $\mu_{\tilde{N}}(j)$, $j \in N$ of the FS $\tilde{N} = \{(j, \mu_{\tilde{N}}(j)) : j \in N\}$ of states. Note that the cardinality of the set Ω is $|\Omega| < n$. It is clear that, when obtaining the α-cut $N_\alpha = \{j \in N : \mu_{\tilde{N}}(j) \geq \alpha\} \neq \varnothing$ of the FS $\tilde{N}$, we can assume that $\alpha \in \Omega$ rather than $\alpha \in (0,1]$.*

Proposition 1 highlights a valuable characteristic of the FS $\tilde{G}$.

Proposition 1. *For each fixed $r = r^* \in \mathbb{R}$, the values of the MF $M_{\tilde{G}}(r^*)$ form the FS $M_{\tilde{G}}(r^*) = \{(u, \mu_{M_{\tilde{G}}(r^*)}(u)) : u \in [0,1]\}$ on $[0,1]$ with the MF*

$$\mu_{M_{\tilde{G}}(r^*)}(u) = \max\{\alpha :\ \alpha \in \Omega,\ u = \mu_{G(N_\alpha)}(r^*)\} \tag{26}$$

for $u \in \operatorname{supp}(M_{\tilde{G}}(r^*))$, where the support of the FS $M_{\tilde{G}}(r^*)$ is given by

$$\operatorname{supp}(M_{\tilde{G}}(r^*)) = \{u \in [0,1] :\ u = \mu_{G(N_\alpha)}(r^*),\ \alpha \in \Omega\}. \tag{27}$$

Proof of Proposition 1. According to (21) and (25), Formula (23) implies that $\mu_{M_{\tilde{G}}(r^*)}(u) = \max\{\alpha : \alpha \in [0,1], u = \mu_{G(N_\alpha)}(r^*)\}$ for $u \in \text{supp}(M_{\tilde{G}}(r^*))$. Then, Remark 5 entails (26). Next, we prove (27). Assume that

$$u^* \in \text{supp}(M_{\tilde{G}}(r^*)). \tag{28}$$

We aim to verify that

$$u^* \in \{u \in [0,1] : u = \mu_{G(N_\alpha)}(r^*), \alpha \in \Omega\}. \tag{29}$$

According to Remark 5, it suffices to show that there exists $\alpha^* \in (0,1]$, such that $u^* = \mu_{G(N_{\alpha^*})}(r^*)$. Assume, on the contrary, that the inequality $u^* \neq \mu_{G(N_\alpha)}(r^*)$ holds for any $\alpha \in (0,1]$, whence $u^* \neq G^{r^*}(N_\alpha)$ by (25). Therefore, $u^* \notin \text{supp}(G^{r^*}(\tilde{N}))$ by (24). An appeal to (21) yields $u \notin \text{supp}(M_{\tilde{G}}(r^*))$, a contradiction to (28). Therefore, (29) holds true.

On the other hand, let us assume that the inclusion of (29) is valid. Then, there exists $\alpha^* \in \Omega$, for which

$$u^* = \mu_{G(N_{\alpha^*})}(r^*). \tag{30}$$

We intend to prove Formula (28). Assume, on the contrary, that the inequality $u^* \notin \text{supp}(M_{\tilde{G}}(r^*))$ holds. Then, Formula (21) implies that $u^* \notin \text{supp}(G^{r^*}(\tilde{N}))$. Therefore, $u^* \neq G^{r^*}(N_\alpha)$ for all $\alpha \in (0,1]$ by (24). Hence, we infer $u^* \neq \mu_{G(N_\alpha)}(r^*)$ by (25), a contradiction to (30). Therefore, (27) holds true. □

Based on Proposition 1, we state that $\tilde{G}$ is a FS on $\mathbb{R}$ with the MF which values form a FS on [0, 1]. Thus, $\tilde{G}$ is the T2FS on $\mathbb{R}$ by [28]. In the manner of vertical slices (see Section 2.3), the T2FS $\tilde{G}$ is given by $\tilde{G} = \{(r, M_{\tilde{G}}(r)) : r \in \mathbb{R}\} = \{(r, \{(u, \mu_{M_{\tilde{G}}(r)}(u)) : u \in U_r\}) : r \in \mathbb{R}\}$, where $\mu_{M_{\tilde{G}}(r)}(u), u \in [0,1]$ is the MF of the FS $M_{\tilde{G}}(r) = \{\{(u, \mu_{M_{\tilde{G}}(r)}(u)) : u \in [0,1]\}$ of values of fuzzy degree of membership of the number $r \in \mathbb{R}$ to the T2FS $\tilde{G}$, and $U_r = \text{supp}(M_{\tilde{G}}(r))$ is the set of primary membership degrees. We can also characterize the T2FS $\tilde{G}$ by the T2MF:

$$\eta_{\tilde{G}}(r,u) = \begin{cases} \mu_{M_{\tilde{G}}(r)}(u), & u \in U_r; \\ 0, & \text{otherwise} \end{cases}$$

(see Section 2.3). Then, the T2FS $\tilde{G}$ of the maximum guaranteed payoff is $\tilde{G} = \{((r,u), \eta_{\tilde{G}}(r,u)) : u \in [0,1], r \in \mathbb{R}\}$.

5. Maximum Guaranteed Payoff for a FS of States

5.1. Maximum Guaranteed Payoff T2FS

The conclusion drawn in Section 4 leads us to introduce the following concept.

Definition 3. *By the maximum guaranteed payoff to the decision-making problem $D(\tilde{N}) = \langle M, \tilde{N}, \tilde{F}\rangle$ for the FS $\tilde{N} = \{(j, \mu_{\tilde{N}}(j)) : j \in N\}$ of states is meant the T2FS.*

$$\tilde{G} = \{((r,u), \eta_{\tilde{G}}(r,u)) : u \in [0,1], r \in \mathbb{R}\} \tag{31}$$

with the T2MF

$$\eta_{\tilde{G}}(r,u) = \begin{cases} \max\{\alpha \in \Omega : u = \mu_{G(N_\alpha)}(r)\}, & u \in U_r; \\ 0, & u \notin U_r; \end{cases} \tag{32}$$

$r \in \mathbb{R}, u \in [0,1]$.

Here,

$$U_r = \{u \in [0,1] : u = \mu_{G(N_\alpha)}(r), \alpha \in \Omega\} \tag{33}$$

is the set of primary membership degrees that coincides with the support $\text{supp}(M_{\tilde{G}}(r))$ (refer to Equality (27)) of the FS $M_{\tilde{G}}(r)$ of fuzzy membership degrees of the number $r \in \mathbb{R}$;

$$\mu_{G(N_\alpha)}(r) = \max\{\min_{j \in N_\alpha} \mu_{F_{ij}}(r_{ij}) : \ r = \max_{i \in M} \min_{j \in N_\alpha} r_{ij}, \ r_{ij} \in \mathbb{R}, \ i \in M, \ j \in N_\alpha\} \tag{34}$$

is the MF of the FN

$$G(N_\alpha) = \{(r, \mu_{G(N_\alpha)}(r)) : r \in \mathbb{R}\} \tag{35}$$

which is the maximum guaranteed payoff $G(N_\alpha) = \max_{i \in M} \min_{j \in N_\alpha} F_{ij}$ to the decision-making problem $D(N_\alpha) = \langle M, N_\alpha, \tilde{F} \rangle$ for the set N_α of states (see (10) and (11) with $J = N_\alpha$);

$$N_\alpha = \{j \in N : \mu_{\tilde{N}}(j) \geq \alpha\} \tag{36}$$

is the α-cut of the FS $\tilde{N} = \{(j, \mu_{\tilde{N}}(j)) : j \in N\}$ of states, $\alpha \in \Omega$;

$$\Omega = \{\mu_{\tilde{N}}(j) : j \in N\} \tag{37}$$

is the set of the positive membership degree values of the FS $\tilde{N} = \{(j, \mu_{\tilde{N}}(j)) : j \in N\}$ of states (see Remark 5).

Remark 6. *In the case of a decision-making problem with a crisp payoff matrix and a fuzzy set of states, the maximum guaranteed payoff is* $\tilde{G} = \{((r, u), \eta_{\tilde{G}}(r, u)) : u \in \{0, 1\}, r \in \mathbb{R}\}$, *which is a special case of a T2FS. Since the primary membership degrees* $u \in \{0, 1\}$ *of the T2FS* $\tilde{G}$ *take only two values, 0 or 1, this yields an interesting interpretation of the T2FS* $\tilde{G}$ *by Remark 1. Similar to a crisp set, there are only two options for each number* $r \in \mathbb{R}$: *either r completely belongs to the T2FS* $\tilde{G}$ *(the primary membership degree is* $u = 1$*) or it completely does not belong (*$u = 0$*). Unlike a crisp set, the degrees* $\eta_{\tilde{G}}(r, 0)$ *and* $\eta_{\tilde{G}}(r, 1)$ *of truth of the identification of these two facts can differ from 1 and take values in the closed interval* [0, 1].

We note that this type of a T2FS is already known (see, for instance, [35]).

Remark 7. *In the case of a decision-making problem with payoffs in the form of crisp numbers, we also use MFs to represent these numbers. For example, we represent a crisp number* $a \in \mathbb{R}$ *by* $\{(a, \mu_a(r)) : r \in \mathbb{R}\} = \{(a, 1)\} \cup \{(r, 0) : r \neq a, r \in \mathbb{R}\}$, *where*

$$\mu_a(r) = \begin{cases} 1, & r = a; \\ 0, & \textit{otherwise} \end{cases}$$

is the MF (the characteristic function) of the crisp number a.

Proposition 2 validates the decomposability, as defined in Definition 2, of a maximum guaranteed payoff T2FS for a decision-making problem involving a fuzzy set of states. This decomposition involves breaking down the T2FS into a collection of embedded T2FSs characterized by constant secondary grades.

Proposition 2. *The maximum guaranteed payoff T2FS* $\tilde{G}$ *to the decision-making problem* $D(\tilde{N}) = \langle M, \tilde{N}, \tilde{F} \rangle$ *for the FS* $\tilde{N} = \{(j, \mu_{\tilde{N}}(j)) : j \in N\}$ *of states is decomposable by secondary grades* $\alpha \in \Omega$ *into the collection*

$$\tilde{G} = \{\tilde{G}_\alpha^{e2} : \ \alpha \in \Omega\} \tag{38}$$

of the embedded T2FSs

$$\tilde{G}_\alpha^{e2} = \{(G(N_\alpha), \alpha)\} \tag{39}$$

and given by

$$\tilde{G} = \{(G(N_\alpha), \alpha) : \ \alpha \in \Omega\} \tag{40}$$

where $G(N_\alpha) = \{(r, \mu_{G(N_\alpha)}(r)) : r \in \mathbb{R}\}$ *is the embedded T1FS* $G_\alpha^{e1} = G(N_\alpha)$ *with the MF* $\mu_{G_\alpha^{e1}}(r) = \mu_{G(N_\alpha)}(r)$ *in Form (34). It is the FN that is the maximum guaranteed payoff* $G(N_\alpha) = \max_{i\in M}\min_{j\in N_\alpha} F_{ij}$ *to the decision-making problem* $D(N_\alpha) = \langle M, N_\alpha, \tilde{F}\rangle$ *for the crisp set* N_α, $\alpha \in \Omega$ *of states.*

Proof of Proposition 2. In accordance with (31), the maximum guaranteed payoff T2FS is $\tilde{G} = \{((r,u), \eta_{\tilde{G}}(r,u)) : u \in [0,1],\ r \in \mathbb{R}\}$. Then, invoking (32) yields

$$\tilde{G} = \{\{((r,u), \max\{\alpha : \alpha \in \Omega, u = \mu_{G(N_\alpha)}(r)\}) : u \in U_r\} \cup \{((r,u),0) : r \notin U_r\} : r \in \mathbb{R}\}.$$

Remark 2 allows us to ignore pairs (*r*,*u*) that have secondary grades that are equal to 0; therefore, $\tilde{G} = \{\{((r,u), \max\{\alpha : \alpha \in \Omega,\ u = \mu_{G(N_\alpha)}(r)\}) : u \in U_r, r \in \mathbb{R}\}$. Then, invoking (33) yields $\tilde{G} = \{(r, \{(\mu_{G(N_\alpha)}(r), \alpha) : \alpha \in \Omega\}),\ r \in \mathbb{R}\}$. Further, regrouping the elements, we obtain

$$\tilde{G} = \{(r, (\mu_{G(N_\alpha)}(r), \alpha)) : \alpha \in \Omega,\ r \in \mathbb{R}\} = \{\{((r, \mu_{G(N_\alpha)}(r)), \alpha) : r \in \mathbb{R}\} : \alpha \in \Omega\}$$

Then, (35) entails (40) and, thereupon, (38) by (39). □

Proposition 2 allows us to represent the T2FS $\tilde{G}$ in a form that is more suitable for calculations and interpretation. Following Remark 1, the T2FS $\tilde{G}$ can be interpreted as the collection of maximum guaranteed payoffs $G(N_\alpha)$ to the decision-making problem $D(N_\alpha)$ for the crisp set N_α of states with the degree of truth of the FN $G(N_\alpha)$ being equal to $\alpha \in \Omega$.

5.2. *Calculation Algorithm of the Maximum Guaranteed Payoff T2FS*

In this section, we consider an algorithm for calculating the maximum guaranteed payoff T2FS.

Step 0. We construct the finite set $\Omega = \{\mu_{\tilde{N}}(j) : j \in N\}$ of membership degrees values of the FS $\tilde{N} = \{(j, \mu_{\tilde{N}}(j)) : j \in N\}$ of states and represent Ω in the form $\Omega = \{\alpha_1, \ldots, \alpha_{|\Omega|}\}$.

Step $k \in \{1, \ldots, |\Omega|\}$. For $\alpha = \alpha_k$, following (36), we construct the α-cut $N_\alpha = \{j \in N : \mu_{\tilde{N}}(j) \geq \alpha\}$ of the FS $\tilde{N}$. We calculate a solution $G(N_\alpha) = \max_{i\in M}\min_{j\in N_\alpha} F_{ij}$ to the problem $D(N_\alpha) = \langle M, N_\alpha, \tilde{F}\rangle$ for the set N_α of states. This is the maximum guaranteed payoff FN $G(N_\alpha) = \{(r, \mu_{G(N_\alpha)}(r)) : r \in \mathbb{R}\}$ (see (35)), which is the embedded T1FS—that is, $G_\alpha^{e1} = G(N_\alpha)$ by Proposition 2. To calculate the FN $G(N_\alpha)$, we use the representation of this FN by its cuts. According to (15) with $J = N_\alpha$, we use the formula

$$G(N_\alpha) = \{([(G(N_\alpha))_u^L, (G(N_\alpha))_u^H], u) : u \in [0,1]\}. \tag{41}$$

The MF of the FN $G(N_\alpha)$ is given by

$$\mu_{G(N_\alpha)}(r) = \max\{u \in [0,1] : (G(N_\alpha))_u^L \leq r \leq (G(N_\alpha))_u^H\},\ r \in \mathbb{R} \tag{42}$$

as a consequence of (14) with $J = N_\alpha$. For each $u \in [0,1]$, we calculate the boundaries

$$(G(N_\alpha))_u^L = \max_{i\in M}\min_{j\in N_\alpha} (F_{ij})_u^L \tag{43}$$

and

$$(G(N_\alpha))_u^H = \max_{i\in M}\min_{j\in N_\alpha} (F_{ij})_u^H \tag{44}$$

of the closed interval

$$[G(N_\alpha)]_u = [(G(N_\alpha))_u^L, (G(N_\alpha))_u^H] \tag{45}$$

according to (13) with $J = N_\alpha$. In these formulae, $(F_{ij})_u^L$ and $(F_{ij})_u^H$ are the lower and the upper bounds, respectively, of the closed interval $[F_{ij}]_u = [(F_{ij})_u^L, (F_{ij})_u^H]$. This interval is the u-cut of the payoff FN F_{ij} of the alternative $i \in M$ for the state $j \in N_\alpha$. For approximate calculations, we choose the values $u = u_s = s/S$, $s = 0, \ldots, S$, where $(S + 1)$ is the number of cut levels.

The final step. Once all FNs $G(N_\alpha)$, $\alpha \in \Omega$ have been obtained, the resulting T2FS $\tilde{G}$ is given by $\tilde{G} = \{(G(N_\alpha), \alpha) : \alpha \in \Omega\}$ according to (40). The T2MF $\eta_{\tilde{G}}(r, u)$ can be calculated with the help of Formulae (32) and (33). According to Remark 1, the T2FS $\tilde{G}$ can be interpreted as follows. The maximum guaranteed payoff T2FS $\tilde{G}$ is equal to the FN $G(N_{\alpha_1})$ with the degree of truth being equal to α_1; the FN $G(N_{\alpha_2})$ with the degree of truth being equal to α_2;...; and the FN $G(N_{\alpha_{|\Omega|}})$ with the degree of truth being equal to $\alpha_{|\Omega|}$.

5.3. Properties of the Maximum Guaranteed Payoff T2FS

Proposition 3 highlights several valuable properties of a maximum guaranteed payoff T2FS to a decision-making problem for a FS of states.

Proposition 3. *Let $\mu_{G(N_{\alpha^*})}(r)$ be the membership degree of a number $r \in \mathbb{R}$ to the FN $G(N_{\alpha^*})$, which is the maximum guaranteed payoff to the decision-making problem $D(N_{\alpha^*}) = \langle M, N_{\alpha^*}, \tilde{F} \rangle$ for α^*-cut, $\alpha^* \in \Omega$ N_{α^*} of the FS $\tilde{N}$ of states. Then $u = \mu_{G(N_{\alpha^*})}(r)$ is the primary membership degree of the number r to the maximum guaranteed payoff T2FS $\tilde{G}$ with the secondary grade not smaller than α^*—that is, $\eta_{\tilde{G}}(r, \mu_{G(N_{\alpha^*})}(r)) \geq \alpha^*$.*

Proof of Proposition 3. Assume that $\alpha^* \in \Omega$ and $u = \mu_{G(N_{\alpha^*})}(r)$. Then, $u \in U_r$ according to (33). Therefore, $\eta_{\tilde{G}}(r, u) = \max\{\alpha : \alpha \in \Omega, \mu_{G(N_{\alpha^*})}(r) = u = \mu_{G(N_\alpha)}(r)\} \geq \alpha^*$ by (32). □

According to Proposition 3, the maximum guaranteed degree of truth of the primary degree of membership of some number $r \in \mathbb{R}$ to the T2FS $\tilde{G}$ is determined by the smallest degree of membership to the FS $\tilde{N}$ of those states for which this number r is the maximum guaranteed payoff.

In Proposition 4, we employ the fuzzy number ordering proposed by Ramik and Rimanek [36].

Definition 4. *Let $\tilde{a}$ and $\tilde{b}$ be two fuzzy numbers and $[\tilde{a}]_u = [(\tilde{a})_u^L, (\tilde{a})_u^H]_u$, $[\tilde{b}]_u = [(\tilde{b})_u^L, (\tilde{b})_u^H]_u$ be their u-cuts, $u \in [0, 1]$. By the fuzzy partial order is meant the relation $\tilde{a} \succsim \tilde{b} \Leftrightarrow (\tilde{a})_u^L \geq (\tilde{b})_u^L$, $(\tilde{a})_u^H \geq (\tilde{b})_u^H$ for all $u \in [0, 1]$. Here $(\tilde{a})_u^L$ and $(\tilde{a})_u^H$ are the lower and upper bounds of $[\tilde{a}]_u$.*

Proposition 4. *Suppose that the maximum guaranteed payoff T2FS $\tilde{G}$ to the decision-making problem for the FS $\tilde{N}$ of states is represented as in (40). Then, for any α', $\alpha'' \in \Omega$ with $\alpha' \geq \alpha''$, the relations $N_{\alpha'} \subseteq N_{\alpha''}$ and $G(N_{\alpha''}) \succsim G(N_{\alpha'})$ hold true, where '$\succsim$' is the fuzzy partial order.*

Proof of Proposition 4. Formula (36) implies that

$$N_{\alpha'} \subseteq N_{\alpha''}. \tag{46}$$

According to Definition 4, to prove the relation $G(N_{\alpha''}) \succsim G(N_{\alpha'})$, it suffices to show that the inequalities $G(N_{\alpha''})_u^L \geq G(N_{\alpha'})_u^L$ and $G(N_{\alpha''})_u^H \geq G(N_{\alpha'})_u^H$ hold for each $u \in [0, 1]$. Assume, on the contrary, that there exists $u^* \in [0, 1]$, such that the inequalities

$$G(N_{\alpha'})_{u^*}^L < G(N_{\alpha''})_{u^*}^L \tag{47}$$

or (and)

$$G(N_{\alpha'})_{u^*}^H < G(N_{\alpha''})_{u^*}^H \tag{48}$$

hold. In the former case, we obtain

$$(G(N_{\alpha'}))^L_{u^*} = \max_{i\in M}\min_{j\in N_{\alpha'}}(F_{ij})^L_{u^*} < \max_{i\in M}\min_{j\in N_{\alpha''}}(F_{ij})^L_{u^*} = (G(N_{\alpha''}))^L_{u^*}$$

This entails $\min_{j\in N_{\alpha'}}(F_{ij})^L_{u^*} < \min_{j\in N_{\alpha''}}(F_{i^*j})^L_{u^*}$ for all $i \in M$ and particularly for $i^* = \text{argmax}_{i\in M}\min_{j\in N_{\alpha''}}(F_{ij})^L_{u^*}$. With this at hand, we conclude that $\min_{j\in N_{\alpha'}}(F_{i^*j})^L_{u^*} < \min_{j\in N_{\alpha''}}(F_{i^*j})^L_{u^*}$ and thereupon $N_{\alpha'} \supset N_{\alpha''}$, a contradiction to (46). We also obtain a similar contradiction in the case where Inequality (48) holds. □

According to Proposition 4, FNs with more favorable maximum guaranteed payoffs, corresponding to smaller cut levels of the FS of states, exhibit larger secondary membership degrees (degrees of truth) to the maximum guaranteed payoff T2FS $\tilde{G}$. This is quite natural, for large degrees of truth correspond to large degrees of membership in a fuzzy set of states.

5.4. Numerical Examples

In this section, we examine examples that demonstrate the construction of a maximum guaranteed payoff T2FS for a fuzzy set of states. Example 1 serves to illustrate the algorithm for calculating a maximum guaranteed payoff T2FS. Example 2 demonstrates the ability of the developed approach to find a solution to a decision-making problem under ignorance in the case where the standard decision-making criteria fail.

Example 1. *We consider the problem of decision-making with the matrix of fuzzy payoffs given in Table 2 in the form of the 'triangular' FNs F_{ij}, $i \in M, j \in N$ with the MFs $\mu_{F_{ij}}(r)$, $r \in \mathbb{R}$, $i \in M$, $j \in N$, respectively, where M = {1, 2, 3} is the set of alternatives and N = {1, 2, 3, 4} is the set of states. The input data are given in the form of 'triangular' FNs only for the purpose of simplification and clarity of the description. Recall that the MF for the 'triangular' FN B = (a, b, c) is given by*

$$\mu_B(x) = \begin{cases} 1-(b-x)/(b-a), & a \le x \le b; \\ 1-(x-b)/(c-b), & b \le x \le c; \\ 0, & \text{otherwise}. \end{cases} \tag{49}$$

The cuts $[B]_u = [(B)^L_u, (B)^H_u]$, $u \in [0,1]$ of the 'triangular' FN B with the MF in Form (49) are calculated using the formula $[B]_u = [a+(b-a)u, c-(c-b)u]$. In this example, we use approximate calculations with the number of u-cuts, $u = u_s = s/10$, $s = 0,\ldots,10$ being equal to 11. The graphs of the MFs $\mu_{F_{ij}}(r)$, $r \in \mathbb{R}$, $j \in \{1, 2, 3, 4\}$ are represented in Figure 1a for the alternative $i = 1$, in Figure 1b for $i = 2$, and Figure 1c for $i = 3$. In Figure 1a–c, for each alternative $i \in \{1, 2, 3\}$, the MFs $\mu_{F_{ij}}(r)$, $r \in \mathbb{R}$ are drawn blue for the state j = 1, yellow for the state j = 2, green for state j = 3, and red for the state j = 4.

Assume that a DM perceives the set N = {1, 2, 3, 4} of states in the form of the FS $\tilde{N} = \{(1,0.7),(2,0.9),(3,1),(4,1)\}$ with the MF values $\mu_{\tilde{N}}(1) = 0.7$, $\mu_{\tilde{N}}(2) = 0.9$ u $\mu_{\tilde{N}}(3) = \mu_{\tilde{N}}(4) = 1$. The DM intends to predict a maximum guaranteed payoff using the algorithm from Section 5.2.

Step 0. According to (37), the set of membership degrees of the FS $\tilde{N}$ is $\Omega = \{0.7, 0.9, 1\}$.

Step k = 1. For $\alpha = 0.7$, according to (36), we construct the 0.7-cut $N_{0.7}$ = {1, 2, 3, 4} of the FS $\tilde{N}$. We intend to find a solution $G(N_{0.7}) = \max_{i\in M}\min_{j\in N_{0.7}} F_{ij}$ to the problem $D(N_{0.7}) = \langle M, N_{0.7}, \tilde{F}\rangle$ for the set $N_{0.7}$ of states. To calculate the FN $G(N_{0.7})$ in Form (41), we represent this FN by its cuts $[G(N_{0.7})]_u = [(G(N_{0.7}))^L_u, (G(N_{0.7}))^H_u]$, $u = u_s = s/10$, $s = 0,\ldots,10$ with the help of Formulae (43) and (44). In these formulae, we use u-cuts $[F_{ij}]_u = [(F_{ij})^L_u, (F_{ij})^H_u]$ of the payoffs F_{ij} of the alternatives $i \in M$ for the states $j \in N_{0.7}$. The MF $\mu_{G(N_{0.7})}$ of the FN $G(N_{0.7})$ is drawn red in Figure 1d. We call the FN $G(N_{0.7})$ 'approximately 350' and denote it by $\widetilde{350}$.

Step k = 2. For $\alpha = 0.9$, according to (36), we construct the 0.9-cut $N_{0.9} = \{2,3,4\}$ of the FS $\tilde{N}$. We intend to find a solution $G(N_{0.9}) = \max_{i\in M}\min_{j\in N_{0.9}} F_{ij}$ to the problem $D(N_{0.9}) = \langle M, N_{0.9}, \tilde{F}\rangle$ for *the set $N_{0.9}$ of states. To calculate the FN $G(N_{0.9})$ in Form (41), we represent this FN by its cuts $[G(N_{0.9})]_u = [(G(N_{0.9}))^L_u, (G(N_{0.9}))^H_u]$, $u = u_s = s/10$, $s = 0, \ldots, 10$ with the help of Formulae (43) and (44). The MF $\mu_{G(N_{0.9})}$ of the FN $G(N_{0.9})$ is drawn green in Figure 1d. We call the FN $G(N_{0.9})$ 'approximately 400' and denote it by $\widetilde{400}$.*

Step $k = 3$. For $\alpha = 1$, according to (36), we construct the 1-cut $N_1 = \{3,4\}$ of the FS $\tilde{N}$. We intend to find a solution $G(N_1) = \max_{i \in M} \min_{j \in N_1} F_{ij}$ to the problem $D(N_1) = \langle M, N_1, \tilde{F} \rangle$ for the set N_1 of states. To calculate the FN $G(N_1)$ in Form (41), we represent this FN by its cuts $[G(N_1)]_u = [(G(N_1))^L_u, (G(N_1))^H_u]$, $u = u_s = s/10$, $s = 0, \ldots, 10$ using Formulae (43) and (44). The MF $\mu_{G(N_1)}$ of the FN $G(N_1)$ is drawn blue in Figure 1d. We call the FN $G(N_1)$ 'approximately 470' and denote it by $\widetilde{470}$.

The final step. Once all FNs $G(N_{0.7}) = \widetilde{350}$, $G(N_{0.9}) = \widetilde{400}$, and $G(N_1) = \widetilde{470}$ have been obtained, the resulting T2FS $\tilde{G} = \{(G(N_{0.7}), 0.7), (G(N_{0.9}), 0.9), (G(N_1), 1)\}$ is given by $\tilde{G} = \{(\widetilde{350}, 0.7), (\widetilde{400}, 0.9), (\widetilde{470}, 1)\}$. The T2MF $\eta_{\tilde{G}}(r,u)$ can be calculated with the help of Formulae (32) and (33). The levels $\eta_{\tilde{G}}(r,u) \in \{0.7, 0.9, 1\}$ are given by blue (for $\alpha = 1$), green (for $\alpha = 0.9$), and red (for $\alpha = 0.7$) lines in Figure 1d. The obtained T2FS $\tilde{G} = \{(\widetilde{350}, 0.7), (\widetilde{400}, 0.9), (\widetilde{470}, 1)\}$ can be interpreted as follows. The maximum guaranteed payoff is equal to the FN $\widetilde{350}$ with the degree of truth being equal to 1, the FN $\widetilde{400}$ with the degree of truth being equal to 0.9, and the FN $\widetilde{470}$ with the degree of truth being equal to 1.

Table 2. Payoffs of Example 1.

Alternatives	States			
	1	**2**	**3**	**4**
1	(300, 400, 500)	(310, 350, 380)	(520, 550, 600)	(500, 600, 650)
2	(270, 300, 450)	(250, 350, 600)	(600, 700, 800)	(620, 650, 700)
3	(400, 600, 800)	(150, 250, 350)	(180, 200, 220)	(450, 500, 550)

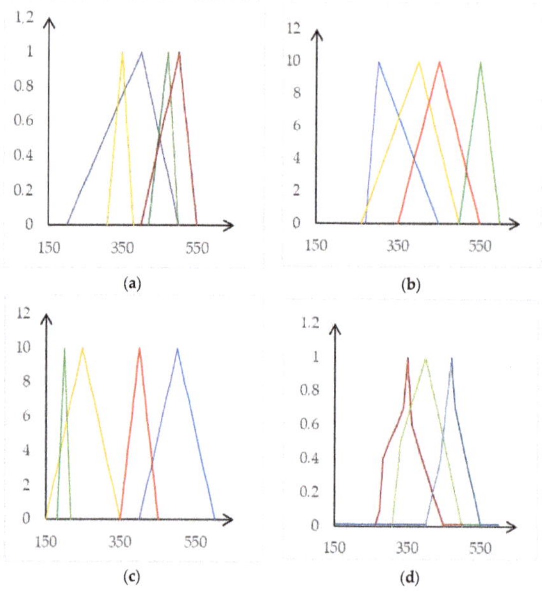

Figure 1. The graphs of the MFs $\mu_{F_{ij}}$ of the payoffs F_{ij}, $j \in \{1, 2, 3, 4\}$: (**a**) for the alternative $i = 1$; (**b**) $i = 2$; (**c**) $i = 3$; (**d**) the levels lines of the T2MF $\eta_{\tilde{G}}$. *For each alternative $i \in \{1, 2, 3\}$, the MFs $\mu_{F_{ij}}(r)$, $r \in R$ are drawn blue for the state $j = 1$, yellow for the state $j = 2$, green for state $j = 3$, and red for the state $j = 4$.*

Example 2. *In this example, we take crisp payoffs to transparently compare the results of solving a decision-making problem using different methods and under different assumptions about a set of states. The payoff matrix F_{ij}, $i \in M = \{1,2,3,4\}$, $j \in N = \{1,2,3,4,5\}$ is given in Table 3.*

We consider the following cases.

In the first case, assume that we make a decision when the probabilities $p_1 = 0.2$, $p_2 = 0.3$, $p_3 = 0.2$, $p_4 = 0.15$, and $p_5 = 0.15$ are available for the states $j \in \{1,2,3,4,5\}$, respectively, and a decision is made sufficiently often so that we can hope for a proper application of statistical criteria. If we use the Bayesian decision criterion, we obtain equal expected utilities $G_i^B = \sum_{j \in N} F_{ij} p_j = 1$ for all alternatives $i \in N$. Therefore, a unique decision is not possible.

In the second case, assume that we make a decision under complete ignorance, when state probabilities are not available and/or a decision is made only once. We consider the following situations:

1. *Suppose that the set $\tilde{N}$ of states is crisp—that is $\mu_{\tilde{N}}(1) = \mu_{\tilde{N}}(2) = \mu_{\tilde{N}}(3) = \mu_{\tilde{N}}(4) = 1$. Then, in the case of using:*
   a. *the maxmin criterion (the Wald criterion), we obtain equal maximum guaranteed payoffs $G_i^W = \min_{j \in N} F_{ij} = 0$ for all alternativesi $\in N$;*
   b. *the optimistic criterion, we obtain equal optimistic payoffs $G_i^O = \max_{j \in N} F_{ij} = 2$ for all alternatives $i \in N$;*
   c. *the compromise criterion (the Hurwicz criterion), we obtain equal compromise payoffs $G_i^H = \lambda \max_{j \in N} F_{ij} + (1-\lambda) \min_{j \in N} F_{ij} = 2$ for all alternatives $i \in N$ for any value of the parameter $\lambda \in [0,1]$ characterizing the DM's propensity to take risks;*
   d. *the minmax regret criterion (the Savage criterion), we obtain equal relative utility losses $G_i^S = \max_{j \in N} (\max_{k \in M} F_{kj} - F_{ij}) = 2$ for all alternatives $i \in N$.*

   Thus, in all these cases, applying basic standard decision criteria does not help us to make a unique decision.
2. *Assume that the set $\tilde{N}$ of states is fuzzy. It is quite possible that we can consider the FS $\tilde{N}$ as 'probable states' and choose degrees of membership to this FS being equal to the corresponding probabilities—that is, $\mu_{\tilde{N}}(1) = p_1 = 0.2$, $\mu_{\tilde{N}}(2) = p_2 = 0.3$, $\mu_{\tilde{N}}(3) = p_3 = 0.2$, $\mu_{\tilde{N}}(4) = p_4 = 0.15$, and $\mu_{\tilde{N}}(5) = p_5 = 0.15$. Using the algorithm from Section 5.2, we infer:*
   $\Omega = \{0.15, 0.2, 0.3\}$ is the set of degrees of membership to the FS $\tilde{N}$;
   $N_{0.3} = \{2\}$, $N_{0.2} = \{1,2,3\}$, $N_{0.15} = \{1,\ldots,5\}$ are the α-cuts, $\alpha \in \Omega$ of the FS $\tilde{N}$ of states;
   $G(N_{0.3}) = \{(2,1)\} \cup \{(r,0) : r \neq 2\}$ (denote it by '2');
   $G(N_{0.2}) = \{(1,1)\} \cup \{(r,0) : r \neq 1\}$ (denote it by '1');
   $G(N_{0.15}) = G(N_{0.1}) = \{(0,1)\} \cup \{(r,0) : r \neq 1\}$ (denote it by '0')

Are the maximum guaranteed payoffs for the α-cuts, $\alpha \in \Omega$ of the FS $\tilde{N}$ of states, respectively; hereinafter, we use Remark 7 to represent crisp numbers using MFs, for example, a crisp number $G(N_{0.3})$ is given by

$$G(N_{0.3}) = \text{'2'} = \left\{(2, \mu_{G(N_{0.3})}(r)) : r \in \mathbb{R}\right\} = \{(2,1)\} \cup \{(r,0) : r \neq 2\}$$

with the MF

$$\mu_{G(N_{0.3})}(r) = \begin{cases} 1, & r = 2; \\ 0, & \text{otherwise.} \end{cases}$$

Once all maximum guaranteed payoffs $G(N_{0.3})$ = '2', $G(N_{0.2})$ = '1', and $G(N_{0.15})$ = '0' have been obtained, the resulting T2FS $\tilde{G} = \{(G(N_{0.3}), 0.3), (G(N_2), 0.2), (G(N_{0.15}), 0.15)\}$ is given by $\tilde{G}$ = {('2',0.3),('1',0.2),('0',0.15)} . The obtained T2FS $\tilde{G}$ can be interpreted as follows. The maximum guaranteed payoff is equal to '2' with the degree of truth being equal to 0.3, '1' with the degree of truth being equal to 0.2, and '0' with the degree of truth being equal to 0.15.

Table 3. Payoffs of Example 2.

Alternatives	States				
	1	**2**	**3**	**4**	**5**
1	0	1	1.25	2	1
2	1.5	1	2	0	0
3	1	2	0	0	4/3
4	2	0	1	2/3	2

6. Discussion and Results

Since the purpose of this article was to demonstrate that, in a fuzzy decision-making problem under ignorance, a FS of states generates a T2FS of the maximum guaranteed payoffs, we directed our attention towards outcomes that facilitated this objective. In Section 4, we provided the rationale supporting the assertion that the maximum guaranteed payoffs for a fuzzy set of states form a T2FS. This enabled us to outline the corresponding definition in Section 5.1. Using a decomposition approach, we represented a maximum guaranteed payoffs T2FS for a FS of states by a collection of embedded T2FSs with constant secondary grades. In Section 5.2, we worked out the algorithm for constructing a maximum guaranteed payoffs T2FS. This study clarified that, while a type-2 fuzzy set (T2FS) is typically a complex mathematical construct, T2FSs with constant secondary grades exhibit simplicity suitable for practical applications. This was illustrated through the examples provided in Section 5.4. In addition, in Example 2 of Section 5.4, we showed how to use our approach for solving a fuzzy decision-making problem under ignorance in the case where the standard decision-making criteria fail. Our investigation of some properties of the maximum guaranteed payoffs T2FS in Section 5.3 showed that:

- The maximum guaranteed degree of truth of the primary degree of membership of some number $r \in \mathbb{R}$ to the resulting T2FS was determined by the smallest degree of membership to the FS $\tilde{N}$ of those states for which this number r was the maximum guaranteed payoff.
- More preferable FNs of maximum guaranteed payoffs (which corresponded to smaller cut levels of the FS of states) had larger secondary membership degrees (degrees of truth) to the maximum guaranteed payoff T2FS. This was quite natural, for large degrees of truth corresponded to large degrees of membership in a fuzzy set of states.

Upon comparing the maxmin criterion with our approach, we draw the following conclusion: Our approach exhibits a notable limitation, namely an escalation in computational complexity when juxtaposed with the maxmin criterion. This is caused by the need of calculating a maximum guaranteed payoff for each α-cut $N_\alpha = \{j \in N : \mu_{\tilde{N}}(j) \geq \alpha\}$ of the FS $\tilde{N}$ of states. This drawback constrains the applicability of our approach to scenarios involving a substantial number of alternatives and states, which may pose challenges for solving optimization Problems (43) and (44). However, this limitation can be mitigated by refraining from undertaking the full computation of the maximum guaranteed payoff T2FS and instead focusing solely on obtaining the T2FS $\tilde{G}^{e2}(N_\alpha) = \{(G(N_\alpha), \alpha)\}$ with the constant secondary grade α corresponding to an acceptable fixed value $\alpha \in \Omega$ of the degree of truth.

7. Conclusions

The present research shows that, in addition to classical decision criteria, a DM can use our approach, which is based on representing a set of states by a FS. This FS can describe some property of the set of states, for example, an expected ability of the states. An application of the FS theory for solving a decision-making problem in such a formulation appears quite rational. Since we use a maximum guaranteed payoff, our methodology accedes to the benefits, drawbacks, and possibility of employment of a guaranteed outcome in practice.

Accordingly, our approach guarantees a risk-free decision and an opportunity to make a decision only once. In addition, using the approach, one constructs a maximum guaranteed payoff depending on the set of states (fuzzy, in general) that are considered during the decision-making process. These techniques enable us to optimize decision-making processes by considering and leveraging the inherent symmetries and patterns present in the decision-making problem. Since the problem formulation is symmetrical with respect to alternatives and states of nature, the results obtained can be used in the case of a fuzzy set of alternatives. Looking ahead, one potential avenue for future research could involve further exploring the integration of symmetry-aware optimization techniques with other decision criteria and to develop a similar approach for decision problems with FSs of alternatives and states. By expanding and refining our approach in this manner, we can continue to advance decision-making theory across various disciplines, including social sciences and artificial intelligence. Ultimately, we anticipate that our approach, alongside contributions from other researchers, will broaden the scope and applicability of decision-making theory in diverse fields of study.

Author Contributions: Conceptualization, S.M.; Methodology, S.M.; Resources, S.B.; Writing—original draft, S.B. and S.M.; Writing—review and editing, S.B. and S.M.; Project administration, S.B. All authors have read and agreed to the published version of the manuscript.

Funding: This research was funded by the Ministry of National Defense of Lithuania as part of the study project Study Support Projects No VI-18, dated 2 December 2021 (2021–2024), General Jonas Žemaitis Military Academy of Lithuania, Vilnius, Lithuania, and was partially supported by the Ministry of Education and Science of Ukraine (grant BF/30-2021 (2021–2025) for the perspective development of the scientific direction "Mathematical Sciences and Natural Sciences" at the Taras Shevchenko National University of Kyiv.

Data Availability Statement: Data are contained within the article.

Conflicts of Interest: The authors declare no conflicts of interest. Any opinions, findings, conclusions, or recommendations expressed in this material are those of the authors and do not necessarily reflect the view of the funding agency.

References

1. Jain, R. Decision-making in the presence of fuzzy variables. *IEEE Trans. Syst. Man Cybern.* **1976**, *6*, 698–703. [CrossRef]
2. Von Neumann, J.; Morgenstern, O. *Theory of Games and Economic Behavior*; Princeton University Press: Princeton, NY, USA, 1944.
3. Savage, L.J. *The Foundations of Statistics*; John Wiley and Son: New York, NY, USA, 1954.
4. Tanaka, H.; Okuda, T.; Asai, K. On decision-making in fuzzy environment, fuzzy information and decision-making. *Int. J. Prod. Res.* **2007**, *15*, 623–635. [CrossRef]
5. Guo, L.; Zhan, J.; Xu, Z.; José Carlos, R.; Alcantud, J.C.R. A consensus measure-based three-way clustering method for fuzzy large group decision making. *Inf. Sci.* **2023**, *632*, 144–163. [CrossRef]
6. Tanaka, H.; Okuda, T.; Asai, K. A formulation of fuzzy decision problems and its application to an investment problem. *Kybernetes* **1976**, *5*, 25–30. [CrossRef]
7. Mashchenko, S.O. Generalization of Germeyer's Criterion in the Problem of Decision-making under the Uncertainty Conditions with the Fuzzy Set of the States of Nature. *J. Autom. Inf. Sci.* **2012**, *44*, 26–34. [CrossRef]
8. Whalen, T. Decision-making under uncertainty with various assumptions about available information. *IEEE Trans. Syst. Man Cybern.* **1984**, *14*, 888–900. [CrossRef]
9. Watson, S.R.; Weiss, J.J.; Donnell, M.L. Fuzzy decision analysis. *IEEE Trans. Syst. Man Cybern.* **1979**, *9*, 1–9. [CrossRef]
10. Freeling, A.N. Fuzzy sets and decision analysis. *IEEE Trans. Syst. Man Cybern.* **1980**, *10*, 341–354. [CrossRef]
11. Yager, R.R. Possibilistic decision making. *IEEE Trans. Syst. Man Cybern.* **1979**, *9*, 388–392.
12. Whalen, T.H. Risk minimization using L-fuzzy sets. In Proceedings of the International Conference on Cybernetics and Society, Hyatt Regency, Cambridge, MA, USA, 8–10 October 1980; pp. 821–825.
13. Mashchenko, S.O.; Bovsunivskyi, O.M. Effective alternatives of decision-making problems with the fuzzy set of preference relations. *J. Autom. Inf. Sci.* **2013**, *45*, 32–42. [CrossRef]
14. Mashchenko, S.O. Non-dominated alternatives of fuzzy set of experts. *Cybern. Syst. Anal.* **2023**, *59*, 407–416. [CrossRef]
15. Zadeh, L.A. A note on Z-numbers. *Inf. Sci.* **2011**, *181*, 2923–2932. [CrossRef]
16. Larbani, M. Multiobjective problems with fuzzy parameters and games against nature. *Fuzzy Sets Syst.* **2010**, *161*, 2642–2660. [CrossRef]
17. Dubois, D.; Prade, H. Operations on fuzzy numbers. *Int. J. Syst. Sci.* **1978**, *9*, 613–626. [CrossRef]

18. Heilpern, S. Representation and application of fuzzy numbers. *Fuzzy Sets Syst.* **1997**, *9*, 259–268. [CrossRef]
19. Ambrosio, R.; Martini, G.B. Maximum and minimum between fuzzy symbols in noninteractive and weakly non-interactive situations. *Fuzzy Sets Syst.* **1984**, *12*, 27–35. [CrossRef]
20. Fung, L.W.; Fu, K.S. An axiomatic approach to rational decision-making in a fuzzy environment. In *Fuzzy Sets and Their Applications to Cognitive and Decision Processes*; Academic Press: New York, NY, USA, 1975; pp. 227–256.
21. Klir, G.J.; Yuan, B. *Fuzzy Sets and Fuzzy Logic: Theory and Applications*; Prentice-Hall PTR: Englewood Cliffs, NJ, USA, 1995.
22. Zhang, K.L.; Hirota, K. On fuzzy number lattice (R, <). *Fuzzy Sets Syst.* **1997**, *92*, 113–122. [CrossRef]
23. Tahayori, H.; Tettamanzi, A.G.; Degli Antoni, G.; Visconti, A. On the calculation of extended max and min operations between convex fuzzy sets of the real line. *Fuzzy Sets Syst.* **2009**, *160*, 3103–3114. [CrossRef]
24. Chiu, C.H.; Wang, W.J. A simple computation of MIN and MAX operations for fuzzy numbers. *Fuzzy Sets Syst.* **2002**, *126*, 273–276. [CrossRef]
25. Shirin, S.; Saha, G. Graphical representations of membership functions of maximum and minimum of two fuzzy numbers using computer program. *GANIT J. Bangladesh Math. Soc.* **2012**, *31*, 105–115. [CrossRef]
26. Mashchenko, S.O. Minimum of fuzzy numbers with a fuzzy set of operands. *Cybern. Syst. Anal.* **2022**, *58*, 210–219. [CrossRef]
27. Skalna, I.; Rebiasz, B.; Gawel, B.; Basiura, B.; Duda, J.; Opila, J.; Pelech-Pilichowski, T. *Advances in Fuzzy Decision-Making. Theory and Practice*; Springer: Cham, Switzerland, 2015. [CrossRef]
28. Zadeh, L.A. Quantitative fuzzy semantics. *Inf. Sci.* **1971**, *3*, 159–176. [CrossRef]
29. Mizumoto, M.; Tanaka, K. Some properties of fuzzy sets of type-2. *Inf. Control* **1976**, *31*, 312–340. [CrossRef]
30. Karnik, N.N.; Mendel, J.M. Introduction to type-2 fuzzy logic systems. *IEEE Int. Conf. Fuzzy Syst.* **1998**, *2*, 915–920. [CrossRef]
31. Mendel, J.M.; John, R.I. Type-2 fuzzy sets made simple. *IEEE Trans. Fuzzy Syst.* **2002**, *10*, 117–127. [CrossRef]
32. Harding, J.; Walker, C.; Walker, E. The variety generated by the truth value algebra of T2FSs. *Fuzzy Sets Syst.* **2010**, *161*, 735–749. [CrossRef]
33. Mendel, J.M. Type-2 fuzzy sets: Some questions and answers. *IEEE Connect. Newsl. IEEE Neural Netw. Soc.* **2003**, *1*, 10–13.
34. Zadeh, L. The concept of a linguistic variable and its application to approximate reasoning—I. *Inf. Sci.* **1975**, *8*, 199–249. [CrossRef]
35. Bekesiene, S.; Mashchenko, S. On Nash Equilibria in a Finite Game for Fuzzy Sets of Strategies. *Mathematics* **2023**, *11*, 4619. [CrossRef]
36. Ramik, J.; Rimanek, J. Inequality relation between fuzzy numbers and its use in fuzzy optimization. *Fuzzy Sets Syst.* **1985**, *16*, 123–150. [CrossRef]

MDPI AG
Grosspeteranlage 5
4052 Basel
Switzerland
Tel.: +41 61 683 77 34

Symmetry Editorial Office
E-mail: symmetry@mdpi.com
www.mdpi.com/journal/symmetry

www.ingramcontent.com/pod-product-compliance
Lightning Source LLC
Chambersburg PA
CBHW040819250926
51850CB00007BA/1216
9783725872787